"This powerful and humane book is a brea[l] which launched the environmental movemen.... .... own spirits, and that an ugly misuse of thousands of women – and very young children – is the dark and criminal underside of this industry. I hope this is the point where we turn away from pornography – from using it, from condoning it, from allowing it."
  – STEVE BIDDULPH, AUTHOR OF *THE NEW MANHOOD* AND *THE SECRET OF HAPPY CHILDREN*

"At a time when so many celebrities, academics and free speech fundamentalists are siding with the sex industry to deny that pornography is violence against women, *Big Porn Inc* is the voice of reality – a strong indictment; an epic work."
  – JANICE G. RAYMOND, PROFESSOR EMERITA OF WOMEN'S STUDIES AND MEDICAL ETHICS; PAST CO-DIRECTOR OF THE INTERNATIONAL COALITION AGAINST TRAFFICKING IN WOMEN (CATW)

"*Big Porn Inc* is a first-rate book: comprehensive and thoroughly researched. Porn does not liberate sexuality. What is it that men enjoy in porn: humiliation, degradation, control, sexual violence, submission …? Fortunately, this anthology considers the possibilities of resistance and offers hope for transformative futures."
  – RICHARD POULIN, PROFESSOR OF SOCIOLOGY AT THE UNIVERSITY OF OTTAWA AND AUTHOR OF *SEXUALISATION PRÉCOCE ET PORNOGRAPHIE* AND *PORNOGRAPHIE ET HYPERSEXUALISATION: ENFANCES DÉVASTÉES*

"If you care about social justice, buy this book. *Big Porn Inc* is a must read for anyone interested in the human rights of women and children. The book is cogent and alarming, yet hopeful that together we can create a world where women and children are not hurt and degraded. *Big Porn Inc* is a much needed blueprint for ending the global porn industry."
  – CHRISTINE STARK, AUTHOR OF *NICKELS* AND CO-EDITOR OF *NOT FOR SALE*

"When anthropologists from Planet Upsilon report on how civilization failed, *Big Porn Inc* will probably be Exhibit One. I thank the authors for the courage it took to wade through this material and put together this awesome book that drags us kicking and screaming to what so many do not want to know about corporate sex. *Big Porn Inc* may be our last chance to grasp porn ideology before it slips in and becomes the very fabric of our lives."
  – MARTIN DUFRESNE, ANTI-SEXISM ACTIVIST, CANADA

"Global media have infused the culture with sexually objectified and commodified women and girls, mainstreaming pornography with ever-increasing harms to females everywhere. *Big Porn Inc* is a clarion call to action against this gross violation of women's human rights. Brilliant, insightful, essential."
  – KATHLEEN SLOAN, BOARD OF DIRECTORS, NATIONAL ORGANIZATION FOR WOMEN (NOW) USA; CONVENOR, UN PANELS ON THE MEDIA'S SEXUAL COMMODIFICATION OF WOMEN AND GIRLS

"Woman or man, ignore this book at your peril. A remarkable international collection of insightful essays on the growing, poisonous role Big Porn plays in global culture, economics, mores, and violence against women and children. Brava to Spinifex Press for publishing this gift to thoughtful readers."
  – ROBIN MORGAN, AUTHOR AND ACTIVIST

"Big Food, Big Oil, Big Pharma and, yes, Big Porn – global corporate giants that shape and exploit human needs and desires, profiting while furthering injustice and denying toxic effects. *Big Porn Inc* is a hugely necessary, radical and rousing work, full of big thoughts and big truths about the all-consuming pornographic worldview."

– JANE CAPUTI, CREATOR OF DVD *THE PORNOGRAPHY OF EVERYDAY LIFE*

"Many people, for all sorts of reasons, have preferred to avoid thinking about the porn industry and its manifold negative impacts. The invasion of Big Porn throughout mainstream culture makes moving beyond such denial long overdue. *Big Porn Inc* offers clear and topical chapters from a range of thinkers who are uniquely well-equipped to explain why. This is a profoundly important book."

– EMMA RUSH, LEAD AUTHOR *CORPORATE PAEDOPHILIA: SEXUALISATION OF CHILDREN IN AUSTRALIA*; LECTURER IN ETHICS, CHARLES STURT UNIVERSITY

"In *Big Porn Inc* feminists lay down the gauntlet to pornographers by exposing the hate and harm of their man-dated sexuality which has become normative behavior. *Big Porn Inc* not only contests pornographic harm and hate. It will, I predict, incite a new bold wave of global activism in which we reclaim our future."

– KATHLEEN BARRY, AUTHOR OF *FEMALE SEXUAL SLAVERY*, *PROSTITUTION OF SEXUALITY*, AND *UNMAKING WAR, REMAKING MEN*

"*Big Porn Inc* represents a powerful and growing reaction against the influence of the porn merchants and society's willingness to let them get away with one outrage after another. The book unleashes a cascade of emotions – shock, disgust, guilt, rage, and heart-felt admiration for the victims of the porn industry … A landmark publication sure to help open the eyes of the public to the modern scourge of porn and amplify the call for greater decency and respect. Because without them, there can be no true liberation."

– CLIVE HAMILTON, PROFESSOR OF PUBLIC ETHICS AT CHARLES STURT UNIVERSITY

"*Big Porn Inc* is a brilliant exposé on how the porn industry has sold us big fat lies about sex and sexuality. No previous generation has had to navigate such a flood of porn inspired imagery and concepts. Essential reading for everyone, especially the deluded defenders who remain willfully blind to the harmful impacts. I hope *Big Porn Inc* helps to create the seismic shift humanity needs."

– JULIE GALE, ACTIVIST AND FOUNDER OF KIDS FREE 2B KIDS

"*Big Porn Inc* is a courageous book, brilliantly undertaken. Based on impressive research and experience, the collection provides a disturbingly convincing portrayal of the multi-billion dollar global pornography industry. The pornography industry's assault on women, girls and our culture is real. This is the book we need to understand how and why and the means by which it can be halted."

– MARY LUCILLE SULLIVAN, AUTHOR OF *MAKING SEX WORK: A FAILED EXPERIMENT WITH LEGALISED PROSTITUTION*

Melinda Tankard Reist is a writer, speaker, blogger, media commentator and activist against violence against women, objectification of women and sexualisation of girls. Melinda is author/editor of 4 books including *Defiant Birth: Women Who Resist Medical Eugenics* (Spinifex Press, 2006) and *Getting Real: Challenging the Sexualisation of Girls* (Spinifex Press, 2009). Melinda's opinion pieces appear frequently in Australian media and she is a regular on morning television and current affairs programs. She is a co-founder of Collective Shout: for a world free of sexploitation. Melinda is named in the *Who's Who of Australian Women* and the *World Who's Who of Women*. Her Website is <melindatankardreist.com>.

Dr **Abigail Bray** is a Research Fellow at the Social Justice Research Centre at Edith Cowan University. She has published widely in leading international academic journals on anorexia, child sexual abuse, moral panics, and child pornography. She is the author of *Hélène Cixous: Writing and Sexual Difference* (2004) and *Body Talk: A Power Guide for Girls* with Elizabeth Reid Boyd (2005). She was an inaugural inductee into the Western Australian Women's Hall of Fame in 2011. Her forthcoming book *Misogyny Re-Loaded* will be published by Spinifex in 2012. She is a member of Socialist Alliance and the Marxist collective Das Argument.

Other books by Melinda Tankard Reist
Giving Sorrow Words (2000)
Defiant Birth: Women Who Resist Medical Eugenics (2007)
Getting Real: Challenging the Sexualisation of Girls (2009)

Other books by Abigail Bray
Hélène Cixous: Writing and Sexual Difference (2004)
Body Talk: A Power Guide for Girls (2005) with Elizabeth Reid Boyd

BIG PORN INC

EXPOSING THE HARMS
OF THE GLOBAL
PORNOGRAPHY INDUSTRY

edited by
Melinda Tankard Reist and Abigail Bray

First published by Spinifex Press 2011, Reprinted 2011, 2012, 2015

Spinifex Press Pty Ltd
504 Queensberry St
North Melbourne, Victoria 3051
Australia
women@spinifexpress.com.au
www.spinifexpress.com.au

Edited in-house by Renate Klein
Copy edited by Maree Hawken
Indexed by Kath Harper
Cover design by Deb Snibson, MAPG
Typeset by Palmer Higgs
Printed by McPherson's Printing Group

The National Library of Australia Cataloguing-in-Publication data:

Big Porn Inc: exposing the harms of the global pornography industry / Melinda Tankard Reist; Abigail Bray editors.
9781876756895 (pbk)
9781742195407 (ebook: pdf)
9781742195414 (ebook: kindle)
9781742195438 (ebook: epub)

Includes bibliography and index.

Pornography. Internet pornography. Sex in popular culture. Sex role in children. Mass media and sex. Sex-oriented businesses.

Other Authors/Contributors:
Tankard Reist, Melinda.
Bray, Abigail, 1966-

306.742

PEFC

PEFC/21-31-16

Contents

PART 3: HARMING CHILDREN

PART 4: PORNOGRAPHY AND THE STATE

PART 5: RESISTING BIG PORN INC

Acknowledgements

Melinda Tankard Reist

Firstly, my gratitude to some of the best women in the country for working on this book with me.

My co-editor Abigail Bray – the way your mind works and the way you put words together, is a wonder to behold. Thank you for significant support and solidarity.

This book is also the product of the brilliance and dedication of a number of women, primary among them Renate Klein, Helen Pringle and Caroline Norma.

To the contributors – counted among the bravest people I know. I am indebted to you for your willingness to contribute and for continuing to speak out in the face of unrelenting opposition. Your names make an impressive and compelling line-up.

To those who shared their personal stories of suffering harm and damage from their own or another's pornography use, deepest gratitude.

To Renate Klein and Susan Hawthorne at Spinifex Press for your belief in this project (even a cyclone couldn't stop you!). Renate, thanks for keeping us on track and reminding us that there really was a deadline. And also for your special friendship over many years. Susan, for massive help with proofing (and so much more). Special acknowledgement to Deb Snibson for the strong cover design, Maree Hawken for careful and intelligent copy editing, Kath Harper for a comprehensive index, Nikki Anderson and Kate Page for publicity, along with Maralann Damiano, Jo O'Brien and Bernadette Green.

To our wonderful endorsees. Your support means so much.

I have been blessed with the support and friendship of great women: Abigail, Renate, Susan, Helen, Caroline – as well as Deborah Malcolm, Melinda Liszewski and my other Collective Shout colleagues. Significant thanks to Julie Gale for almost daily de-briefs and laughter, without which I'm not sure I would still be standing. To everyone who sent a word of encouragement through my blog and social network pages. Do not underestimate how much this means.

Finally, to my family who make significant sacrifices for my work. One day I hope to make it up to you.

Abigail Bray

First of all, I would like to salute the contributors for their integrity and life work; without them this book would not be possible, and I have learnt a great deal from all of them. Thank you Melinda for your courage, fortitude and friendship, for bearing the 'terrible knowledge' and staying strong. A special thank you to Renate, Susan, Helen, Julie, Caroline and the Collective Shout team, for immeasurable things, for the gift of such intelligent friendship, and for your passionate integrity. I would like to acknowledge the Edith Cowan University Social Justice Research Centre for supporting this book. Gabby, your infectious laughter and cool subversive mind is the best cure for the misogyny blues. Thanks Jonathan for large bottles of vitamin C, 500 soy smoothies, bags of health food and hysterical laughter. Thank you Charity for your integrity and wisdom, and for always being there for me. Thanks Peter, Sam and Martin for many interesting conversations about capitalism and pornography. Thanks also to my scattered and talented family for much support.

Vagelis – your solidarity, humour, courage, wise and kind advice, help with research, and inspiring political passion through difficult times, helped me stand when the knees of my soul were cut. This book is for you, comrade.

Melinda Tankard Reist and Abigail Bray[1]

Introduction: Unmasking a Global Industry

We live in a world that is increasingly shaped by pornography. The signs are everywhere:

- A urinal at the Clock Hotel on the Gold Coast in Queensland, shaped as a woman's mouth with huge painted red lips.
- A music video by Kanye West featuring semi-naked women's corpses hanging from chains, with West holding the head of a decapitated woman in scenes of eroticised carnage.[2]
- Ejaculation-themed images in advertising for face cream and alcohol.[3]
- Porn-inspired t-shirts depicting women naked, bound and blood spattered, sold in youth fashion stores.[4]
- A 'Pippa Middleton Ass Appreciation Society' Facebook page set up in honour of the sister and bridesmaid of Kate Middleton, attracting over 200,000 members. Men describe what they want to do to the 29-year-old: knock her up, bash her 'back doors' in, cause her injury such that she would need 'straw and a wheelchair'.[5]
- A Facebook page dedicated to the facial cum shot titled 'Smile or it's going in your eye' ("make sure every girl gets the message!") had almost 12,000 members.[6]
- In the children's holiday movie *Hop*, the cartoon teenage boy-bunny asks Hugh Hefner about spending the night at the Playboy mansion.[7] It's where all the sexy bunnies stay, replies the pornography mogul through the mansion's intercom.

1   We would like to acknowledge the significant input of Dr Helen Pringle to this introduction.
2   <http://melindatankardreist.com/2011/01/so-decapitated-women-are-fine-with-you-kanye-west/>
3   <http://thesocietypages.org/socimages/2008/07/10/ejaculation-imagery-in-ads/>
4   <http://www.facebook.com/pages/Say-no-to-porn-t-shirts/163212907070593>
5   <http://melindatankardreist.com/2011/05/pippa%e2%80%99s-arse-has-become-porn-for-the-slobbering-masses/>
6   <http://www.facebook.com/group.php?gid=241705237082&ref=mf>
7   <http://melindatankardreist.com/2011/04/playboy-pushes-global-porn-brand-to-kids-in-easter-bunny-film/>

Big Porn Inc documents the proliferation and normalisation of pornography, the way it has become a global industry and a global ideology, and how it is shaping our world and the harm this causes. The global pornography industry is expected to reach US$100 billion in the near future.[8] In 2009, the UN estimated that the global child pornography industry made a profit of up to $20 billion (M'jid Maalla, 2009). Pornography money is buying governments, academic research, national and international corporations and law enforcement agencies.

This largely unregulated pornography industry has colonised private and public spaces at a rate that presents significant challenges to women's and children's rights. The mainstreaming of pornography is transforming the sexual politics of intimate and public life, popularising new forms of anti-women attitudes and behaviours and contributing to the sexualisation of children. The pornification of culture is leading to a form of hypersexism that entails an increase in physical, sexual, mental, economic and emotional cruelty towards women and children. This radical cultural shift is shaping the way we understand ourselves and others, both personally and politically.

Big Porn Inc demonstrates why a comprehensive and uncompromising intervention – first to expose, and second to rein in – is needed to challenge the global pornography industry. Drawing on empirical, legal, political, ethical, and philosophical arguments, this collection presents the work of leading international experts and activists who are combating the toxic industries and cultures of Big Porn.

Our book provides a powerful challenge to libertarian conceits that pornography is simply about pleasure, self-empowerment and freedom of choice. Challenges to the pornography industry that call attention to evidence of harm and the destruction of human dignity and rights are frequently derided as 'moral panics', a term designed to silence and humiliate political critics who threaten vested financial, political and ideological interests. Those who use the term 'moral panic' as an insult set up a reactionary conflict between 'wowser' types who have issues with 'sex' as against the more relaxed fun-loving sexual sophisticates. But challenging the sexist and racist pornographic industrialisation of intimacy is not an anti-sex position. Pornography is a distortion of respect-based sexuality.

---

8 <http://www.morssglobalfinance.com/the-economics-of-the-global-entertainment-industry/>

The real picture

As we worked on *Big Porn Inc*, it was difficult to be confronted with hardcore violence on a daily basis. In 1980, Andrea Dworkin wrote: "The visceral experience of a hatred of women [in pornography] that literally knows no bounds has put me beyond anger and beyond tears; I can only speak to you from grief (p. 287)." She continued: "And how can it go on like this, senseless, entirely brutal, inane, day after day and year after year, these images and ideas and values pouring out, packaged, bought and sold, promoted, enduring on and on, and no one stops it" (1980, p. 290).

We found ourselves relating to Andrea Dworkin's words many times as we put this book together. We had to negotiate our own distress, but we also discovered that speaking out in opposition to pornography brings a deluge of online bile and e-hate (Jackman, 2011). Ironically, defenders of pornography who claim to be in favour of freedom of speech often engage in answering critiques of the pornography industry with personal attacks.

As we discussed what we wanted to include in *Big Porn Inc*, we questioned whether it was ethically appropriate to publish some of the content. The chapters on child-rape and 'incest'-themed pornography were especially disturbing. Other opponents of pornography have faced a similar dilemma. For example, Robert Wosnitzer and Chyng Sun (a contributor to this volume), included disturbing images in their film, *The Price of Pleasure*. Wosnitzer (n.d.) justified their use in this way:

> To not include these images would have distorted the reality of what is being actively consumed by viewers – a distorted version of reality that, interestingly, benefits the porn industry, enabling the industry to continue to construct an image of pornography that is harmless, sexual representations of consensual sexual activity, and masks the ideological world that pornography depicts.

We share this rationale in deciding to include descriptions and written representations of pornography and harm here.[9]

We also wanted to correct the pornography industry's distorted version of reality by clearly saying: Here is why you shouldn't believe the myths about pornography being simply 'naughty pictures' and 'sex between consenting adults'. Here is how pornography creates and shapes appetites and demands. Here is how it operates to acclimatise and condition boys and men to demand the 'Porn Star Experience' from women and girls. Here is how men and boys have come to see the 'money shot' on a woman's face as the climax to sex. Here is how

---

9   We did, however, exclude some of the most extreme porn Websites so as not to promote them.

boys develop a sexual taste for coercion. Here is how they learn predatory sexual attitudes. Here are some possible factors contributing to sex crimes committed by younger men (Malamuth and Pitpitan, 2007, p. 139; see also Nakasatomi, this volume).[10] Here is how men are socialised into eroticising and sexualising children through Pseudo Child Pornography (Dines, 2010). Here is why demand for child sexual assault images – including of babies – is increasing.[11] Here is how women have been turned into 'human toilet bowls'. Here is how pornography and torture often look the same (see Dines 2010; and Kendall, Masson, Hawthorne, Farley, this volume).[12] As Rebecca Whisnant observed: "In today's mainstream pornography, aggression against women is the rule rather than the exception … hostile, aggressive content is so prevalent in contemporary pornography that it would be hard for a regular consumer to avoid it" (2007, p. 115).

In *Big Porn Inc* we illustrate Whisnant's claim.

Pornography's training ground

We also wanted to explore how sex industry themes and messages have come to infiltrate the world of girls and boys. In toys and games, clothing, music videos, in the billboards wallpapering their daily lives, children are growing up in the shadow cast by pornography (see Hamilton, this volume). The globalisation of sexual imagery means that children become "valid participants in a public culture of sex" (Durham, 2008, p. 115). Little girls read in girls' magazines where American pop singer Lady Gaga will be appearing next. When they go, they see her perform simulated sex acts on stage. Children's cartoon characters are appropriated and turned into porn sites.

Children and young people are exposed to pornography at increasingly early ages. Pornography has become a global sex education handbook for many boys, with an estimated 70% of boys in Australia having seen pornography by the age of 12, and 100% by the age of 15 (Sauers, in Scobie 2007; see also Bryant,

---

10 Exposure to porn has been linked to sexual crimes among young people in Japan. "Japan's sex crime victims are predominantly teenagers. Of all indecent assault victims, 41 percent are aged 13 to 19, while a further 21 percent are of elementary school age or younger. The 13–19 age group also accounts for 44 percent of rape victims, a figure far higher than for any other demographic group. At 23 percent, nearly a quarter of all Japan's convicted rapists are aged 19 or under" (Malamuth and Pitpitan 2007, p. 139).

11 Detectives from Britain's Child Exploitation and Online Protection Centre (CEOP) are uncovering evidence that paedophiles are focusing on 'pre-verbal' victims whose inability to describe their abuse makes them attractive targets (Townsend, 2008).

12 See also anti-pornography activist Nikki Craft's collection of pornography and torture from *Penthouse*, <http://www.nostatusquo.com/ACLU/CFMRWL/Pent1.html>.

2009).[13] In Michael Flood's study of 16 and 17-year-old teenagers in Australia, 73% of boys had watched an X-rated video, with 1 in 20 watching on a weekly basis, and more than 1 in 5 watching at least once a month (Flood, 2010, p. 165). Girls are also exposed to pornographic images; Joan Sauers found that 53.5% of Australian girls aged 12 and under have seen pornography, with the figure rising to 97% by the age of 16 (2007, p. 80).

Michael Flood describes the potential harms to young people of these patterns of pornography use:

> What are the effects of showing sexual violence without negative consequences? ... [I]t is possible that such depictions result in beliefs that people like to be slapped or insulted during sex; that double penetrations and gagging are erotic, and that treating a partner as a sexual object is arousing ... [Y]outh may expect that these behaviours *should* feel erotic and arousing and, if they hurt, may choose to ignore that or avoid saying something to a partner, for fear of being seen as prudish or inexperienced (2010, p. 47).

Gail Dines (2011) similarly notes the impact of pornography use on a boy's developing sexuality:

> Porn is actually being encoded into a boy's sexual identity so that an authentic sexuality – one that develops organically out of life experiences, one's peer group, personality traits, family and community affiliations – is replaced by a generic porn sexuality limited in creativity and lacking any sense of love, respect or connection to another human being.

Children are being transformed into living advertisements for the global pornography industry. Branded by *Playboy* and other sexed-up corporations, they are taught that consumer obedience is a form of rebellion, and that the only authority worth following and imitating is the very corporate culture that creates and feeds off their hopes, fears and desires while repackaging their feelings as hypersexualised consumer products (see also Quart, 2004). We should oppose this industrialisation of children's bodies and minds by a pornified corporate culture just as we continue to campaign against the exploitation of children everywhere, whether in the mines and chimneys of yesteryear or the sweatshops, carpet factories and garbage heaps of today.

For many girls, naming and expressing emotional or physical pain is the new taboo because it transgresses the fake porn script of the continually up-for-it girl who takes it with a smile. The message is that men and boys *must* be able to get sexual release whenever they need to, and that women should accept men's need for porn.

---

13 See Ropelato (n.d.) for compelling 2005/2006 global Internet pornography statistics, <http://internet-filter-review.toptenreviews.com/internet-pornography-statistics.html>.

A 20-year-old university student expresses her misgivings on an Australian blog, but makes herself accept that even though she has sex with her boyfriend 5–7 times a week, she just cannot meet his 'needs':

I found some porn on my bf's laptop a while ago and i hit the roof….i spoke to girl and guy friends about whether i overreacted and every guy i spoke to said that i had and that is normal and i would never find a guy who doesnt do it, where as all the girls agreed with me and said since he has a girlfriend and we have a very active sex-life then he shouldnt need to. I felt like if i was serving his needs and he was still watchn porn then obviously i wasnt enough or good enough….all the girls i discussed this with said this was the same reason they hated their boyfriends watchn porn.

I spoke to my boyfriend about it and he explained that while he thought we had a great sex life (usually 5-7times a week) he had a pretty high sex-drive and still wants it more but doesnt want to pressure me when im not in the mood/busy/whatever so uses porn to masterbate with instead…So while still dont really like it, i understand that my sex drive is not on par with his and i guess unless im willing to do it whenever he gets the urge (which he says he would always prefer to watchn porn) then i cant really object to him watchn porn.[14]

Many women express their dissatisfaction with damaged relationships that are blighted by the pornography use of their partners.[15] Michael Flood summarises the research on this aspect:

In a US study, one quarter of women saw their partner's pornography use as a kind of affair, one-third felt that it had had negative effects on their sexual lives and relationships, and over one-third agreed that they felt less attractive and desirable and more like a sexual object. Other studies find that partners of adult pornography users report decreased sexual intimacy, lowered esteem and demands that they participate in activities they find objectionable (2010, p. 172).

Women as sex robots: artificial and living dolls

Pornography is producing a more de-personalised, alienated and transactional sexuality. Sex doesn't even have to involve an actual person. The film *Hardcore Porn Profits* shows a man who develops an artificial vagina for men to feel and put their hands into while watching a woman performing sex acts.[16] "Always turned on and ready to talk and play", Roxxxy is "a life-size robotic girlfriend," complete with artificial intelligence and flesh-like synthetic skin. The doll's creator, Douglas Hines, says: "She can't vacuum, she can't cook but she can do almost anything

14 Anonymous (7 July, 2010), <http://www.mamamia.com.au/weblog/2010/07/naomi-wolf-porn-feminism-sex.html>.
15 See also the personal account by Caroline, this volume; and Whisnant (2010); Rothbart (2001); Cochrane (29 October, 2010). See more broadly Jensen (2007).
16 <http://www.youtube.com/watch?v=f3HSyLee74k>

else if you know what I mean."[17] Roxxxy is programmed to say "I love it in the arse!"[18] This bizarre trend is connected to a broader pornographic cultural logic that views women as things, objects, holes, as 'living dolls'.

Of course our main concern is with flesh-and-blood women providing the raw material for the pornography industry. The pro-pornography assumption that the production of pornography does not harm women, or that it is merely their 'choice' if they are harmed, is as callous as the indifference to the rapid rise of women's sexual degradation within new pornography cultures.

The lived experience of pornography actors is the human face of research showing that physical and verbal aggression is "the norm rather than the exception in popular pornographic film" as noted by Ana J. Bridges (2010, p. 46). Bridges completed a content analysis of best-selling and best-renting pornographic videos available by catalogue in the USA, and found that

[p]hysical aggression occurred in 88 per cent of scenes ... Across all acts of aggression – both physical and verbal – 94 per cent were directed towards women ... When aggressed against, 95 per cent of targets responded with either expressions of pleasure (encouragement, sexual moans, and so forth) or neutrally (e.g. no change in facial expression or interruption of actions) (Bridges 2010, p. 46; see also Sun, this volume).

An insight into the abuse and violence visited on porn performers is graphically depicted in the photo documentary account 'They shoot porn stars don't they?' by Susannah Breslin (2009). She describes how a woman, pulled into the porn industry to support her children, is subjected to verbal abuse and torture:

He threatens to beat her, threatens to torture her, pulls up her shirt, pulls up her skirt, hits her breasts, hits her thighs, throttles her by the neck with both hands, humiliates her, degrades her, makes her cry, chokes her until she is gasping for air. He gets her to tell the camera she is 27 years old and the only reason she's here doing this particular job on this particularly day in this particular hotel room in the Valley is for the money, and the fact of the matter is she has two young children to support, of whom the man asks rhetorically, and seemingly for the sole purpose of screwing with her head, 'They're going to grow up to be proud of you, right?'

The woman is becoming unmoored. He orders her on her hands and knees, and begins beating her with a leather strap that *cracks!* across the bared skin of her backside every time he hits her, leaving angry pink welts, until, finally, in a futile attempt to protect herself, the woman reaches her arm around herself, her hand turned upwards, her palm facing outwards, and the man stops ... 'To steal a Quentin Tarantino line,' he muses, mockingly, 'Was that as good for you as it was for me?'

---

17 'Sexbot's here, and what a doll she is' (11 January, 2010), <http://www.news.com.au/adelaidenow/story/0,1,26574881-5006301,00.html>.

18 <http://www.truecompanion.com/tv/>

We give space in this book to the experience of girls and women used to make pornography and how their suffering doesn't end because their images are circulated for eternity (see Pringle, and Amy's Victim Impact Statement, this volume). As Amy, whose sexual abuse is known as the 'Misty Series' of child pornography images, writes: "I did not choose to be there, but now I am there forever in pictures that people are using to do sick things."

An industry unregulated and uncontrolled

Compounding the abuse so often involved in the making of pornography is a lack of regulation of the industry in all its forms. The shelves of corner stores and petrol stations are stacked with pornography promoting sex with 'live young girls', rape and incest, while pornography distributors continually flout Australia's classification laws (see Tankard Reist, 2008). Abigail Bray has described an Internet site called *Passed Out Pussy* which incites crimes of violence against women and girls, and endorses rape, torture and hatred upon the bodies of young women (Bray, 2009). Other sites revel in the torture and enslavement of women.

For example, Ken Franzblau has written about photos on the 'Slavefarm' site: "These are pictures of naked women bound, gagged, chained, in a stock, and drinking from a dog's dish. If there is a distinction between pornography and torture, it's not detectable from these pictures" (2007, p. 262). There are sections on the site for auctions and rentals where you can sell, rent and purchase women, as 'Female Slaves for Sale'. These representations of women and the hatred expressed in them are reminiscent of propaganda for the 19th century slave trade (see Hawthorne, this volume).

However, against this background, attempts to bring Internet content into line with existing classification laws and the treatment of illegal material in Australia have met with virulent objection by vested interests. Requiring Internet Service Providers (ISPs) to filter out a blacklist of URLs containing extreme and violent pornography has been proposed by the current (Labor) Government. This material can be legally viewed in no other medium. As Australian author and Professor of Public Ethics, Clive Hamilton, has argued:

> We live in a democracy where citizens ask their governments to impose restrictions on certain types of content that are regarded as harmful to individuals or to the community more broadly. We have a censorship system governing films, television and magazines, defined by law, enforced by government bodies and with widespread community support. There is nothing special about the Internet that puts it beyond community standards (Hamilton, 2009).

But those who demand a right to view 'legal and illegal' pornography protested against the filtering proposal. In February, 2010, Australia's Parliament House and Federal Government Websites were shut down in a cyber-attack and inboxes of members of parliament were flooded with pornography (Davis, 2010). This sense of entitlement to 'our pornography' entails defending the 'right' of the pornography industry to market child rape, violation of women and girls, and female slavery to anonymous consumers, all in the name of freedom of speech. If we consider this ethically acceptable, whose rights are we defending?

The Swedish scholar, Max Waltman, has analysed the shielding of these kinds of abuses behind the screen of 'free speech'. He details numerous cases where law makers, judges, and other arbiters dismiss claims against even some of the most violent pornography, or where those in breach of various laws in various countries are only given 'penalties', such as community service.

Waltman responds to the common refrain of pornography defenders to 'avert your eyes' or to 'turn it off' if you are offended by it. He points out that such a response assumes that the harm of a pornographic world is no more than 'offensive' to the observer:

> Closing your eyes will not prevent women from being raped, battered, or tortured by intimate partners being inspired and impelled by pornography though. Nor will it help adolescent girls forced out on streets, coerced into imitating pornography upon thousands of clients' requests, to escape the sexual abuse. Defining harm as an offence to observers silences and denies these women their rights (Waltman, 2009, p.12).

Like Waltman, our primary concern with pornography is not that it is offensive (although it often is), but that it is subordination and degradation – mostly of women. It is a human rights issue.

'Capturing Men in a Wide Net'

The global pornography industry shows little concern for subordination, degradation or human rights violations; indeed powerful elements in the industry market the violation of human rights. Meanwhile Big Porn continues to devise new ways of catching men in a global and very sticky web. In her chapter 'To catch a curious clicker', Jennifer A. Johnson describes how the online porn industry captures men in a vast web:

> Upon his arrival, he is entangled in a series of click manoeuvres and marketing gimmicks calculated to further reduce his agency and transform him from the 'curious clicker' into the 'member clicker' (p. 148) ... men are drawn into the online commercial pornography network, where they find themselves enmeshed in a well constructed set of relationships designed to extract maximum profits through the circumscription of consumer choice. The structure of the network is designed to prevent 'leavers' ... by restricting and/or obfuscating (male) consumer choice (2010, p. 153).

It is remarkable that civil libertarians can see this level of manipulation into industrialised sex as something for freedom-loving people to celebrate.

Nothing radical about mass market masturbation

People on the 'Left' have opposed 'Big Pharma' and more recently 'Big Food' and 'Big Society', but many seem to fall silent in the face of 'Big Porn' and its predatory profit-driven practices.[19] Long-time US anti-porn campaigner, Nikki Craft, takes 'progressive' anti-globalisation campaigners to task for ignoring the global profit machine of Big Porn.[20] There is, however, nothing to be celebrated in the dehumanising global commodification of women in pornography. There is nothing revolutionary about mass-marketed masturbation. Radical big-picture thinking requires that we connect the global pornography industry to other social justice issues, in order to acknowledge the lack of justice in the reduction of human beings to objects of exchange.

Pornography today presents elements of every kind of barbarism imaginable – from overt fascist celebrations of racial hatred, to the killing of animals for sexual entertainment. And yet, for many people it still passes as 'cool', as just a bit of fun, as sexual 'lulz', something to emulate and celebrate. In the brave new world of pornochic, ethical boundaries are for wowsers and bores.

Contributors to *Big Porn Inc*

Our contributors are from diverse backgrounds and countries, with a range of views on social and ethical issues. But they are in broad agreement on the harms of pornography. We have divided *Big Porn Inc* into 5 Parts: Pornography Cultures, Pornography Industries, Harming Children, Pornography and the State, and lastly, a section on global activism, Resisting Big Porn Inc.[21] Each Part opens with extracts from personal accounts shared with us during the writing of this book (and some sourced online) so that we remember that real people suffer real harm through pornography.

We begin the book with a personal reflection by Caroline (a pseudonym) who remembers the impact that finding her partner's pornography had on their relationship. She captures the ordinariness and the normalisation of pornography in women's lives as she states: "I'm the woman behind you in the supermarket

---

19 Gail Dines exposes the mainstream companies which benefit from pornography profits (see Dines, 2010, chapter 3). The porn profit trail is also a feature in the film *Hardcore Porn Profits*, <http://www.youtube.com/watch?v=f3HSyLee74k>.
20 See Nikki Craft, '*Hustling the Left*', <http://www.hustlingtheleft.com/index.html>.
21 The English language has a range of spelling conventions and this diversity is reflected in individual contributions.

queue." In Part 2, Stella (a pseudonym) describes the destructive impact of dancing in a strip club and her grief that continues 12 years later. In Part 3, 'Amy' writes of how the abuse of pornography is re-experienced over and over. All 3 women voice the profound sense of loss, shame and humiliation they experienced in reflecting on how pornography touched their lives. But they also give voice to the courage to expose what happened to them – for the sake of others.

These contributions illustrate how pornography has become integrated into our cultural norms. In Part 1, Pornography Cultures, Gail Dines argues that Pseudo Child Pornography, in which girls over the age of 18 are represented as children, normalises and eroticises child abuse. Dines believes that this form of sexualisation weakens the norms that define children as off-limits to sexual use by men. Catharine A. MacKinnon writes about living in a world made by pornographers, and explores the many ways in which pornography has colonised our world, such that "[t]he cultural politics of pornography become normalised to the point of invisibility." Maggie Hamilton focuses on how sexualised marketing targets children so they see pornography as a consumer good. Hamilton offers a passionate analysis of the ways in which children are sexually groomed, and in which childhood itself is controlled and defined by corporations.

Robert Jensen identifies rape culture and pornography as forms of propaganda by which the powerless are kept in line. He points out that pornography is not only sexist, but that it is also the most openly racist form of mass media today. Nina Funnell looks at how communication technologies, sexting and peer-to-peer porn affect the intimate lives of teenagers, especially how technology has multiplied the ways in which they are humiliated and abused. Diane L. Rosenfeld offers insights into an emerging extreme culture of pornography-inspired sexism on North American college campuses. She concludes that a 'pimp and ho' culture is glorified on campuses as exciting and desirable, creating a backdrop to sexual negotiations among college students.

Women bear the brunt of pornography culture, but men are not immune to its objectification and dehumanisation. In his chapter on the harms of gay male pornography, Christopher N. Kendall argues that sexual subordination is enforced through extreme forms of torture and violence which celebrate a masculinity founded on the abuse of vulnerable others – often feminised – in the name of sexual pleasure. Jeffrey Moussaieff Masson takes on pornography and animals, exploring the academic and aesthetic condoning of women engaging in bestiality in the name of a 'post-feminist' self-empowerment.

Research on effects on consumers is critical to our understanding of how society is affected by pornography. Robi Sonderegger's chapter analyses the ways in which pornography grooms consumers into accepting the eroticisation of inequality. A number of industries have taken up the new business opportunities provided by pornography. Meagan Tyler examines how pornsex is legitimised through the industry of sex therapy and how its presentation as sexual authority threatens women's equality. Renate Klein looks at the ideological and business links between Big Porn and Big Pharma, specifically the harms created by pornsex and reproporn. Klein calls for a future which is not a plastic 'porn-and-pill saturated world' where medicalisation rules, but a world full of possibilities for a creative and just life for all.

Susan Hawthorne's chapter on lynching and torture opens Part 2, Pornography Industries. Hawthorne connects pornography to broader structures of global inequality, and identifies how porn culture feeds off the torture of people living under repressive regimes. Hawthorne also critiques 'lesbian' pornography while co-editor, Abigail Bray, explores how 'post-feminist' sex shops appropriate feminist rhetoric about sexual liberation and empowerment in order to promote and sell sex industry products. In an examination of *The Porn Report*, Helen Pringle provides an incisive discussion of the growing business of academic defences of pornography, and the striking indifference to harm on which they rest. Co-editor, Melinda Tankard Reist, investigates the marketing of pornography in her chapter on the Sexpo trade fair, which describes the open racism and misogyny promoted at such events.

Sheila Jeffreys, Stella and Melissa Farley articulate the ways in which prostitution, strip clubs and pornography intersect. Jeffreys argues that pornography and strip clubs overlap in ownership and customers, with the clubs acting as 'free billboards' for pornography. Stella offers a heart-breaking account of her life in the sex industry and provides an insight into the brutal assault of this industry on minds and bodies: "I left with my self-esteem in shreds, my pockets empty, my body damaged." Melissa Farley argues that pornography is infinite prostitution, with similar kinds of violence in each, even involving acts that international conventions define as torture, a crime against humanity.

Abigail Bray refers to the Internet as a 'porn factory', and argues that women working in pornography are not only exploited, but that images of their prostituted bodies often continue to be exchanged on the Internet after they have died, such that pornography becomes the 'prostitution of the dead'. Hiroshi Nakasatomi from Japan shows how the pornification of the computer gaming industry is exemplified by the simulation of rape in the game of *Rapelay* in which women are gang-raped and beg to be abused by their rapists. The final contribution in Part 2 is by Chyng Sun who traces the making of her documentary film, *The Price of Pleasure*. She offers an understanding based on 7 years of rigorous research and concludes that pornography has become much more violent and hence disturbing in its implications for sexual equality.

Part 3 focuses on child pornography and its growing availability. Diana E.H. Russell summarises her decades-long work to show how child pornography is linked to, and part of, the sexual abuse of children. Russell argues that child pornography works to undermine inhibitions against cruelty and violence to children, just as the training of soldiers for war breaks down inhibitions against doing harm to others. S. Caroline Taylor examines intra-familial rape and shows how the popular 'incest' genre of pornography promotes the sexual assault of children by family members in the home, where most child abuse takes place. Caroline Norma presents a compelling analysis of the links between pornography and child sexual assault, based on records of criminal cases that show how pornography is used in child sexual assault.

Helen Pringle's chapter on restitution for victims of child pornography discusses some groundbreaking legal approaches in the USA which represent the emergence of a 'civil rights' approach to child pornography, perhaps able to be used in other countries to address the global trade in abuse. Amy's Victim Impact Statement is an account of the social, emotional and psychological harms sustained by a victim of child pornography. Amy's account indicates that pornography use is not just a form of voyeurism on an already-committed harm, but itself a crime scene of harm to children.

Part 4 is concerned with how governments and other state actors contribute to, support and participate in the pornography industry, and provides an exploration of the role of 'free speech' advocates in justifying the ready accessibility of pornography.

Anne Mayne explores the impact of the sex industry's colonisation of South Africa since the end of apartheid, as pornography exploits an already vulnerable population of women through promoting sexual violence. Asja Armanda and Natalie Nenadic's chapter is a gruelling analysis of the role of pornography in the genocidal sexual crimes during and after the collapse of Yugoslavia. Sexual atrocities were recognised under international law as acts of genocide through the effort of the authors and others, such as Catharine A. MacKinnon, in a landmark civil suit in the USA against Radovan Karadzic, leader of the Bosnian Serbs. Moving to Asia, Ruchira Gupta argues that the spread of violent pornography in India is linked to an increase in sexual assault, paedophilia and sex tourism, and to India's emergence as a global 'porn capital'.

Betty McLellan takes up the important issue of freedom of speech and provides ways of rethinking the relationship between free speech and the right to equality, dignity and respect. She outlines the importance of seeing fair speech as an analytical tool for maximising social justice, in an analogy with fair vs free trade.

In the final section, Part 5, anti-pornography activists from around the world contribute short essays on resistance to porn culture. Julia Long is optimistic about new forms of grassroots feminist activism in the UK, with a new generation of feminists emerging around this issue. Gail Dines's 'Stop Porn Culture!' introduces the new wave of US feminist activism against porn. Linda Thompson in Scotland describes the challenges confronting activists and educators who are frequently vilified by defenders of the global porn industry. Anna van Heeswijk describes the activities and strategies of OBJECT, a formidable UK activist group in opposition to the objectification and dehumanisation of women. In Australia, Melinda Liszewski writes about the dynamic new movement, Collective Shout, with its inspiring and powerful grassroots campaign combating the sexploitation of girls and women by exposing and boycotting companies that market sexist and degrading products. And Caroline Norma writes about the 10-year history of the Tokyo-based Anti-Pornography and Prostitution Research Group (APP) in combating pornography and prostitution.

Men too are organising against pornography. Matt McCormack Evans writes about The Anti Porn Men Project in the UK, explaining how men can challenge pornography. Finally, Susan Hawthorne in her Quit Porn Manifesto asks us to reflect on why people use pornography, and why refusal to participate in the industry is an issue of social justice.

Signs of hope

In our efforts to challenge the global pornography industry, we need signs of hope. In writing this book we have found many signs. The activist section of *Big Porn Inc* is a beginning. New and exciting forms of action are emerging in many parts of the world. Susan Hawthorne offers us strategies to Quit Porn. The increasing number of men speaking out against the commercial exploitation of sexual expression in many countries is encouraging – and see Robert Jensen, Christopher Kendall, Jeffrey Masson, Robi Sonderegger, Hiroshi Nakasatomi and Matt McCormack Evans in this volume.

Big Porn Inc is a call to action, to begin to assert our human rights to dignity, respect and justice at every level. In 'Pornography is What the End of the World Looks Like', Robert Jensen has argued that forms of domination like pornography "diminish our ability to contribute to a just and sustainable future"

(Jensen 2010, p. 112). By eroticising oppression, pornography cultures and industries undermine our ability to imagine and create a just future for all people.

Such a future is a non-negotiable goal for us. We want women to experience real justice, and to live free from all forms of oppression. For us, opposition to pornography is a question of social justice. We either allow subordination or freedom: there is not room for both.

We invite you, the readers of this book, to join our resistance to Big Porn Inc.

Bibliography

Adelaide Advertiser (11 January, 2010) 'Sexbot's here, and what a doll she is', <http://www.adelaidenow.com.au/news/world/sexbots-here-and-what-a-doll-she-is/story-e6frea8l-1225818031211>.

Bray, Abigail (24 August, 2009) 'Googling S*x' *Online Opinion*, <http://www.onlineopinion.com.au/view.asp?article=9344>.

Breslin, Susannah (2009) 'They shoot porn stars, don't they?', <http://susannahbreslin.blogspot.com/2011/04/they-shoot-porn-stars-dont-they.html> and <http://theyshootstars.com>.

Bridges, Ana J. (2010) 'Methodological considerations in mapping pornography content' in Karen Boyle (Ed) *Everyday Pornography*. Routledge, Abingdon, Oxon, UK, pp. 34–49.

Bryant, Colleen (February, 2009) 'Adolescence, pornography and harm' *Trends and Issues in Crime and Criminal Justice* No 368, Australian Institute of Criminology, Canberra, <http://aic.gov.au/upload/aic/publications/tandi2/tandi368.pdf>.

Cochrane, Kira (29 October , 2010) 'Men who hate porn' *The Age*, <http://www.theage.com.au/national/men-who-hate-porn-20101027-173wm.html>.

Craft, Nikki (n.d.) 'Torture photos from *Penthouse*' (1985), <http://www.nostatusquo.com/ACLU/CFMRWL/Pent1.html>.

Craft, Nikki (n.d.) 'Hustling the Left', <http://www.hustlingtheleft.com/index.html>.

Davis, Mark (13 February, 2010) 'Porn fans attack website to protest against censorship' *Sydney Morning Herald*, <http://www.smh.com.au/technology/technology-news/porn-fans-attack-website-to-protest-against-censorship-20100213-ny3b.html>.

Dines, Gail (2010) *Pornland: How Porn Has Hijacked Our Sexuality*. Beacon Press Boston; Spinifex Press, North Melbourne.

Dines, Gail (28 February, 2011) 'On Pornography' Lecture presented at Harvard University, Cambridge, MA.

Durham, Meenakshi Gigi (2008) *The Lolita Effect: The Media Sexualisation of Young Girls and What We Can Do About It*. The Overlook Press, New York.

Dworkin, Andrea (1980) 'Pornography and Grief' in Laura Lederer (Ed) *Take Back the Night*. William Morrow, New York, pp. 286–291.

Flood, Michael (2010) 'Young men using pornography' in Karen Boyle (Ed) *Everyday Pornography*. Routledge, Abingdon, Oxon, UK, pp.164–178.

Franzblau, Ken (2007) 'Slavefarm, Sex Tours and the Pimp John T.: Using Pornography to Advance Trafficking, Sex Tourism and Prostitution' in Guinn, David E. with Julie Di Caro (Eds) *Pornography: Driving the Demand in International Sex Trafficking*. Captive Daughters Media, Los Angeles, pp. 261-273.

Hamilton, Clive (16 February, 2009) 'Web doesn't belong to net libertarians', <http://www.theaustralian.com.au/australian-it/web-doesnt-belong-to-net-libertarians/story-e6frgakx-1111118869227>.

Jackman, Christine (4 June, 2011) 'A War of Words' *The Weekend Australian*, <http://www.theaustralian.com.au/news/features/war-of-words/story-e6frg8h6-1226068173588>.

Jensen, Robert (2007) *Getting Off: Pornography and the End of Masculinity*. South End Press, Cambridge, MA.

Jensen, Robert (2010) 'Pornography is what the end of the world looks like' in Karen Boyle (Ed) *Everyday Pornography*. Routledge, Abingdon, Oxon, UK, pp. 105–113.

Johnson, Jennifer A. (2010) 'To catch a curious clicker: A social network analysis of the online pornography industry' in Karen Boyle (Ed) *Everyday Pornography*. Routledge, Abingdon, Oxon, UK, pp. 147–163.

Malamuth, Neil M. and Eileen V. Pitpitan (2007) 'The effects of pornography are moderated by men's sexual aggression risk' in David E. Guinn with Julie Di Caro (Eds) *Pornography: Driving the Demand in International Sex Trafficking*. Captive Daughters Media, Los Angeles, pp. 125–143.

M'jid Maalla, Najat (2009) 'Report of the Special Rapporteur on the sale of children, child prostitution and child pornography' A/HRC/12/23 Human Rights Council, Geneva.

Quart, Alison (2004) *Branded: The Buying and Selling of Teenagers*. Basic Books, New York.

Ropelato, Jerry (n.d.) 'Internet Pornography Statistics', <http://internet-filter-review.topten reviews.com/internet-pornography-statistics.html>.

Rothbart, Davy (30 January, 2001) 'He's just not that into anyone' *New York Times Magazine*, <http://nymag.com/news/features/70976/>.

Sauers, Joan (2007) *Sex Lives of Australian Teenagers*. Random House, Sydney.

Scobie, Claire (6 February, 2007) 'Wild Things', *The Bulletin* p. 35, <http://clairescobie.com/static/files/assets/0a6c7553/040607_Sex_Lives_of_Teenagers_BTN.pdf>.

Tankard Reist, Melinda (5 December, 2008) 'Incensed about censorship' *Online Opinion*, <http://www.onlineopinion.com.au/view.asp?article=8176&page=3>.

Townsend, Mark (24 August, 2008) 'Babies are new target, Met warns as paedophile threat spirals', <http://www.guardian.co.uk/society/2008/aug/24/childprotection>.

Waltman, Max (2009) 'The Civil Rights Equality Deficit: Legal Challenges to Pornography and Sex Inequality in Canada, Sweden, and the U.S.' Paper presented at the annual meeting of the Canadian Political Science Association, Ottawa, 27–29 May, 2009, and the Law and Society Association, Denver, 28–31 June, 2009, <http://www.cpsa-acsp.ca/papers-2009/Waltman.pdf> (accessed 29 May, 2011).

Whisnant, Rebecca (2007) 'From Jekyll to Hyde: The grooming of male pornography consumers', in Karen Boyle (Ed) *Everyday Pornography*. Routledge, Abingdon, Oxon, UK, pp. 114–133.

Wosnitzer, Robert (n.d.) *The Price of Pleasure*, <http://thepriceofpleasure.com/pdf/robert_statment.pdf>.

Caroline

The Impact of Pornography on My Life

I'm anxious about writing this. Anxious that although I know rationally there is no way you can know who I am, I am still afraid.

In one sense you will know me. I'm the woman behind you in the supermarket queue or sitting opposite you on the train. Middle aged, middle class, educated, professional. Ordinary. Yet there is something in my life I will hide from you, no matter how close we are.

When I first met my partner, way back when, one quiet afternoon on my own in his flat I came across 3 dog-eared copies of *Playboy* in the back of his wardrobe. Flicking through the images of women in silk lingerie reclining in misty boudoirs, I was held. I could breathe these pictures to life with my own sexual imagination. They were mysterious, partial, hinting. It was a brief encounter with pornography. We stayed together, the paper pictures long thrown out.

Fast-forward many years. It happened like this. I borrowed my partner's laptop and as the cursor rolled slowly over the Internet history it revealed a trail of regular porn viewing. Panic. I clicked on to a couple of the sites. For someone who had never seen Internet porn, the sudden imagery of women displayed arse up, faceless, with orifices, raw, red and black, open and roughly penetrated was deeply, deeply distressing. These were explicit; viciously invading my sexual identity and choking it with images distorted, ugly, degraded. The click speed, the slickness of the connections revealed that this was no occasional or unwanted intrusion but a regular search on my partner's part to view.

How can I convey to you the way the stomach lurches and sickens with the discovery? A long-term loving relationship is built on things that are shared, unspoken, gathering over time. Love and making love; intimate, hidden, soft, warm and lingering; ruddy and boisterous; funny and fumbled. Trust, a commitment, ways of relating, a sexual life that you believe – oh, but believed until now – you both treasured. To discover suddenly that your partner has been visiting a secret, voyeur's world, and has sought out these other images of women for arousal; many, many women, is devastating.

I looked. Perhaps I shouldn't have done. But I looked because I needed to know what I was dealing with. I needed to know how far it extended. Who is this person I no longer recognise? I confronted. A wild, visceral, rage. His first reaction was to lie; to lie about the extent and to downplay it. I wasn't supposed to know. For how long? Three, maybe four years – three, four times a week. And maybe more than that when working away, alone in hotels. A rare few men may be so addicted that the viewing has become compulsive, but many more, much more insidiously across society as a whole, have become habitual viewers. Ordinary men, with ordinary partners. You and me.

I was repulsed. In this climate of permissiveness, we are not supposed to confess to repulsion. It sounds censorious, prim, prejudiced. We are supposed to be open-minded, extending our boundaries of acceptance. Rampant individualism, the free market, the liberal gods of freedom and choice, insist on each to his own by right. But where does another's supposed right infringe upon mine? Values of equality, respect, social responsibility, ethical concern for others – these are tossed aside; indifferent to the distress of others. But what is thought to be a question of freedom and choice, is in reality far from being free but instead is rigidly determined by the dominant, masculinist belief systems of our own society.

Once discovered he sought to justify and minimise the situation by one-sided arguments that ranged from – "it's just guys' stuff, a bit of fun, all guys look at porn, hey, get real – it's the way the world is now." The implication being that I was a prude, over-reacting and out of date. "It was just 'fantasy'", he said, and therefore not related to the real sex that we shared. My reply: "it's obvious fakery for the women – you can see that" was met with "no, no, you have that wrong, they are genuinely enjoying it." He knew. So it wasn't fantasy then? I was supposed to believe it was just a mild diversion, when for the women it had to be real. Any suggestion though of the reality that women were coerced or treated badly was dismissed. They were fine, they were well paid. Self-delusional and ambiguous arguments ran amok. He seemed to have gone to a different place; to comment about the women in porn and me in a cold and detached way, to say things about women's bodies, about sexual acts which came out of his mouth with swingeing bluntness. A layer of empathy had been ground away. My man. The one I had promised to love and cherish.

There is social-wide acceptance that an affair for a monogamous relationship is wrong, or at least if not wrong as such, certainly not conducive to the continuation of a trusting relationship. But with pornography there is no such clear line, with many levels of self-justification ready-made in a male dominated culture that the man can summon up to avoid having to look at its real impact on a loving relationship with cold, hard honesty. The male discourse provides justifications, minimisations that enable the man to deaden any lingering doubts.

We attended counselling. To my initial relief the counsellor acknowledged my enormous distress, and likened it to the discovery of an affair. This is a familiar approach, but while it helpfully acknowledges the degree of distress and the similar elements of secrecy, betrayal, hurt, there are some important differences. While I certainly wouldn't have wished my partner to have had an affair, it would have been one-person related sex (who would naturally have found him adorable), intimate, secret, warm-bodied in a form I recognised. What caused me immense distress was the considerable shift in sexuality brought about by the porn viewing, the nature of the sexuality that the porn represented and the thought that he had looked at probably hundreds of women engaged in the most intimate of acts – using them to harness his own desire, allowing it to romp through scenarios created out of the imaginations of the porn makers. The most intimate parts of myself that I share with him, and only him, now seemed worthless. Porn-centred sex is a selfish activity that denies and thus destroys connections with anything outside itself. The porn-viewing partner needs help in re-connecting and with being less obsessed by their own wants and desires. The partner of a porn-viewer needs help with the profound sense of being cast aside, not good enough, mixed with conflicting emotions of being degraded and defiled.

The counsellor, however, changed tack to frame our relationship as co-dependent. My partner was supposedly dominating, an addictive personality, and I was the weak, co-dependent partner. Her efforts focussed on endeavouring to convince me that the relationship was in negative territory. In a fragile, emotional state when the pieces of my relationship were broken and I needed help in carefully reassembling them, I took more than I should of what she said seriously.

We changed counsellors. The next took a different line. Men, I was to understand, were visual, wired differently. Implicitly they 'could not help it' poor things – a message of the biological imperative. I was to show compassion and understanding. Did he know before that 'no porn' was one of the relationship rules. No? Well, then, how could he know I would impose this restriction on him? Restriction? Restriction! Despite the fact that little compassion and understanding seemed to come my way, I tried. What I *have* discovered by hard experience is that run-of-the-mill relationship guidance has inadequate resources for dealing with the emotional fallout and relationship damage caused by today's Internet porn. I asked one of my counsellors if she had seen contemporary Internet pornography – she confessed she had not – they are working with out-of-date ideas. The result is that it's very difficult to get the kind of support and help that you need to recover – particularly if the relationship is long-term and loving and you are trying to repair after the crisis.

I needed to mourn the loss of my relationship as I knew it and thought of it, and of my sexual self. I needed help in knowing how I – we – could rebuild a relationship with someone who could view and talk of women in those terms and still hold respect for him and for myself. To some extent I've managed to live with that dilemma, not as I would have liked it by his reflective and remorseful analysis of what has happened, but by trying to understand the process myself whereby affectionate, intelligent, kind and thoughtful men can become hooked, for want of a better word, in this strange, isolated, distorted world.

In the end I found a confidential online counselling service dedicated to women whose partners are involved with habitual Internet porn the most helpful. My long screeds of email message would be carefully responded to with insightful understanding and practical suggestions. Whoever you are out there who wrote replies to my emails, often frenetically tapped in the small dark hours, I thank you.

I have no time whatsoever for those who see pornography as liberating or empowering to women's sexuality as this is absolutely not my experience at all. The distress caused sleepless nights, lots of crying, a constant feeling of being on edge, an anger that was all consuming.

A while on now, is it better? Carefully reassembling a relationship, mourning and accepting what has been lost, trying to make some parts anew, takes much time and patience. I still have enormous anger. Anger at him for, as I see it, being so easily drawn in to it. Some of my anger has, as I come to understand the psychology of porn viewing more, moved on to the industry. Yes he was responsible for his actions, but the industry is so slick at inveigling its way in. It toys with the masculine mind as our culture has made it. It quickly becomes a habit, desensitising, a siren pulling men in to dare to look at increasingly edgy images. Secret, exciting, elicit, nefarious. All the elements necessary to relationships – care, respect, responsibility, empathy, are not only deliberately negated in porn, but alternative reassurances and flatteries are subliminally implanted in their place.

Yes, my partner promised not to view again, and has kept to that. But only after a long period can I relax and trust him again. In the early days of abstinence, although he declared he did not need porn, and invited me to search his Internet history any time, the hidden cache files still told the truth of glimpses at porn here and there. So shifting the habit was not as easy as he had declared. The topic is sensitive and raw still. If it resurfaces in our conversation, he often has another newly minted justification to offer that is supposed to convince me of the innocuousness of the porn and his viewing of it – never the real acknowledgement of responsibility or the harm to our relationship. I wait for the day he'll say he thinks he understands and that he's sorry.

PART ONE

Pornography Cultures

"Each time I found porn photos on his PC or his iPod I would begin to feel less and less attractive and more worried that I was never going to be good enough for him." – Jade

"There is no glory in trying to make love to men who only know how to f**k – man after man after man raised on porn … A lot of guys have come to expect P.S.E. [the 'Porn Star Experience'] as a common thing … A few [women] might enjoy it, but for most it's harrowing. I think there's a fear that if they can't make it happen, their boyfriend will retreat online." – Sadie[1]

"The fact that I trusted him with my physical and emotional self has left me shattered especially when he did not deny my body DISGUSTED him because I did not look like the internet [surgically enhanced and airbrushed] females he spent every night with …" – Chantelle

"I was completely shattered. I felt disgusted and also ashamed, like it must in some way be my fault. Clearly I, his wife, was not satisfying him sexually. Worse than this, was the betrayal. He had lied to me for years. How could I trust him again? I started to think about times when he was in his study and I was somewhere else in the house. Had he been looking at pictures of naked women when I was there? Did he wish I looked like them, would do what they did? I felt sick." – Gina

---

1   <http://nymag.com/news/features/70976/>

Gail Dines

The New Lolita: Pornography and the Sexualization of Childhood

In 2008, Miley Cyrus was photographed for *Vanity Fair* wearing a bed hairdo, a provocative gaze, and not much else. She was 15 years old. Even though these photos caused a stir at the time, just a year later – when she appeared in *Elle* sprawled across a table wearing S&M gear – barely a voice of protest was heard. These images, together with the thousands of others that bombard us daily, are part of what media scholars call 'image-based culture'[1] a term used to describe a society in which images have replaced the spoken or written word as the major form of communication. From billboards to 24-hour television, the staple of this image-based culture is the youthful, sexualized female body. Advertisements, movies, TV shows, music videos, and pornography are just some of the ways in which this image is delivered to us, and as we become more desensitized to such depictions, the producers need to ramp up the degree to which the female body is sexualized as a way to get our attention. This has led to an increasingly pornographic media landscape, where the codes and conventions that inform pornography filter down to such a level that the images we now see in mainstream media are almost on a par with those that were found in softcore porn just a decade ago.

As pop culture begins to look more and more pornographic, the actual porn industry has had to trend more hardcore as a way of distinguishing its products from those images found on MTV, in *Cosmopolitan*, and on billboards. Often called 'gonzo' by the industry, this subgenre is made up of acts that are designed to dehumanize and debase the woman with cruel and brutal sex that includes gagging with a penis and multiple men ejaculating onto her face and body. The problem for the pornographers is that consumers are becoming increasingly desensitized to such hardcore porn and are always on the lookout for something new and fresh. Porn director, Jules Jordan, who is known for a particularly violent brand of porn, said that even he is "always trying to figure out ways to do something different" since the fans "are becoming a lot more demanding about

---

1   For a more extensive analysis, see Jhally (1990).

wanting to see the more extreme stuff" (in Jensen, 2007, p. 70). So one of the big challenges pornographers constantly have to grapple with is how to keep their customers interested.

It is this need to find new niche products that provides insight into why, in 2002, the Free Speech Coalition (the lobbying organization for the porn industry) worked to change the 1996 Child Pornography Prevention Act that prohibited any image that "is, or appears to be, of a minor engaging in sexually explicit conduct." Arguing that the words "appears to be" limited the free speech of the pornographers, the coalition successfully got this 'limitation' removed. The law was thus narrowed to cover only those images in which an actual person (rather than one who appears to be) under the age of 18 was involved in the making of the porn. Thus, the path was cleared for the porn industry to use either computer-generated images of children or real porn performers who, although 18 or over, are childified to look much younger.

Since that 2002 decision, there has been an explosion in the number of sites that childify women, as well as those that use computer-generated imagery. Pseudo Child Pornography (PCP) sites that use adults (those people defined by the law as 18 or over) to represent children is never called child pornography by the industry. Instead, almost all of those sites that childify the female porn performer are found in the subgenre called 'teen-porn' or 'teen-sex' by the industry. There are any number of ways to access these sites, the most obvious one being Google. Typing 'Teen Porn' into Google yields over 30 million hits, giving the user his[2] choice of thousands of porn sites. A number of the hits are actually for porn portals where 'teen porn' is one sub-category of many, and when the user clicks on that category, a list of sites comes up that runs over 90 pages. Moreover, teen porn has its very own portal,[3] which lists hundreds of sub-subgenres such as 'Pissing Teens', 'Drunk Teens', 'Teen Anal Sluts', and 'Asian Teens'.

The competition for customers is fierce in the porn industry, since the user, sitting at his computer and eager to begin his masturbatory session, has a cornucopia of sites, themes, images, and narratives to choose from. The

---

2   I refer to the user in the masculine since the majority of porn consumers are men. While it is impossible to give an accurate breakdown of male and female consumers, Mark Kernes, senior editor of the pornography trade magazine *Adult Video News*, stated that "Our statistics show that 78% of the people that go into adult stores are men. They may have women with them, but it's men, and 22%, conversely, is women or women with other women or women alone." (Author interview at the Adult Entertainment Expo in Las Vegas with Robert Jensen, 7 January, 2005).

3   <http://www.ultraenlist.com> (accessed 18 December, 2007).

pornographers know this, so they attempt to pull the user in quickly by giving the sites names that are short, to the point, and unambiguous. It is therefore not surprising that many of the sites in this category actually have the word 'teen' in the name, for example, *Solo Teen*, *Solo Teen Babe*, *Sexy Teen Girl*, *Teen Cuties*, and *Solo Teen Girls*. When the user clicks on any one of these sites, the first and most striking feature is the body shape of the female porn performers. In place of the large-breasted, curvaceous bodies that populate regular porn Websites, there are small-breasted, slightly built women with adolescent-looking faces that are relatively free of make-up. Many of these performers do look younger than 18, but they do not look like children, so the pornographers use a range of techniques to make them appear more childlike than they actually are. Primary among these is the use of childhood clothes and props such as stuffed animals, lollipops, pigtails, pastel-colored ribbons, ankle socks, braces on the teeth and, of course, the school uniform. It is not unusual to see a female porn performer wearing a school uniform, sucking a lollipop, and hugging a teddy bear while she masturbates with a dildo.

Another technique for childifying the woman's body is the removal of all pubic hair so that the external genitalia look like that of a pre-pubescent female. What is interesting is that over the years, this technique has lost much of its signifying power, as it is now commonplace in porn for women to remove all their pubic hair. One of the results of this is that today, virtually every female porn performer has genitalia that look like a pre-pubescent female. This is a shift that, in itself, is cause for concern, as those porn users who are not looking for pseudo-child images nonetheless are exposed to them when they surf the porn sites. This normalization of a shaved pubic area is filtering down increasingly into mainstream pop culture, with regular articles in women's magazines discussing the best way to remove pubic hair, TV shows such as *Sex and the City* publicizing and eroticizing the Brazilian Bikini Wax, and beauty salons across the country promoting the Brazilian as a way to spice up sex. The effect this is having on adolescent girls was made evident to me when I spoke to the Sexual Assault Nurse Examiner (SANE) Conference in Boston in 2007. These nurses administer rape kits on adolescents who are the victims of sexual assault, and one of their tasks is to check for the markers of puberty, with pubic hair being a key marker. However, I was informed that this is no longer effective, as girls are removing the hair as soon as it grows, something that the nurses had never seen before. In my interviews with college-age females, I hear repeatedly that pubic hair is considered unhygienic and a sexual turnoff by their boyfriends, so they now wax or shave. This is probably one of the clearest examples of how a porn-generated practice slips into the lives of real women, no doubt because a good percentage of the male partners have become accustomed to, and are aroused by, images of women in porn.

For all of the visual clues of childhood surrounding the women in PCP sites, however, it is the written text accompanying the images that does most of the work in convincing the user that he is masturbating to images of sexual activity involving a minor. The words used to describe the women's bodies (including their vaginas) – tiny, small, petite, tight, cute, teeny – not only stress their youthfulness but also work to separate them from women on other sites, since these are adjectives rarely used to describe women in regular porn. Most striking is how many of these PCP sites refer to the females as sweeties, sweethearts, little darlings, cutie pies, honeys – terms of endearment that starkly contrast with the abusive names the women on other sites are called (slut, whore, cumdumpster, and cunt being the most popular). The use of kinder terms on the PCP sites is a method of preserving the notion for the user that these girls are somehow different from the rest of the women who populate the world of porn in that they are not yet used-up whores deserving of verbal abuse. This would explain why so many of these Websites have the word 'innocent' in their names, for example, *Innocent Cute*, *Innocent Dream*, *Innocent Love*, and *Petite Innocent*.

The reason why innocence is so central to the marketing of the sites and why the girls are portrayed as not yet sullied, dirtied, soiled, or tainted by sex is that the promise on offer on the Website is a witnessing of their loss of innocence. One fan of this genre, writing to a porn discussion forum, calls this a "knowing innocence," which he defines as "the illusion of innocence giving way to unbridled sexuality. Essentially, this is the old throwback of the Madonna and the Whore. Therein lies the vast majority of my attraction to this genre."[4] This fan and indeed many others (if their posts are to be believed) make clear that for them, the pleasure is in watching the (sweet, cute, petite) Madonna being coaxed, encouraged, and manipulated by adult men into revealing the whore that lies beneath the (illusionary) innocence.

The pornographers reveal their understanding of the nature of this spectatorial pleasure when they offer the guarantee to their consumers that the 'girls' they are watching are "first timers," having their "first sexual experience," which, of course, leads to their "first orgasm ever." The *Solo Teen* site goes so far as to promise that "[h]ere you will ONLY find the cutest teen girls ... Our

---

4   <http://forum.adultdvdtalk.com/forum/topic.dlt/topic_id=108072/forum_id=1/cat_id=1/108072.htm> (accessed 19 January, 2008).

girls are fresh and inexperienced and very sexy in an innocent kind of way." It is thus no surprise that most of these sites advertise "fresh girls added each week," since using the same performer twice would cut into the sexual excitement of the viewer. How, after all, does one defile an already-defiled girl?

The story of the 'defilement' told on these sites is genre-bound in that it almost always starts with an eager but innocent girl who is gently and playfully coaxed by off-camera adult men into performing sexually for the pleasure of the viewer. This is the narrative informing most of the images on the *SoloTeengirls.com* site, which has hundreds of movies available to members, as well as hundreds of still photographs posted on the site as a teaser for non-members. Each woman has 5 photographs and a written text detailing her supposed first sexual experience. For 'Natasha' the story goes as follows:

> This lil cutie came in pretending that she couldn't wait to be naked in front of the camera. And … we couldn't wait to see her. As she started to take off her clothes and show off she giggled and smiled but we could tell she was nervous and when she found out that naked meant showing off her snug little teen pussy she blushed! But showing off her pussy proved to be too much of a turn on and when *we encouraged* her to play with it she could not resist. This beautiful teen girl really *did have her first time* on camera and we got to watch her stroke that velvety teen pussy (my emphasis).

The message that the written text conveys in this story can be found throughout the Websites in this category, as it embodies the way in which the pornographers carefully craft a story of who is really innocent and who is really culpable in the scenario. For all the supposed innocence of the 'lil cutie', as evidenced by her nervousness, giggling, smiling, and blushing, it really only took a bit of encouragement to get her to masturbate for the camera, which in porn-world language is another way of saying that it didn't take much for her to reveal the slut she really is. It is this very culpability on the part of the girl that simultaneously divests the user of his culpability in masturbating to what would be, in reality, a scenario of adult men manipulating a naïve girl into masturbating for the pleasure of other adult men, himself included.

The obvious question here is: what effect could these sites have on the viewers? Once they click on these sites, users are bombarded – through images and words – with an internally consistent ideology that legitimizes, condones, and celebrates a sexual desire for children. The norms and values that circulate in society and define adult–child sex as deviant and abusive are wholly absent in PCP, and in their place is a cornucopia of sites that deliver the message (to the viewer's brain, via the penis), that sex with children is hot fun for all.

There is a wealth of research within media studies that shows that people construct their notions of reality from the media they consume, and the more consistent and coherent the message, the more people believe it to be true.[5] Thus, the images of girls in PCP do not exist within a social vacuum, but rather are produced and consumed within a society where the dominant pop culture images are of childified women and hypersexualized, youthful female bodies. Encoded within all of these images is an ideology that encourages the sexual objectification of the female body, an ideology that is internalized by both males and females, and has become so widespread that it normalizes the sexual use and abuse of females. This does not mean that all men who masturbate to PCP will rape a child, or even be sexually attracted to a child. What it does mean, however, is that on a cultural level, when we sexualize the female child, we chip away at the norms that define children as off limits to male sexual use. The more we undermine such cultural norms, the more we drag girls into the category of 'woman', and in a porn-saturated world, to be woman is to be a sexual object deserving of male contempt, use, and abuse.

Bibliography

Gerbner, George (1998) 'Cultivation Analysis: An Overview' *Mass Communication and Society* 1 (3&4), pp. 175–194.

Jensen, Robert (2007) *Getting Off: Pornography and the End of Masculinity*. South End Press, Boston.

Jhally, Sut (1990) 'Image-Based Culture: Advertising and Popular Culture' *The World and I*, July, pp. 506–519.

Quayle, Ethel and Max Taylor (2002) 'Child Pornography and the Internet: Perpetuating a Cycle of Abuse' *Deviant Behavior* 23 (4), pp. 331–361.

Russell, Diana and Natalie J. Purcell (2006) 'Exposure to Pornography as a Cause of Child Sexual Victimization' in Nancy E. Dowd, Dorothy G. Singer, and Robin Fretwell Wilson (Eds) *Handbook of Children, Culture and Violence*, pp. 59–82. Sage Publications, Thousand Oaks, CA.

---

5   For a discussion of the findings of over 30 years of studies on how media shapes the social construction of reality, see Gerbner (1998).

Catharine A. MacKinnon

X-Underrated: Living in a World the Pornographers Have Made[1]

The belief that pornography inhabits its own physical and mental world is an illusion. Nothing restricts its effects. Yet the protective myth of its spatial separation and cognitive confinement endures, even as pornography visibly takes over more and more public and private space, invading homes and offices and transforming popular culture.

There is such a thing as pornography, as its producers and consumers well know. No one is making tens of billions of dollars from, or masturbating to, the Bible, for example. This is only to notice that the pornography industry and mass media have long operated in separate spheres defined by content. In the name of taste, values or division of labour, legitimate cinema, books and media have traditionally eschewed or coyly skirted the sexually explicit. The 'adult' movie industry, cable television and 'men's entertainment' magazines have frontally specialised in it. This mutually clear line, quite precisely and effortlessly observed in practice, coexists with the common cant that pornography cannot be defined or distinguished from anything else.

Pornography is increasingly making popular culture more pornographic. This effect is routinely observed and sometimes deplored, whether for sexually ob-jectifying women yet more inescapably, or for taking away the sexiness of the forbidden. But if this movement is rarely documented, and even more seldom explained, the fact that pornography itself has been a popular feature of culture – the most mass of media – for some time is never faced.

Society's ideology of compartmentalisation – that the rest of life can go on unaffected – never seems to be embarrassed by pornography's ubiquity. It has been in plain sight all along. In reality, pornography's place is just down the street, right there on the rack in the convenience store, not to mention in the bedrooms and bathrooms of homes where its users seldom live alone. Yet even as the industry has burgeoned, taking over more public space and penetrating more deeply into private life at home and at work with each advance in technology, it is considered to be somehow not really there.

---

1   This is an edited version of 'X underrated' published in the UK *Times Higher Education,* <http://www.timeshighereducation.co.uk/story.asp?sectioncode=26&storycode=196151>.

The same dissociative logic structures the legal regulation of pornography.

Obscenity, one meaning of which is off stage, is located in some neighbour-hoods and not others. The question of where is politically fought over locally like the placement of noxious waste, as if its effects can be so confined. Pornography has to be somewhere, the attitude is, the only question is where. (One reading of the law of this subject in the USA revolves around how far a man has to travel to get his fix before it becomes unconstitutional.) Pornography is considered addressed by the legal sleight of hand through which it is imagined placed in some demimonde: over there rather than right here.

Beyond the geographical, the psychological disconnect is perhaps most socially potent: the delusion that pornography is 'fantasy'. 'No woman was ever ruined by a book', as the slogan goes. This gives using pornography a certain deniability. Never mind that someone has to be sexually used to make the visual materials that form the vast majority of the industry's output. Never mind that among the first and most robust of the results of consumption is the spontaneous generation of rape fantasies, or that people often do what they imagine they want to do. Never mind that 'fantasy' is the word used by a man convicted of being about to make a snuff film of a boy, to describe the detailed plans he was intercepted discussing, or what the media reported a man was having with a prostitute whom he drowned in a bathtub.

One telling episode in these annals of denial arose in the publication of *American Psycho*, an upmarket, high-concept work of fiction in which one woman after another is sexually slaughtered. Women are skinned alive, mutilated, raped and one dismembered head is used for oral sex, all in graphic and explicit terms. Simon and Schuster, in an exceptional move, rescinded its contract of publication shortly before the book was due out.

It was rumoured by insiders that women on the staff refused to have it published in their house.

The publishing industry has long coexisted with – at times affirmatively defended – the pornography industry. This includes the film *Snuff*, a sex movie available since 1972 right down the street from Simon and Schuster, in which a woman is shown being disemboweled while alive. The shock of, hence the opposition to, *American Psycho* was apparently that it was here, in mainstream publishing. As long as sexual killing is happening 'over there', it is as if it is not happening at all. *American Psycho* seemed to shatter that illusion of context for some people, at least momentarily. The book was quickly bought and published by Vintage, a division of Random House.

A similar magical framing move occurred in connection with the scandal surrounding Abu Ghraib in 2004. The photos of naked Arab men being abused by American soldiers while in their custody were routinely termed pictures of torture and sexual humiliation in the press. If the fact that the photos were identical to much pornography (although mild by its standards) was noticed at all, it was more often to excuse the crimes than to indict the pornography. Then a mass-market US newspaper was duped into publishing photos said to be of an Iraqi woman being raped by American soldiers that turned out to come from pornography. The public was upset by the pictures – until they found out that it was pornography. The newspaper apologised for not properly authenticating the picture.

The photos, had they been what they were thought to have been, would have documented criminal atrocities. The identical picture, framed as pornography, became masturbation material that a legitimate outlet had been cleverly tricked into putting on its front page in another blow for sexual freedom of expression. As pornography, the conditions of its making – who was she? how did she get there? was she being raped? – were not subject to inquiry. They never are.

The assumption that the violence, violation and abuse that is shown in pornography is somehow 'consensual' is just that: an assumption. It coexists with much evidence of force and coercion, beginning with the materials themselves. Mass emails advertising photos of 'hostages raped!' are spammed to Internet accounts without generating inquiry into whether they are either. A Website called Slavefarm offered women for sale as 'sexual slaves', complete with contracts signing away all human rights and explicit photographs of the slave being tortured. Authorities stonewalled.

Live feed provides direct sexual use of prostituted women onscreen. No matter how real and harmful it gets, pornography, in reality a form of trafficking in women, is this parallel universe in which everything that happens becomes harmless and unreal.

Long overlapping sub rosa with legitimate entertainment, pornography has been a criminal underworld pursuit. Making it still is. But as it has exploded to an industry approaching earnings of US$100 billion globally, its distributors no longer live under rocks. Legitimate corporations now traffic pornography, often through subsidiaries, their financial stake as immense and established as it is open.

Certainly the level of threat and damage to women's status and treatment and to equality of the sexes worsens as pornography has gone mainstream and is seen as more legitimate. Venue does matter. That does not mean that pornography has not been a dangerous, damaging and real part of social life all along. As its effects worsen, the more widespread and visible pornography becomes, the view – as tenacious and pernicious as it is baseless – that it has no effects as long as it stays underground – makes its march into the open possible. If the spatial separation of pornography into its own little world has been dubious, its mental isolability is pure delusion. Pornography changes its consumers, who then go everywhere under its influence. Nothing contains them.

Excellent social science research over the past 25 years has documented the effects of exposure to pornography, providing a basis to extrapolate the predictable consequences of mass social saturation. The catharsis hypothesis – the notion that the more pornography men use, the less abusive sex they will seek out elsewhere – has been scientifically disproved.

Closer to the reverse has been found: it primes the pump. As women have long known, use of pornography conditions consumers to objectified and aggressive sex, desensitising them to domination and abuse, requiring escalating levels of violence to achieve a sexual response. Use of pornography is also correlated with increased reports by perpetrators of aggressive sex and with increased inability to perceive that sex is coerced. Consumers thus become increasingly unable to distinguish rape from other sex. Some become addicted, virtually none is unaffected, the evidence as a whole suggests.

Consuming pornography, with some individual variation, produces attitudes and behaviours of discrimination and violence, particularly against powerless others. By extension, the more pornography is consumed, the more difficult it will become, socially, to tell when rape is rape, even for some victims. An increase in sexual assault, accompanied by a drop in reporting and low conviction rates, is predictable. All this has happened.

Mass desensitisation of a major segment of the viewing public has a corresponding effect on the rest of popular culture. The audience for popular culture is the same as the audience for pornography. Ten winos in raincoats are not producing the industry's revenue figures. Popular culture, from advertising to legitimate film and books, has to become correspondingly more explicitly sexual – specifically more sexually aggressive and demeaning to women – to get the desired rise out of the same audience. Advertising is a particularly sensitive barometer of this effect.

How that public buys, what it demands, how it responds and what it wants to see are being significantly controlled, skewed by pornographers. Soft pornography blurs into light entertainment. The powerful conditioning of huge proportions of the male public makes them demand that the women around them look and act in conforming ways. We increasingly live in a world the pornographers have made.

High culture is affected as well. Women writers who present young girls loving being sexually initiated by old men, daughters feeling ambivalent about sex with their fathers, pornography being part of the old world of freedom rather than a future dystopia of totalitarianism, rocket to success. It is not that they are not fine writers. It is the fact that their work converges with pornographic conditioning, affirms it in a classy woman's voice that catapults them to the top, makes their work suddenly catch on as exciting. It is the moment of, and precondition for, their success. Academic women who breathlessly defend pornography benefit from the same response. Criticising pornography, or writing so that rape is experienced by the reader as abuse, produces the opposite reaction: detumescent shunning. When feminists unmask pornography effectively, those who support it suddenly become favourites du jour. It works for men, too.

Excuse sexual assault ever more openly, present women who oppose pornography as befuddled if well-intentioned moralists, attack serious approaches to the problem as evil censorship and you too may receive a Nobel prize for literature.

Tracking the escalation in sexual explicitness and sexual violence in mainstream cinema is child's play. More to the point, why was Sharon Stone's vaginal flash in *Basic Instinct* so electrifying, such a sensation? Far more than that was available in any softcore pornography film or magazine right down the street. It was context: a mainstream actor, doing it here, in a mainstream film in a family cinema. Breaking the frame on sex gives a frisson of power, it seems, for which you first have to believe that the frame is there. Why was it shocking when Janet Jackson's breast popped out in a dance-attack on her in the Superbowl halftime show? *Playboy* has scores monthly; page three, at least 2 a day. But this was a mainstream singer, here, in family time during one of masculinity's public ritual events. Audiences are thrilled, scandalised, titillated. Barriers broken. Pundits juiced. Territory gained. Freedom reigns.

Who pays? Stone was told when she shot that scene that the footage would not be used (hence its grainy first-take outtake quality); she reportedly suffered considerably when it was. Jackson more or less apologised for the 'wardrobe malfunction'. However, they felt they had to be good sports for the sake of their careers, a pressure that continues. Pornographic portrayals of feminist antipornography writer, Andrea Dworkin, lowered the floor on how she was seen and treated for life.

In pornography, women are publicly construed as members of an inferior sex-based group and constructed, some individually, before they are ever known personally. Sexual arousal, excitement and satisfaction are harnessed to that portrayal, reinforcing it, naturalising it, making it unquestionable and irrefutable. So, too, for all the nameless women used in pornography – society's 'whores'. Pornography is a mass instrument for creating how women in general, specific women and groups of women in particular, are seen, treated and received. It constructs their status as unequal and their reputation as inferior. Few weep for a 'whore's' reputation.

Meanwhile, progressive people, whatever they really think, defend pornography's right to exist and other people's right to use it, in tones pious and terms high-minded. Esoteric debates about aesthetics and causation take place amid periodic convulsions of moral fervour, producing occasional convictions for obscenity or restrictions on indecency. The industry shapes itself to law, and, more crucially, law to it. Most fundamentally, pornography changes culture to protect its existence and extend its reach, so finally it will be true that there is no distinction between pornography and anything else. The best camouflage of all is being able to lie around in plain sight.

People who do not want to be accosted by pornography visually are expected to avert their eyes. Having fewer and fewer places to avert their eyes to, with fewer means of escape in public and none in private, women specifically – who are most endangered by these materials and often know it – are segregated, painted into ever smaller corners. The female version of the male compartmentalisation myth is, 'pornography has nothing to do with me'. Pornography is thus at once increasingly everywhere and yet protected from direct scrutiny and effective abolition by seeming not to be there at all.

In 1983, Andrea Dworkin and I proposed a civil law that would empower anyone who could prove they are hurt through pornography to sue the pornographers for human rights violations. We defined pornography as what it is – graphic sexually explicit subordination of women through pictures and words that also includes specified presentations – and defined causes of action for coercion, force, assault and trafficking. We documented its effects and predicted its impact if nothing was done. Our law was found unconstitutional in the USA in a ruling that held that pornography had to be protected as 'speech' because it is so effective in doing the harm that the opinion conceded it does. Since then, although the law could have been re-passed and this blatantly wrong and arguably illegal ruling challenged, pornography has not only exploded, it has changed the world around us. Even the determinedly blinkered cannot evade noticing. It is colonising the globe.

The pornography industry is a lot bigger, more powerful, more legitimate, more in everyone's face today than it was a quarter of a century ago. To the degree that it cannot exist without doing real damage, it could still be stopped in its tracks anywhere by this law. Sexual objectification and violation does not happen all by itself. Real social institutions drive it. Pornography does, powerfully, in capitalist mass-mediated cultures.

If nothing is done, the results will keep getting worse. We told you so.

Maggie Hamilton

Groomed to Consume Porn: How Sexualised Marketing Targets Children

The pornification of our children and teenagers is a dark tale of greed, exploitation, and corporate muscle, orchestrated by those whose sole focus is on how much money they can make from our kids. Little or no thought is given to the devastating impact this trend has on them.

The level of exposure of children to porn, and the young age at which many are viewing this material – accidentally or otherwise – is cause for grave concern. Symantec's 2009 study of children online revealed the word 'porn' ranked as the fourth most popular search word for children aged 7 and younger, and was in the top 5 words googled by children under 18 (Campbell, 2010).

The explosion of new technologies gives children access to the best and worst of online content. Aside from home computers, pornographic content is now accessible to kids on their mobile phones. They may view porn at their friends' place or at less than vigilant Internet cafes. The advent of wireless technologies also means that as long as they can get a connection, children can download porn on buses or trains, in parks, out with friends, or wherever they choose. The presence of porn in our children's lives has happened in a few short years, and is radically changing childhood and teenage life. When we fail to come to terms with this changing landscape, we leave children vulnerable in ways never-before-experienced.

Less obvious, but of equal concern, is the direct link between the increasing sexualisation of girls and boys, and their interest in and exposure to porn. The fallout from the countless sexual images seen in ads, on TV screens, posters and billboards, in MTV clips, movies, video games and sitcoms, on clothing and accessories, and on the Internet, is real and impacting. This constant stream of hypersexualised imagery and sexual expression that boys and girls are subjected to daily lowers their inhibitions, discourages empathy towards others, and reshapes their sexual aspirations and expression often in risky, violent or unhelpful ways.

Whether or not the use of sexual images and messages to market products is intended to prepare children for the consumption of porn, this is one of the most concerning outcomes. When the intense sexualised marketing to children is put under the microscope, we see that the methods corporations use to reach children are the very same techniques employed by sexual predators to home in on unsuspecting kids, as they meticulously groom them for their own ends. Like the sexual predator, corporations market their products to young people by pretending to be their friend. Using the same techniques as a predator, they work hard at cultivating a one-on-one relationship with our children, offering gifts and incentives, flattering them, talking in their language, and assuring kids that they understand. Like the sexual predator, corporations deliberately use sexualised content in their products and/or advertising, because they know how irresistible sexualised material can be. And, like the sexual predator, corporations actively ramp up the sexualised images and products they use, to lower kids' inhibitions around sex, to get them to do what they want.

Perhaps most insidious of all is the way a predator works to separate a child victim from his/her parents and other gatekeepers, leaving them isolated and vulnerable. Again, corporations use this same technique. So even though increasing numbers of parents complain about the sexy tops and skirts, padded bras and sexy underwear available to young kids, still the corporations rule. Sexualised marketing is now so prevalent among manufacturers of teen products most of us scarcely give it a thought. What would have been inconceivable a decade ago has very quickly become an integral part of teenagers' lives. As noted media critic Professor Mark Crispin Miller puts it, "The official advertising worldview is that your parents are creeps, teachers are nerds and idiots, authority figures are laughable, nobody can really understand kids except the corporate sponsor" (Miller, PBS, undated).

When a girl or boy grows up in a toxic sexual atmosphere, their inhibitions are lowered to the point that accessing porn seems a natural progression. The sexualised climate our children are growing up in is a *manufactured* process, not an organic one. The sexualised landscape children are now forced to inhabit reshapes their attitudes to sex and their desires, and it starts long before they learn to read or write. During my research for *What's Happening to Our Girls?* and the subsequent presentation of this material to thousands of parents, so many voiced their concern at the sexualised behaviour and language they are seeing in children aged 3 and up. Jacki, a health professional and mother of a 5-year-old boy, spoke with concern at her son talking of 'sexing' girls, when referring to girls he liked, after day care (Hamilton, 2008/2009, p. 19). Gemma, also a mum and kindergarten teacher, talked of the level of sexualised behaviour she was seeing, to the point that she and other teachers were having to be extra vigilant around the toilets and out-of-the-way parts of the pre-school grounds

(Hamilton, 2008/2009, p. 19). Another grandmother was worried to find her young granddaughter accessing porn sites on her computer when she stayed over. It transpired that the little girl had been told about these sites by a friend at school (Hamilton, 2008/2009, p. 52).

Whether intentional or not, the sexualised marketing to children is negatively impacting their lives, attuning them to pornographic themes and behaviour. Alongside relatively innocuous online games, such as *Club Penguin*, young boys can now access the Play Games Club, for example, which in amongst action games offers boys such raunchy games as *Hot Gllrs*, where the screen explodes with large-breasted young girls. There's *Naughty Classroom* and *Naughty Office* where points are awarded for a variety of moves including players viewing women's panties and breasts. There's also the *Funny Red Carpet* game where boys have to join various objects together. Their reward? To systematically strip the girls of their clothes. These games encourage boys to be voyeuristic, to have denigrating attitudes towards girls and women. And having sampled this kind of material, young boys could be forgiven for assuming porn is the 'natural' next step.

One of the many concerns around this active sexualising of small children is their desire to re-enact the scenarios they've been exposed to on their peers, creating a new level of child abuse. Add to this the plethora of sexualised images on billboards and in ads, and MTV clips and it's not hard to see how their attitudes are being shaped in unhealthy ways as they are actively encouraged to take part in predatory and/or risky behaviour. This early sexualisation of little boys is nothing short of abusive. It collapses vital parts of their humanity and erodes their ability to connect meaningfully with others. As professor of nursing, Ann Burgess from the University of Pennsylvania, reminds us that the formation of sexual identity is a gradual process that develops through the childhood and adolescent years. Left to their childhood, boys and girls generally do not have a *natural* sexual sense until they are between 10 and 12 years old. Previously, most children came to understand the sexual landscape and their own emerging sexuality in age-appropriate stages, which are now hastened and distorted by the sexualised climate our children are immersed in. According to Burgess, this leaves boys and girls "confused, changed, and damaged" (Burgess, 1997).

Rowan, a youth worker, told me: "We are now seeing children grooming younger kids for sex, there's a real seduction pattern going on" (in Hamilton, 2010, p. 64).

> We're now seeing kids sexually active way under 10, because of access to porn or their parents' own behaviour. I've seen many cases where porn is readily left around the home, where it's part of the family culture. Then you've got parents who carefully stash their porn away, and kids have a way of finding it (in Hamilton, 2010 p. 68).

These incidents are happening in homes across the socio-economic spectrum.

As boys grow, so does the desensitisation. The challenge for boys in the popular *Grand Theft Auto* is to progress as far as they can in the world of organised crime. To win, boys have to commit a range of crimes from killing cops to getting involved in prostitution. In the Microsoft and console versions of the *San Andreas* game there's a sex mini-game, the 'hot coffee mod', where players can have sex with their online girlfriend. In the fantasy and science fiction online games MUDs (multiple user dungeon virtual games), and MMORPGs (massively multiple player online role-playing games) such as *Rune Scape*, there are opportunities for any boy able to find his way around this game to take part in virtual sex or cybering. Here, their avatars (online personas) can simulate sex with other consenting avatars. Those in the know can also highjack someone else's avatars and use them in violent or sexual ways (Hamilton, 2010, p. 162). While some games have an MA15+ classification, there is nothing to prevent younger children in Australia purchasing and playing these games as long as they have a parent's consent.

In virtual worlds such as *Second Life*, there are thousands of sex workers willing to perform virtual sex for 'Lindens' (Second Life currency) or for real money. Other sites have been set up purely to offer virtual sex (Ruberg, 2007). On YouTube there are several highly lucrative porn equivalents. Here millions of viewers can watch endless video clips of live sex. Some videos are professional, many homemade. While some content is free, others charge people to view every sexual act imaginable. Children and teenagers are accessing virtual sex sites, viewing live sex via web cams and chat roulette, amateur porn through such sites as redtube (one of a number of YouTube porn sites), and sharing sexual images on mobile phones and through email.

A Canadian study of 13 to 14-year-old boys in urban and rural areas revealed that more than a third of these boys viewed pornographic movies and DVDs 'too many times to count'. Just over 7 out of 10 of these boys accessed pornography on the Net. More than half saw it on a specialty TV channel. In this same study 2 out of 10 boys viewed porn at the home of a friend (Betkowski, 2007).

In a few short years, porn has become a 'natural' part of teen life for a significant number of boys. This was borne out in my research for *What's Happening To Our Boys?* As Hunter, 18, explained, "Porno is so easy to access now with technology, to access and to buy" (in Hamilton, 2010, p. 221). Harrison, 15, agreed:

There's the porno aspect of the Internet now. Kids don't have to buy it off older boys like they used to do. It's readily accessible too. Some boys use it quite regularly. There's quite a culture of it. Inside jokes and words. A lot of boys talk about it in an open and relaxed manner. Most of my peer group admit to doing it. It can change the way boys talk in groups (in Hamilton, 2010, p. 222).

The boys I spoke with were very relaxed when talking about their experiences around porn. They had no sense that this mass access is a new phenomenon.

Dr Michael Flood, who headed up the Violence Against Women Program, a partnership between VicHealth and Latrobe University from 2008 to 2010, points out that the Internet is an ideal medium for boys wanting to access porn, as there's an almost endless amount of material they can view anonymously, customise, and store for on-going access (Flood, 2007, p. 48). Like many professionals, he is at pains to emphasise that pornography is a poor sex educator (Flood, 2007, p. 58). Porn shuts down a boy's natural feeling, as it places little value on intimacy, empathy or respect of partners in pornographic material. A growing body of research also shows that viewing porn is likely to make boys more sexually aggressive, to do whatever they feel they can get away with, and to want to act out what they have seen (Flood, 2009, p. 390). One Canadian study of teen boys revealed that those who regularly accessed porn tended to think it was okay to hold a girl down and force her to have sex (Wellard, 2001, pp. 26–27). A 2008 White Ribbon Foundation report found 1 in 7 boys thought it was OK to force a girl to have sex if she had been 'flirting' with him (Flood and Fergus, 2008, p. 24).

Educators are very aware of the fallout from porn and the wider hyper-sexualised landscape boys now inhabit. "It all starts with the language – how sex is referred to. Young boys talking about 'fucking a girl', 'having a fuck'," Sara, a young high school teacher, told me. "They wander around the school grounds saying 'I'd tap that', or 'I wouldn't tap that'. Or they talk openly about 'fingering her'. It's this grotesque, yet casual way they talk in a demeaning way about girls as sex objects" (Hamilton, 2008/2009, pp. 207–208). This exposure can impact a boy's life in ways it's hard to retreat from. Bryan Duke, himself a dad, who runs a juvenile regional mentoring program for young men and boys, has real concerns about porn.

> It awakens boys too soon to respond in a healthy way to sexual situations. They're too young to make commonsense decisions. It's like kids who have suffered sexual abuse. Their sexual experiences come out in their drawings, their thinking, their perspective. Sex is now part of the perspective of a growing number of kids 10, 11 and 12 (Hamilton, 2010, p. 69).

Studies back this up, showing that children who view porn on the Net become desensitised to this material and may then become sexually abusive towards others (Flood, 2009, p. 393).

Academic and activist, Gail Dines, reminds us of the impact on women and girls as well. "Porn culture doesn't only affect men. It also changes the way women and girls think about their bodies, their sexuality and their relationships" (in Bindel, 2010). This was evident in my research for *What's Happening to Our Girls?* Many professionals expressed their concerns at the level at which girls are now objectifying themselves. "When you talk to girls about sex, they don't have sex for pleasure or because they've got a special boyfriend," one high school teacher told me. "Most of the time it's just spread your legs for a boy" (Hamilton, 2008/2009 p. 158). Under-age girls were engaging in oral and anal sex, threesomes and group sex. One of the most poignant stories one teacher told was of an at-risk girl who was having a great deal of difficulty holding things together. Eventually the girl opened up, talking of her many sexual encounters with boys and with her stepfather. As she talked about her life, she had no sense of being violated in any way.

Then there are the young girls who have a 'friend with benefits' or a 'f**k buddy' – a boy they like as a friend, with whom they have no-strings-attached sex. Others are attracted to, or peer pressured into, more risky situations, such as 'randoming', where they see a guy they like the look of but have never met, and make a beeline for him in the expectation they'll have casual sex.

"Rainbow kiss is an oral sex party game" explains Slight, on the Net. "All the girls put on a different shade of colorful lipstick and the guy with the most colors on his dick by the end of the night usually wins a drink or something along those lines" (Slight, 2006). There are no prizes for the girls it seems.

When *Girlfriend* magazine conducted an online survey into girls and sex, it revealed that 1 in 4 participants had had sex before they were 14. Twenty-eight per cent of these girls had caught sexually transmitted diseases; 58 per cent had regretted their last sexual encounter (*Girlfriend*, February 2007, pp. 124–130). Journalist, Caitlin Flanagan, says "[w]hat's most worrisome about this age of blasé blowjobs isn't what the girl may catch, it's what the girls are most certainly losing: a healthy emotional connection to their sexuality and their own desire" (Flanagan, 2006).

With the ready access young children have to porn we're seeing an increase in sexual predators who are the same age as their victims (Hamilton, 2010, p. 64). It's sobering to talk with professionals counselling sexual assault victims, who are now dealing with ever more incidents amongst primary school-age children. For decades, research literature has indicated that children act out behaviours they have viewed or experienced. Sexual assault units also report that girls are presenting who have been subject to the kinds of sexual assaults previously only seen with adult women. Australian psychologist, Michael Carr-Gregg, sums up the situation when he says:

> One of the greatest problems we face is that many adults lack the skills, knowledge or strategies to critically analyse and understand the longer term impacts that sexualisation/pornification have on the behaviour of boys towards girls and, eventually, men towards women. The evidence is potentially one of the most toxic elements in society and it is time that those responsible for propagating this material be held accountable. When the history of public health is written, I am sure that this battle will sit alongside the struggle against the tobacco industry, infant food formula manufacturers and elements of the alcohol industry, in significance (correspondence with Hamilton, January, 2010).

One of the many outcomes of the regular consumption of porn is that often users no longer gain the satisfaction they once did with run-of-the-mill material. In a quest to experience continued arousal they begin to seek out more deviant and violent pornographic material. Gemma, a senior clinical psychologist who heads a sexual assault support team at a major hospital, spoke of her concerns about this new climate.

> We see a lot of 12-to-14 year-olds, targeted by boys 17 to 18 years. These are young girls wanting to be grown up, who're still very young and trusting, who fall prey to pre-planned situations. They're plied with alcohol, and possibly drugs, and often raped anally. In the past it was rape by one boy, but now it's 2 or 3 boys, and often filmed. The severity of assaults is also growing (Hamilton, interview September, 2008).

Neuroscience pulls few punches when examining the effects of porn. As medical researcher, Norman Doidge, reminds us, "[s]oftcore pornography's influence is now most profound because, now that it is no longer hidden, it influences young people with little sexual experience and especially plastic minds, in the process of forming their sexual tastes and desires" (Doidge, 2007, p. 103).

We have to act. As writer, TV and radio host, and former presidential speechwriter, Colleen Caroll Campbell reminds us,

> [i]n a society where pornography is so pervasive, it's intimidating to face the truth about how it endangers our children, destabilizes our families and distorts our views of sex and one another. It's easier to shout down the occasional unexpected criticism of pornography than to ponder its validity and change behaviour accordingly (Campbell, 2010).

Mary Eberstadt, a research fellow at the Hoover Institute, describes pornography as "sexual obesity – the widespread gorging on pornographic imagery" (Eberstadt, 2010).

Surely the measure of a healthy society is the level to which it nurtures and protects its young? The current climate is abusive to boys and girls. If we don't speak out against the corporate sexualisation of our children and teens, and fight the pornification of our communities, what will the landscape be like for our children's children? How will this new generation fare as adults and parents? How will *their* relationships fare?

We need to reclaim the hearts and minds of our children, our public spaces, and control over the products, games and clothing marketed to them, so children can have healthy, stress-free childhoods, and develop a positive sense of their sexuality as teenagers. Perhaps this issue is best summed up by British philosopher and academic, Roger Scruton: "This, it seems to me, is the real risk attached to pornography. Those who become addicted to this risk-free form of sex run a risk of another and greater kind. They risk the loss of love, in a world where only love brings happiness (Scruton, 2007).

Bibliography

Betkowski, Bev (2 March, 2007) 'Study Finds Teen Boys Most Likely To Access Pornography' *Folio*, University of Alberta, <http://www.ualberta.ca/~publicas/folio/44/13/09.html>.

Bindel, Julie (2 July, 2010) 'The Truth About The Porn Industry' *The Guardian*.

Interview with Ann Burgess, professor of nursing, University of Pennsylvania, 15 January, 1997 on 'Pornography – Victims and Perpetrators', Symposium on Media Violence & Pornography, Proceedings Resource Book and Research Guide, edited by D. Scott (1984).

Campbell, Colleen Carroll (27 May, 2010) 'Freedom From Porn' *St Louis Post-Dispatch*.

Doidge, Norman (2007) *The Brain That Changes Itself: Stories of Personal Triumph form the Frontiers of Brain Science*. Penguin, London.

Eberstadt, Mary (June/July, 2010) 'The Weight of Smut' *First Things*, <http://www.firstthings.com/article/2010/05/the-weight-of-smut>.

Flanagan, Caitlin (January/February, 2006) 'Are You There God? It's Me, Monica: How Nice Girls Got So Casual About Oral Sex' *The Atlantic Online*, <http://www.theatlantic.com/doc/200601/oral-sex>

Flood, Michael (2007) 'Exposure to Pornography Among Youth in Australia' *Journal of Sociology*, Vol 43 (1).

Flood, Michael (2 November, 2009) 'The Harms of Pornography Exposure Among Children and Young People' *Child Abuse Review*, Vol 1.

Flood, Michael and Lara Fergus (2008) 'An Assault on Our Future', A White Ribbon Foundation Report.

Girlfriend (February, 2007) 'Girlfriends Fess Up: The Original Sealed Advice: This Month's Hot Topic: We Explore the Risks, the Consequences and the Long-Term Effects of Being a Promiscuous Girl'.

Hamilton, Maggie (2008/2009) *What's Happening To Our Girls? Too Much, Too Soon, How Our Kids are Overstimulated, Oversold and Oversexed*. Penguin, Melbourne.

Hamilton, Maggie (2010/2011) *What's Happening To Our Boys? At Risk, How the New Technologies, Drugs and Alcohol, Peer Pressure and Porn Affect Our Boys*. Penguin, Melbourne.

Miller, Mark Crispin (undated) 'Merchants of Cool', transcript, *Frontline*, PBS, <http://www.pbs.org/wgbh/pages/frontline/shows/cool/interviews/crispinmiller.html>.

Ruberg, Bonnie (28 August, 2007) 'Peeking Up the Skirt of Online Sex Work: Topless and Proud', *villagevoice.com*, <http://www.villagevoice.com/2007-08-28/columns/peeking-up-the-skirt-of-online-sex-work/>.

Scruton, Roger (17–19 May, 2007) 'Profit as a By-Product Versus Profit as a Goal, Rethinking Business Management' Witherspoon Institute Conference, Princeton University.

Slight (13 November, 2006), <http://www.answerbag.com/q_view/82582>.

Wellard, Sally (15–21 March, 2001) 'Cause and Effect' *Community Care*, pp. 26–27.

Robert Jensen

Stories of a Rape Culture: Pornography as Propaganda[1]

We live in a pornography-saturated culture in which women are routinely targets of sexual violence and intrusion. We live in a rape culture that is increasingly pornified. Pornography is a form of propaganda for a rape culture.

But wait – we can hear voices rising up immediately to object that pornography does not cause rape.

In simplistic terms, pornography does not cause rape. There are men who use pornography and don't rape. There are men who rape and don't use pornography. There was rape before pornography was widely available, and there would be rape if pornography magically disappeared tomorrow.

Pornography doesn't cause rape, if by 'cause' we mean that a specific man's specific act of sexual violence can be established as the direct result of pornography use and would not have happened if he had not used pornography.

However, a rigorous analysis of the nature and effects of human communication, including propagandistic communication, does not begin and end with simplistic assertions about mechanistic notions of cause-and-effect. In the study of propaganda, we do not ask whether one specific message, or series of messages, was the sole cause of one specific person committing one specific act. Instead we investigate the way in which the style of human communication labelled 'propaganda' encourages certain ways of thinking about the world and makes inviting certain behaviors that flow from those ways of thinking.

An examination of *pornography as propaganda for a rape culture* leads to more complex and productive questions. For example, how are gender, power, and sexuality typically constructed in the contemporary industrial pornography that is widely available? How do these themes support or undermine the ideology of a rape culture? By whom and how is that pornography typically used? When such material is readily available to young people, what is the effect on their sexual development? What are the effects of the habitual use of pornography on

---

1   A longer version of this essay appeared in *The Propaganda Society* edited by Gerry Sussman (2011).

people's intimate experiences? Is there a relationship between those constructions and the levels of sexual intrusion and violence in contemporary culture? How is pornography racialized? And how does pornography train us to understand who we are in an industrial capitalist society?

In addressing such questions, I offer the following assumptions to situate a study of propaganda in general, and pornography as propaganda in particular:

(1) Human beings are storytelling animals; stories are a primary way we communicate what it means to be a person in the world. When we tell stories, we not only report on our experiences in the world but also contribute to a collective understanding of that world, which will influence the experiences and understandings of others. Stories matter. In any culture, the stories that people tell will reveal things about how they collectively make sense of the world, and that sense of the world will shape how people act. Stories shape attitudes, and attitudes affect behavior.

(2) In flourishing societies with a relatively egalitarian distribution of power, storytelling tends to be dialogic and creative, a way for people to engage each other with respect and explore ways of understanding the world. In contrast, in societies marked by inequality and concentrations of power, storytelling can be a vehicle to control and dominate, a way for people to shut down that dialogic and creative process in the service of maintaining or taking power. This type of human communication is called propaganda.

Special attention to propaganda is especially crucial in societies with concentrations of power that undermine the dialogic and creative aspects of human communication. In heavily mass-mediated societies such as the USA, Canada, Australia and European countries, this inquiry is vital.

Again, a comparison to make this point: when critics speak of commercial advertising as propaganda for capitalism, we are not asserting that a specific advertisement viewed by a person is the direct cause of that person's decision to purchase a good or service. Even advertisers recognize this, reflected in the common quip, 'We know half our ads don't work, but we don't know which half'. Critics cannot explain exactly how a specific advertisement or series of advertisements cause people to think of themselves as consumption machines rather than human beings. Instead, we recognize that in a larger culture which encourages that sense of self, the endless barrage of commercial advertising carrying the same message plays a role in that process.

This is the sense in which we can see pornography as propaganda for a rape culture.

Pornography

The term 'pornography' is used by many people to describe all sexually explicit books, magazines, movies, and Internet sites, often with a distinction made between softcore (nudity with limited sexual activity not including penetration) and hardcore (graphic images of actual, not simulated, sexual activity including penetration). Pornography also is often distinguished from erotica, with pornography used to describe material that presents sex in the context of hierarchical relationships. Laboratory studies often construct categories of pornography according to their degree of violence and degradation.

The associated terms 'indecency' and 'obscenity' have specific legal meanings. In the United States, for example, indecency concerns only broadcast television and radio, while the case of *Miller v. California* (1973) established a three-part test for obscenity in any media – material that appeals to the prurient interest (an unhealthy interest in sex); portrays sexual conduct in a patently offensive way; and does not have serious literary, artistic, political, or scientific value – and identified contemporary community standards as the measure. Pornography using children is a separate category that is banned.

In this essay, I focus on the heterosexual commercial pornography industry which produces a significant portion of the pornography available and whose codes and conventions have shaped much of the pornography produced by others.

Rape Culture

My analysis is rooted in feminist critiques of male dominance and hierarchy. By feminist, I simply mean an analysis of the ways in which women are oppressed as a class in this society – the ways in which men as a class hold more power, and how those differences in power systematically disadvantage women. Gender oppression plays out in different ways depending on social location which makes it crucial to understand the oppression of women in connection with other systems of oppression such as heterosexism, racism, class privilege, and histories of colonial and postcolonial domination.

In patriarchy, men are trained through a variety of cultural institutions to view sex as the acquisition of pleasure by the taking of women. Sex is a sphere in which men are trained to see themselves as 'naturally' dominant and women as 'naturally' passive. Women are objectified and women's sexuality is commodified. Sex is sexy because men are dominant and women are subordinate. Power is eroticized.

The predictable result of this state of affairs is a world in which violence, sexualized violence, sexual violence, and violence-by-sex is so common that it must be considered to be normal – an expression of the sexual norms of the culture, not violations of the norms. A recent review of the data by well-respected researchers concluded that in the United States, at least 1 of every 6 women has been raped at some time in her life, a figure that is now widely accepted (Tjaden and Thoennes, 2006).

The term 'rape culture' describes ideas and practices beyond those legally defined as rape. As one researcher suggests, we should " ... broaden the definition of violence against women to include not just violent acts, such as physical assault, sexual assault, and threats of physical and sexual assault, but also nonviolent acts, such as stalking and psychological and emotional abuse" (Tjaden, 2004, p. 1246).

I use the term 'sexual intrusion' to describe the range of unwanted sexual acts that women experience in contemporary society – obscene phone calls, sexual taunting on the streets, sexual harassment in schools and workplaces, coercive sexual pressure in dating, sexual assault, and violence with a sexual theme. In public lectures on these issues, I often tell the audience that I have completed an extensive scientific study on the subject and determined that the percentage of women in the United States who have experienced sexual intrusion is exactly 100%. Women understand the dark humor; no study is necessary to describe their routine collective experience.

The Ideology of Hierarchy and the Role of Propaganda

No society would let happen what happens to women, and children, if at some level it did not have contempt for them. A rape culture is a woman-hating culture. But most people's stated philosophical and theological systems are rooted in ideas of justice, equality, and the inherent dignity of all people. So, how do we explain all the violence, exploitation, and oppression? Only a small percentage of people in any given society are truly sociopaths, those incapable of empathy who engage in cruel and oppressive behavior openly and with relish.

Maintaining a claim to naturalness is essential for the maintenance of unjust hierarchies, and the illegitimate authority that is exercised in them. Oppressive systems work hard to make it appear that the hierarchies – and the disparities in power and resources that flow from hierarchies – are natural and, therefore, beyond change. If men are naturally smarter and stronger than women, then patriarchy is inevitable and justifiable. If white people are naturally smarter and more virtuous than people of color, then white supremacy is inevitable and justifiable. If rich people are naturally smarter and harder working than poor people, then economic injustice is inevitable and justifiable.

One of the key functions of propaganda is the naturalizing of hierarchy and authority in the minds of people at all places in the hierarchy. For elites at the top of the hierarchy, propaganda reinforces a sense of natural superiority and justifies a sense of entitlement. For those in the middle, propaganda promotes identification with the goals of elites above and discourages solidarity with oppressed people below. And propaganda also tries to persuade those on the bottom of the hierarchies that they deserve their fate, which can create a sense of futility about the prospects for change.

The Ideology of Pornography

Pornography is one of the dominant sexual-exploitation industries in the contemporary world, along with prostitution and stripping. These are the primary ways in which objectified female bodies are presented to men for sexual pleasure, typically for profit. The vast majority of people used in these industries are girls and women.

While women in prostitution and stripping tell stories in the course of their interactions with men, it is in pornography – the mass-mediated sexual-exploitation industry – that we see the ideology of sexual exploitation most fully developed. My analysis is that pornography (used to describe the genre of sexually explicit mass media) is routinely pornographic (used in a feminist sense, to describe the naturalizing of the social subordination of women).

Any discussion of the ideology of pornography should start with a sketch of the industry. The 2 main categories in today's pornographic movie industry (whatever its form or outlet) are 'features' and 'wall-to-wall/gonzo'. Features most resemble a Hollywood movie, with plot and characters. Wall-to-wall movies are all-sex productions with no pretense of plot or dialogue. Many of these movies are shot gonzo style, in which performers acknowledge the camera and often speak directly to the audience. In addition, there are specialty titles – movies that feature sadomasochism and bondage, fetish material, transsexuals – that fill niche markets. Heterosexual material dominates the pornography industry, with a thriving gay male pornography market and a smaller lesbian pornography market (much of it for a heterosexual male audience).

The majority of hardcore movies include oral, vaginal, and anal sex, almost always ending with ejaculation on the woman. A 1993 study of pornographic heterosexual videotapes (Brosius et al., 1993) found that the tapes typically presented a world in which women were younger, more sexually active, and more expressive than men; women were frequently depicted in subordinate positions (e.g. kneeling down in front of a partner); and sexual contact was usually between strangers. A 2007 content analysis of 50 best-selling adult videos (Wosnitzer and Bridges, 2007) revealed a similar pattern of inequality and violence. Nearly half of the 304 scenes analyzed contained verbal aggression (for example, name calling or verbal threats), while over 88% showed physical aggression (including hair pulling, open-hand slapping or spanking, choking, and whipping). Seventy percent of aggressive acts were perpetrated by men and 87% of acts were committed against women. Fewer than 5% of the aggressive acts provoked a negative response from the target, such as requests to stop. This pornographic 'reality' was further highlighted by the relative infrequency of more positive behaviors (verbal compliments, embracing, kissing, or laughter), portrayed in fewer than 10% of the scenes.

As pornography depicting conventional sexual acts has become commonplace, gonzo producers have pushed the limits of social norms and women's bodies with painful and body-punishing pornsex (Dines, 2010). Nearly every scene ends with the 'cum shot' or 'money shot' – male ejaculation into a woman's mouth or on her face or body. As one pornography director put it, "it's like a dog marking its territory" (Sun and Picker, 2008). Another veteran pornographic director and actor put it more bluntly: "I'd like to really show what I believe the men want to see: violence against women ... [but] the most violent we can get is the cum shot in the face. Men get off behind that, because they get even with the women they can't have" (Stoller and Levine, 1993, p. 22).

Combining such quantitative studies with qualitative analyses using more interpretive methods (Dworkin, 1979; Jensen, 2007), the main propagandist messages of pornographic films can be summarized as:

1. All women always want sex from men;
2. Women like all the sexual acts that men perform or demand, and
3. Any woman who does not at first realize this, can be persuaded by force.

Such force is rarely necessary, however, for most of the women in pornography are the 'nymphomaniacs' of men's fantasies. Women are the sexual objects, whose job it is to fulfill male desire.

Summarizing insights from the feminist critique of pornography, we can describe the ideology of pornography, and hence its propagandist use, as:

1. We all must be sexual all the time.
   Sex must be hot.
   Hot sex requires inequality
   and
2. Men are naturally dominant.
   Women are naturally submissive,

therefore

3. While specific sexual scenes in pornography are 'fantasy', pornography portrays men and women in their natural roles free from unnatural constraints imposed by repressive social norms,

and all this can be reduced to one conclusion:

4. Women are whores.

No matter what a woman's role or status, all women are for sex at the discretion of men. Men's desires not only define women's value to men, but women's fulfilling of that male desire defines their essence. Women not only owe it to men to service them sexually, women owe it to themselves. Women can find their authentic selves only by acknowledging – indeed by embracing – this status as whores.

In the pornographic world, women are allowed to fill a variety of professional and social roles, as long as they recognize that they are made women not by pursuing the variety of goals that come with those roles, but by *not* allowing those roles to impede their core function as whores, as beings who exist primarily to provide sexual pleasure to men.

Complimentary Ideologies of Racism and Industrial Capitalism

Contemporary pornography is not only sexist but also the most openly racist mass-media genre in contemporary society. In mainstream movies and television, the most blatant and ugly forms of racism have disappeared, although subtler patterns of stereotyping continue. *Pornography is the one media genre in which overt racism is still routine and acceptable.* Not subtle, coded racism, but old-fashioned racism – stereotypical representations of the sexually primitive black male stud, the animalistic black woman, the hot Latina, the Asian geisha.

The pornography industry uses the term 'inter-racial' for the category of overtly racist material. This category contains most every possible combination of racial groups, but the dominant mode of interracial pornography is black men and white women (Dines, 2010, chapter 7). If the sexual charge of pornography is in the sexual degradation of women, for some consumers that sexual charge can be heightened by images of white women submitting to the sexual demands of the demonized black man. The degradation is intensified by the racism: the white male consumer can go 'slumming' and experience the sexual pleasure that is rooted in the patriarchal and white-supremacist ideology.

Pornography also dovetails with industrial capitalism. The advertisers and marketers of mass-consumption society train us to think of ourselves as consumption machines. Such a cultural climate provides added support for the idea that as sexual beings we are little more than pleasure-seeking machines. In a world dominated by the industrial model, it's not surprising that a view of sexuality as primarily pleasure-acquisition by a body-as-machine flourishes. So, while pornography constructs women as objectified bodies for male pleasure, it also reduces all humans – men and women – to industrial objects, bodies devoid of any deeper humanity. It is dehumanizing in the same sense that the industrial model is dehumanizing.

The pornography industry in capitalism is engaged not in the exploration but in the exploitation of sexuality. The DVDs and Internet sites to which men are masturbating are not being made by struggling artists who work in lonely garrets, tirelessly struggling to help us understand the mysteries of sexuality. In abstract discussions about sexually explicit material – the kind pornographers prefer we get lost in – a focus on the reality of pornography drifts off into musings about the nature of 'sexual expression' that ponder the 'transgressive' nature of pornography. Such discourse obscures the reality that the vast majority of pornography is produced to turn a profit.

Conclusion: Reading the Resistance

It is interesting to note, however, the resistance from the Left to this critique of pornography as propaganda. Leftists who otherwise pride themselves on analyzing systems and structures of power can turn into extreme libertarian individualists on the subject of pornography. The sophisticated, critical thinking that underlies the best of Left politics often gives way to simplistic, politically naïve, and diversionary analysis that leaves far too many leftists playing cheerleader for an exploitative industry. That analysis is all about individual choice, not about the culture's ideology and how it shapes people's perceptions of their 'choices'. A critique of pornography doesn't imply that freedom rooted in an individual's ability to choose isn't important, but argues instead that these issues can't be reduced to that single moment of choice of an individual. Instead, we should ask: What is meaningful freedom within an industrial capitalist system that is racist and sexist? Leftists, who challenge the contention of the powerful that freedom comes in accepting one's place in a hierarchy, need to make the same challenge to the sexual hierarchy of pornography.

Leftists who take women's well-being seriously should recognize that pornography, along with other forms of sexualized exploitation – primarily of women, girls, and boys, by men – in capitalism is inconsistent with a world in which ordinary people can take control of their own destinies. This critique focuses our attention on *systems*. It offers an analysis of the failure of our dominant systems rather than misdiagnosing the problem as individual failures within otherwise healthy systems. It also asks us to critique not only those systems but ourselves, to examine how the values of those systems live within us.

There is a powerful argument from justice – the obligation to act on the principles we claim to hold – to inspire men to engage in this kind of critical self-reflection. There also is a compelling argument from self-interest – our desire to be fully human. My own experience has been that when I face these questions, no matter how painful the struggle, my life is richer and fuller for that struggle. For those of us socialized to be 'real men' in patriarchy – or to be white in a white-supremacist society, or middle/upper class in a society based on economic exploitation – the struggles are always there. If we ignore that struggle out of fear of the pain, we not only impede progressive political struggles but surrender some of our own humanity.

Bibliography

Brosius, H.B., J.B. Weaver III and J.F. Staab (1993) 'Exploring the social and sexual "reality" of contemporary pornography' *Journal of Sex Research*, 30, pp. 161–170.

Dines, Gail (2010) *Pornland: How Porn Has Hijacked Our Sexuality*. Beacon Press, Boston; Spinifex Press, North Melbourne.

Dworkin, Andrea (1979) *Pornography: Men Possessing Women*. Perigee, New York; reprinted 1989 Dutton, Boston.

Jensen, Robert (2007) *Getting Off: Pornography and the End of Masculinity*. South End Press, Cambridge, MA.

Jensen, Robert (2011) 'Pornography as Propaganda' in Gerry Sussman (Ed) *The Propaganda Society*. Peter Lang, New York.

Koss, Mary P. (1988) 'Hidden rape: Sexual aggression and victimization in a national sample of students in higher education' in Ann Wolbert Burgess (Ed) *Rape and Sexual Assault: II*. Garland, New York, pp. 3–25.

Stoller, Robert J. and I.S. Levine (1993) *Coming Attractions: The Making of an X-rated Video*. Yale University Press, New Haven.

Sun, Chyng and Miguel Picker (2008) *The Price of Pleasure: Pornography, Sexuality, and Relationships*. Media Education Foundation, Northampton.

Tjaden, Patricia (2004) 'What is violence against women? Defining and measuring the problem: A response to Dean Kilpatrick' *Journal of Interpersonal Violence* 19 (11), pp. 1244–1251.

Tjaden, Patricia, and Nancy Thoennes (2006) 'Extent, nature, and consequences of rape victimization: Findings from the National Violence Against Women Survey' US Department of Justice Office of Justice Programs, National Institute of Justice, <http://www.ncjrs.g/pdffiles1/nij/210346.pdf>.

Wosnitzer, Robert J. and Ana J. Bridges (2007) 'Aggression and sexual behavior in best-selling pornography: A content analysis update'. Paper presented at the 57th Annual Meeting of the International Communication Association, San Francisco.

Nina Funnell

Sexting and Peer-to-Peer Porn

Historically, debates about children and pornography have typically played out in 2 directions: either children are discussed as being the victims used in illegal child pornography or, alternatively, they are constructed as the damaged consumers of adult pornography which they inadvertently or deliberately access.

Both the 'exploited victim' and 'damaged consumer' approaches have produced a wealth of research that has contributed to public debates about pornography. However, while these approaches have offered important frameworks for understanding and discussing the harm caused to children, they have not been able to account for a recently emerging trend whereby young people are not merely accessing and consuming pornography, but are now the active producers of pornography.

Youth, sex and technology

In recent years, academics have been focussing on the ways in which young people are incorporating technology into their dating, courtship and sexual social-isation practices. While many young people report that technology has enhanced their social lives, girls have also expressed distress over the ways in which tech-nology (such as digital photography, mobile phone cameras and web cams) has contributed to making them feel increasingly exposed and visually vulnerable.

The ease with which photos are now produced, the speed at which they travel, combined with the permanence of those photos once online, has meant that young people's private lives are now being shared and recorded in ways never seen or imagined before. The advent of the smartphone which allows users to access the World Wide Web directly from their personal phones also means that young people are now able to upload and retrieve digital information from anywhere and at anytime, with few time-delay barriers that might otherwise give an opportunity for reflective thought.

Of particular concern is the way in which young people are now uploading sexualised personal content which is then immediately available for peers and others. According to one study[1] completed by the 'National Campaign to Prevent

---

1   <http://www.thenationalcampaign.org/sextech/>

Teen and Unplanned Pregnancy in America', as many as 1 in 5 teenagers have electronically sent a nude or semi-nude image or video of themselves. This statistic which has been widely reproduced in media articles, has alarmed parents and children's rights groups everywhere. Blended with the concern that young people may be jeopardising their reputations and employment prospects is the fear that such photos could fall into the hands of paedophiles, as once those photos are online it is virtually impossible to control how they circulate or where they end up.

But beyond reputational and personal safety fears, there are additional concerns regarding why these images are being produced in the first place, and what motivations underscore the actions of those who make them. In the above study it was found that 51% of teen girls say "pressure from a guy" is one reason girls send sexy messages or images, and 52% of girls who had sent images said they did so as a 'sexy present' for their boyfriend.

When considering the enormous pressure placed on young women to appear attractive and to participate in a hypersexualised culture which rewards exhibitionism, it is not surprising to learn that so many girls and young women are producing nude or sexualised images of themselves. These photos then become the currency that young women use to gain access to a culture that affords social approval to those who are willing to perform within tightly constructed sexual scripts that privilege the male gaze.

But while girls are often taught to equate their self-worth with their sexual desirability, paradoxically, they are also taught that women who seek out and enjoy lots of sex (or lots of sexual partners) are somehow 'dirty' or 'slutty'. The result is that girls learn that they must appear desirable, but be lacking in any desire of their own; they are taught that male sexual pleasure is considered the goal, while female sexual pleasure, desire and sexual expression are often pathologised as polluting or dangerous.

Deborah Tolman, a professor of human sexuality at New York's City University, suggests that rather than enjoying their own erotic pleasure, girls are becoming most concerned about how they looked during sex.

> By the time they are teenagers, the girls I talk to respond to questions about how their bodies feel – questions about sexuality or desire – by talking about how their bodies *look*. They will say something like, 'I felt like I looked good'.[2]

---

2   Cited in 'Girls, what you see is not what you are, or what you can achieve' published in *The Age*, 12 March (2011) by Suzy Freeman-Greene, <http://www.theage.com.au/opinion/society-and-culture/girls-what-you-see-is-not-what-you-are-or-what-you-can-achieve-20110312-1brps.html>.

And it is against this cultural backdrop which devalues sexual intimacy and female pleasure (while excusing and promoting the objectification and commodification of female bodies) that young women are being culturally groomed to produce sexual representations of themselves as 'sexy presents' for the gratification of others.

While there is a need to continue to discuss the competing pressures bearing down on young women, there is another set of risks of an entirely different nature facing young people who produce such images; namely that sending or receiving a nude photo could result in a conviction or jail term for a teenager.

The Pennsylvania Case Study

In 2009, 3 teenage girls in Greensburg Pennsylvania took nude and semi-nude photos of themselves on their mobile phones before reportedly sending those photos on to 3 boys. When the images were discovered on the boys' phones, the girls (for photographing their own bodies) were threatened with charges relating to the production and distribution of child pornography, and the 3 boys were threatened with charges relating to the possession of child pornography.

In the media commentary that followed, a debate erupted over the definition of child pornography and the application of the law in cases involving teens who 'willingly'[3] photograph their own bodies. On the one hand, some claimed that prosecution was an appropriate response that would serve to deter other teenagers from engaging in a behaviour now known as sexting.[4] But others raised a series of probing questions: Why are laws which were initially intended to protect children now being used to criminalise teenage sexuality? Is it appropriate to group sexually curious teenagers in with convicted paedophiles? How can a girl be both the victim and the perpetrator of the same crime? And what possible good can come from labeling these teens as sex offenders and putting them on a sex offender registry for the rest of their lives?

Eventually the Pennsylvania case was dismissed after the American Civil Liberties Union launched a countersuit against the District Attorney for threatening to lay the charges against the teenage girls. But the significance of the case was clear: the law had been utterly outpaced by the speed at which the technology had evolved and was now woefully ill-equipped to respond to the

---

3   For a photo to be sent 'willingly' it must be sent of one's own volition without any pressure, force or coercion. 'Pressure' under this definition does not only include pressure deliberately or inadvertently exerted by an individual, but it also includes pressure that results from cultural paradigms, peer groups or social contexts.

4   'Sexting' refers to the production and distribution of sexualised personal photos via mobile phone or online.

current paradigm. Clearly, at the time when these laws were first developed, no one had comprehended the possibility of children (or young people) themselves being the ones to produce the pornography. Beyond this, the case also demonstrated a need to differentiate between cases of 'agreed' sexting (where a photograph is willingly produced and does not travel beyond the intended recipient) and situations where images are produced and/or distributed without the permission of the subject.

Just kids being kids?

There is a long history of children expressing curiosity over bodies and sex. While there is nothing inherently unnatural or dangerous about expressing an age-appropriate interest in bodies and nudity, there is growing evidence that technology has accelerated the rate at which young people access and consume sexualised material with added concern that this material is more sexually graphic, violent and exploitative than ever before. Against this backdrop young people are now emulating and authoring their own pornographic images and movies, simultaneously performing the roles of porn star, director, producer, distributor and audience.

While authorities are dealing with the legal dilemmas arising around sexting, there is another far darker side and set of consequences to this behaviour which needs urgent attention.

In May 2008, a young woman named Jesse Logan appeared on a Cincinnati television station to tell her story. She had sent nude photos of herself to her boyfriend who sent them on to other classmates after the relationship ended. Logan was harassed and repeatedly labeled a 'slut' and a 'whore'. She became depressed, withdrawn and avoided school. Two months after agreeing to talk about her experience on television Jesse was found hanging in her bedroom. She was only 18.

In 2010, another 18-year-old student, Tyler Clementi, committed suicide by jumping from the George Washington Bridge. Clementi, who was not openly gay, had recently had a sexual encounter with a man in his dorm room. His roommate, Dharun Ravi, and another student had secretly filmed and streamed the footage of the encounter. Clementi's Facebook status at the time of his death read: "jumping off the gw bridge sorry." His body was found a short time after.

In 2011, an 18-year-old female cadet in the Australian Defence Force engaged in consensual sex with a fellow cadet. Unbeknown to her, the sex was being streamed live via Skype web cam to 6 male cadets in an adjacent room. Still photos were also taken and distributed to other people. On learning what had transpired, the cadet known as 'Kate' stated that her "whole world came crashing down"[5] and that she was physically ill. After speaking out publicly, Kate was then subjected to further harassment from fellow cadets who labeled her a 'slut' and a 'whore'. Meanwhile, those who produced, distributed and consumed this non-consensual pornography continued on for a month before being charged, and, at the time of writing (May 2011), were still attending classes with their peers. Kate, meanwhile, was excused on 'compassionate leave'.

When these various stories broke, the public responded with a mix of shock, disgust and outrage. Commentators struggled to make heads or tails of each situation, describing the events as utterly incomprehensible. And to an extent they are.

But when we look further afield, the practice of individuals filming or distributing sexually explicit footage of individuals without their knowledge or consent has a longer history and one that, in certain spheres, has gone largely uncontested.

Captured girls in popular culture

Twelve years before the ADF web cam scandal, the teen hit comedy *American Pie* (1999) was released. In it, the main character, Jim, is convinced by a fellow student to set up a web cam in his room to film a female exchange student changing her outfit. As the girl strips down, unaware that she is being filmed, Jim and his friends watch on in jocular amusement from a neighbouring home. Jim then returns to the room and attempts to have sex with her. At no point in the film is there any consideration of the legal or ethical issues or the likely emotional ramifications for the girl. Indeed, in the sequel *American Pie 2* (2011), the girl returns as a love interest for Jim.

There is a long history of boys in films bonding through the collective consumption of naked women. In *Milk Money* (1994), three 11-year-old boys who watch pornography after school go on a mission to see a naked woman. They achieve this by paying $100 to a sex worker in exchange for seeing her breasts. In *Sleepers* (1996), pubescent boys bond by spying on naked women through a hole in a wall of a female change room. In *The Virgin Suicides* (1999), teen boys take turns on a telescope spying on a teen girl having sex across the street. In *Dead Poets' Society* (1989), male students gather in a cave and collectively pore over a pornographic image of a nude woman. In these 'coming of age' movies, the collective consumption of female nudity is depicted as a type of rite of passage

---

5   <http://www.abc.net.au/news/stories/2011/04/05/3183128.htm?site=canberra>

that all heterosexual boys are expected to go through in their journey into adult male sexuality.

Likewise, in films about adult male sexuality, the collective consumption of nude women is depicted as a means by which men maintain and entrench their homosocial bonds. In *Knocked Up* (2007), Seth Rogen's character and his mates spend their days sitting on a couch trawling through movies looking for female nudity. Their dream is to run a Website that states the exact point in a movie that you can expect female nudity. In *The Hangover* (2009), and various other films, men bond on a bucks' night filled with nude women.

While such movies seek to naturalise male bonding through shared sexual desire, these films also serve to normalise bonding processes which exclude women. That is, a woman's body may be served up as an object that men can bond through, but an integral feature of this bonding process is the assumed absence – and agency – of all other women.

Similarly, while ostensibly these films set up male pleasure as something tied to nudity and titillating images of women, arguably male pleasure is really derived from the power imbalance which results from the voyeuristic consumption of nude women without their knowledge or consent. Of course, this isn't limited to film.

In 2009, an ESPN (worldwide leader in sport) reporter named Erin Andrews was surreptitiously filmed nude while alone in her hotel room. The videotape soon surfaced online showing various video grabs of Andrews as she put on make-up and walked around nude. The video quickly became one of the most searched Google items. Video-blogging on *Feministing*, US writer, Jessica Valenti, made the following comment:

> You know you can see plenty of hot naked ladies on the Internet. It's not that hard to find. But folks want to watch this and people are interested in this precisely because Erin Andrews doesn't know she is being filmed. I think that reveals something incredibly fucked up about the way American culture views women. That what we consider hot and sexy is looking at naked pictures of women without their consent.[6]

Looking further afield again we can see many other examples where Internet users have swarmed to download sex tapes of women which have been produced or distributed without the consent of the women involved. Aside from the infamous Paris Hilton sex tape (which was released in 2004 without her consent), in 1995 a sex tape of Pamela Anderson and husband Tommy Lee on their honeymoon was stolen from their home and released online. Model Katie

---

6   <http://www.youtube.com/watch?v=n2-Yy2pMsnQ>

Price, and her then boyfriend, Dane Bowers, had a sex tape stolen from their flat and leaked during their 2-year relationship between 1998 and 2000. Severina Vučković, a Croatian pop star, had a tape of her having sex stolen and released in 2004. Mexican-American singer, Jenni Rivera, also had a tape stolen from her home and released in 2008.

Then in 2010, a non-authorised sex tape featuring former *Playboy* Playmate, Kendra Wilkinson, was released. The film had been made in 2003 when she was 18 years old and before she had breast implants. In the footage it is clear that she doesn't want to be videotaped and she says so on a number of occasions. In virtually all these cases, the women have been subjected to vicious character attacks, while those responsible for distributing and consuming the images have gone largely uncommented on.

Aside from the impacts on the individual women, the danger in these cases is that they reaffirm the idea that it is acceptable to pressure a woman (including a drugged woman) into sex, to film that sex against her wishes, and to circulate that footage without her knowledge, let alone consent. The other implicit message in these cases is that women who have sex or who live or work in the public eye, have somehow surrendered their right to privacy and respect – and worse – that individuals who download and watch such material are somehow absolved of all personal and ethical responsibility.

It is against this backdrop that condones female degradation as sport, that teenagers are now picking up cameras and filming themselves.

So while digital technology and social media have no doubt enhanced many aspects of our lives, they have also extended the ways in which women and girls can be violated, humiliated and abused. To deal with this will require more than mere education for young people about the risks associated with technology. It will require an entire cultural shift which, as its starting point, acknowledges and seeks to redress the ingrained misogyny, sexism and degradation of girls and women that underscores so much of our current culture.

Diane L. Rosenfeld[1]

Who Are You Calling a 'Ho'?: Challenging the Porn Culture on Campus

In the fall of 2008, a fraternity rush chairman (the individual responsible for recruiting new members) at a small, liberal arts college, sent out an email intended for potential 'rushees'[2] that leaked to and was forwarded to others, and quoted in the school newspaper (Rosenfeld, 2008). In describing the party scene for the upcoming weekend and bragging that his fraternity threw the best 'lodge' parties, he wrote, "Off-campus party at our house … So bring your favorite freshman skeezas[3] so they can get a cock thrown in em by whoever. Hopefully, if you brought em u can finish the deal."

In October 2010, 45 men, members and pledges of the Yale chapter of the Delta Kappa Epsilon (DKE) fraternity, surrounded the dorms that house most female freshman students, and loudly chanted: "NO MEANS YES! YES MEANS ANAL!" and "My name is Jack, I'm a necrophiliac, I fuck dead women and fill them with my semen!" (Gasso and Greenberg, 2010). As the pledges

---

1   Much inspiration for this article comes from working with my student Laura Jarrett, Harvard Law School, Class of 2010, and a brilliant paper she wrote for my Title IX seminar entitled 'The Blueprint for Sexual Harassment: How Schools Can Combat Sexual Misconduct As Required Under Title IX by Addressing the Harm of Pornography' (hereinafter 'Jarrett') (on file with author, December, 2009). The author wishes to thank Jennifer Dein, my teaching and research assistant who provided primary editorial assistance, shared insights about the Greek system and contributed enormously to the overall writing of the chapter. Other students, former students and colleagues who contributed thoughts, insights and editorial help include Krista Anderson, Laura Jarrett, Michelle Katz, Renate Klein, Rebecca Leventhal, Kimberly Lucas, Maris Rosenfeld, Roberta Oster Sachs, Anne Catherine Savage, Tamara Schulman, Kamilah Willingham, and Elizabeth Wol.

2   'Rush' refers to the initial process men go through to pledge a fraternity. Men are invited to 'rush' a fraternity; they then become 'pledges'. After meeting the pledging requirements, the pledges become brothers, or full-fledged members of the fraternity. A significant amount of hazing behavior is required for the pledges to achieve brotherhood.

3   The fact that the email specified 'freshman skeezas' is consistent with David Lisak's work on 'undetected rapists'. As he explained on NPR (3 April, 2010), rapists target the most vulnerable women on campus – freshmen. "The predators on campus know the women who are new to campus," he said, "they are younger, they're less experienced" (see Shapiro, 2010; see also Lisak and Miller, 2002).

repeated these taunting chants, other men in the background instructed "Louder!" and the pledges complied. The account of this aggression was widely circulated through listservs, and the chanting was posted on YouTube.[4]

In March 2011, a Kappa Sigma brother at the University of Southern California began a weekly 'Gullet Report' email to educate his brothers on how to be a 'Cocksman'. The primary purposes of the 'Report' were to "strengthen brotherhood and help pin-point sorostitiutes [sic] more inclined to put out." 'Sorostitute' is a term used by fraternity brothers as shorthand to refer to sorority members as prostitutes. The author included a note to explain his reference to females as 'targets': "They aren't actual people like us men," he explained, "Consequently, giving them a certain name or distinction is pointless." The email goes on to define pertinent terms (such as 'Blackberry', meaning a 'black target'), a rating system (women ranked below 4 are 'filth'), and important tips: for example, "Non-consent and rape are two different things" (Hartmann, 2011).

Each of these examples provides a glimpse into the current social climate on US college campuses.[5] Adding to this culture of an aggressive and threatening atmosphere is a socially accepted practice on many college campuses called 'pimp and ho' parties. At these gatherings, men dress in 'pimp' outfits – long coats, jewelry, 'bling', fur, fake gold teeth, black curly wigs (stereotyping African American males), and women often dress up in revealing clothing, lingerie, stilettos, fishnet stockings and heavy make-up.

Dressed as pimps, the men evaluate the women at these parties, rate, and rank women and their potential economic value as 'hos', and offer to buy and sell them as commodities. These events are usually held at fraternity houses where the balance of gender power favors the men who live there – they control the guest list, they know the architecture of the building, they control the access to alcohol and they control the social hierarchy. The men also determine which freshmen women are going to be targeted. Like large animals in the wild, these upperclassmen often target and prey on the younger, smaller, weaker, and more vulnerable members of their society (Lisak, 2011).

---

4   'Student Footage of Frat Pledges on Old Campus' YouTube (13 October, 2010), <http://www.youtube.com/watch?v=CLh0RMpit1k> (accessed 7 May, 2011).

5   Similar stories emerge from Australia. In 2009, the highly prestigious St Paul's College of the University of Sydney came under fire after it was exposed that a group of male college students had created and participated in a Facebook group titled 'Define statutory' described as being 'pro-rape, anti-consent'. The same college had previously come under fire for a slogan in their bar reading 'they can't say no with a cock in their mouth' and for awarding an 'animal act of the year' trophy to a male student accused of committing rape. See <http://www.abc.net.au/news/video/2009/11/13/2742684.htm> and <http://www.smh.com.au/opinion/society-and-culture/bachelors-who-major-in-abhorrent-behaviour-20091109-i58t.html>.

Pornography plays a powerful role in creating images that glorify 'pimp and ho' culture as sexual, exciting, and desirable. It creates a critical backdrop to sexual culture on campus. The 3 examples offered above are united by the sexually derogatory way in which the men refer to women as objects to be raped, used, and whose will is to be disregarded. What is striking, but not immediately apparent, is the role that pornography plays in the construction of these attitudes.

The reason this violent sexual campus culture matters is twofold. First, these attitudes contribute to the astoundingly high level of rape and sexual assault on campus. Government studies in the United States estimate that 1-in-4 or 1-in-5 women will be sexually assaulted during her time in college (Krebs et al., 2007). There is an "inextricable correlation between men's consumption of pornography and corresponding misogynist attitudes about women, sexual harassment and rape" (Jarrett, 2009, p. 1). When such attitudes are allowed to exist – if not prevail – unaddressed on a college campus, women are clearly at risk of sex discrimination that will affect their educational experience.

This chapter interrogates the current sexual culture on US campuses. First, it asks what men mean when they refer to women as 'hos', and how they construct female sexuality in all-male spaces, such as fraternities and in pornography, as reflected in the 3 examples. It focuses on the ubiquitous theme of 'pimp and ho' parties as representative of the cultural attitudes and social behavior relating to sexuality on campus.[6]

Second, it asks what it means for women to participate in a culture that refers to them as 'hos'? The constant designation of women as 'hos' leaves little space for alternative definitions of female sexuality. Moreover, participation in this party culture makes women more vulnerable to being sexually assaulted, while simultaneously diminishing their ability and entitlement to complain about their victimization. If she dresses up as a 'ho' to attend a party and is assaulted, she is more likely to face victim-blaming questions than to be respected and feel comfortable asserting her rights to bodily integrity and sexual autonomy.

Third, the chapter asserts that women have a right *not* to be prostituted. Quite simply, referring to women in sexually derogatory terms fosters inequality. In the United States, Title IX of the Civil Rights Act confers a right to equal access to educational opportunities. Vice President Joseph Biden recently articulated this important civil right when he announced new guidelines to schools

---

6   There are many variations on this theme, such as 'CEO's and Office Hos', 'Golf Pros and Tennis Hos'. In each, women are designated as the 'ho'. 'Ho' is slang for 'whore'.

on preventing and addressing sexual violence.[7] The establishment of the new guidelines coincided with the Department of Education's Office for Civil Rights announcement that it was investigating Yale University in response to a complaint filed by 16 current and former students detailing the sexually hostile environment on campus, culminating in the 'No Means Yes' chanting described above. Thus, the chapter concludes with the recommendation that women bond together, supported by their schools, to reject the designation of themselves and one another as 'hos' – sexually devalued objects rather than humans with equal rights.

1 'Bros before Hos': How Men Talk About Women in Male-Dominated Spaces

To change the culture of pornography use on campus, we need to confront directly what goes on in all-male spaces. Fraternities and locker rooms, as key spaces for male bonding, are important places to examine, as attitudes towards women and gay men are often the basis of jokes and male bonding activities. The privacy men have in these spaces allows them to talk uninterrupted and without consequence, ensuring unimpeded transmission of misogynist attitudes.

Athletes and fraternity members are more likely to commit gang rapes (Kimmel, 2008, pp. 238–239). Membership in these exclusive groups "confers on them an elite status that is easily translated into entitlement, and because the cement of their brotherhood is intense, and intensely sexualized, bonding" (Kimmel, 2008, pp. 238–239). I have seen a tremendous rise in the number of multi-perpetrator sexual assaults over the past few years,[8] correlative with the rise in 'gonzo' porn, that involves several men taking turns penetrating, or penetrating all at once, one woman (see also Jensen, 2007, p. 59). Rather than being spontaneous cases of drunken misbehavior, evidence indicates that the vast majority of these rapes (around 71%) are premeditated and even scripted (Kimmel, 2008, p. 239). Acts of sexual violence appear not to be random, unrelated events, but rather central,

---

7   The new guidelines clarify schools' responsibilities to prevent and address sexual harassment on campus as well as articulate the importance of the civil rights to equality in education. Dear Colleague Letter, Assistant Secretary's Office for Civil Rights, Department of Education (2011), <http://www2.ed.gov/about/offices/list/ocr/letters/colleague-201104.html (last accessed 19 May, 2011).

8   A common pattern presented in 4 recent cases I have worked on involved a young woman partying with friends who is either left in a room with 1 male friend who calls another to join him, or finds herself with 2 or more men who were friends of hers, who then rape her. Later, the men inevitably claim she consented, while she was caught completely off-guard, having been with people she'd considered her friends. See, e.g. Laura Dunn, featured on *Headline News* <http://www.cnn.com/video/#/video/bestoftv/2011/04/08/exp.jvm.rape.victims.courage. hln>; Beckett Brennan, featured on *60 Minutes*, 11 April, 2011, <http://www.cbsnews.com/ video/watch/?id=7363066n&tag=related;photovideo> (accessed 7 May, 2011).

even necessary, to the bonding that supports the sexual culture. The men seem to be operating on the principle that 'Ain't no fun unless we all get some'.[9]

A particularly troubling aspect of the Yale example was that it required men to proclaim the willingness to rape and disregard a woman's will in order to gain admission into the exclusive all-male group. It also reflected the proliferation of anal sex that is increasingly common in mainstream pornography (Jensen, 2007, pp. 58–59).

Michael Kimmel, evaluating porn use by college men, reports: "The guys I interviewed consistently spoke of women more with contempt than desire. Women were 'hos', 'bitches', and 'sluts'..." (Kimmel, 2008, p. 182). Men's attitudes were, "You don't have sex with women because you desire them; sex is the weapon by which you get even with them, or, even, humiliate them" (Kimmel, 2008, p. 182).

Pornography is intricately related to other forms of commercial sexual exploitation, such as strip clubs, escort services and other forms of prostitution (see Jeffreys; Bray; Farley; this volume). Some commercial sexual exploitation is marketed particularly towards fraternities. For example, Centerfold Strips, an adult entertainment booking agency, tweeted in February, 2011 (an important month for fraternity spring recruitment): "Frat rush party specials available – impress your pledges with hot strippers from Centerfold Strips!" Fraternities throughout the nation incorporate 'Stripper Nights' into their 'rush' recruitment week, despite Interfraternity Council (IFC) regulations that ban such practices. One Website, Bachelor Party HQ, provides a list of colleges and universities where fraternity members have hired women to perform at rush events. The list includes over 80 campuses.

During these rush shows, women who strip typically engage in interactive behavior with highly pornographic themes. One performer, Nevaeh, who strips at Cornell rush parties, has described some of the acts in detail. "The guy will lay down," she explained, "and we'll get them into 69 position and someone will pour beer down my back and into their mouths." In addition to the 'anal butt chug', the boys might also compete to eat a Hostess cupcake out of the performer's crotch the fastest, or watch as the women engage in, or simulate, girl-on-girl conduct, such as oral sex (Ensign, 2007).

---

9   In a popular Nelly song called 'Tipdrill' the lyrics include the lines: "Now baby girl bring it over let me spit my pimpjuice, I need a tipdrill ... I said it ain't no fun less we all get some," <http://www.lyrics007.com/Nelly%20Lyrics/Tip%20Drill%20Lyrics.html> (accessed 7 May, 2011). A 'tipdrill' is a term for basketball players lining up and taking turns scoring. In this context, it refers to 'running train' on a woman – men lining up to take turns having sex with the same woman.

Pornographic themes do more than simply sexualize gender inequalities. They often work to sexualize racism and other forms of degradation as well. At Princeton, fraternity brothers were required to travel to Philadelphia for the express purpose of, among other things, "receiving a lap dance from a black stripper" (Westmoreland and Wolff, 2010). Similarly, the author of the USC email distinguished each potential 'target' by race: a 'Blackberry' is a 'black target', a 'Lemon Meringue' is Asian, a 'Pumpkin Pie' is Latina or Mexican and so on.

Racist references to women sometimes garner more public criticism than merely sexist ones, such as when the radio host, Don Imus, referred to the Rutgers women's basketball players as 'Nappy Headed Hos', a term taken directly from pornography (Picker and Sun, 2008). Yet, the racist and sexist messages in mainstream pornography often escape critical analysis because they are about sex, thus deemed private sexual behavior, shielded from public scrutiny. However, we must breach this imaginary boundary in order to stop the perpetuation of the discriminatory attitudes expressed in pornography.

2 'Sorostitutes' and Theme Parties: Pornography and the Party Scene

The party scene on college campuses provides an important lens into sexual relations. Fraternity-sponsored theme parties often dominate the social scene because of easy access to alcohol and social spaces. According to 'College OTR: Your Online Frathouse', "[w]hen it comes to frat parties, a good theme is everything. If the theme is right, the girls will get drunk, naked, and you'll have more ass than you know what to do with" (College OTR, 2009). Furthermore, the 'right' themes have highly pornographic elements. One aspect of the seemingly infinite iterations of the 'pimp and ho' party remains constant: men remain in a position of power while the women are simply 'hos'.

The nickname of sorority women as 'sorostitutes' says it all. This term directly equates sorority sisters with prostitutes. What do women do in response to being referred to as prostitutes? If they object, they risk being derided as 'too serious', unable to take a joke, or just not the right kind of feminist.[10] In order to rationalize their designation as sexual objects for use by their male counterparts, they choose to believe that the men are just kidding, and can tell them apart

---

10 In response to the Yale chanting, the Yale Women's Center objected, and then was derided in the *Yale Daily News* editorial entitled 'The Right Kind of Feminism', <http://www.yaledailynews.com/news/2010/oct/18/the-womens-center-must-continue-to-break-the/>. Following that criticism, however, hundreds of Yale students, alumni, and others signed a petition objecting to the editorial and addressing the seriousness of the rape chants.

from the 'real' prostitutes. They are the good girls having fun — and, as such, do not expect to be subject to unwanted sex or violation by their friends. Byron Hurt challenges the reality of the attempt to reconcile this conflict. In his 2006 film, *Beyond Beats and Rhymes*, Hurt looks at misogyny, homophobia and racism in hip hop music. The segment called 'Sistahs and Bitches' includes an interview with a woman who claimed that when men refer to women as bitches and 'hos' "[t]hey're not talking about us. We know who we are." But unbeknownst to this woman, just moments earlier, a man in the documentary had been talking about her and her friend when he discussed his plan to be "getting up on those bitches." Hurt makes an apt comparison to racist remarks, stating that if "George Bush said something about all those N**s, you wouldn't say, well, he's not talking about me. He is. He is talking about you!" (Hurt, 2006).

Anne,[11] a recent college graduate who was active in the Greek system, said:

> Theme parties were the easiest way of coercion. Like my boyfriend's fraternity would bring in a dump truck filled with sand and pour it all over the first floor of their mansion so they could get the girls to come over in bathing suits in the middle of winter. Another fraternity had a 'Saran Wrap' party where you literally had to create an entire outfit out of Saran Wrap. These were the cool guys, not just the dirtbags. It was really everyone, athletes, smart guys, everyone. Theme parties could be the conduit to sexual coercion, but at the time, you don't think of it that way. It's only if you step back (interview with Anne, on file with author, March 2011).

Jen, another recent Greek graduate, describes her sorority activities in a highly academic environment, like Anne's:

> Even in that environment … we gladly embraced pornographic messages. We sang songs about our willingness for sex and dressed as 'playboy bunnies' or any variation of 'hos' when the party called for it. One night, the sorority had a mixer with a fraternity. As with many fraternity parties, the police broke up the mixer due to noise complaints. When they arrived, they were horrified to find the girls in various states of undress. They questioned the boys, trying to discern what sexual coercion, harassment, or abuse must have occurred for the girls to be in this state. The fraternity boys were equally confused. 'They came like this' they desperately tried to explain. The unbuttoned shirts, the short skirts, and the exposed cleavage — that was simply how the girls dressed to attend the night's themed party.

In light of the dominance of fraternity culture on so many college campuses, it is perhaps unsurprising that sororities tend to conform to the pornographic themes and stereotypes introduced by the fraternities. Sororities sing songs about sisterhood and friendship. Many, however, also rewrite these songs to sing drunkenly at mixers and formals, on busses and at frat houses. Alpha Sigma Alpha, for example, incorporates the language of pornography into their songs.

---

11 I am using a pseudonym for Anne, who wishes to remain anonymous.

In the following tune, they embrace the theme of women as willing and eager for sexual activity under conditions of questionable consent:

Take me up to a fraternity house,
Take me up to your room,
Buy me some beer and vodka too,
Get me drunk and I'll surely screw you,
For it's grunt, grunt, grunt goes the Alpha Sig as the [fraternity name] shoves it in
For it's one, two, three times a night, thanks for getting me laid!

Sorority members embracing the porn culture in such a way is an example of what Ariel Levy explores in her book *Female Chauvinist Pigs: A Rise in the Raunch Culture*. She comments, regarding similar behavior by other young women, "[t]hat women are now doing this to ourselves isn't some kind of triumph, it's depressing" (Levy, 2005, p. 44). Apparent self-objectification does not make it less objectifying; objects are less than human. As Tamara Schulman writes (Schulman, 2009, p. 29):

Just because some women may enjoy their chains, does not mean that subordination does not exist. Consent does not eliminate harm. Accepting pornographic roles mean valuing male pleasure and devaluing female pleasure. Sexual pleasure is unequal. Young girls today feel expected to perform oral sex on boys, but feel that it would be abnormal for them to ask for their partners to pleasure them. Sex has become casual to kids, and the 'hook-up' culture centers around male pleasure.

3   Creating a Campus Culture of Sexual Respect

Sexual harassment at schools represents a barrier to equality in education. The role of schools is to educate, putting schools in the best position to counter sexually hostile environments through education on sexual respect. Regardless of the civil rights involved in ensuring equal access to educational opportunities, schools everywhere train leaders for the next generation. It is in everyone's best interest to teach affirmatively the values of respect, that women are not the 'other' – the objectified enemy, but rather are future colleagues and collaborators.

We are at a pivotal moment in the United States regarding sexual violence on campus. The US Vice President, in announcing new guidelines for schools in April 2011, looked at the auditorium filled with over 600 students, faculty and community members, and stated: "Look guys. It doesn't matter what a girl does, no matter how she's dressed, no matter how much she's had to drink, it is never okay to touch a woman without her consent … Rape is rape is rape … and no means no."[12]

The new guidelines seek to enforce the provisions of Title IX of the Civil Rights Act that provide for equal access to educational opportunities.[13] While not directly controlling what schools do, the guidelines present a strong incentive for schools to take a proactive role in preventing sexual violence before it happens by focusing on preventative education. Schools play an enormous role in creating campus community, and have a great deal of power to shape norms based on sexual respect. This requires schools to take steps to prevent pornographic messages from dominating the social scene on campus, and to confront and dismantle the resultant harmful attitudes that degrade women permeating campus culture today. Pornography has been recognized in other contexts to contribute to hostile work environments – it is no less harmful on college campuses and should be treated accordingly.

Just before the publication of the new guidelines, the US Department of Education's Office for Civil Rights, the enforcement arm of Title IX, announced an investigation of Yale University for tolerating a toxic sexual culture, which the earlier mentioned rape chants demonstrated, that routinely fostered loud expressions of male dominance on campus. The case has received national attention and has provoked a long-overdue conversation about what we can do to prevent the astoundingly high number of acquaintance rapes on college campuses.[14] In a most promising development, Yale announced in May, 2011, that it is suspending all activities and affiliation with the Delta Kappa Epsilon fraternity for at least 5 years, as well as disciplining some individual members for sexually harassing and intimidating behavior (Miller, 2011).

This is consistent with what I believe schools must do to enable cultures of sexual respect. The project on which I have been working with my students is called the 'Acquaintance Rape Prevention Project', and is formulated to transform college campuses to places where equal access to education is a reality. It is an educational project with the following components.

---

12 Vice President Biden spoke at the University of New Hampshire on 4 April, 2011 to address sexual violence on campus. National Public Radio covered the press conference at <http://www.npr.org/2011/04/05/135135544/federal-effort-targets-sexual-assaults-at-colleges> (accessed 7 May, 2011).

13 The guidelines are contained in a 'Dear Colleague Letter' at <http://www2.ed.gov/about/offices/list/ocr/letters/colleague-20100420.pdf> (accessed 7 May, 2011).

14 See, e.g. 'At Yale: Sharper Look at Treatment of Women', *New York Times*, 7 April, 2011 found at: <http://www.nytimes.com/2011/04/08/nyregion/08yale.html> (accessed 8 May, 2011); 'Hostile Sexual Environment at Yale?' *CBS Early Show*, 4 April, 2011, found at: <http://www.cbsnews.com/stories/2011/04/04/earlyshow/living/parenting/main20050348.shtml>.

First, it focuses on consciousness-raising. As in the first example with the fraternity email suggesting men rape their 'favorite freshman skeezas', when the author of the email was confronted about it, he quickly saw how offensive and degrading it was. Having personally interviewed him, I believe that he was not fully conscious of the implications of his suggestions, but rather reflecting the party scene on campus. After realizing the implications of his harmful email, he agreed to become part of the change through educational programs aimed at men at his college.

The program involves sex-segregated education to develop safe spaces in which to address sensitive issues (Jarrett and Johnson, 2009). The short film *The Undetected Rapist* by David Lisak demonstrates how many acquaintance rapes are premeditated and planned (Lisak, 2002) and would be shown to both groups early in freshman orientation. The education aimed at men focuses on healthier forms of male bonding that do not involve the sexual exploitation of women. As well, it offers tools for bystander intervention, the brilliant program developed by Jackson Katz called 'Mentors in Violence Prevention' (Katz, 2006).

The Acquaintance Rape Prevention Program includes an 'Empathy Inversion Scale' for women and men. Studies have shown that men need to develop more empathy in order to prevent them from coercing or forcing sex on another person (Foubert and Perry, 2007). Women, on the other hand, need to decrease the level of empathy for male acquaintances so that they might be better equipped to self-defend when aggressed upon, instead of trying to make sense of why their 'friend' would be doing this to them (Rosenfeld, 2011).

The education aimed at women includes reaffirming one's right to bodily integrity and sexual autonomy. It also raises self-esteem through education about one's rights (Fallon, 2010). It includes a self-defense program specifically tailored to acquaintance rape situations, as these assaults are much more common on college campuses. Finally, teaching self-defense to individual women promotes a sense of entitlement that reifies one's rights to bodily integrity. This in turn leads women to feeling both competent and entitled to defend one another.

I refer to this idea of collective self-defense as the 'Bonobo Principle' based on the model of bonobo primates. Through strong female–female alliances, bonobos have eliminated male sexual coercion (Rosenfeld, 2009). If a female bonobo is aggressed upon by a male, she lets out a cry, other females descend from the trees to fend off the aggressor, whom they then isolate and ostracize for a few days until he is reintroduced to the troop. They seem to operate on a principle that if one female can be assaulted, then they are all at risk.

The Acquaintance Rape Prevention Project provides a perfect opportunity to apply the Bonobo Principle on college campuses. Female students can forge alliances with one another to reject the designation of women as 'hos'. As women, we have to realize that being called a 'ho' is neither funny nor harmless, and that if men can designate some of us as 'hos', they can designate any of us that way. Women must understand that we are stronger together than we are when divided against ourselves, and that when we participate in judging other women as 'hos', believing that we are somehow above that designation, we are only hurting ourselves. We must realize that we do not even have to *like* one another to achieve strong alliances; rather, we just need to agree that we are stronger if we embrace a sense of basic female solidarity. A collective self-defense, challenging loudly the male sexual entitlement to prostitute women, is the first step towards defining a new, affirmative sexuality; one based on the Bonobo Principle.

Bibliography

College OTR (2009) 'The Top 5 Frat Party Themes', <http://www.collegeotr.com/college_otr/top_5_frat_party_themes_18285> (accessed 10 April, 2011).

Ensign, Rachel (2007) 'Taking It Off: Declothing the Dynamic Between Strippers and their Student Clientele' *Kitsch*, <http://kitschmag.com/index.php?Itemid=26&id=161&option=com_content&task=view> (accessed 10 April, 2011).

Fallon, Elizabeth (2010) 'Framing a Positive Right to Sexual Autonomy: Self Esteem and Community Building on University Campuses,' Harvard Law School, Title IX Seminar, Fall 2010 (on file with author).

Foubert, John and Bradford Perry (2007) 'Creating Lasting Attitude and Behavior Change in Fraternity Members and Male Student Athletes' *Violence Against Women* 13 (1), pp. 70–86.

Gasso, Jordi and Sam Greenberg (2010) 'DKE Apologizes for Pledge Chants' *Yale Daily News*, <http://www.yaledailynews.com/news/2010/oct/15/dke-apologizes-for-pledge-chants/> (accessed 10 April, 2011).

Hartmann, Margaret (2011) 'Frat Email Explains Women Are "Targets," Not "Actual People"', *Jezebel* <http://jezebel.com/#!5779905/usc-frat-guys-email-explains-women-are-targets-not-actual-people-like-us-men> (accessed 10 April, 2011).

Hurt, Byron (2006) 'Beyond Beats & Rhymes' DVD, Media Education Foundation: Northampton, MA.

Jarrett, Laura (2009) 'The Blueprint for Sexual Harassment: How Schools Can Combat Sexual Misconduct as Required Under Title IX by Addressing the Harm of Pornography' (on file with author).

Jarrett, Laura and Stefani Johnson (2009) 'Standing Up for Sexual Respect', American Association of University Women, *Outlook Magazine*, Spring/Summer, p. 16. Washington, DC.

Jensen, Robert (2007) *Getting Off: Pornography and the End of Masculinity.* South End Press, Cambridge, MA.

Katz, Jackson (2006) *The Macho Paradox: Why Some Men Hurt Women and How All Men Can Help.* Sourcebooks Inc., Naperville, Illinois.

Kimmel, Michael (2008) *Guyland.* HarperCollins, New York.

Krebs, Christopher, Christine H. Lindquist, Tara D. Warner, Bonnie S. Fisher and Sandra L. Martin (2007) The Campus Sexual Assault Study: Final Report xii (Nat'l Criminal Justice Reference Serv.), <http://www.ncjrs.gov/pdffiles1/nij/grants/221153.pdf>.

Levy, Ariel (2005) *Female Chauvinist Pigs: Women and the Rise of Raunch Culture*. Free Press, New York.

Lisak, David (2011) 'Changing Paradigms of Title IX Enforcement' Keynote Address, U.S. Department of Education, Office for Civil Rights Conference, Region One, Boston, MA (March, 2011).

Lisak, David and Paul M. Miller (2002). 'Repeat rape and multiple offending among undetected rapists' *Violence and Victims* 17, pp. 73–84.

Miller, Mary (17 May, 2011) 'Regarding the Disciplinary Charges Against DKE' Memo to Faculty and Staff from Dean of Yale College (on file with author).

Office for Civil Rights (2007) 'Sexual Harassment Guidance: Harassment of Students by School Employees, Other Students, or Third Parties', *Federal Register* 62. Washington, DC.

Picker, Miguel and Chyng Sun (2008) 'The Price of Pleasure: Pornography, Sexuality, and Relationships', DVD. Media Education Foundation, Northampton, MA.

Rosenfeld, Diane (2008) 'Concluding Remarks: Changing Social Norms? Title IX and Legal Activism' *Harvard Journal of Law and Gender* 29 p. 407.

Rosenfeld, Diane (2009) 'Sexual Coercion, Patriarchal Violence and Law' in Martin N. Muller and Richard W. Wrangham (Eds) *Sexual Coercion in Primates and Humans: An evolutionary perspective on male aggression against females*. Harvard University Press, Cambridge, MA, p. 424.

Rosenfeld, Diane (2011) 'Changing Paradigms: Acquaintance Rape Prevention Project' Keynote Address, U.S. Department of Education, Office for Civil Rights, Region One Conference, Boston, MA.

Schulman, Tamara (2009) 'Talking Back to Porn: Starting a Dialogue, Speaking Up, and Changing Sexual Scripts', Harvard Law School, Gender Violence Seminar (on file with author).

Shapiro, Joseph (2010) 'Myths That Make It Hard to Stop Campus Rape'. *National Public Radio*, <http://www.npr.org/templates/story/story.php?storyId=124272157> (accessed 15 April, 2011).

'Student Footage of Frat Pledges on Old Campus' (2010) YouTube, <http://www.youtube.com/watch?v=CLh0RMpit1k> (accessed 10 April, 2011).

The Center for Public Integrity Project (2010) 'Sexual Assault on Campus: A Frustrating Search for Justice', <http://www.publicintegrity.org/investigations/campus_assault/> (accessed 7 May, 2011).

Twitter (2010), <http://twitter.com/centerfoldstrip/status/36086856013586432> (accessed 10 April, 2011).

Westmoreland, Matt and Josephine Wolff (2010) 'In the Hot Seat: Hazing at Princeton' *The Daily Princetonian*, <http://www.dailyprincetonian.com/2010/04/26/25997/> (accessed 10 April, 2011).

Yale Daily News (2010) 'The Right Kind of Feminism', <http://www.yaledailynews.com/news/2010/oct/18/the-womens-center-must-continue-to-break-the/> (accessed 10 April, 2011).

Christopher N. Kendall[1]

The Harms of Gay Male Pornography

Introduction

Justified as a source of gay male liberation, self pride and a valued source of much needed sex education, some (indeed, far too many) gay male academics and activists have gone to great lengths to promote and sell gay male pornography as 'harm-free' and 'different from' heterosexual pornography.

This paper rejects this trend, arguing that when we examine what gay male pornography presents and what it actually says about being gay and male today, what we find is a model of behaviour more concerned with self-gratification and the right to dominate and control than with self-respect and respect for others. Indeed, the identity politics on offer sexualises a role play that rejects compassion, affection and equality between gay men and instead promotes (through sex) homophobia and sexism, self-hate, hate for others and harm to others. As such, it must be rejected and any rights strategy that depends on it re-thought.

Gay Male Pornography: The Reality

In early 2000, I was part of the legal team for the human rights lobby group Equality Now in litigation before the Supreme Court of Canada in the case of *Little Sisters Book and Art Emporium*.[2] In that case, Canada's highest court accepted Equality Now's argument that the production and distribution of same-sex pornography causes the same harms to equality that the Court had previously recognised within the context of heterosexual pornography in the case of *R v Butler*.[3]

The pornographic materials at issue in *Little Sisters*, and others like them, have been defended and promoted as gay male identity and a source of equality and

---

1   BA(Hons), LLB (Queen's); LLM, SJD (Michigan); Barrister, John Toohey Chambers: Perth, Western Australia. The writing that appears in this paper first appeared in an expanded version in the author's book on the harms of gay male pornography. See Christopher N. Kendall (2004) *Gay Male Pornography: An Issue of Sex Discrimination*.
2   *Little Sisters Book and Art Emporium v Canada (Minister of Justice)*, [2000] 2 SCR 1120; see <http://www.canlii.org/en/ca/scc/doc/2000/2000scc69/2000scc69.htm> to access details of this case.
3   *R v Butler*. [1992] 1 SCR 452 (SCC).

liberation by pro-pornography and pro-gay advocates alike. An analysis of what these materials actually say about gay male identity, however, reveals that this commitment to pornography is short-sighted, anti-equality and anti-liberation.

In answering this question, it is worth noting the quotation below, found in an article in *Manscape Magazine*, not an issue in *Little Sisters*, but available nonetheless from the Plaintiff's bookstore prior to the case being heard. It, like many of the materials defended in *Little Sisters*, reminds the reader that to be 'male' is to be empowered, but that to be male requires conformity to a clearly defined, gendered norm – a gender role according to which some are entitled to sexually abuse and control, while others, because they are descriptively less 'male', are socially less relevant, less equal, and not entitled to the respect, compassion, and human dignity that only true equality can provide:

> I pushed him lower so my big dick was against his chest; I pushed his meaty pecs together. They wrapped around my dick perfectly as I started tit-fucking him like a chick. His hard, humpy pecs gripped my meat like a vice. Of all the things I did to him that night I think he hated that the most. It made him feel like a girl. I sighed, 'Oh, my bitch got such pretty titties! They was made for tittie fuckin, made to serve a man's dick'.[4]

As in a great deal of written or pictorial gay male pornographic presentations, what one gets from the above is a 'source of liberation and equality' in which the physically more powerful, ostensibly straight male is glorified. This linking of manliness with heterosexuality and overt masculinity is a common theme throughout many of these materials with masculinity often gained at the expense of a woman or ostensibly gay male's safety and self-worth – all in all, the antithesis of both equality and liberation.

To the extent that women are not used or ridiculed in the pornography sold as gay male (and women frequently *are* ridiculed and used as objects of sexual debasement), the effects of sexism and misogyny are not eliminated. These materials, while free of biological femaleness, continue to promote violence and/or the sexual degradation of others along the lines of gender as socially defined, interpreted, and imposed through systems of sex inequality. They often sexualise large, hyper-masculine men – many of whom are described as 'straight' men who find sexual arousal through the infliction of pain on socially feminised sexual subordinates (read: gay men) who, in turn, are shown enjoying the pain, humiliation and degradation to which they are subjected.

Frequently, sexual subordination is enforced through extreme forms of torture and violence, with masculinity again epitomised and celebrated in men

---

4   William Willcox, 'That Old Time Religion' (1995) 10:11 *Manscape Magazine* at 15–18.

who ridicule and emasculate others in the name of sexual pleasure. Humour, we are told, is found in the sexual debasement of another, assertiveness tied to aggression, resulting in an identity politics that creates, packages and re-sells a sexuality that epitomises male supremacy. Femininity in turn is linked with emasculation, linked with inferiority, linked with inequality on the basis of sex. Indeed, those who are emasculated in these materials are often specifically described as gay male, while those who abuse them and who are iconised as sexual role models are described as heterosexual.

Note, for example, *MAC II 19: A Drummer Super Publication, Volume 19.*[5] This magazine contains an article entitled 'Prisoner' that details the torture and sexual mutilation of prisoners of war during a fictional military coup. Many of the prison officers are described as 'straight' and 'real men' whose masculinity is shown through the sexual abuse of their prisoners, most of whom are belittled as gays, queers, sissies etc.[6]

A similar theme is found in *Bear: Masculinity Without the Trappings.*[7] The emphasis in this magazine is on overt, hyper-masculinity. Like *MAC II 19*, many of the stories mock gay men, describing them as 'too feminine', 'sissy' or 'queer'. One article, for example, quotes a trucker who, while bragging about the men who have 'serviced' him at truck stops, says:

> ... truckers sure know about the clean finger nail faggots taking up stalls all day playing footsies, tossing toilet paper and love notes at any pair of boots along side. Most truckers ignore them. Some want to kill them and others figure a blowjob for free is one hell of a lot better than tossing dollars at a whore.[8]

This publication, like many others, promotes violence and aggressive, non-egalitarian behaviour. The theme throughout is hyper-masculinity found at the expense of someone else's liberty and self-worth. Merit is found in degradation. Rewards attached to one's ability to use or be used. Equality, if at all, is found only in reciprocal abuse.

What all of these examples provide is a sexualised identity politic that relies on the inequality found between those with power and those without it; between those who are dominant and those who are submissive; between those who are

---

5   Little Sisters Trial Exhibits, Exhibit number 49, *MAC II 19: A Drummer Super Publication*, Volume 19, January 1990.
6   Ibid. at 24.
7   Little Sisters Trial Exhibits, Exhibit number 197, *Bear: Masculinity Without the Trappings*, Issue 9, 1989.
8   Ibid.

top and those who are bottom; between straight men and gay men; between men and women.

From these and other materials, we are told to glorify manliness and those who meet a hyper-masculine, muscular ideal. The result is a sexual and social reality in which men who are more feminine, less male, are degraded as 'queer' and 'faggots' and subjected to degrading and dehumanising epithets usually used against women, such as 'bitch', 'cunt' and 'whore'. These men are in turn presented as enjoying this degradation. In sum, these materials reinforce a system in which, as Catharine A. MacKinnon explains, "a victim, usually female, always feminized" is actualised (1989, p.141).

In examining the exhibits before the Supreme Court of Canada in the *Little Sisters* case, we also get materials that sexualise racist stereotypes and degrade members of racial minorities for the purpose of sexual arousal. The message conveyed is one in which gay Asian men, for example, are presented as smaller and more feminine than their Caucasian counterparts and thus willing to be sexually subordinated by a more dominant, more stereotypical white male. An example of this type of publication is found in the magazine *Oriental Guys (OG)*. This magazine is, as its title indicates, a pictorial and written collection of articles and photographs of, and about, Asian men. A quick review of the magazine makes it clear, however, that, although 'about' Asian men, the magazine is directed at the Caucasian gay male market.

OG presents photographs of young Asian men, usually posing by themselves. These photo spreads are often accompanied by articles with titles like 'Be My Sushi Tonight'[9] or 'Behind Bars in Thailand'[10] which discusses sex for sale in that country – a country where the sale and sexual use of young boys, via sex tourism, is rampant. The magazine does not present more than one young man at any one time. There is no apparent presentation of violence or physical pain. The magazine does, however, focus on and sexualise the youth and race of those used to produce this publication with the stories throughout the magazine describing, among other things, older white men cruising Asian boys and male prostitutes. In this context, young Asian men are described as 'pearls of the orient', 'easy to find', 'accessible' and 'available.' Often, the photo spreads of young Asian men, shown face down with buttocks elevated, are accompanied by 'news' articles that tell the reader how, for example, to recruit young Balinese men.[11] These, in turn,

---

9   Little Sisters Trial Exhibits, Exhibit number 262, *Oriental Guys*, Issue 4, Spring 1989, p. 10.
10   Little Sisters Trial Exhibits, Exhibit number 6, *Oriental Guys*, Issue 6, Spring 1990, p. 10.
11   *Oriental Guys*, above note 10.

are accompanied by 'letters to the editor' that detail the success of the magazine's Caucasian readers' 'foreign' sexual conquests.

The focus and content of this publication sexualises racism and sexual exploitation. This is its intended result and it is marketed as such. While degrading to Asian gay men, the theme promoted also justifies through sex the types of attitudes and inequalities that make racism and sexism a powerful and interconnected reality. The white male is described as one who seeks out an inferior Asian other; the young Asian is described and presented as ready and willing to serve his sexual needs and fantasies. The white male is superior; the Asian male inferior. The resulting harm is an affront to all persons seeking equality.

In a similar vein, the reader is offered materials in which African-American men are presented as violent sexual predators with large sexual organs who care only to emasculate white men through rape or in which the same men are presented as sexually desiring to be the slaves of white men needing to reaffirm a masculinity threatened by the Black male.

With titles like 'Native American Drifter Hustles Man in Abandoned Mall' and 'Hawaiian Cocksucker Licks Cum From Peepshow Booth Floor', the collection of essays in *Sex Stop: True Revelations and Strange Happenings*,[12] is typical of this type of gay male pornography. Many of the stories contained in it sexualise racial difference, sex with or between young boys and incest. In the story, 'Boy Buys Bicycle by Riding Man's Face', for example, the author describes how he and his friend were paid by an older Black male for sex when they were boys. The story concludes with an editorial comment in which the editor of this collection of stories explains that "this gentleman is married and has grandchildren. He says he has no regrets and just loves to chase old Black men when he can get away from his wife to do it."

Throughout many of these materials rape is also normalised, consent implied. For example, in the story, 'Sucks Brother Off Before Wedding' from *Juice: True Homosexual Experiences*, the writer describes being raped by his older brother and other men. Explaining that these experiences formed the basis of his preferred sexual experiences as an adult, the reader then details another of his sexual encounters as follows:

> Once when I was about 25 I got raped by a powerful young guy that I had taken home to blow. I always say that was the best sex I ever had. Rape at that stage of the game was enjoyable. God

---

12 Little Sisters Trial Exhibits, Exhibit number 200, *Sex Stop: True Revelations and Strange Happenings From Wheeler, Volume 3.*

he was good. He knew just what to do to a willing asshole that kept saying no. He took me with force and I fought him right to the bitter end and – thank God – he won out. When he got through with [me] I knew I had had it. The bastard never came back though.[13]

The identity sold is one in which violence by one man against another man or men is normalised through sex for the persons involved and for the consumer of these materials.

This is a common theme. The magazine *Dungeon Master – The Male S/M Publication*,[14] for example, presents men torturing other men in sexually explicit ways with hot wax, heat and fire, while sexualising this abuse as sexually arousing for the abusers, the persons injured, and, again, for the consumer. The magazine *Mr S/M 65*[15] presents photographs of men being defecated on and who derive pleasure from eating and drinking excrement. The film *Headlights and Hard Bodies*[16] includes footage of men sexually using other men who are being pulled by neck chains, hit and whipped while tied to poles, penetrated by large objects and/ or subjected to clamping, biting and pulling of their nipples and genitals. Men presented as 'slaves' are shown in considerable pain but finding sexual enjoyment from the abuse inflicted on them by others. Those released from bondage kiss the man or men who have just beaten them and thank them for putting them in their place with whips and verbal degradation. *MACII* magazine,[17] in turn, glorifies sexually explicit torture in a military setting, while detailing the kidnapping, torture and sexual mutilation of prisoners of war. In a photograph in the same magazine, two young men are shown confined in a cage. One, face down and bent over, is being slapped by an older man in a Nazi military uniform. Another is chained and hung in stirrups with a hand shoved down his throat.

What one sees in these materials is an almost pervasive glorification of the idealised masculine/male icon. Through them, inequality is sexualised, homophobia entrenched, sexism normalised. Dominance and non-mutuality, submission and inequality remain central to the sexual act and in those photos where men are alone, positioned, posed, humanity is removed and replaced with an object. As 'Men Against Rape and Pornography' (a US activist group) accurately explain, the man exposed becomes a non-human, an object waiting for you to do something to it or wanting to do something to you because he has what it takes to do so. The message sent is that some people want and deserve to

---

13 Ibid.
14 Little Sister Trial Exhibits, Exhibit number 48, *Dungeon Master: The Male SM Publication*, No. 39.
15 Little Sister Trial Exhibits, Exhibit number 216, *Mr SM 65*.
16 Little Sister Trial Exhibits, Exhibit number 192, Film: *Headlights and Hard Bodies*.
17 Little Sister Trial Exhibits, Exhibit number 49, *MACII 19: A Drummer Super Publication*.

have sex forced on them. They solicit this and they deserve this.[18] Either way, the result is a sexuality that is hierarchical and rarely compassionate, mutual or equal.

No Women, Just Men: Harm-Free?

Some have argued that any perceived inequality evident in gay male pornography is rendered non-harmful because in it, unlike in heterosexual pornography, women are not sexually exploited within the heterosexual context. That is, men are presented with men, not men with women, and the sexuality presented is used and experienced by gay men, not straight men.

Arguments that focus predominantly on the use of men in gay male pornography risk claiming that what makes heterosexual pornography harmful is the use of biological females by biological males and that it is this biological polarity that makes women unsafe and unequal. This is misleading, as well as sexist and homophobic: sexist because it implies that harm to men isn't harm, and homophobic because it implies that harm is avoided if it is done to gay men. Gay male pornography does not eliminate harm simply because there are no women in it. At a basic level, this argument assumes that there is something about men hurting and violating men that makes the resulting assault non-harmful, normal and acceptable – an assumption that only reinforces already dominant assumptions about acceptable male behaviour and male aggression generally. Sexualised violence *is* violence and the biological capabilities of the person who harms or who is harmed are irrelevant.[19]

Moreover, any analysis that rests on biology is dangerously naive. Power does not depend on the biology of those who assert it. Straight pornography is harmful not simply because it presents a biological male violating a biological female, but because of the model of behaviour offered the biological male and presented/ sexualised as normal, male gender behaviour. The mere absence of biological 'opposites' does little to undermine the very real harms of rape, abuse, assault, harassment and discrimination resulting from materials in which 'male' equals masculine, equals dominant, equals preferable. The fact that a biological male can also be a 'bottom' is in many ways irrelevant if in order to be that bottom, he is required to assume those characteristics which ensure that those who are 'men', socially defined, remain on top.

The coupling of two biological males does nothing to destabilise sexual and social power inequalities divided along gender lines if those behaviours –

---

18 Men Against Rape and Pornography, *Looking at Gay Porn* (1993).
19 See generally, Christopher Kendall (2004) 'Gay Male Pornography and Sexual Violence: A Sex Equality Perspective on Gay Male Rape and Partner Abuse'.

central to the preservation of gender hierarchy (cruelty, violence, aggression, homophobia, sexism, racism and ultimately compulsory heterosexuality through which heterosexual male dominance is preserved) – are not themselves removed from the presentation of sexuality as power-based. Because gay male pornography sexualises gender stereotypes and the inequalities inherent in them, it reinforces those behaviours and characteristics that ensure that heterosexuality remains the norm and is compulsory, because it does little to advance a model of gay identity that subverts those socially prescribed gender roles that ensure and enforce heterosexual male privilege.

Playing Top and Bottom: Reciprocal Abuse Marketed as Equality

It has also been argued that any inequalities evident in straight pornography are undermined in gay male pornography because the men in gay male pornography, and gay men generally, have the 'option' of participating in a role reversal not normally afforded women – that is, they can 'take turns' being top and bottom. As a result, they further challenge the idea that gender roles are fixed or immutable and thereby question the assumption that men must always be on top (see Burger, 1995).

Central to arguments of this sort is the idea that you can somehow subvert gender's harms if you simply 'play' with it. You can't. If gay men and men generally were willing to give up male privilege, then *maybe* playing with gender would work. But they are not. Accordingly, many gay men seem obsessed with getting, and taking advantage of, that which their straight counterparts have had all along, including pornography. For many, gender and male privilege promise a great deal in a world in which being a man still means something. As such, any medium that promises validation through gender conformity tends to lose its subversive potential and, on the contrary, ensures that those constructs that constitute and construct male supremacy, that make it what it is, remain in place. For many gay men, pornography is not a game. It offers them something very real: power. Over men, as men. There is nothing particularly challenging about this bit of 'theatre', regardless of the biological attributes of those who 'perform' it.

What this focus on role play and role reversal as a means of undermining gender hierarchies overlooks is the fact that the pleasure found remains the pleasure derived from dominance and submission. Although these roles can be reversed, there are still clearly defined roles. There is always a top and there is always a bottom, articulated along gender lines so as to differentiate between those with and those without power. Hierarchy – inequality – thus remains central to the sex act. While there is mutuality, it is in the 'pleasure' found in shared degradation – the pleasure derived from controlling or being controlled by someone else. Mutual abuse does not eradicate abuse. It doubles it and risks trivialising it through sex.

Conclusion

Pornography tells gay men that they too can be real men. But at what cost? Becoming 'a man' does nothing for gay male liberation. It does, however, do a lot for male supremacy. It ensures that the rejection of male dominance, necessary for gay male liberation, will be more difficult and that those of us who do choose to do so will face more hostility from both straight men and those in our community who have sold out. It ensures that the 'groveling faggot', aware that he can never be the man he is supposed to be, will be just what gay male pornography and society says he should be: the object of scorn and male aggression. It ensures that the closeted youth, already attacked for being different, will stay closeted, afraid to express any 'difference' that might reveal his secret and make him the target of more hatred.

While pornographic reality, cloaked as fantasy, might promise the gay male vindication because he too can be on top, the struggle to become that top will only reinforce a social hierarchy straight men have supported all along – the result being gay male silence and subordination, male superiority and female inferiority. And any liberation strategy that normalises this inequality in the name of freedom is not really a politic worthy of celebration, despite the considerable efforts of those who continue to promote it.

Bibliography

Burger, John (1995) *One Handed Histories: The Erotic-Politics of Gay Male Video Pornography.* Harrington Park Press, New York.

Kendall, Christopher N. (2004) *Gay Male Pornography: An Issue of Sex Discrimination.* University of British Columbia Press, Vancouver.

Kendall, Christopher N. (2004) 'Gay Male Pornography and Sexual Violence: A Sex Equality Perspective on Gay Male Rape and Partner Abuse' *McGill Law Journal* 49 (4) pp. 877–923.

Little Sisters Book and Art Emporium v Canada (Minister of Justice), [2000] 2 SCR 1120.

R v Butler. [1992] 1 SCR 452 (SCC).

Little Sisters Trial Exhibits (January 1990) Exhibit number 49, *MACII 19: A Drummer Super Publication,* Volume 19, published by Desmotis Publishers, USA (no longer in existence).

Little Sister Trial Exhibits, Exhibit number 192, Film: *Headlights and Hard Bodies,* A Zeus Video Production.

Little Sisters Trial Exhibits, Exhibit number 200, *Sex Stop: True Revelations and Strange Happenings From Wheeler, Volume 3.*

Little Sister Trial Exhibits, Exhibit number 216, *Mr SM 65.*

Little Sisters Trial Exhibits (1989) Exhibit number 197, *Bear: Masculinity Without the Trappings,* Issue 9, published by COA Publishers, USA (no longer in existence).

Little Sister Trial Exhibits (1990) Exhibit number 48, *Dungeon Master: The Male SM Publication,* No. 39, published by Desmotis Publishers, USA (no longer in existence).

Little Sisters Trial Exhibits, Exhibit number 262, *Oriental Guys,* Issue 4, Spring 1989 at 10.

Little Sisters Trial Exhibits, Exhibit number 6, *Oriental Guys,* Issue 6, Spring 1990 at 10.

MacKinnon, Catharine (1989) *Toward a Feminist Theory of the State.* Harvard University Press, Boston.

Men Against Rape and Pornography, *Looking at Gay Porn* (1993), available from MARAP, PO Box 8181, Pittsburgh, PA 1517.

Willcox, William (1995) 'That Old Time Religion' *Manscape Magazine* 10 (11) pp. 15–18.

Jeffrey Moussaieff Masson

Pornography and Animals

Some things are incomprehensible. Why would anyone derive sexual pleasure from seeing a video of scantily clad women in high heels squashing, stomping, and torturing small animals (including puppies and kittens) who squeal in horror as they die? How could that be 'sexual' in any way where the word makes sense? Perhaps just as incomprehensible is the far larger number of people who insist that such videos are, or can be, 'art', or are examples of freedom of expression which must be defended even if, and perhaps especially if, we personally do not like the content.

These are snuff videos.[1] But how, one might ask, can anyone find this 'sexy'. There is a wide body of feminist literature over the past 30 years that answers this question in detail. I merely wish to make some common-sense observations. Such as the fact that we go to zoos, and rodeos and circuses where we see animals exploited in ways that are not as obvious as in snuff videos. We may not find sexual pleasure in watching these animals forced to behave in ways that are completely unnatural, but something about the total control over them appeals to us. Or we would not attend such spectacles. (As people become more aware of the harm to the animals, attendance is falling off, I am happy to say.)

---

1   They are similar to those far more dangerous, illegal and hard to find snuff films of women being killed for sexual pleasure of the person who watches the film. Just a rumor, some will say. Others call it an urban myth. But I have no reason to doubt that such films exist, are produced by killing real women and are watched by men (pretty much exclusively the audience for such films) from all walks of life. Much like incest, this is not something that happens only in the poorest of neighborhoods. Businessmen, lawyers, doctors, college professors and other elite members of society throughout the Western world pay to see these films in private showings. People who say there are no such things are being willfully blind. Even the daily news brings proof that they exist. Even as I write these lines the commander of Canada's largest Air Force base, Colonel Russell Williams, who once flew prime ministers and served as a pilot to the Queen during a 2005 visit, pleaded guilty to 2 first-degree murder charges, 2 sexual assaults and 82 breaking-and-entering charges. Prosecutors warned the court that details of the killings were horrific before explaining how Williams bound, beat, raped, photographed, videotaped and asphyxiated Marie Comeau, a 38-year-old corporal, and Jessica Lloyd, 27. No mention is made of the purpose of the videotapes, but it is beyond doubt that such 'movies' are made-for-profit films and can be ordered on command, just as can animal crush videos.

Some men obviously take pleasure, sexual pleasure, in control, sadistic control. If they cannot exercise it themselves, they want to see other men exercise it. Pornography involving animals satisfies both the urge to see women as animals, and to see animals as under the control of a dominating male. Some males wish to see both suffer. This is true even when there is a cover, for example pretending that the woman or the animal *likes* the suffering or in some sense *deserves* it. This is also behind the inexplicable suggestion that human/animal sex is consensual, that the animal chooses to have sex with the human and enjoys it. Again, male fantasy is at work. We see this in the whole genre of 'incest' or intra-familial child sexual abuse pornography where grown men rape young girls (or young boys) and insist that the children enjoy it. They have 'chosen' to have sex with these men. Some animal rights activists, notably Peter Singer, are on record as saying that there are some animals who freely 'choose' (or at least are not forced) to have sex with humans. But a moment's reflection reveals that animals cannot make such a free choice, any more than can a child. The very words 'free choice' lose all meaning when we apply them in such situations. In law, but also in common sense, we recognize that a child is *not* free to make any such decision, because children cannot be expected to foresee all the ramifications of such an act, including physical, emotional, mental and social harm, a sexually transmitted disease, or even, for older children, pregnancy.[2] And of course, needless to say, the very power imbalance makes 'no' often impossible. The animal in question, of course, is even less able to understand the consequences of the act.

Here is what Peter Singer wrote (Singer, 2001):

> Some men use hens as a sexual object, inserting their penis into the cloaca, an all-purpose channel for wastes and for the passage of the egg. This is usually fatal to the hen, and in some cases she will be deliberately decapitated just before ejaculation in order to intensify the convulsions of its sphincter. This is cruelty, clear and simple. (But is it worse for the hen than living for a year or more crowded with four or five other hens in a barren wire cage so

---

2   I would make the same point about the sexually suggestive photographs by Sally Mann of her young naked children. There is no way for a child to know how they will feel about such photographs when they are adults. It is disingenuous to claim, as Sally Mann and her supporters do, that her children, now adults are 'fine' with the photos and even proud of them. That may well be. But it cannot be known in advance. And what if those same children, as adults, eventually change their mind? The photos cannot be recalled. There is no meaningful way to speak of 'consent' for young children who are being viewed in ways they cannot yet understand. I really don't care how good the photographs are. That would be like saying the crush videos of the animals have nice color composition. Tell that to the dead animals. And what of the children of the children? How might *they* respond? Why should 'art' trump all other ethical considerations? When I was a university student in France, a friend told me he found the holocaust, apart from its moral dimension, a 'superb spectacle'. He was Jewish, as was I. I stared in disbelief at him. I later learned he was hardly alone.

small that they can never stretch their wings, and then being stuffed into crates to be taken to the slaughterhouse, strung upside down on a conveyor belt and killed? If not, then it is no worse than what egg producers do to their hens all the time.) But sex with animals does not always involve cruelty. Who has not been at a social occasion disrupted by the household dog gripping the legs of a visitor and vigorously rubbing its penis against them? The host usually discourages such activities, but in private not everyone objects to being used by her or his dog in this way, and occasionally mutually satisfying activities may develop.

The comparison is actually not a good one: yes, the way chickens are generally kept for eggs is cruel (which is why I am a vegan). But the people who practice this are often not aware of the cruelty involved (and certainly the vast majority of people who eat eggs do not recognize how terrible the conditions are for the vast majority (99%) of hens who lay eggs. People are not *deliberately* looking for a way to cause suffering. In the case of sex with hens, on the contrary, the whole point is to cause the maximum amount of suffering, culminating in death. It is the death and the agony that are the source of the male's pleasure. Singer should not simply omit this important distinction. Moreover, to say that what happens between a dog and a person is 'mutually satisfying' is to degrade the use of the word mutual. Something is mutual only if it is consensual, and sex between humans and animals can never be consensual, because animals cannot consent. Singer also misunderstands the gesture of the dog: it only appears to be sexual; in actual fact, dogs engage in mounting behavior in order to test or display dominance. Much as I admire Peter Singer for his groundbreaking work on animal rights, his views on this topic (and I might add, on human euthanasia and infanticide for babies with disabilities) are open to serious criticism.

Just how common are crush (or squish, as they are also called) videos? In the USA, they are still, for the moment at least, common. Alas, so called 'soft' crush videos using invertebrates is legal, protected under the First Amendment as 'free speech'. It is a shadowy world, similar to the world of snuff videos where hard information is difficult to find. A Humane Society investigation found that 'customers' can request a video over the Internet with a specific type of animal and a specific torture, and the video will be sent with 48 hours.

I had presumed it was a world inhabited by the dregs of society. That assumption may not be justified. Consider the fact that these videos have influenced 'higher' art. Many artists in England, America and Australia, have found their art to be highly appreciated when it involves the suffering of a living animal. A notorious example is the British artist Damien Hirst, the most celebrated of the 'Young British Artists' and Britain's richest living artist. Many of his installations involve animals: *Away from the Flock*, consists of a dead sheep in a glass tank full of formaldehyde, and *Mother and Child Divided*, consists of a mother cow and a calf sliced in half in a glass tank of formaldehyde (it won the prestigious Turner Prize). *The Physical Impossibility of Death in the Mind of Someone Living* consists of a shark in a vitrine, preserved in formaldehyde. Commissioned in 1991, the piece was sold in 2004 for $12 million to an American art collector who donated it to the Metropolitan Museum of Modern Art. It is considered the iconic work of art of Britart. The Australian art critic, Robert Hughes, in a well-deserved attack on his work, called Hirst's shark the world's most over-rated marine organism.

More examples abound. In 2000, the Chilean artist Marco Evaristti exhibited at the Trapholt Art Museum in Denmark. The display, entitled *Helena*, featured 10 blenders containing goldfish. Evaristti said that he wanted people "to do battle with their conscience" (why there would be a battle is not explained) so visitors to the exhibition were invited to turn on the blenders.[3] (As if any invitation had to be accepted.) How many is not clear, but some people liquidized the fish. Singer might claim this is no worse than eating fish for dinner, but he is wrong. It *is* worse, because it is deliberate cruelty masquerading as high art. (Fish were also part of an installation by the Brazilian artist Cildo Meireles at the Tate Modern, where many of them died during the 13-week-long exhibition.)

Victorian artist, Ivan Durrant, is enjoying a retrospective of his work in Melbourne under the title 'Paddock to Plate' at the Monash Art Gallery. He is best known for having butchered a cow and left it on the steps of Parliament House in Melbourne.

In 2008, Parisian artist, Adel Abdessened, opened an exhibit called 'Don't Trust Me'. Among other things, the show included something that has been correctly described as a snuff film using animals. The 'art' consisted of six video screens showing a loop of various animals being beaten to death with a sledgehammer. The animals included a pig, goat, horse, sheep, and ox. The point?

All of these artists claim that they are trying to hold up a mirror to society, basically saying: 'You are all hypocrites. Look at what you do to animals'. But of course the problem is that they are doing exactly that, even as they say it. The hypocrisy belongs as much to the artist as to the society. And what about the gallery or museum that condones the exhibit, or the viewer who stands in front of the piece? None of these artists (Durrant is a wealthy farmer who owns a bull ranch) is doing this as an animal rights activist; rather the artist very much participates in the society he supposedly denounces.

---

3   Arts Law: Animal Rights and Artistic Freedom <http://www.artslaw.com.au/articles/entry/animal-rights-and-artistic-freedom/>.

If you put 'bestiality porn' into Google, you do not get Websites where such matters are discussed. You get hundreds and hundreds of sites containing the actual stuff. I confess I did not go to them to see exactly what they offered. It was enough to see the phrase 'includes cruel fucking' to know that what they offered would make me ill. (I made the same confession when I wrote a book about the feelings of farm animals: I could not bring myself to visit a slaughterhouse – but others have done it for me.)

However, Abigail Bray alerted me to a new trend, 'pet love' as some call it, a lucrative porn genre. One company, run by Doctor X and an animal sex prostitute 'Stray', sells 200–400 DVDs through their Website every day. New subscribers join daily; the majority are aged between 18 and 45. The owners have moved from the UK to a European country where they say "you can freely buy animal porn in shops and from news-stands … Pet love videos are routinely in the top three bestselling DVDs at sex shops" where expos screen "doggy sex shows on giant TVs" and the government is "very helpful with the business side of things." University educated, Doctor X decided to market porn videos of women with dogs as a cool, sexually self-empowering practice for transgressive liberated women. His business partner, Stray, also frames 'sex' with dogs with post-feminist sexual self-empowerment rhetoric: "Getting fucked by dogs allows me to take charge of my own sexuality. I don't have to rely on a man." Stray says that it was reading pornographic bestiality fantasies by the libertarian writer, Nancy Friday, that encouraged her to explore bestiality. The online 'pet love' community normalizes her abuse of dogs.

> Suddenly information was available, chat rooms, forums … Pet love sites would frequently get closed down, but I learned to recognise insider lingo – plus, as a single woman into pet love, I was a popular community member and fellow enthusiasts would ensure I was kept in the loop! Posts on an internet group drew my attention to one of Doctor X's websites, which had been running for three years, and I thought it really spoke to women. It was classy and upmarket, not degrading … Money isn't my main motivation, but I earn a good amount of cash too, and no-one takes a bigger cut than me from the productions I star in. *Every aspect of what I do is liberating and empowering* (emphasis added).

Stray also argues that Peter Singer's argument validated her bestiality prostitution especially as the president of the animal group PETA, Ingrid Newkirk, endorsed his 'ethics,' although Newkirk later retracted the endorsement.[4]

Pornography, in all its many variations, is the attempt to take away the

---

4   See <http://www.animalrights.net/2005/peta-and-bestiality-round-2/> and for a feminist critique of PETA see <http://melindatankardreist.com/2011/02/porn-masquerading-as-an-anti-animal-cruelty-video/>.

personhood or subjective identity of whatever is depicted. So it is not surprising that it is primarily used against women. Perhaps the first us/them in history consists of men feeling different and superior to women. Nor is it surprising that it would then pass over to animals: possibly the second us/them in history consists of men and women feeling different and superior to animals. Common cause should be the default position of feminists and animal rights activists; we are all fighting for the same thing: dignity and the abrogation of cruelty. Pornography is violence against women, children, animals, and all those who are falsely believed to have no claim to a soul. We are all, as the philosopher, Tom Regan, reminds us, the subject of a life.

Bibliography

Animal Rights (2005) 'PETA and bestiality Round 2', <http://www.animalrights.net/2005/peta-and-bestiality-round-2/>.

Arts Law (2003) 'Animal Rights and Artistic Freedom', <http://www.artslaw.com.au/articles/entry/animal-rights-and-artistic-freedom/>.

Singer, Peter (2001) 'Heavy Petting' (*Nerve*, 2001) and <http://www.utilitarian.net/singer/by/2001----.htm>.

Tankard Reist, Melinda (2011) 'Porn masquerading as an anti-animal cruelty video', <http://melindatankardreist.com/2011/02/porn-masquerading-as-an-anti-animal-cruelty-video/>.

Robi Sonderegger

Neurotica: Modern Day Sexual Repression

At the height of the 1960s American counterculture revolution, folklorist and social critic Gershon Legman coined the slogan 'Make love not war'. Notwithstanding the popular use of the term by activists in opposition to the Vietnam War, the slogan originated from Legman's deeply held views that sexual repression and censorship of erotic publications were the cause of escalating violence and sadism in American culture (in Landesman, 1999). Despite Legman's best intentions, however, the sexual revolution delivered more than he bargained for. As sexual and interpersonal norms were challenged in pursuit of 'sexual freedom', new types of repression emerged in the form of the capitalist commercialisation of sex. The 'sexual freedom' that people aspired to in the 1960s was exploited by big business in the 70s and 80s with the production of pornography en masse (Jong et al., 2003). Any notion of 'Make love not war' quickly became 'Make money not love'.

Renowned political theorist and philosopher on the sexual revolution, Herbert Marcuse, argued that the notion of 'sexual freedom' was almost oxymoronic. Despite being an advocate for sexual expression in art and literature in its true form, he challenged the Freudian-style thinking of the day that suggested the commercialisation of sexual liberty would only result in social enslavement. Indeed, contrary to the myth that pornography could somehow enhance intimacy, free the libido, or grant a liberating outlet for sexual expression, sexualised media has ultimately became a source of addiction and bondage (US Attorney General's Commission on Pornography, 1986). In his classic *One-Dimensional Man* (1964/1994) Marcuse describes this as a process of Repressive Desublimation: when the best sellers of oppression defile authentic sexuality by replacing relational intimacy with a commodity to be consumed. The sexual revolution was supposed to throw off outdated constrictions. However, in an endeavour to cheapen and profane what so many consider sacred, 'sexual freedom' has been hijacked by industrialised, mass-produced, stereotyped pornography which only represses authentic sexual expression and intimacy. Marcuse contends that hope and truth preserved in the sublimations of higher culture are both betrayed and destroyed (1994/1994, p. 60).

Paradoxically, with the relaxation of laws relating to the commercial availability of sexually explicit material and the increasing demand to satisfy newly cultivated sexual appetites, greater liberality has been taken in the production of hardcore and violent content. In a recent investigation of pornographic subject matter (Bridges et al., 2010), almost 90% of scenes in the most popular adult films incorporated verbal aggression (48%: name calling/insults; threatening physical harm; and/or using coercive language) and physical aggression (88.2%: pushing/ shoving; biting; pinching; pulling hair; spanking; open-hand slapping; gagging; choking; threatening with weapon; kicking; closed-fist punching; bondage/ confining; using weapons; torturing, mutilating and attempting murder). Such aggression (averaging 11.52 acts per scene) was mostly perpetrated against women, by both men (72.7% of offences) and women (27.0% of offences).

While not everyone who views pornography goes on to develop sexual behaviour problems, for many pornography seems to both create and exacerbate pathology. Similar to other mental health professionals, I've observed a disturbing trend among pornography consumers towards both compulsive behaviours and the development of abnormal interests, over which clients report having little control. According to Dr William Struthers, Associate Professor in Biopsychology, pornography creates significant confusion for the human brain. As pornography consumption increases, autonomy (freedom over what a person thinks and pursues) decreases, leaving one's sexual drive screaming for an outlet. "Sexually acting out in response to pornography creates sexual associations that are stored as hormonal and neurological habits. These associations are seared into the fabric of the brain" (2009, p. 59).

As the brain's limbic system becomes dependent on the neurological rewards[1] of viewing pornography, many consumers need to employ cognitive defence strategies to deal with the resulting dissonance and identity confusion. Over time, defence mechanisms mutate to justify more extreme sexual interests and behaviours. According to Dr Struthers, pornography consumers start with *denial* (avoiding disclosure due to cultural stigma), and progress to *minimisation* (asserting control over viewing habits and playing down its impact), to *normalisation* (arguing everyone is doing it so it must be acceptable), to *rationalisation* and *justification* (endeavouring to use logical arguments to excuse viewing, or acting out after viewing, pornography), and ultimately end up in *celebration* (embracing sexual exploitation and revelling in one's habitual behaviour). Emeritus Professor in

---

1   A complex neurochemical interplay (incorporating Serotonin, Norepinephrine, Oxytocin and Vasopressin) with Dopamine (the primary neurotransmitter that most addictive drugs release) ultimately terminating in the Nucleus Accumbens (the brain's pleasure centre).

Psychology, Dr Victor Cline, reports a similar progression from pornography consumption to sexually deviant interests and delinquency.[2] Based on observations over the course of treating hundreds of clients with sexual behaviour problems, Dr Cline has identified 4 progressive phases in the aetiology of sexually abhorrent interests and behaviours (2001, pp. 3–4):

1. Compulsive pornography viewing accompanied by masturbation and subsequent sexual release;

2. Escalation of explicit content (more violent, extreme or deviant) to achieve the same sexual high through masturbation and sexual release;

3. Desensitisation to material that initially may have been repulsive, shocking or even illegal (despite being contrary to previously held moral beliefs and personal standards), coming to see it not only as common place, but also justifying, rationalising, and defending it; and

4. An intense desire or propensity to sexually act out a range of abhorrent behaviours viewed in pornography (e.g. compulsive promiscuity, exhibitionism, voyeurism, violence, child molestation, rape). As sexually deviant behaviours take hold, clients find themselves locked into a neurotic addiction cycle that is pursued at all costs – irrespective of potential negative consequences.

The state of being neurotic or engaging neurotic behaviour stems from a psychiatric condition known as neurosis. Characteristics of neurosis typically manifest as obsessional thoughts and compulsive behaviours. To varying degrees, neurotic thoughts dominate one's personality and result in interpersonal maladjustment. Interestingly, such patterns of neurotic thoughts and behaviours are widely reported in explorative research on the role pornography consumption plays in the development of sexual dysfunction. Is there a connection between pornography and neurosis?

The empirical literature refers to sexually neurotic thoughts and behaviours as paraphilia. According to the Diagnostic and Statistical Manual of Mental Disorders (DSM-IV-TR) "… paraphilia is characterised by recurrent, intense sexual urges, fantasies, or behaviours that involve unusual objects, activities, or situations." More specifically, paraphilia generally involves "1) nonhuman objects, 2) the suffering or humiliation of oneself or one's partner, or 3) children or other nonconsenting persons …" (American Psychiatric Association, 2000, pp. 535, 566).

---

2 A list of reports and articles highlighting the progression from pornography to delinquent interests can be found in Peters, 2009, pp. 11–13.

Given that many of these paraphilia are also criminal activities, research parameters make it difficult to conclusively ascertain how such sexual dysfunction and deviancy develop. Nevertheless, it should be noted that there are strong parallels between sexual dysfunction and published pornographic materials. Most pathological conditions are also common pornographic sub-genres.[3] Table 1 provides a breakdown of some of the most common online pornographic sub-genres, their descriptions and their popularity both in the number of available Webpages (generated through a Google Web search) and the average number of searches performed globally each month (calculated by Google AdWords). These sub-themes almost perfectly match the clinical forms of sexual paraphilia acknowledged in forensic psychiatry.

Table 1: Online pornographic sub-genres (listed in order of predominance)

Online search terms	Description	Total Web pages[a]	Total monthly searches[b]
Teen sex	Involving actual post-pubescent adolescents	81,700,000	N/A[c]
Animal sex	Involving the sexual engagement of animals (Bestiality)	50,300,000	6,120,000
Bondage	Involving sadism & masochism	29,400,000	5,000,000
Spankwire	Involving the violent mutilation of reproductive organs	16,600,000	7,480,000
Bukkake	Involving numerous men (10+) having sex with one wo(man)	17,900,000	1,500,000
Voyeur sex	Involves filming & spying on people while dressing/showering	15,900,000	135,000
Twink porn	Involving younger/slender looking boys	8,210,000	135,000
Crush sex	Involving the killing of small animals (also called Hard Crush)	7,740,000	5400
Vomit sex	Involving vomiting & gagging (Emetophilia pornography)	3,790,000	9900

---

3   A comprehensive outline of sexual paraphilia as recognised in forensic psychiatry is reported in Hucker (2010); a parallel outline of pornographic sub-genres is published by Wikipedia.

Online search terms	Description	Total Web pages[a]	Total monthly searches[b]
Rough sex	Involving humiliation, choking, hair-pulling	3,250,000	368,000
Scat porn	Involving defecation, manipulation/consumption of feces	3,050,000	165,000
Lolita sex	Involving underage-looking performers (appearing 15-18 years)	2,200,000	N/A[c]
Rape sex	Involving real or portrayed forced unconsensual sex	2,770,000	550,000
Diaper porn	Involving performers pretending to be infants	1,730,000	27,100
Wired porn	Involving electrical shocks & use of electrocution devices	1,690,000	2400
Pre-teen sex	Involving actual pre-pubescent children	1,560,000	N/A[c]
Exhibitionist sex	Involves public genital exposure (from flashing to intercourse)	1,360,000	2900
Snuff sex	Involving actual death of participants, consenting or otherwise	1,280,000	6600
Menstrual porn	Involving menstruating women (with focus on menstrual blood)	531,000	9900
Felching sex	Involving the suction of recently-ejaculated semen from the anus	480,000	170
Guro sex	Involving blood, gore, disfiguration, mutilation, urine or feces	278,000	480

a   Total number of pornography sub-genre Google generated Webpages in 2010 (accessed 15 December, 2010).
b   Average number of global monthly Google searches in 2010: Data specific to Keyword Match Type (derived from Google AdWords, calculated 15 December, 2010).
c   Number of Google AdWords searches publicly restricted. However Google Trends reports juvenile sex search terms were, by far, the most popular of all requests in 2010 (derived from Google Trends, calculated on 20 December, 2010).

The mere parallel between deviant sexual pathology and popular pornography sub-themes does not warrant the conclusion that one is determined by the other. According to Kingston et al. (2008) other relevant moderating variables, such as family background and transient emotional states, may also contribute to an individual's predisposition in relation to sexualised media. Yet, the socially corrosive power of unregulated commercialised pornography is clearly acknowledged throughout scientific literature.

Not only does pornography activate and reinforce inappropriate cognitive representations (fostering sexual preoccupation), repeated exposure to pornography has been found to "help shape an individual's fantasies, perceptions, rationalizations, and deeper core beliefs" (Kingston et al., 2008, p. 349). Empirical studies[4] into the effects of pornography have consistently shown that the degradation encouraged by pornography encourages negative attitudes and dominant behaviours towards women, including the heightened proclivity towards coercive sex. This is especially true of pornography that advocates aggression and violence towards women, which, based on findings that aggression rates in pornographic scenes have nearly tripled in recent years (Bridges et al., 2010), can be considered the overwhelming majority.

According to social, operant, and classical learning theories,[5] consumers model what they learn from sexually explicit media when the sexual acts they observe are positively reinforced. Most disturbingly, Bridges et al. (2010), found that when aggressed against, 95.9% of female pornography actors responded with approving (expressions of pleasure) or condoning (expressions of neutrality) responses.[6] To the extent that consumers of mainstream pornography learn that verbal and physical sexual aggression is rewarding, they are more likely to incorporate coercive aggression in their own sexual encounters. An overwhelming number of empirical studies have now established a significant relationship between the consumption of sexually explicit media and sexual delinquency. Irrespective of additional mediating/moderating variables, pornography contributes directly to pro-sexual-offending attitudes, intimate relationship difficulties, sexual callousness, disinterest in the suffering of others, and desensitisation to violence against women, acceptance of male dominance and female servitude, leniency toward rapists in legal proceedings, accepting various rape myths (that rape can be justified), self-assessed proclivity to force sex on women, and the

---

4   A summary of studies and findings can be found in Bridges et al. (2010).
5   Theories developed and made popular by Ivan Pavlov (1927/1960), Burrhus Skinner (1953) and Alan Bandura (1977).
6   Of course, the signs of approval are required of the women appearing in pornography.

direct instigation of sexual assault (Dèttore and Giannelli, 2008; Marshall, 2000; Waltman, 2008). Pornography has been rendered "instrumentally causal in the aetiology of sex offending" (Itzin, 2002, p. 21).

Violence against women is a human rights violation, yet the industry that fuels the production and distribution of pornography continues unabated in the denigration of women and the indirect facilitation of the most heinous of crimes. Meta-analyses of published research show consistent and reliable evidence that exposure to explicitly violent as well as so-called non-violent pornography has a direct influence on gender violence. This is true not only for adults, but also minors. In one study, an overwhelming majority (97%) of juvenile sex offenders disclosed their involvement with pornography (Wieckowski et al., 1998). It has also been demonstrated that juvenile sex offenders who consume pornography have a greater propensity to engage in rape, forced oral or digital penetration, verbal aggression, exhibitionism and bestiality (Alexy et al., 2009). In fact, research into developmental harm from pornography exposure is so conclusive, that the empirical literature now considers it to be beyond question (Oddone-Paolucci et al., 2000).

Juvenile sex crime victims are also exposed to pornography by perpetrators in an endeavour to normalise sexual behaviours and facilitate subsequent grooming. Research studies conducted with child sex offenders (convicted for indecent assault, rape and buggery) have repeatedly found pornography to be used as part of the crime, with prevalence rates ranging from 33% (Elliot et al., 1995) to 55% (Langevin and Curnoe, 2004). Yet just as sex offenders groom their victims, so it appears the pornography industry inconspicuously grooms consumers. With pornography gaining unrestricted access into the homes and minds of ordinary people, more than at any other time in human history, unsuspecting consumers are undeniably conditioned. Therefore, it is reprehensible for policy makers to remain idle on the issue of pornography. Based on the empirical research reviewed in this chapter, it could well be argued that to produce, distribute, consume, or even passively condone pornography, is to endorse sexual violence against women. The discrepancy between the sex industry's spin about 'sexual freedom' and our actual human liberty is so great that it is legitimate to suggest Legman's ideology has ultimately become 'Make war not love'.

Bibliography

Alexy, Eileen, Ann Burgess and Robert Prentky (2009) 'Pornography use as a risk marker for an aggressive pattern of behavior among sexually reactive children and adolescents' *Journal of the American Psychiatric Nurses Association* 14 (6), pp. 442–453.

American Psychiatric Association (2000) *Diagnostic and Statistical Manual of Mental Disorders; Fourth Edition, Text Revision (DSM-IV-TR)*. Jaypee Brothers Medical Publishers, New Delhi.

Bandura, Allan (1977) *Social Learning Theory*. General Learning Press, New York.

Bridges, Ana, Robert Wosnitzer, Erica Scharrer, Chyng Sun and Rachel Liberman (2010) 'Aggression and sexual behaviour in best selling pornography videos: A content analysis update' *Violence Against Women* 16 (10), pp. 1065–1085.

Cline, Victor (2001) 'Pornography's Effects on Adults and Children' *Morality in Media,* pp. 3–4, <http://www.obscenitycrimes.org/cline_unabridged.pdf> (accessed 13 December, 2010).

Dèttore, Davide and Alberto Giannelli (2008) 'Explorative survey on the level of online sexual activities and sexual paraphilias' Abstracts of the 9th Conference of the European Federation of Sexology 17 (1), S15–S15.

Elliott, Michelle, Kevin Browne and Jennifer Kilcoyne (1995) 'Child Sexual Abuse Prevention: What Offenders Tell Us' *Child Abuse and Neglect* 19 (5), pp. 579–594.

Hucker, Stephen (2010) 'Forensic Psychiatry: Paraphilias'. Law and Mental Health Program, University of Toronto, <http://www.forensicpsychiatry.ca/paraphilia/overview.htm> (accessed 8 December, 2010).

Itzin, Catherine (2002) 'Pornography and the construction of misogyny' *Journal of Sexual Aggression* 8 (3) pp. 4–42.

Jong, Erica, Jeffrey Escoffier and Fred McDarrah (2003) *Sexual Revolution*. Thunder's Mouth Press, New York.

Kingston, Drew, Paul Fedoroff, Philip Firestone, Susan Curry and John Bradford (2008) 'Pornography use and sexual aggression: The impact of frequency and type of pornography use on recidivism among sexual offenders' *Aggressive Behavior* 34 (4) pp. 341–351.

Landesman, Jay (1999) Gershon Legman (d.1999). *The Independent (London)*, <http://www.independent.co.uk/arts-entertainment/obituary-gershon-legman-1083016.html> (accessed 13 December, 2010).

Langevin, Ron and Suzanne Curnoe (2004) 'Use of pornography during the commission of sexual offenses' *International Journal of Offender Therapy and Comparative Criminology* 48, (5) pp. 572–586.

Marcuse, Herbert (1964/1994) *One-dimensional Man: Studies in ideology of advanced industrial society*. Routledge, London.

Marshall, William (2000) 'Revisiting the use of pornography by sexual offenders: Implications for theory and practice' *Journal of Sexual Aggression* 6 (1/2) pp. 67–77.

Oddone-Paolucci, Elizabeth, Mark Genius and Claudio Violato (2000) 'A meta-analysis of the published research on the effects of pornography' *Medicine, Mind and Adolescence* 7 (1/2) pp. 101–112.

Pavlov, Ivan (1927/1960) *Conditional Reflexes*. Dover Publications, New York.

Peters, Robert (2009) 'How adult pornography contributes to sexual exploitation of children' *Morality in Media,* pp. 1–215, <http://www.obscenitycrimes.org/news/HowAdultPornographyHarmsChildren.pdf> (accessed 13 December, 2010).

Skinner, Burrhus (1953) *Science and human behavior*. Macmillan, Oxford.

Struthers, William (2009) *Wired for intimacy: How pornography hijacks the male brain*. IVP Books, Downers Grove (Illinois).

US Attorney General's commission on pornography (1986), <http://www.porn-report.com/> (accessed 8 December, 2010).

Waltman, Max (2008) 'Rethinking Democracy: Pornography and Sex Inequality' (University of Michigan Law School) Paper presented at the Western Political Science Association (WPSA) San Diego, pp. 1–41.

Wieckowski, Edward, Peggy Hartsoe, Arthur Mayer and Joianne Shortz (1998). 'Deviant sexual behaviour in children and young adolescents: Frequency and patterns' *Sexual Abuse: A Journal of Research and Treatment* 10 (4) pp. 293–303.

Wikipedia, the free Encyclopaedia (2010) *List of pornographic sub-genres: Fetish,* <http://en.wikipedia.org/wiki/List_of_pornographic_sub-genres> (accessed 8 December, 2010).

Meagan Tyler

Pornography as Sexual Authority: How Sex Therapy Promotes the Pornification of Sexuality

Pornography is increasingly infiltrating various aspects of our lives. Most often in discussing this 'pornification' (Paul, 2005), we raise examples that we can easily see and recognise: fashion, art, advertising, television shows, movies. But pornography is also infiltrating areas which are not so obvious in everyday, public life, from the business practices of global corporations (Davies and Wonke, 2000; Lane, 2000; Rich, 2001) to the sex practices of our intimate relationships (Dines, 2010; Häggström-Nordin et al., 2005; Paul, 2005; Tydén and Rogala, 2003, 2004). These public and private processes of pornification not only involve the increasing exposure and influence of the pornography industry but also its increasing legitimacy. One of the most prominent ways in which pornography is now presented as legitimate is in the area of sex therapy. In sex therapy today, pornography is deemed to be not just an acceptable part of everyday sexual practice, but an ideal model of sexuality for people to imitate. This is pornography being presented as the ultimate sexual authority and it poses serious harms to women's equality.

The recommendation of pornography can be found in many sex self-help books, even those written by well-known and respected sex therapists (see for example Heiman and LoPiccolo, 1992; Morrissey, 2005; Zillbergeld, 1993). Pornography is most often recommended as an aide for couples. According to therapists Striar and Bartlik, writing on the use of 'erotica' in sex therapy, pornography should be seen as a way of "adding diversity to a monogamous relationship" (Striar and Bartlik, 1999, p. 61). In particular, they state that it can be beneficial for "couples with incompatible sexual fantasies" (p. 61). This is one of the most common ways in which pornography is introduced as part of sex therapy. Pornography is used "to introduce a partner to a new mode of sexual experience that he or she might find otherwise distasteful or unacceptable" (p. 61). In cases such as this, pornography, under the guidance of therapists, is promoted as a tool to be used when trying to convince an unwilling partner to perform a sex act that they do not wish to engage in.

The idea that women should 'experiment' and perform sex acts that they do not want to has become a popular model for women's sexual behaviour in heterosexual relationships since the 'sexual revolution' of the 1960s. It is an idea frequently reinforced and legitimated through sex therapy (see Jeffreys, 1990). Women are still encouraged by therapists to sexually fulfill their male partners, even if they have no desire to do so, or experience pain or discomfort (Tyler, 2008). For example, in the widely recommended self-help manual for women *Becoming Orgasmic*, therapists Heiman and LoPiccolo encourage women to try anal sex (an increasingly ubiquitous sex practice in pornography) if a male partner is interested in it. The advice from the therapists is: "If any discomfort does occur, try again some other time" (Heiman and LoPiccolo, 1992, p. 187). The central premise is that pain and discomfort for women are not acceptable reasons for discontinuing a sexual practice, but, rather, are reasons for women to undergo further 'training', 'modelling' and coercion. Instead of understanding that using pornography as a coercive strategy is harmful, sexologists extol pornography's virtues, stating for example that it is useful for "giving the viewer permission to model the behavior" (Striar and Bartlik, 1999, p. 61).

Exactly what type of behaviour women are expected to model from pornography further exposes the way in which the promotion and legitimation of pornography in sex therapy poses harms to women's equality. Even at the most respectable end of therapist-recommended pornography, sadomasochistic practices and acts such as double penetration, or DP as it is known in the porn industry, can be easily found. Take for example, the Sinclair Intimacy Institute, run by a "well known and respected sexologist, Dr Mark Schoen" (Black, 2006, p. 117). It consists mainly of an online store that sells therapist-recommended pornography. On the Institute's Website, customers are assured that the pornography available is reviewed and approved by therapists who choose only "high quality sex positive productions" (Sinclair Intimacy Institute, 2007a, n.p.). Among the list of "sex positive productions" are the mainstream pornography titles *The New Devil in Miss Jones*, *Jenna Loves Pain*, and *Deepthroat*.

The choice of *Deepthroat* is particularly revealing given the amount of publicity surrounding the circumstances of its production. Linda Marchiano (Linda Lovelace at the time of filming) detailed her extensive abuse at the hands of her husband and pimp in her book *Ordeal*, explaining how she was forced, sometimes at gun point to perform in pornography (Lovelace, 1980). She once stated that: "every time someone watches that film, they are watching me being raped" (quoted in Dworkin, 1981). That such a film is labelled 'sex positive' by therapists should be serious cause for concern. But *Deepthoat* is not an isolated case.

The New Devil in Miss Jones and *Jenna Loves Pain* both received rave reviews in the prominent US porn industry magazine *Adult Video News*. The editors of *Adult Video News* (*AVN*) gave *Miss Jones* a glowing recommendation, stating: "The sex is universally good and downright edgy, with piercing, double penetration and flogging in the closing scene ..." (Pike-Johnson, 2005b, n.p.). Keep in mind, these are titles recommended for couples to watch and then model their behaviour on. *Jenna Loves Pain*, as if the title is not problematic enough, also received a hearty endorsement from *AVN*. Readers were informed that the title contained not only mild sadomasochism but that "*Jenna Loves Pain* raises the bar for what is possible in pure BDSM titles" (Ramone, 2005b, n.p.). To be clear, we are talking about fetish titles which contain acts of bondage, discipline and sadomasochism (BDSM), and sadly therapists do actually expect women to model this BDSM behaviour. Striar and Bartlik, for example, inform their fellow therapists that accessories to facilitate domination and submission fantasies such as "whips, restraints and blindfolds" (1999, p. 61) should be recommended to clients and can easily be found in sex stores.

The promotion of domination, submission, and other sadomasochist practices can even be found in therapist-endorsed 'sex education' videos. The Sinclair Intimacy Institute produces and distributes some of the most well known titles in the sex education genre. According to Dr Judy Seifer, one of the therapists involved in developing the Institute's *Better Sex* series, couples should use the videos "like a textbook. Stop the tape; freeze the frame, like re-reading a chapter" (quoted in Eberwein, 1999, p. 193). This 'textbook', however, contains many, if not all, of the stereotypical conventions of mainstream pornography (Eberwein, 1999), including themes of BDSM.

The promotion of sadomasochism in sex education videos is particularly obvious in the Institute's *Better Sex* Kits which include videos and also sex toys. One kit is titled 'Smart Maid'. Potential customers are told via the Website that: "Dressing up and looking sexy for your partner is part of any healthy relation-ship ..." (Sinclair Intimacy Institute, 2007b). The dressing up, however, is only expected of women: the kits offer no outfits for men. In this particular instance, women are supposed to dress up in an "upstairs maid costume". The sexual excitement that men are expected to experience from a woman's servitude is high-lighted in the accompanying details: "At your service! Playful and sexy fantasies will come alive when she wears this sheer maids [sic] set" (Sinclair Intimacy Institute, 2007b). Themes of dominance and submission are also obvious in the 'Tie Me Up, Tie Me Down' kit, which includes "Japanese wrist and ankle cuffs" in addition to a leather blindfold. The accompanying photograph for the kit, rather unsurprisingly, shows a woman modelling the so-called educational BDSM wear (Sinclair Intimacy Institute, 2007c).

The promotion of pornography in sex therapy, however, only explains part of how pornography is increasingly seen as an authority on sexual matters. As a consequence of the legitimacy that sex therapists have afforded pornography over the years – holding it up as an ideal model on which to base heterosexual sex – porn stars are increasingly being positioned as 'sex experts'. For example, in the 1999 collection *Sex Tips: Advice from women experts around the world* edited by Australian sex therapist Jo-Anne Baker, porn stars, sadomasochist practitioners and prostituted women appear alongside therapists as the designated 'experts' (Baker, 1999). Also in keeping with this trend, a number of men's magazines in the UK and US have revamped their sex advice sections to feature porn stars instead of sex therapists (Attwood, 2005, p. 85; mediabistro.com, 2007a, 2007b).

Some porn stars and prostituted women have even begun to release their own sex advice literature. Recent titles include: *How to Have A XXX Sex Life* (Anderson and Berman, 2004), which is based on advice from women who are contracted to the Vivid pornography production company in the United States; *Sex Secrets of Escorts: Tips from a Pro* (Monet, 2005), written by Veronica Monet, a former prostitute and porn star; and *How to Tell a Naked Man What to Do: Sex advice from a woman who knows* (Royalle, 2004), by Candida Royalle, a high profile former porn star, turned pornographer. Rather than competing with the advice offered by medically trained therapists, the sex advice given in these works frequently draws on 'medical' ideas about sex and, furthermore, often reinforces these ideas with supportive examples from pornography and prostitution. Pornography and prostitution are promoted in these texts as the ultimate authority on sex and, in these texts, the eroticising of women's submission and degradation are recurring themes.

The sex advice books written by porn stars all assert that being involved in prostitution and pornography makes you an authority on sex, in particular, good sex, sex that should be emulated. Flowing from this premise are sections that offer hints and tips to women on how to improve their own sex lives, based on the experiences of women in prostitution and pornography. As Monet puts it: "You will learn the sexual techniques that are the staple of the paid sexual services" (Monet, 2005, p. viii). This poses a serious problem for women as these are sex tips based on a system which involves inherent power imbalance, a system where for the most part, men are the buyers and women are the bought (Barry, 1995; Jeffreys, 1997). It is a system in which women are paid to sexually service men with no regard for their own pleasure (Barry, 1995). A system in which women are often terribly physically abused, suffer from dissociation, and frequently also post-traumatic stress disorder (Farley, 2003). It is a system in which women's inequality is fixed (Jeffreys, 1997). And yet it is this model that is held up for women to mimic in their own sexual lives.

There are some, including the authors of these pro-pornography texts, who try to argue instead that prostitution and pornography are liberating and can accommodate and promote women's pleasure and equality (see for example McElroy, 1995; Monet, 2005; Royalle, 2004; Strossen, 1995). But the advice offered in these texts so often shows just how misleading such arguments are.

Mirroring the sex therapy literature, there are frequent messages in porn star authored texts that reiterate the importance of trying something for a partner or questioning certain inhibitions. One example of this comes from Royalle's *How To Tell a Naked Man What To Do*. She states: "Don't ever feel like you must do something that you don't want to do. However, it's always good to be open and at least give something a try. You might want to ask yourself exactly why you don't want to watch x-rated movies ..." (2004, p. 65). Royalle then explains to women, that once they have agreed to watch pornography, they will most likely be required to watch things they do not want to: "Maybe he wants something nasty and you want something softer ... It's simple: take turns! And don't do it begrudgingly" (Royalle, 2004, p. 70). Indeed the assumption that women will initially not want to participate in the type of sex acts that are recommended is evident in most of this sort of sex advice literature. For example, Monet advises women to "[g]ive yourself a chance to get past your initial embarrassment or perhaps feelings of distain" (Monet, 2005, p. 130). The authors of *How to Have a XXX Sex Life* also offer advice on "freeing yourself of guilt and inhibitions" (Anderson and Berman, 2004, p. x). The suggestion is, of course, that these feelings of distain or unease about re-enacting acts of prostitution, or mimicking pornography, are somehow unfounded. Women are not entitled to feel this way, and need to work on overcoming their 'inhibitions'. Pornography is the predictable tool suggested to help women learn more appropriate 'sex positive' reactions.

In *How to Have a XXX Sex Life* the authors actively encourage women to copy dialogue straight from pornographic films. They are also rather blunt in declaring the sexual appeal of the degradation involved, explaining that: "When most people think of 'talking dirty' they think of using nasty, even *degrading* language to make it hot. When it works, it works well" (Anderson and Berman, 2004, p. 49, my emphasis). For useful examples, readers are directed to watch the pornographic film *Swoosh* because "the talk is raunchier, with lines 'Is that what you want, you filthy fucking whore?' Or 'Take it bitch' " (Anderson and Berman, 2004, p. 49).

In a further cross over between pornography and sex therapy, similar advice on 'dirty talk' is given by the renowned Australian sexologist Gabrielle Morrissey in her popular sex self-help book *Urge: Hot secrets for great sex* (2005). Morrissey states that dirty talk is "designed to arouse", and to support this contention she offers the scenario of a man telling his female partner to: "Bring your wet cunt over here, I want to fuck it good …" (Morrissey, 2005, p. 442). It is not made clear if Morrissey believes this statement to be arousing to men, women, or both, but she does acknowledge that in non-sexual contexts women may find such a statement deeply offensive. She notes: "A woman in the bedroom may find it horny for her man to shout *'Fuck you're a nasty bitch yeah'*, but if he growled anything like that in the kitchen, he'd probably receive a walloping …" She further explains: "Tone, intent and context are everything" (p. 424). The context is important because, according to both sex therapists and the pornographers, the degradation and subordination of women is acceptable as long as it is sexual. While Morrissey claims women should not be degraded or verbally abused in the kitchen, the bedroom is placed beyond claims of respect and equality.

Which returns us again to the problem of basing sex advice on a model of sexuality that is not about women's sexual pleasure but about women's sexual subordination. While sex therapy has long afforded pornography some form of legitimacy, the processes of pornification seem to have fuelled this to a point where porn stars are now becoming understood as the ultimate sex experts. As pornography and sex therapy continue to provide mutually reinforcing understandings of what sex should be, it makes it increasingly difficult for women to step outside this model and make claims to a sexuality which is based on equality and respect, one that fundamentally rejects pornography as an authority on sex. But while it may be increasingly difficult to challenge this model, it is also increasingly important that we try.

Bibliography

Anderson, Dan and Maggie Berman (with The Vivid Girls) (2004) *How to Have a XXX Sex Life*. Harper Collins, New York.

Attwood, Feona (2005) 'Tits and Ass and Porn and Fighting: Male heterosexuality in magazines for men' *International Journal of Cultural Studies* 8 (1), pp. 77–94.

Baker, Jo-Anne (Ed) (1999) *Sex Tips: Advice from women experts around the world*. Allen and Unwin, London.

Barry, Kathleen (1995) *The Prostitution of Sexuality*. New York University Press, New York.

Black, Jules (2006) 'The Joy of Erotic Massage: Review' *Sexual and Relationship Therapy*, 21 (1), pp. 117–118.

Davies, Guy and Anthony Wonke (13 July, 2000) 'We Want Porn' *The Guardian*, London.

Dines, Gail (2010) *Pornland: How Porn Has Hijacked Our Sexuality*. Beacon Press, Boston, MA; Spinifex Press, North Melbourne.

Dworkin, Andrea (1981) *Pornography: Men possessing women*. The Women's Press, London.

Eberwein, Robert (1999) *Sex Ed: Film, video and the framework of desire*. Rutgers University Press, Piscataway, NJ.

Farley, Melissa (Ed) (2003) *Prostitution, Trafficking and Traumatic Stress*. Harworth Press, New York.

Häggström-Nordin, Elisabet, Ulf Hanson and Tanja Tydén (2005) 'Associations between pornography consumption and sexual practices among adolescents in Sweden' *International Journal of STD and AIDS* 16 (1), pp. 102–107.

Heiman, Julia and Joseph LoPiccolo (1992) *Becoming Orgasmic: A sexual growth program for women*. Revised ed. Fireside, New York.

Jeffreys, Sheila (1990/2011) *Anticlimax: A feminist perspective on the sexual revolution*. The Women's Press, London; reprinted and available as e-book from Spinifex Press, North Melbourne.

Jeffreys, Sheila (1997/2008) *The Idea of Prostitution*. Spinifex Press, North Melbourne.

Lane, Frederick (2000) *Obscene Profits: The entrepreneurs of pornography in the cyber age*. Routledge, New York.

Lovelace, Linda (1980) *Ordeal*. Citadel Press, Secaucus, NJ.

mediabistro.com (7 April, 2007a) '*Spin*'s Newest Hire? The 'Madame of Punk Rock Porn' of Course', <http://www.mediabistro.com/fishbowlny/magazines/spins_newest_hire_the_madame_of_punk_rock_porn_of_course_35066.asp> (accessed 19 October, 2007).

mediabistro.com (19 July, 2007b). '*FHM* Hires Adult Film Star To Write Weekly Sex Blog', <http://www.mediabistro.com/fishbowlny/magazines/fhm_hires_adult_film_star_to_write_weekly_sex_blog_40442.asp> (accessed 19 October, 2007).

McElroy, Wendy (1995) *XXX: A woman's right to pornography*. St. Martin's Press, New York.

Monet, Veronica (2005) *Sex Secrets of Escorts: What men really want*. Alpha Books, New York.

Morrissey, Gabrielle (2005) *Urge: Hot secrets for great sex*. Harper Collins, Sydney.

Paul, Pamela (2005) *Pornified: How pornography is transforming our lives, our relationships and our families*. Times Books, New York.

Pike-Johnson, Heidi (2005b) 'The New Devil in Miss Jones – Review' *Adult Video News* (December), <http://www.adultvideonews.com/editch/edch0905_01.html> (accessed 17 September, 2006).

Ramone, Mike (2005b) '*Jenna Loves Pain* – Review' *Adult Video News* (November), <http://www.adultvideonews.com/editch/edch1105_05.html> (accessed 17 September, 2006).

Rich, Frank (20 May, 2001) 'Naked Capitalists' *The New York Times*, New York.

Royalle, Candida (2004) *How to Tell a Naked Man What to Do*. Fireside, New York.

Sinclair Intimacy Institute (2007a) 'Movies: Sinclair Select', <http://www.bettersex.com/movies-c-5.aspx> (accessed 5 March, 2007).

Sinclair Intimacy Institute (2007b) *'Better Sex* Kits: Smart Maid Kit', <http://www.bettersex. com/Better-Sex-Kits/sp-better-sex-kits-smart-maid-kit-2527.aspx?categoryid=2> (accessed 5 March, 2007).

Sinclair Intimacy Institute (2007c) *'Better Sex* Kits: Tie Me Up, Tie Me Down', <http:// www.bettersex.com/Better-Sex-Kits/sp-better-sex-kits-tie-me-up-tie-me-down-kit-2393. aspx?categoryid=10> (accessed 5 March, 2007).

Striar, Sharna and Barbara Bartlik (1999) 'Stimulation of the Libido: The use of erotica in sex therapy' *Psychiatric Annals* 29 (1), pp. 60–62.

Strossen, Nadine (1995) *Defending Pornography: Free speech, sex and the fight for women's rights.* Scriber, New York.

Tydén, Tanja and Christina Rogala (2003) 'Does pornography influence young women's sexual behavior?' *Women's Health Issues* 13 (1), pp. 39–43.

Tydén, Tanja and Christina Rogala (2004) 'Sexual behavior among young men in Sweden and the Impact of Pornography' *International Journal of STD and AIDS* 15 (9), pp. 590–593.

Tyler, Meagan (2008) 'Sex Self-Help Books: Hot Secrets for Great Sex or Promoting the Sex of Prostitution?' *Women's Studies International Forum* 31 (5), pp. 363–372.

Zillbergeld, Bernie (1993) *The New Male Sexuality.* Bantam Books, New York.

Renate Klein

Big Porn + Big Pharma: Where the Pornography Industry Meets the Ideology of Medicalisation[1]

Introduction

As the pornification of culture continues to engulf our daily lives, so too does the normalisation of medicalisation. Increasingly, all aspects of our health are deemed in need of medical scrutiny and 'personalised' attention. We are checked, screened and tested from before birth to old age and when (invariably) found deficient and straying from the 'holy' average (which, in fact, changes quite frequently), we are plied with a bewildering array of ever more tests, drugs and procedures. In 2006, global revenues for 'Big Porn' were reported to be approaching US$100 billion, and 'Big Pharma' has projected profits of US$1000 billion (1 trillion) by 2013.[2] These 2 industries are linked in many ways and it is some of these connections that I will examine in this article. I include the cosmetic and reprogenetic industries under the rubric of Big Pharma and will discuss the medicalisation of (porn)sex, the need for bodies to conform to pornsex, the medical hazards of pornsex, reproporn, and lastly, what to make of the new disease 'porn addiction'.

1 The Medicalisation of (Porn)Sex

Pornsex portrays women as horny 'hos' with an insatiable appetite for oral, anal and vaginal penetration, and men as domineering studs whose erections need

---

1   My heartfelt thanks go to Susan Hawthorne, Helen Pringle, Abigail Bray, Melinda Tankard Reist, Diane Bell and Maree Hawken who have all commented on this chapter. I really value your input; just occasionally I had to leave one of my 'Swissisms'. When working on such distressing issues as this book contains, good friends are crucial. All shortcomings in this chapter are of course my own.

2   'Global pornographic revenues are approaching $100 billion …', <http://www.morssglobal finance.com/the-economics-of-the-global-entertainment-industry/>; 'Global pharmaceutical market value is expected to expand to $975+ billion by 2013', <http://www.pharmaceutical-drug-manufacturers.com/articles/pharmaceutical-market-trends-2010.html>.

to be bigger and 'last longer'[3] so as to fill female orifices and spill their 'cum'. These portraits create anxieties for many 'ordinary' women and men who feel ill-equipped to live up to porn industry standards.

'Luckily', Big Pharma has come to their rescue by, first, creating new diseases of sexual dysfunction and, second, offering a cure for them. For men with less than pornsex erections in size and duration, Viagra (meaning 'tiger' in Sanskrit) brings salvation. Initially prescribed for 'erectile dysfunction' – but now also used as an 'enhancement drug' easily available online for any man who wants more prowess in his ordinary, pornographic, or prostitution sex – Pfizer's little blue pill has raked in close to US$2 billion since 1998.[4] Viagra works by increasing blood flow to the penis, but carries the short-term risk of possibly fatal stroke and heart attack.[5]

Diagnosing – and 'curing' – female sexual dysfunction (FSD) has proven a far greater challenge for Big Pharma. To repeat the commercial success of blue Viagra for men, pink Viagra, and later Cialis (manufactured by Eli Lily), seemed a lucrative answer. But in order to attract female customers, women first had to be convinced they suffered from FSD. The republication of earlier findings in a 1999 article in the *Journal of the American Medical Association* did just that (Laumann et al., 1999). Seven survey questions were asked of a group of 1500 US women, including: did they lack interest in sex? did they not have an orgasm? were they anxious about their sexual performance? – even if it was only *once* in the past year. A 'yes' response to just one of these questions branded the respondent as suffering from FSD. Adding up these one-time events, the researchers concluded that a whopping 43% of US women suffered from female sexual dysfunction.[6]

Viagra, Cialis, testosterone patches, and more recently, the fast-acting antidepressant Flibanserin, were all Big Pharma dreams to cure FSD (and one of its

3 'Want Longer Lasting Sex?' is one of the many slogans by the Advanced Medical Institute (AMI) that are exhibited on towering billboards in Australian cities, <http://amiaustralia.rtrk.com.au/?scid=46607&kw=3828705&pub_cr_id=6221612116> despite an order by the Advertising Standards Authority (ASA) in 2009 to remove them; see <http://www.dailymail.co.uk/news/article-1109523/Nasal-spray-advert-slogan-Want-Longer-Lasting-Sex-banned-watchdogs.html>.

4 In March 2011, Pfizer reported global sales of $1.93 billion for Viagra, with Viagra Jet, a chewable, its latest offering, now selling in Mexico, <http://www.newslocale.org/health/hnews/pfizer_to_introduce_chewable_viagra_jet_in_mexico_2011031911513.html>.

5 Long-term use of Sildenafil (Viagra) may lead to difficulty breathing, vision problems, headaches and flushing. Erections can last longer than 4 hours. Meika Loe (2006) has documented the less than happy reactions by female partners of Viagra users.

6 A similar British study published in 2007 found that only 18% of women perceived a one-time lack of orgasm and interest in sex as a problem. The figure fell to 6% when the women were asked if they were distressed by these events (King et al., 2007).

sub-disorders, hypoactive sexual desire disorder or HSDD). But unfortunately for Big Pharma, female sexuality does not follow the male hydraulic model. Pumping blood into women's genitals does not do the trick. Even research projects sponsored by pharmaceutical companies did not come up with increased sexual satisfaction when compared with placebos.

Moreover, since 2000, well-publicised grassroots activism against pornsex by New York University feminist psychiatrist and sex therapist, Leonore Tiefer, is gaining ground. Tiefer argues that the 'corporate-backed idea of sex-as-function' needs to be replaced with a 'humanistic vision' of sexuality which she puts forward in her New View Campaign[7] (Kaschak and Tiefer, 2002; see also Moynihan, 2010, p. 148). In a similar way, the 2011 film *Orgasm Inc.: The Strange Science of Female Pleasure*, directed by Liz Canner, reveals the manufacturing of the 'disease' FSD by profit-hungry pharmaceutical companies (see Laureano, 2011). Nevertheless, encouraging as these critiques of Big Pharma's union with Big Porn are, it would be naïve to conclude that the pharmaceutical quest for a miracle pill or patch for this elusive 'disease' has come to an end; new drugs are in the pipeline and the magic number '43%' continues to haunt women and to 'normalise' FSD.

2   Pornsex Needs Pornready Bodies

The continuing hypersexualisation of women and girls demands that their bodies fit the ideology of pornsex and a male-centred model of sexual activity. Their breasts need to be augmented, any real or imaginary wrinkles Botoxed, and their hairless labia and vaginas surgically redesigned. 'Pornochic' has become the norm of the beauty industry.

Injuries and death from breast augmentation have long been noted by feminist writers.[8] Adverse effects from silicone breast implants have led to hundreds of product liability litigation cases (Cohen, 1994). Notwithstanding such docu-

---

7   Leonore Tiefer deserves a medal for her decade-long, feisty resistance to the medicalisation of sex ('sex for our pleasure or their profit?'), see <http://www.newviewcampaign.org/>. Tiefer regularly attends FDA hearings and puts the alternative view (as Shere Hite did 25 years ago in *Women and Love*, 1987) that satisfying sex for women has as much (or more) to do with intimacy and connection as with the actual sex act.

8   For example, see Sheila Jeffreys (2005, pp. 158–161) on the tragic death of German Lolo Ferrari in 2000. Ferrari was pimped by her husband for prostitution and pornography. Before she died from an overdose of prescription drugs, Ferrari weighed a mere 48 kg. She was a heavy user of pain killers as each breast had been surgically augmented and weighed more than 3kg, which meant she could barely stand up, and she rarely slept because of not being able to find a comfortable position. Eleven years after her death, a quick Google search locates hundreds of porn pictures of Ferrari. Pornography is indeed infinite prostitution (see Farley, this volume).

mented damage, the pornification of women's lives has normalised breast augmentation surgery as a way to attain the required 'ho' look.

A case in point is the death of German porn star, Carolin Berger, during her 6th breast enhancement surgery at age 23 in January, 2011. Her heart stopped during the operation and she sustained severe brain damage. Bloggers expressed sadness over Carolin's death on the Website JustBreastImplants.com which describes itself as a 'Breast augmentation patient education resource' where you can locate a surgeon. One post reads: "Oh how sad! My heart goes out to her loved ones" followed, however, by the same woman writing "5'1 almost at 5'2, 103lbs, 350 mod+ saline, started as 34aa, now a 34c or a 32d!!!!" Other bloggers post their own revealing photos with augmented breasts and a full list of enhanced body parts, followed by the name of their cosmetic surgeon. The postmodern ideology of bodies-as-text, here to be inscribed, meets the demands of a pornified society for medically enhanced women's bodies.

The same ideology was reflected in a 2009 Channel 4 TV Program in the UK. Four hundred teenagers from 14 to 17 had been surveyed. A group of boys from Sheringham High School in Norfolk was shown photographs of 10 pairs of breasts. All said that the most attractive breasts were those that had been surgically enhanced. As TV presenter, Anna Richardson, commented: "Alarmingly, a posse of their female classmates says the same thing. Both sexes are unimpressed with normal breasts, which – unlike porn stars' silicone-boosted chests – are often not symmetrical and sit down, not up." And 45% of girls from Sheringham High School were unhappy with their own breasts, and almost a third said they might consider surgery (*The Guardian*, 30 March, 2009).

The Guardian report continues:

> When the programme makers show boys and girls a woman opening her legs to reveal hair, there are gasps, some born of disgust. In porn, females are always shaved down below. Girls admit that they are starting to shave their lower regions and that boys expect them to do so. The pupils' reaction shows how their expectations of what bodies should look like are framed by watching porn. Freakish ideas of physicality are mainstream.

Indeed, there is now a seemingly non-negotiable demand to be hairless and 'pert' in the vaginal department. Unruly vaginal lips and body hair are frowned upon by men who like their (porn) women to look like little girls: clean, and definitely hairless. Hence the commercial success of celebrity surgeon David Matlock's trademarked procedures at his Institute in Los Angeles: the 'Designer Laser Vaginoplasty®' ("for the aesthetic enhancement of the vulvar structures") and 'Laser Vaginal Rejuvenation®' ("for the enhancement of sexual gratification, vaginal tightening"). Other must-have surgeries include 'Brazilian Butt Augmentation' demonstrated by Dr Matlock himself in a video on his Website to, as he puts it, "artistically enhance your buttocks to give it a more rounded, toned, lifted, athletic look that compels people to look and admire" (<http://www.drmatlock.com/>).

Leonore Tiefer and colleagues call such procedures FGCS (Female Genital Cosmetic Surgery) and compare them to FGM (female genital mutilation, see <http://www.newviewcampaign.org/video.asp>). They decry the increasing lack of diversity in women's bodies – including labia of all sizes and shapes – as creating a monoculture of pornsex bodies. Retail medicine and global medical tourism offer a plethora of exotic places where women can submit their bodies to FGCS: from Australia's Gold Coast to Bangkok or Florida.

As pornography critic, Gail Dines, observes:

> Something has shifted so profoundly in our society that the idealized, pop culture image of women in today's pornified world is no longer a Stepford Wife but rather a plasticized, scripted, hypersexualized, surgically enhanced young woman. The media world we live in today has replaced the stereotyped Stepford Wife with the equally limiting and controlling stereotype of a Stepford Slut (in Rivers, 2010. See also her comment on 'sluts' in Griffin, 2011).

3 Medical Hazards of Pornsex

In addition to the damage from cosmetic surgery, there are daily health risks from engaging in increasingly violent pornography acts – be it as paid 'porn stars' or as Stepford Sluts in the privacy of millions of homes. For potential porn recruits the Website of the Adult Industry Medical (AIM) Healthcare Foundation (<http://www.aim-med.org/>) with 2 clinics in Los Angeles, acts as a Health Care provider, and will tell you all there is to know about starting your 'career' in 'the Industry'. In the video *Porn 101*, you are guided by Sharon Mitchell (Dr Mitch) who introduces herself as having been "an actress and a producer, director, stripper and just about anything else you can possibly think of in the Adult Entertainment Industry for over 21 years" (such as waging a battle with drug addiction for 18 years, as she tells viewers in *Porn 102*). The potential porn 'professional' is introduced to the Pornography Industry in a matter-of-fact, friendly and non-threatening way. The most important message is to be tested for sexually transmitted infections (STIs) before you start performing, and to be re-tested every 30 days. Easy – and just what you would do in any other 'job'.

Joined by an equally friendly and non-threatening male doctor, the pair then goes through some of the 25 sexually transmitted infections (STIs) that awaits you in your new 'profession' including chlamydia, syphilis, gonorrhea (including of the throat), hepatitis A, B and C (A is transmitted by faeces from anal to mouth). You are told to avoid sharing razors, and also needles, with others, to avoid hepatitis C. HIV is another infection you might contract during your professional porn performances, and Dr Mitch particularly cautions about HIV in breast milk "for those milk movies." Genital warts are talked about at length – where to spot them, how to treat them – and novices are instructed to have regular pap smears. Women as well as men are strongly urged to get the 3-shot HPV vaccine Gardasil at $400 – without any warnings as to its serious adverse effects.[9]

The idea is created that if you follow this health advice, life in the pornography industry is without danger to your health. Indeed, 'the Industry' is depicted as so safe that you are admonished to watch your private sex life so you won't infect your fellow 'clean' porn performers.

Condom use is encouraged ("switch condoms for every hole") but 'unprotected sex' is mentioned so frequently that it is clear that condom use is wishful thinking rather than daily reality. The follow-up video, *Porn 102*, is interspersed with short video clips that show how exciting porn shoots are, while Dr Mitch and Nurse Nina – a jolly blond woman and former porn performer too – instruct you, with lots of laughs, how to start working in the Industry. Their advice includes: "don't do anything you haven't already tried out with your partner", "don't fuck under water, very bad for your tender parts." Some of what they say sounds eminently sensible: "you can say no"; "[y]ou are in charge of your career"; and "make sure you get paid properly." You are also advised to bring "some knitting, puzzles, a robe, slippers ... because you will have to wait a lot on the set." If, despite these precautions, you get sick, AIM promises plenty of drugs they can treat you with. The clear message is that ongoing medical supervision and treatment is part of your life in the porn industry: medicalisation and pornification joined at the hip (pocket).

Ultimately, despite – or precisely because of – the easy camaraderie between Dr Mitch, Nurse Nina and other ex-porn stars in *Porn 101* and *Porn 102*, the AIM Website acts as a grooming site for inexperienced girls and women who are attracted to the promise of stardom and big money. The health care aspect normalises the Porn Industry, with potential porn performers being reassured repeatedly that it is a lucrative 'job' and that they will be in charge ("your pussy is

9   The so-called cervical cancer vaccines Gardasil and Cervarix are experimental vaccines against 2 strains of the human papillomavirus (HPV) that are associated with many, but not all, cervical cancers. At the time of writing (May 2011), there have been 94 deaths and 21,634 adverse effects associated with these vaccinations. There were 8,733 emergency room visits and 2,159 hospitalisations; 4,346 girls and young women did not recover. See <http://sanevax.org/#top>, an international women's group that promotes safe vaccination practices.

your business – are you going to incorporate?"). In spite of all of this down-to-earth talk, we must remember that only sex industry 'jobs' accept dangerous STIs, as well as violence through rough handling and vaginal, anal and throat tears, as part of their 'regular' occupational health and safety (OHS) requirements. Add to these dangers the well-documented problems of substantial drug and alcohol abuse to cope with the demands of the 'job'. Unintended pregnancies are not mentioned on the AIM Website, but the Australian Sex Worker Outreach Project (SWOP) recommends the use of the morning-after pill after unprotected sex or condom breakage. If used on a regular basis, the morning-after pill can adversely affect a woman's health (see Sullivan, 2007, pp. 298–299).[10]

The pornography industry's continuous medicalisation via 30-day STI testing and repeated courses of potent drugs for infections consolidate the link between Big Pharma and Big Porn. Pornsex is a health hazard, an 'industrial disease' (Sullivan, 2007, p. 303), and women are reduced to 'industrial vaginas' (Jeffreys, 2009).

4 Reproporn[11]

Similar to the way in which women are reduced to body parts that become 'service stations'[12] for men in pornsex, the ideology of 'assisted' reproductive technologies normalises the dissection of women into body parts for breeding. In 'Fertility Inc' – the thousands of IVF clinics proliferating around the globe – dozens of eggs are extracted from ovaries dangerously extended by high doses of drug cocktails; single sperm – ejaculated by men in fertility clinic cubicles with porn mags – are forced into egg cells;[13] wombs-for-hire, surrounded by real live women, are implanted with petrie-dish embryos to 'house a pregnancy', 'function as an oven', 'bake the bun'. Cut the child out of the woman's womb

---

10 Mary Sullivan's groundbreaking research into the failures of the legalised prostitution industry in the state of Victoria, Australia, documents the problems with OHS policies and the many health hazards of the sex industry (2007, chapters 6 and 7).
11 Space (and good taste) prevents me from discussing 'old-fashioned' pornography movies with doctor-and-nurse themes, or pornography with "depictions of damaged and dead foetuses in a sexual context" as documented by Norwegian researchers Marianne Erikkson and Eva-Britt Svensson (2006). See also Hilkens (2010).
12 I am borrowing the term 'service stations' from Jennifer Drew's comment on Melinda Tankard Reist's blog about Bill Henson's photographs (4 April, 2011): "Pornography is not a moral issue, it is about the normalisation and acceptance that women and girls are not human but just men's disposable sexual service stations," <melindatankardreist.com>.
13 This refers to intracytoplasmic sperm injection (ICSI), a technique that enables subfertile men to pass on their fertility problems to the males in the next generation. See Klein (2008) for an in-depth review of the fertility business since the world's first test-tube baby, Louise Brown, was born in 1978, and Klein (2011a) for an update on the fertility business in Australia.

after it has been sex selected and disease-screened, hand it to the commissioning couple (woman and man or 2 men; rarely 2 women), insert their names on the birth certificate as parents – and the birth mother is obsolete with one stroke of the pen. Women become dehumanised objects and are exploited as 'gestational carriers': for money in commercial surrogacy, or for love in so-called altruistic arrangements. In 1983, Andrea Dworkin foresaw the use of reproductive brothels for controlled eugenic reproduction (Dworkin, 1983); in 1985, US investigative journalist, Gena Corea, predicted that poor women would be used as breeders in reproductive brothels in the 'Third World' (1985, pp. 301–302).

In the 21st century, this practice is now widespread. In a raid on 'Baby 101', a clinic in Thailand, in February 2011, police found 15 pregnant women from Vietnam who had been trafficked (Winn, 2011). Their passports had been taken away and they were kept locked up as reproductive slaves: Margaret Atwood's *The Handmaid's Tale* (1986) gains new meaning. Despite the police raid, the clinic continues to operate and advertises its eugenic services specifically to Western women: "Unnecessary to worry about out of shape on your stature, neither to fear the intimacy fading [with husband]" (<http://www.baby-1001.com/eng/about.htm>).[14]

Pregnancies are medically outsourced to the wombs of poor women by an increasing number of Western couples who appear to see no ethical problem in medical tourism and renting a woman's body for 9 months for their made-to-order child;[15] after all, many argue, the woman is paid much more than she would earn in any other 'job'. In the jarring Israeli documentary *Google Baby* (2009) by Zippi Brand Frank (see Kung, 2010), embryos made with quality-checked 'white' eggs from the USA (sourced online) and sperm from the commissioning fathers in Israel (gay or with infertile wives), are frozen and flown to India to be implanted in Indian women (often 'pimped' by their husbands) in an IVF clinic located in Gujarat, a poor state. Here the women are required to live assembly-line style in the clinic for the whole 9 months of their pregnancy and are not allowed to visit their families. The entrepreneurial businessman who hatched this

---

14 The Website <http://www.baby-1001.com/eng/about.htm> has been changed from Baby-101 to Baby-1001 and no longer contains scantily clad women. It is now called Babe-101 [sic] 'Eugenic Surrogate'. See Klein (2008) for a discussion of eugenics underpinning the ideology of reprogenetic technologies.

15 Children, too, are victims of the Surrogacy Industry. There are heartbreaking tales of women forced to abort a less than perfect child; babies no longer wanted, as the commissioning couple has divorced; children rejected as citizens of countries, such as France and Germany, who do not permit commercial surrogacy.

plan in Israel, and the IVF doctor in India, pocket most of the money. Should the 'surrogate' miscarry, she will only receive a part payment.[16]

The Surrogate Industry has particularly taken off in India, where reproductive tourism was expected to bring in half a billion US dollars in 2010, and surrogacy services are offered in 350 clinics across the country. Women's wombs are cheap; as the Medical Tourism Corporation (2010) claims: "Surrogacy can cost up to $100,000 in the United States, while many Indian clinics charge $22,000 or less (<http://www.medicaltourismco.com/assisted-reproduction-fertility/low-cost-surrogacy-india>).

Some countries are now trying to regulate the practice: France and Germany prohibit surrogacy and the states of Queensland and New South Wales, and the Australian Capital Territory, recently passed legislation that makes going overseas to any countries for surrogacy a criminal offence (see Klein, 2011b).

Such human rights abuses mirror sex industry practices where husbands with 'indisposed' wives buy a prostituted woman, gorge themselves on online pornography and visit lap dancing clubs. Pornsex and reproporn both harm women, while men fulfil their desires, or profit as pimps and club owners.

The similarities between Big Porn and Fertility Inc do not end here. Good looks and glamour are as important for so-called surrogates and egg 'donors' (to provide egg cells for stem cell research and infertile women) as they are in the sought after slut-and-porn-star look for today's girls and women.

On eggdonation.com which calls itself "the premier fertility agency in the United States since 1991," a group of 'Donor Angels' entices prospective egg buyers with their photos: a cheerful blond Caucasian, an Asian girl in a 'sexy' pose, a red-headed beauty with pouting lips and seductive look, and a woman of colour, smile from the Webpage for you. The founder of the site, Shelley Smith, writes that "[t]he Agency for 'Super Donors' is known for representing the brightest, most beautiful and accomplished donors in the country. The Agency accepts less than 3% of the 1,200–1,500 applications we receive every month" (email from eggdonation.com, 13 May, 2011).

In *Confessions of a Serial Egg Donor* (2004), green-eyed, tall and blond Swede, Julia Derek, tells of her life as a 12-time egg 'donor'. Derek moved to the USA as a student. She was not allowed to engage in paid work and was lured into the egg industry by promised fees of thousands of dollars. She became seriously ill from stuffing herself with hormones and then 'popping' dozens of eggs as a

---

16 Apart from *Google Baby, Made in India* (2010) by Rebecca Haimowitz and Vaishali Sinha also shows the exploitation of so-called surrogates, see <http://www.madeinindiamovie.com/>.

Super Donor. Twice, she nearly died from ovarian hyperstimulation and other fertility-drug induced problems.

Julia Derek was lucky to survive the ordeal. Many women do not and there are sad stories of strokes, brain damage, heart attacks, ovarian and other cancers, and death as 'side effects' of the business of egg harvesting.[17] In Eastern Europe, particularly Romania and the Ukraine, poor women who prostitute themselves in the local sex industry are also exploited as egg providers for UK clinics who have set up egg-collecting franchises in this unregulated market (Sexton, 2005; Barnett and Smith, 2006).

All of these examples represent the systemic structural abuse of women (and their commodified children) in the power relations inherent in Big Porn and Fertility Inc. For decades, these abuses have been documented and researched by anti-pornography activists and feminist critics of reprogenetic science. The latter have exposed dangerous practices and shoddy research, and challenged the IVF Industry to prove that their lucrative business, and link with Big Pharma through multi-drug use, does not harm women.[18] Their answer has either been silence or to produce one-sided pharmaceutical-funded research that does not pass even the first test of sound and ethical research methodology.

Postmodern ideology, the ease of advertising medical entrepreneurship on the Internet, rampant capitalism and the increasing commodification of life converge to lead to personal and political *dissociation*: the individual (female) body is ceasing to exist as anything but 'other' – a mere shell 'out there' that can be commercialised and cut, modified, drugged, penetrated – all in the name of 'choice' and 'it is my right'.[19]

But there are signs of hope. There is an international groundswell of new activist groups coming together to challenge dehumanising practices. For example, 80 public health organisations, health networks, medical professionals, human rights and women's groups protested against experiments with the

---

17 See the Egg Donor Project initiated by the Alliance for Human Biotechnology, <http://www.humanebiotech.com/eggdonorsproject/considerthesewomen.html>, and the 2011 award-winning documentary *Eggsploitation* by US bioethicist, Jennifer Lahl, <http://www.eggsploitation.com/>. Diane Beeson and Abby Lippman (2006) discuss the many medical risks and ethical problems of egg provision.

18 The Website <http://finrrage.org> contains all volumes of *Reproductive and Genetic Engineering: Journal of International Feminist Analysis*; see also Klein (2008 and 2011a) for a detailed summary of 25 years of reprogenetic science.

19 The growing practice of allowing children as young as 10 to harm their bodies through hormones and surgery as they 'transit' from patriarchal masculinity to patriarchal femininity (or sometimes the other way around) is another alarming example of such practices (see Jeffreys, 2006).

'cervical cancer' vaccine Gardasil on Indian tribal girls in 2010, and against the surrogacy industry in 2011 (see <http://samawomenshealth.wordpress.com/>). Young women and men are part of these movements and it is crucial that 'the mainstream' understands that the ecology of the body is as important as the ecology of the globe, and that our bodies *are* ourSelves; we have to look after our bodies and cannot afford to trash them.

There is, however another problem that puts new obstacles in the way of these encouraging developments: the return of biological determinism and the increasing tendency to reify behaviours such as compulsive porn use and the obsession with baby making as genetically determined, hard-wired in the brain, or even 'addictions'.

5   Porn Brains: who profits from 'porn addiction'?

When I type 'porn addiction' into Google I get 1,780,000 results in 0.15 seconds. Entries range from 'Addicted to Porn', 'Can't stop watching porn? – Why is it so difficult to stop?' to 'Dealing with Porn Addiction – Ask Men', 'Porn Addiction Treatment' and 'Freedom from Porn Addiction'. Offers to liberate the sufferers from their addiction span a bewildering array of treatments: individual and group therapy; counselling for co-dependency and porn addiction; addictive voice recognition technique (AVRT) also called 'Rational Recovery'; a 're-sensitization model'. The idea that pornography can become addictive is being turned into a lucrative business proposition. Expensive clinics are expanding their treatments for alcohol, gambling and sex addiction to include 'porn addiction'. And there are already drug treatments for pornography 'addicts' such as the SSRI antidepressant Zoloft (sertraline), manufactured by Pfizer[20] and long associated with suicidal behaviour, for co-occurring anxiety and depression, and Naltrexone, approved by the FDA for use in alcoholism treatment, and used off-label for withdrawal from heroin (Bostwick and Bucci, 2008).[21]

But 'Porn Addiction' is rarely defined. In the mainstream media and by many in the 'helping professions', it is simply accepted as a new medical condition that

---

20 See Alan Hesketh's indictment for trading photos of 'Amy' in Helen Pringle, 'Civil Justice for Victims of Child Pornography', this volume. Hesketh was a vice-president and global patent director of the pharmaceutical firm Pfizer.

21 Michael Bostwick and Jeffrey A. Bucci base their endorsement of Naltrexone on a case study with 1 patient who was a life-long porn user (2008). Naltrexone produced by Sun Pharmaceuticals based in Mumbai is an opiate receptor blocker which is said to block excessive dopamine release in response to the 'reward' of watching pornography. (The generic ReVia is produced by the multinational DuPont Pharma.) Its long list of adverse effects range from chest pain to excessive sweating and pain in joints. Liver and kidney checks are essential. It inhibits male orgasm, <http://admin.safescript.com/drugcgic.cgi/INGR?68714689+0>.

is spreading like wildfire among the male population of the universe. Writing on this issue, Joel Tozer quotes ongoing online research of Internet Pornography Addiction by the Australian Centre for Addiction Research (ACAR): "many are becoming addicted to the safety of online pornography to the point where some are unable to achieve orgasm during intercourse" (Tozer, 2011). That pornography has devastating consequences for sexual behaviour has been extensively documented by feminist researchers over decades (see Dines, 2010), but does this *prove* that pornography (over)consumption is an addiction?

Research studies – often case studies with very few participants and an add-on to sex addiction research – indicate that the study of 'porn addiction' is attracting intense attention from a diverse group of experts including biological psychiatrists, geneticists, endocrinologists, bioengineers, and the ever more prominent neuroscientists whose new scanning toys make us gaze in amazement at their experiments with lit-up brains during porn use, despite the lack of clear analysis of what such lit-up brain areas actually mean.

Might there be a chemical imbalance or 'defect' in the brains of the growing numbers of porn users who say they are suffering from 'porn addiction'? Or even perhaps a 'porn gene'? After all, for a long time, scientists have been talking about (controversial) gay genes, genes for happiness, for depression etc. In December 2010, a team of researchers led by Justin Garcia at Binghamton University looked at infidelity and sexual promiscuity, then matched the behaviour of the 181 research subjects to their genes and found the dopamine receptor D4 polymorphism, or DRD4 gene, to be the 'culprit' for such behaviour (Garcia et al., 2010). This gene had already been linked to sensation-seeking behaviours such as alcohol use and gambling; will 'porn addiction' be next?

Then there are developments in neuroscience – including recent technologies of brain imaging – that tell us that our behaviours are mirrored in different parts of the brain and can be observed.[22]

In his bestseller, *The Brain that Changes Itself* (2007/2008), Freudian psycho-analyst and psychiatrist, Norman Doidge, endorses the addiction theory of pornography (chapter 4), using neuroscience to back up his claims. He explains that because of brain plasticity, repeated porn use is visible on functional magnetic resonance imaging (fMRI) scanning. Looking at gonzo porn (and Doidge has a good understanding of the violent nature of current pornography), makes "the pleasure-giving neurotransmitter dopamine more active in the brain" (p. 106).

22　In *Delusions of Gender: How our Minds, Society and Neurosexism Create Difference* (2010), Cordelia Fine cautions about limitations in neuroimaging research: "fMRI doesn't measure neuronal activity directly. Instead it uses a proxy: changes in blood oxygen levels" (p. 134).

New brain maps are developed and, Doidge says, "[b]ecause it is a use-it-or-lose-it brain, when we develop a map area we long to keep it activated" (p. 108). The increased surges of dopamine "are thus wired into our brains" and "[n]eurons that fire together wire together" (p. 114). Put differently, it follows that on a fMRI scan you can see how watching pornography fries your brain.

However, Doidge argues that such wiring together of neurons can be undone. Men without serious childhood trauma, once they understand the problem of dopamine activation and "how they were plastically reinforcing it" (p. 131), can go cold turkey and stop "using their computers for a period to weaken their problematic neuronal networks, and their appetite for porn withered away" (p. 131). Even one of his difficult patients was able to unlearn his addiction to pornography once he understood that it was his childhood (e.g. his drunken, abusive mother) and later his sexual partner who forced her S&M practices on him, that made his sexual and violent dopamine-charged neurons get 'fired and wired together'.[23]

Norman Doidge is optimistic: the brain is so flexible that every bad habit can be unlearned with the help of a therapist. Big Pharma, on the other hand, welcomes the medicalising of 'porn addiction' – defining it as an illness – as a promising market expansion. The use of tablets (or patches or injections), in particular, antidepressants and opioid antagonists, for the new 'epidemic' of 'porn addiction' is increasing. Prescriptions for conditions such as anxiety and depression have been skyrocketing. In 2007, the USA spent $25 billion on antidepressants and antipsychotics (Whitacker, 2010, p. 3). It is now quite common to hear even young people explain: "I've been diagnosed with depression; it's a chemical imbalance in my brain, but the antidepressant I was prescribed will fix it."[24] We are dutifully becoming 'patients' and swallowing the pills doled out by the 'Sickness Industry' (Moynihan and Cassels, 2005) to fix the 'defect' supposedly detected in our bodies. Perhaps we will soon hear the biological determinist explanation: "I have a porn addiction which is due to excessive dopamine in my brain because of a genetic defect, but my Naltrexone controls it"?

The American Psychiatric Association (APA) is considering adding sex addic-

---

23 Norman Doidge's blaming of women for male porn sufferers' predicaments in chapter 4, and his reliance on Freud for explaining childhood trauma, is disappointing and detracts from many interesting observations in his book, in particular, how intensely flexible the brain is which gives hope to brain-injured people.

24 While I welcome the de-stigmatisation of the term 'mental illness', I am concerned about the many adverse effects of antidepressants due to (over)diagnosis of depression-as-mental-illness, particularly in children and adolescents (see Klein, 2009).

tion to the Diagnostic and Statistical Manual of Mental Disorders (DSM).[25] As Russell Brand reports (2011): "The United Kingdom's health service is starting a preliminary project for sex addiction treatment, which experts say, could spark a boom in drug companies repackaging antidepressants and sex-drive-suppressants." If this were to happen, it would lead to a further explosion in experimental treatments as we have seen for female and male sexual dysfunction (see section 1). John Cloud from *Time Magazine* notes:

> APA recognition of sex addiction would create huge revenue streams in the mental-health business. Some wives who know their husbands are porn enthusiasts would force them into treatment. Some husbands who have serial affairs would start to think of themselves not as rakes but as patients (Cloud, 2011).

So why should we be critical of these developments to define pornography use as an illness and medicalise it? The problem is that ordinary men who use pornography in an obsessive way would be turned from 'perpetrators' who indulge in watching the degradation of women for their sexual gratification, into 'sufferers' who cannot really help themselves – and hence have to be excused, pitied, put on medication and supported. That is, being 'hooked' on the misogyny that is pornography – and expecting their partners to perform pornsex – would be excused as a 'personal' illness rather than as part of the much bigger problem of women's continuing subordination in society. 'Ordinary blokes' with supposedly 'ordinary desires' are let off the hook for indulging in watching other men violating women. Such convenient thinking – followed by an abdication of responsibility by the 'addicted' man – is a worrisome development.

The co-dependency Website 'Porn Addict Hubby' is illuminating. A female partner is turned into the 'jailer' to police every move of her addicted husband or partner:

> Albeit an extreme case, let's look at the example of a German woman who uses a shock collar on her husband to keep him from getting out of bed at night to surf for porn. The husband doesn't have to take any responsibility for his actions or the consequences of poor job performance due to lack of sleep. The wife says they are willing to do whatever it takes to save their 12-year marriage.

In other words, the acceptance of 'pornography-as-addiction' could lead to the reversal of agency so that women rather than men become the problem. "Why can't you keep me off this stuff? It's your fault", a relapsing husband might say. As 'Porn Addict Hubby' continues, quite rightly indignant: "How about some ac-

---

25 For years, there have been many concerns expressed about APA members who decide which 'condition' will become the latest disease added to the DSM and their links to the pharmaceutical industry (e.g. see Moynihan, 2011).

countability software[26] and boundaries? How about regular men's support groups and joint counseling?" (<http://www.pornaddicthubby.com/index.html>).

Even more problematic are developments in legal cases where pornography 'addiction' is cited in an attempt to mitigate the crime of sexual abuse. For example, on 12 April, 2011, in the Victoria County Court, Craig Coleman blamed 'his sex and pornography addiction' for violating his 3-year-old daughter with 3 counts of sexual penetration (Lowe, 2011a).

In her judgment on 13 May, 2011, Judge Frances Millane sentenced Coleman to 7 years in prison and ordered him to undergo 'offense specific' treatment to 'contain strong sexual deviancy' towards female children (Lowe, 2011b). His pregnant wife has since left him and his abused daughter has developed a fear of men, including her grandfather, and is displaying sexual behaviour.

These examples show the need to be extremely wary of jumping on the bandwagon of 'pornography-as-addiction'. Accepting the medicalisation of yet another area of life gives more power to Big Pharma. As new drugs come on the market for this latest disease, so will experimental treatments with dangerous adverse advents.

But it is the industry, Big Porn Inc, that benefits most from this development. As the number of 'addicts' continues to grow (added to by men in treatment programmes who relapse), pornography users will demand new, even stronger gonzo, more risqué pornography. The acceptance of 'porn-as-illness' appears to assist some men who genuinely want to free themselves from this soul-destroying predicament through looking for (medical) help. However, I believe we set ourselves up to be further colonised by both Big Porn and Big Pharma.

Any discussion of 'pornography-as-addiction' must first and foremost hold the pornography industry accountable for their multi-billion dollar profits from sexual violence and abuse that brings up the question 'is it an addiction?' in the first place.

Conclusion

The topics covered in this chapter expose areas where Big Pharma and Big Porn reinforce one another. They are all intense commercial growth areas and rely on exploiting people's desires – be it for the longest erection, the most alluring body, the 'personalised' perfect child, or power and control over the infinite offerings of 24/7 online porn domination of women.

---

26 The mind boggles at the idea of using 'accountability software' to check on your partner's every move!

Because they are presented as benevolent relief of suffering (e.g. of sexual problems, of infertility, of 'addiction'), and are called issues of personal 'choice' in a postmodern age where nothing is 'real' anymore – and truth does not exist – it can be difficult to uncover the violence of patriarchy and capitalism that is driving Big Porn and Big Pharma. A feminist analysis focusing on the continued subordination of women is crucial if we are to understand how the medicalisation of every aspect of our lives in a culture saturated with pornography is taking away 'real choices' when it comes to living in harmony in our bodies – however imperfect they might be.

The global corporations of Big Pharma and Big Porn are reshaping before our eyes what it means to be human. Big Pharma has a long and well-documented history of manufacturing illness in order to sell pills. Feminist writers like Phyllis Chesler were among the first to identify the political investments in the corporate production of illness when she wrote *Women and Madness* in 1972. This radical suspicion is beginning to filter into the mainstream; there are increased critiques of antidepressants and of Ritalin (to drug unruly children), for instance. But the covert, implicitly ideological nexus of Big Pharma and hypersexual Big Porn – as I have exposed it in this chapter – has not received due attention.

Together Big Porn and Big Pharma represent the corporate policing of intimacy. To cling to neoliberal ideologies of 'choice' as an explanation for people's obedience to these limited definitions of 'a good life' is to radically underestimate the impact of these multinational corporations on everyday commonsense understandings of health, happiness and well-being. We have to resist being turned into dissociated 'Chemical Citizens'[27] and being under the spell of cut-and-paste babymakers, cutters with knives, and cutters of words who tell us we are all wowsers and prudes who want to spoil their party of 'just a bit of fun'. The future of children who grow up in this porn- and pill-saturated world is too important to be left to the laissez-faire ideology of free markets. There has to be real joie de vivre again – not plastic, not porn-infused, not misogynist, not racist, but instead full of possibilities for life-loving everyday politics for all.

Bibliography

Atwood, Margaret (1986) *The Handmaid's Tale*. Houghton Mifflin Company, Boston.
Babe-101 (2011) 'Eugenic Surrogate', <http://www.baby-1001.com/eng/good.htm> (accessed 15 May, 2011).

---

27 This is Abigail Bray's term (2009) and I thank her and Helen Pringle for input into Conclusion. And Susan Hawthorne for practising *Wild Politics* (2002) in our daily lives.

Barnett, Anthony and Helena Smith (30 April, 2006) 'Cruel cost of the human egg trade' *The Observer*, <http://www.observer.guardian.co.uk> (accessed 15 May, 2011).

Beeson, Diane and Abby Lippman (2006) 'Egg harvesting for stem cell research: medical risks and ethical problems' *Reproductive BioMedicine Online* 13, pp. 573–57.

Bostwick, Michael and Jeffrey A. Bucci (February 2008) 'Internet Sex Addiction Treated with Naltrexone' *Mayo Clinical Proceedings* 83 (2), pp. 226–230, <http://yourbrainonporn.com/internet-sex-addiction-treated-with-naltrexone> (accessed 22 May, 2011).

Brand, Russell (15 March, 2011) 'It's official: Sex addiction is a psychiatric illness', <http://articles.timesofindia.indiatimes.com/2011-03-15/science/28691288_1_addiction-psychiatric-disorder-therapists> (accessed 22 May, 2011).

Bray, Abigail (2009) 'Chemical Control™ ®: from the Cane to the Pill' in David Savat and Mark Poster (Eds) *Deleuze and New Technology*. Edinburgh University Press, Edinburgh, pp. 82–103.

Chesler, Phyllis (1972/2005). *Women and Madness*. Avon Books, New York; Palgrave Macmillan, London and New York.

Cloud, John (28 February, 2011) 'Sex addiction: real disease or excuse for men to cheat?' *Time Magazine*, <http://www.time.com/time/magazine/article/0,9171,2050027,00.html>.

Cohen, Kerith (1994) 'Truth & Beauty, Deception and Disfigurement: A Feminist Analysis of Breast Implant Litigation' *William and Mary Journal of Women and the Law* 149, <http://scholarship.law.wm.edu/wmjowl/vol1/iss1/7>.

Corea, Gena (1985) 'How the new reproductive technologies could be used to apply the brothel model of social control over women' *Women's Studies International Forum* 8 (4) pp. 299–305.

Derek, Julia (2004) *Confessions of a Serial Egg Donor*. Adrenaline Books, New York.

Dines, Gail (2010) *Pornland: How Porn Has Hijacked Our Sexuality*. Beacon Press, Boston; Spinifex Press, North Melbourne.

Doidge, Norman (2007/2008) *The Brain That Changes Itself*. Penguin Books, New York and Toronto; Scribe Publications, Melbourne.

Dworkin, Andrea (1983) *Right-wing Women: The politics of domesticated females*. Perigree Books, New York; The Women's Press, London.

Erikkson, Marianne and Eva-Britt Svensson (2006) *Sex Slavery in Our Time*. Red EU Special Features Series nr 3, <www.guengl.eu/upload/EU-trafficking.pdf>.

Fine, Cordelia (2010) *Delusions of Gender: How Our Minds, Society and Neurosexism Create Difference*. W.W. Norton & Company, New York and London.

Garcia, Justin R, James MacKillop, Edward L. Aller, Ann M. Merriwether, David Sloan Wilson, J. Koji Lum (30 November, 2010) 'Associations between Dopamine D4 Receptor Gene Variation with Both Infidelity and Sexual Promiscuity' *PLoS ONE* 5 (11), <http://www.plosone.org/article/info%3Adoi%2F10.1371%2Fjournal.pone.0014162> (accessed 19 May, 2011).

The Guardian (30 March, 2009) 'Porn: the New Sex Education', <http://www.guardian.co.uk/society/joepublic/2009/mar/30/teenagers-porn-sex-education>.

Griffin, Michelle (13 May, 2011) 'Slutwalk campaign harms' *The Age*, <http://www.theage.com.au/national/slutwalk-campaign-harms-20110512-1ekva.html>.

Haimowitz, Rebecca and Vaishali Sinha (2010) *Made in India* Documentary IMDbPro Distribution, <http://www.imdb.com/title/tt1505349/>.

Hawthorne, Susan (2002) *Wild Politics: feminism, globalisation and bio/diversity*. Spinifex Press, North Melbourne.

Hilkens, Myrthe (2010) *McSex Die Pornofizierung unserer Gesellschaft*. Orlanda, Berlin.

Hite, Shere (1987) *Women and Love: A Cultural Revolution in Progress*. Alfred A. Knopf, New York.

Jeffreys, Sheila (2005) *Beauty and Misogyny: Harmful Cultural Practices in the West*. Routledge, London and New York.

Jeffreys, Sheila (2006) 'Judicial Child Abuse: the Family Court of Australia, gender identity disorder and the "Alex" case' *Women's Studies International Forum* 29 (1), pp. 1–12.

Jeffreys, Sheila (2009) *The Industrial Vagina: The Political Economy of the Sex Trade.* Routledge, London and New York.

JustBreastImplants.com (2011) 'Carolin "Sexy Cora" Berger Dead: Porn Star Dies After Sixth Breast Enlargement Surgery', <http://www.justbreastimplants.com/forum/general-breast-augmentation-discussion/110136-porn-star-dies-during-operation-inject-silicone-into-her-breasts.html> (accessed 1 May, 2011).

Kaschak, Ellyn and Leonore Tiefer (2002) *A New View of Women's Sexual Problems.* New View Campaign, New York.

King, Michael, Victoria Holt and Irwin Nazareth (2007) 'Women's views of their sexual difficulties: Agreement and disagreement with clinical diagnoses' *Archives of Sexual Behavior* 36, pp. 281–288.

Klein, Renate (2008) 'From Test-Tube Women to Bodies Without Women' *Women's Studies International Forum* 31 (3), pp. 157–175.

Klein, Renate (2009) 'The Harmful Medicalisation of Sexualised Girls' in Melinda Tankard Reist (Ed) *Getting Real: Challenging the Sexualisation of Girls.* Spinifex Press, North Melbourne, pp. 131–148.

Klein, Renate (2011a) 'From the Cutting Edge to "Business as Usual": What does the future hold for women in Australia's mainstreaming of reprogenetic technologies?' in Proceedings of International ART Conference (2010) edited by SAMA Resource Group for Women and Health. SAGE Publications, New Delhi (in press).

Klein, Renate (June, 2011b) 'Surrogacy in Australia: New legal developments' *Bioethics Research Notes* 23 (2) (in press).

Kung, Michelle (2010) '"Google Baby" Documentary Sheds Light on Outsourcing Surrogacy', <http://blogs.wsj.com/speakeasy/2010/06/16/google-baby-documentary-sheds-light-on-outsourcing-surrogacy/> (accessed 15 May, 2011).

Laumann, Edward, Anthony Paik and Raymond Rosen (1999) 'Sexual dysfunction in the United States' *Journal of the American Medical Association* 281, pp. 537–544.

Laureano, Bianca (5 April, 2011) 'How the Pharmaceutical Industry is Monetizing the Female Orgasm', <http://www.alternet.org/story/150510/how_the_pharmaceutical_industry_is_monetizing_the_female_orgasm?page=1>.

Loe, Meika (2006) *The Rise of Viagra.* New York University Press, New York.

Lowe, Adrian (12 April, 2011a) 'Porn addict Christian father admits to abusing 3-year-old', <http://www.theage.com.au/victoria/pornaddict-christian-father-admits-to-abusing-3yearold-20110411-1db3m.html>.

Lowe, Adrian (13 May, 2011b) 'Man jailed for seven years for sex act with girl, 3', <http://www.theage.com.au/victoria/man-jailed-for-seven-years-for-sex-acts-with-girl-3-20110513-1elhl.html>.

Medical Tourism Corporation (2010) 'Cheap Surrogacy in India', <http://www.medicaltourismco.com/assisted-reproduction-fertility/low-cost-surrogacy-india>.

Moynihan, Ray and Alan Cassels (2005) *Selling Sickness: How drug companies are turning us all into patients.* Allen & Unwin, Sydney.

Moynihan, Ray (2010) *Sex, Lies and Pharmaceuticals.* Allen & Unwin, Sydney.

Moynihan, Ray (3 May, 2011) 'A new deal on disease definition' *British Medical Journal* 342:d2548, <http://www.bmj.com/content/342/bmj.d2548.full?keytype=ref&ijkey=6pXberf82XwzLlM> (accessed 23 May, 2011).

New View Campaign (n.d.) 'Challenging the Medicalization of Sex', <http://www.newview campaign.org/> (accessed April 15, 2011).

Porn Addict Hubby (n.d.) 'Co-Dependency and Porn Addiction', <http://www.pornaddicthubby. com/CoDependency-and-Porn-Addiction.html> (accessed 22 May, 2011).

Rivers, Caryl (7 November, 2010) 'The soft war against women', <http://www.salon.com/news/ opinion/feature/2010/11/07/caryl_rivers_soft_war>.

Sexton, Sarah (2005) 'From Women's Eggs to Economics for Women' *The Cornerhouse UK*, <http://www.thecornerhouse.org.uk/resource/transforming-waste-resource> (accessed 15 May, 2011).

Sullivan, Mary Lucille (2007) *Making Sex Work. A Failed Experiment with Legalised Prostitution*. Spinifex Press, North Melbourne.

The Center for Bioethics and Culture (2011) *Eggsploitation*. DVD, San Ramon, California, <http:// www.eggsploitation.com/>.

Tozer, Joel (20 May, 2011) 'Demonising porn use unleashes more evil' *The Sydney Morning Herald*, <http://www.smh.com.au/opinion/society-and-culture/demonising-porn-use-unleashes-more-evil-20110519-1eusw.html>.

Whittaker, Robert (2010) *Anatomy of an Epidemic: Magic Bullets, Psychiatric Drugs, and the Astonishing Rise of Mental Illness in America*. Crown Publishers/Random House, New York.

Winn, Patrick (18 March, 2011) 'Underworld: upending an Asian baby farm', <http://www. globalpost.com/dispatch/news/regions/asia-pacific/thailand/110310/thailand-surrogacy-human-trafficking> (accessed 15 May, 2011).

PART TWO

Pornography Industries

"I blame pornography and the industry – for making this sexualised life seem so normal, so easy to do, no consequences to family or health, no problems just fun. We go to counselling once a week. Do they put that in *Playboy*? Is that sexy and fun?" – Marina

"It seems to me that a lot of women that are 'pro-porn' are not really aware of the sort of degrading material that is out there, nor the fact that they are supporting such damaging practices. Just wait until you are in a relationship with a porn addict who wants to orgasm onto your face, or calls you a dirty whore, or tells you there is something wrong with you because you do not want to swallow his orgasm or that your breasts are not big enough! That you are the one with the problem because you are uncomfortable with porn. This is not love or intimacy or even enjoyable sex. PORN IS ABUSE!" – Casey

"It almost lodges itself into your mind, like a parasite sucking away the rest of your inner life and you kind of use it to answer everything and anything. It's a drug." – Malcolm[1]

"Pornography turned my sex life into a form of science fiction/fantasy. I became unreal to myself in sex. I was unable to link these fantasies to any real human dynamic or intimacy. Objectifying myself, my sexuality, my lovers' bodies and sexuality, destroyed any opportunity to 'stay in the moment'. When I did stay in the moment, I found I was unable to experience arousal, except on very rare occasions ... pornography colonized my sexuality and did it so thoroughly that I have never been able to undo the damage. I feel tremendous anger, frustration and sorrow over this." – Anon (female)[2]

---

1   <http://www.emeleus.org/BBCprogramme.htm>
2   <http://www.voicesmatter.org/about.html>

Susan Hawthorne

Capital and the Crimes of Pornographers: Free to Lynch, Exploit, Rape and Torture

Underpinnings

We live in a world where the economic system is structured around global capitalism.

The global capitalist system relies on patriarchal social structures, including militarism to maintain control.

Under patriarchy, male symbolic systems prevail.

Patriarchal systems rely on putting men's perceived needs ahead of all others (women, children, the poor, the colonised, the unknown, animals, plants, the earth).

Patriarchy is supported by male-centred religions in which the male is deemed inviolable.

Research on consumption shows that men spend money on luxury items such as gambling, alcohol, petrol, tobacco and sex.

The third largest illegal trade in the world after armaments and drugs is the trade in women.

Colonisation of poor nations by rich nations has resulted in significant power differentials across countries and ethnicities as well as across the sex divide.

Colonisation and theft of resources, lives and livelihood from the colonised people constitutes structural racism that supports the economies of the rich. Women are the poorest of the poor.

Wars are declared against those among the colonised who get uppity or rebel against imposed systems.

Violence is perpetrated against groups and individuals who resist.

Torture against resisters is normalised.

The history of European slavery is intertwined with the growth of capitalism. Economic forces rather than humanitarianism inspired the abolition of slavery.

Economic forces inspired the increased participation of women in the workforce.

Feminism has been a significant face of resistance to patriarchal capitalism for the last four decades.

Violence against women is a structural weapon of patriarchal systems.

Depictions of tortured women have become so normalised they are regularly used by advertisers and entertainers.

In 2006, the global pornography industry was worth US$96 billion.

The order of the above propositions is not intended to be causal; it is a complex and dynamic matrix made up of systems that support and perpetuate one another. The global pornography industry has the form of a monoculture, a system out of balance supported by economic, symbolic, attitudinal and institutionalised systems.

Global capitalism is a relatively new phenomenon, although capitalist forms have been around for many centuries.[1] Capitalism has been built upon the theft of resources for the creation of wealth. Initially, this was done through plundering of nations by mainly European seafarers. As Maria Mies (1986/1999) argues, the wealth of Europe – and later of the USA and other rich nations – could not have come about without access to free labour, free resources (minerals), free land, access to knowledge about new plants, and the transfer of new ideas and concepts from the colonised world to the old world. Included among the free goods are women. This is the point at which racism and sexism meet and often result in violence against women. The women of the poor nations are 'there for the taking'. The colonist regards it as the moment when the colonised man is truly crushed. Colonists rape the women and impregnate them as a way of weakening the colonised people, and targeting the esteem of the men. When local men abuse the women of their own communities, they share a kind of reflected power of the colonists. This creates a staircase of violence and profit. Capitalism depends on a staircase: the lowest profits and the greatest violence are on the bottom step; the highest profits at the top with impunity from responsibility for violence.

Pornography and lynching

When the slave trade was in full swing and in the hundred years that have followed its abolition, the practice of lynching shifted from one that was 'acceptable' to one that is now considered criminal.

---

1   By capitalist forms, I mean instances of systematic profit-making. The bankers of the Italian City States were among early capitalists and the Slave Trade was yet another manifestation of capitalism.

What is lynching?

'Any act of violence inflicted by a mob upon the body of another person which results in the death of the person,' with a 'mob' being defined as 'the assemblage of two or more persons, without color or authority of law, for the premeditated purpose and with the premeditated intent of committing an act of violence upon the person of another'. Lynching in the second degree is defined as 'Any act of violence inflicted by a mob upon the body of another person and from which death does not result' (Wikipedia, 2011, http://en.wikipedia.org/wiki/ Lynching).[2]

Lynching has two elements. It is a) premeditated violence against a person; b) inflicted by a mob.

Let's look at this in relation to pornography. A premeditated act is one in which a person plans an act. Pornography readily fits this, since in order to produce pornography one has to have a camera, a mobile phone or a video recorder. Taking photos and recording videos involves intention. The second part of pornography is distribution. Putting images onto a phone, Facebook, YouTube, or anywhere on the Internet, is an intentional act. Creating pornography therefore involves at least two layers of intention.

The mob: the definition above considers a mob to be made up of at least two people. This definition was created long before the Internet, mobile phones and video porn turned the idea of a mob into a virtual mob. Pornographers will deny the mob part of lynching, however, if a mob is as small as two people, then the intent to share images with more than one other person should amount to a mob. Indeed, in many instances of pornography the images are shared with a very large mob: hundreds, thousands, even millions of viewers.

And yet, pornography is not considered to be a form of lynching. One of the powerful effects of lynching was the photographing of the lynched bodies – black men and women who, through the distribution of these photographs, were put into a state of fear. Fear changes behaviour and when a particular group of people, such as freed slaves in the USA, are made fearful, then the behaviours of this group change: either by increased compliance to the expectation of the dominant group; or by increased aggression against the dominant group.

The production of fear responses in music videos has escalated over the years. Eminem's violent song lyrics from the late 1990s onwards have morphed into a new genre of music pornography which attempts to pass itself off as art. In late 2010, a video by Kanye West was leaked and created an immediate storm. In an article on *Unleashed*, Melinda Tankard Reist (2010) includes a still which, upon

2   Wikipedia cites the following legal reference for the above quotation: S.C. Code of Laws Title 16 Chapter 3 Offenses Against the Person.

seeing for the first time, reminded me of the photographs of slaves lynched in the years following the abolition of slavery.

From the video by Kanye West – Monster *ft. Jay-Z, Nicki Minaj & Rick Ross [Official Music Video]. Still reproduced from: <http://www.abc.net.au/unleashed/42078.html>.*

Thomas Shipp and Abram Smith, lynched in Marion, IN, 7 August, 1930. Photo by Lawrence H. Beitler. This image is reproduced from: <http://en.wikipedia.org/wiki/Lynching>.

The video has had thousands of hits in the 6 months since it was first leaked, and while this lynching image, which appears near the beginning of the video, is distressing, the video goes on to depict in a luxury gothic setting acts of necrophilia, murder, bondage, strangulation, decapitation, evisceration and execution. All the victims are women. It is difficult to tell whether the women are real or mannequins and I would suggest that this confusion is intentional as it provides a defensive position (maybe) that no women were hurt in the production of this video. However, as others have argued (see Norma, this volume) showing ways in which women can be violated (even in animations) is enough to escalate the desire to hurt real women.

Kanye West is certainly aware of the response to his work, since the latest version of *Monster* appears with a disclaimer: "The following content is in no way to be interpreted as misogynistic or negative towards any groups of people. It is an art piece and it shall be taken as such."[3]

The purpose of showing these 2 images together is so the reader can see for her- or himself just how reminiscent of lynching photography this latest example is. Puzzling over why such images should appear in popular culture at this time, it appears to me that the historical response to ideas of 'women's liberation' might well be just as terrifying to the dominant culture (men) as was the idea of the end

---

3   The video, *Monster*, is available on YouTube and a host of other sites: <http://www.youtube.com/watch?v=XYlyqRQXdtc> (accessed 6 June, 2011). The final cut is available at: <http://www.ballerstatus.com/2011/06/05/kanye-west-ft-rick-ross-jay-z-nicki-minaj-monster-final-cut-video/> (accessed 6 June, 2011).

of slavery to the dominant culture (whites). While the video mixes dominance and subordination across ethnicities, there is no uncertainty in the viewer's eye of which sex is subordinate.

Slavery was finally abolished across the USA in 1865. Mob violence and lynching against African Americans reached its height in the 1890s. Thirty years after the end of slavery, lynching was rife. Did this happen because African Americans had begun to take their freedom for granted, that is, they stepped on the toes of those who would happily have continued the institution of slavery? Is it any accident that 30 to 40 years after feminist analyses of pornography and other violations of women appeared that we are seeing these depictions of woman-lynching?

Since the 1970s, feminists have outlined radical ways of reforming social institutions, outlawing rape in marriage, sexual harassment, even in some places successfully decriminalising prostitution while simultaneously prosecuting the (mostly) male customers. Since the development of the Internet in the 1990s, and increased accessibility of social media, mobile phones and video in the last 10 years, pornography, with the support of finance and industrial-strength publicity, has turned women's bodies into the core of social violence.

Pornography as fodder for a class system

Many on the liberal left adopt a view that says pornographers are not businessmen but are simply there to unleash our sexuality from state-imposed constraints (Gail Dines, quoted in Bindel, 2010)

This is an old left-wing furphy and has no basis in fact. The women who are enticed into the system almost always say that they do it for the money. Working-class boys become soldiers or boxers; many working-class girls are pulled into prostitution or 'just having their photos taken'. I know this latter attitude because I fell for it myself in my late teens. The men had expensive cameras; they had light dissipaters; they came in their suits. The girls – and we were girls – had only themselves and perhaps a boyfriend who thought he might live off her earnings.

Taking photos for pornography does not free anyone; does not unleash any-one's sexuality; least of all the girls'. What it does do is provide fodder for men to exploit the naïvety of young women. What it does for the women is turn them into a saleable commodity. She begins to separate out from herself; she can no longer think of her body as her own; instead it is out there in someone's bottom drawer or, more likely these days, on someone's mobile phone or on the Internet.

We have heard about football clubs wanting to sue a seventeen-year-old schoolgirl for spreading around a photograph of a naked St Kilda footballer.

These same clubs have been rife with sexism for years. When, in Melbourne, the tables are turned and it's naked men instead of naked women, you see finally the concept of humiliation being raised. But only when it is the humiliation of men. While the clubs don't consider it pornography, they do regard the distribution of images of men's nakedness as humiliating. Women do complain about naked photos being spread around, but what feminists are complaining about is not mere nakedness, but depictions of sexualised violence against women. Pornography, these days, as indicated at the beginning of this essay, is about violation, humiliation and sexual gratification at the expense of women.

Is it okay to prod and poke a woman because she is no longer regarded as a human being as soon as she gets her clothes off? Is it okay to anally penetrate a woman and then force the penis into her mouth immediately because only a woman who is a slut would do that? Is it okay to humiliate a woman by ejaculating on her face because clearly she has no pride at all?

These are all statements about status – and we hear them frequently – she's a slut, she's a whore, she's the village mattress who will let anyone lie on her. But what of the men who are the perpetrators of these violations and humiliations? Their status as ordinary guys 'unleashing their sexuality' is secure.

What does pornography do? And to whom does it do that something? Pornography demeans the person at the other end of the camera whose image is then published in a magazine or book or digitally. That person is expected to put up with humiliation, pain, degradation and dehumanisation. That person is expected to accept being portrayed as dirty, as filth, as nothing more than a receptacle, and as a slave. That person is almost always a woman.[4] Pornography treats all women as if they were the same; it homogenises women and makes of women a group to be exploited and put down in all the same repetitive, boring ways. A monoculture of 'receptive' women is presented on Websites around the world.

Who benefits from pornography? Capitalists, individuals after fast money, and corporations with massive publicity budgets. As Gail Dines reports, in 2006 the global pornography industry was worth US$96 billion and in the USA alone $13 billion (Dines, 2010, p. 47). The market is growing significantly every year and 5 years later, it will be worth even more. At the individual end – men benefit because they gain a sense of power or a sense of camaraderie with their peers (see Stark and Whisnant, 2004).

---

4   Or a gay (often feminised) man (see Kendall, this volume).

Pornography and the confusion over free speech

Defending free speech is used by pornographers and the film *The People v Larry Flint* articulates this view. Dines responds that it's not free speech that gets pornographers excited, it "is profit" (in Bindel, 2010). While the Left and Anti-globalisation activists understand the differences between free trade and fair trade, they have not made the link between free speech and fair speech. It took a feminist, Betty McLellan, to see that link. In her book *Unspeakable* (2010) she highlights the parallels between free trade / fair trade and free speech / fair speech (see also McLellan, this volume). Here, in brief, are the arguments she makes:

- free trade / free speech favours the powerful
- free trade / free speech fosters and entrenches inequality
- free trade / free speech focuses on the individual
- free trade / free speech ignores quality of life (McLellan, 2010, pp. 52–58).

McLellan does not specifically illustrate the contrasting axioms, but the consequences of her ideas are as follows:

- fair trade / fair speech decentralises power
- fair trade / fair speech fosters justice and fair treatment
- fair trade / fair speech focuses on the common good and engagement
- fair trade / fair speech highlights the importance of life over profit

Those who promote the idea that pornography is about freeing our sexuality and maintaining free speech have betrayed their political roots. They are no longer on the side of the exploited and the oppressed; they are instead supporting a massive capitalist venture which is based on humiliation, pain and exploitation. Just because those who are exploited are women does not mean that they should be regarded as having no human rights. Freedom is not a get-all-you-can menu. It is about justice and clarity, about who benefits and who loses.

Pornography and the blurring of sex and violence

If it is not about freeing our sexuality, where does sex come in? Does pornography have anything to do with sex? Does it have something to do with violence?

Let's think for a moment about sex: good sex is enjoyable; indeed it can be ecstatic; it's the kind of sex we all hope for and when it happens there is no mistaking it. Mediocre sex is rather disappointing because somehow the people involved have not connected with one another; mediocre sex is probably more common than good sex, but it is not something to make judgements about. Bad sex is when only one person has any enjoyment; it's the kind of sex that happens as a relationship is waning; or when there is cruelty or exploitation on the part of one person.

Let's think about violence: good violence? Is there such a thing? Violence is by necessity negative and only sadists or masochists or people who are severely disconnected from themselves and others would argue differently. Mediocre violence is the sort of thing that lawyers will raise when the issue of self-defence comes up, or perpetrators will claim 'mitigating circumstances' or say 'he only slapped her mildly'. Bad violence is unjustifiable, unprovoked, an example of a massive imbalance in power between the parties. Lynching is bad violence.

Sex and violence don't seem to have much in common, indeed, they appear to be on different ends of the behavioural spectrum. In general, at the good end of sex, it is something that one wants to re-experience. That sense of connection, that release, that overwhelming sensation of pleasure.

Where the two meet is at the bad end. Both are experiences that, if you are the victim – that is you are the one who is used or abused – then you would not wish to re-experience that abuse. When it comes to the user / abuser, it's more complicated. That person often experiences an adrenaline high which arises with the sensation of having power over another being: men of other cultures, women of the same and other cultures, children and animals.

This is the point at which sex and violence blur. Those at the used and abused end are not confused; they can tell the difference. But the user and the abuser can no longer identify whether his enjoyment has come from the high of sex or the high of violence.

Pornographers take this confusion and promote it so that the buyers of pornography will come back again and again. They get addicted to the high of sex/violence; they want more and more hardcore things to do, since they are simultaneously desensitised and need an ever bigger hit to feel the same kick from pornography. Some men recognise the effect that pornography has on them (see Dines, 2010, p. 80), but many are caught in the web and find it difficult to extricate themselves since the confusion between sex and violence blurs their capacity for clarity.

And what of the women? Many of those who are used and abused, do have clarity. However, the original reason for entering pornography – mostly for cash – continues. A considerable number of the used and abused have become hooked on drugs which reduces the pain they experience, whether the social or emotional pain of humiliation, or the physical pain endured by being penetrated or beaten or simply ignored. Some of the used and abused will defend the perpetrators' actions because they too have become desensitised, disconnected from their own sense of pleasure.

Pornography and the normalisation of torture

Torture has an ancient history and the torture of women is a long one (du Bois, 1991). Patriarchal institutions become the purveyors of violence and there are historical instances where religion, politics and medicine become torture fronts. Torture was attested to in Roman times, the church engaged in the torture of women through the witch burnings;[5] more recent histories of the torture of women have occurred in countries in political turmoil, such as Chile and Argentina in the 1970s (with CIA assistance). Naomi Klein (2008) writes of the experiments in torture carried out under the guise of medical treatment. And the well-documented torture of individuals at Abu Graibh have brought the subject of torture into the mainstream.

It is not only these extreme events that have given space for renewed calls for legalisation of torture; it is also the process of normalising violence through the ever-escalated desensitising effect of pornography that makes even torture 'sexy', giving it a kind of social cachet not only in heterosexual contexts – it has become especially de rigueur in Queer Studies.

Margot Weiss, in her article on 'consensual BDSM[6] and sadomasochistic torture', begins with the following description of what she calls 'play' (2009, p. 180):

My copy of the monthly newsletter of a San Francisco SM organization included a scene report, a written description of a consensual BDSM play scene. The scene took place at a San Francisco dungeon in March 2004. It was an interrogation scene, involving a Colonel, a Captain, a General, and a spy. The spy was hooded, duct-taped to a chair, and slapped in the face. As she resisted, the spy was threatened with physical and sexual violence, stripped naked, cut with glass shards, vaginally penetrated with a condom-sheathed hammer, force-fed water, shocked with a cattle prod, and anally penetrated with a flashlight. The scene ended when the spy screamed out her safeword, the word that ends the scene: 'Fucking Rumsfeld!'.[7]

One page later, Weiss goes on to say that "[t]he photographic representation in Abu Ghraib ... effectively transforms a political real – torture – into a safe sexual fantasy" (Weiss 2009, p. 181). She takes no pause to ask whose fantasy and whose pain? The real torture of Abu Ghraib is real to the prisoners, and just like the women abused in pornography, it remains the fantasy of someone who watches from the outside.

---

5 The Papal Bull *Ad Extirpanda* declared by Pope Innocent IV on 15 May, 1252 which authorised the use of torture during the Inquisition, held force until the 19th century when more humanist philosophies entered the Church. In 1994, the Catechism of the Catholic Church condemned torture as a violation of human rights.

6 In this paper I use the abbreviation S/M when speaking generally about sadomasochism, and I use BDSM when discussing the paper by Weiss (2009).

7 The article by Weiss is based on Weiss (2005) which I heard her present at the Transpositions Conference at Purdue University, USA. In Hawthorne (2006) I critiqued her argument based on notes I took. At the time, I unsuccessfully requested a copy of the paper.

The thing about torture is that you do not know whether you will be alive at the end of the day. You do not know when it will end. It is more than just 'powerlessness'; it is subjugation, degradation, abandonment, and dehumanisation. To defend, as Weiss (2009) does, such acts as 'performative' is an instance of moral neglect. Such academic acceptance of torture as a game is deeply offensive. It is appropriative of people living under totalitarian regimes who do not have the 'luxury' of saying 'No', or of saying 'Rumsfeld' as a parody. It misses the entire history of the intersection of the colonisation of women and the colonisation of the 'other'. Because, while Weiss acknowledges that the torture at Abu Ghraib is a "means of imperial control" (2009, p. 191), she fails to see that BDSM in the form she describes is a means of imperial control of women. She writes as if there has never been any difference in access to and exercise of power between women and men.

Sadomasochism and pornography that promote abuse and torture are forms of 'consumerism of experience'. In a way similar to that in which Western culture has appropriated the cultures of Indigenous and non-Western peoples, the practitioners of S/M and the producers of torture pornography are appropriating the experiences of oppressed peoples who have been tortured by dictatorial governments or who have been slaves under racist regimes, or the lesbians who are tortured by fundamentalist and militarised regimes (Hawthorne, 2006). The practitioners of S/M turn an uncontrollable experience of torture into a game that can be stopped. But people undergoing real torture do not have the option of saying no.[8] The woman whose face is splashed by semen is paid to take it. She cannot say no either. And in pornography directed at lesbians, the woman humiliated in S/M porn is degraded. As pro-porn activist Pat Califia writes:

> By reviving the notion that sex is dirty, naughty, and disgusting, you can profoundly thrill some lucky, jaded lesbian by transforming her into a public toilet or bitch in heat (Califia, 1988, p. 52).

Just as the near death experience of S/M can be read as just another consumerist game, pornography and entertainment that focus on the abasement of women are new luxury purchases for the global consumer. As the consuming of material goods is reaching its limits in the West, S/M practitioners and makers of torture pornography attempt to simulate death in the pursuit of yet another thrill. They are luxury games. It is appropriation of experience. It is ultimately full of contempt for others.

---

8   The much-touted rules of S/M, however, need to be adhered to. Anecdotal evidence suggests that the rules are broken in the same way that laws against rape are broken with great regularity.

Conclusion

Pornography is a multi-billion dollar global industry
Pornography is appropriative
Pornography is violence
Pornography is racist
Pornography is very like lynching
Pornography exploits power imbalance between classes
Pornography uses women as sex fodder
Pornography is the free trade of (mostly) women's bodies
Pornography is not about freeing our sexuality
Pornography is very profitable
Pornography is damaging to women
Pornography is damaging to men
Pornography is damaging to children
Pornography damages young people's sense of bodily health
Pornography is a violation of human rights

Bibliography

Bindel, Julie (2010) 'The truth about the pornography industry'. *Guardian*, 2 July, <http://www.guardian.co.uk/lifeandstyle/2010/jul/02/gail-dines-pornography>.
Califia, Pat (Ed) (1988) *The Lesbian S/M Safety Manual*. Boston, Alyson Publications.
Dines, Gail (2010) *Pornland: How Porn Has Hijacked Our Sexuality*. Beacon Press, Boston; Spinifex Press, North Melbourne.
du Bois, Page (1991) *Torture and Truth*. Routledge, London.
Hawthorne, Susan (2006) 'Ancient Hatred and its Contemporary Manifestation: The Torture of Lesbians' *Journal of Hate Studies* 4 (1), pp. 33–58.
Klein, Naomi (2008) *The Shock Doctrine*, Penguin, Camberwell.
McLellan, Betty (2010) *Unspeakable: A Feminist Ethic of Speech*. OtherWise Publications, Townsville.
Mies, Maria (1986/1999) *Patriarchy and Accumulation on a World Scale*. Spinifex Press, North Melbourne; Zed Books London.
Stark, Christine and Rebecca Whisnant (Eds) (2004) *Not For Sale: Feminists Resisting Prostitution and Pornography*. Spinifex Press, North Melbourne.
Tankard Reist, Melinda (2010) 'Who says female corpses aren't sexy?' *Unleashed*, 10 December. <http://www.abc.net.au/unleashed/42078.html>
Weiss, Margot (2005) 'Consensual BDSM and "Sadomasochistic" Torture at Abu Ghraib'. Paper presented at Trans/Positions: A Conference on Feminist Inquiry in Transit, 7–9 April, Purdue University.
Weiss, Margot (2009) 'Rumsfeld!: Consensual BDSM and "Sadomasochistic" Torture and Abu Ghraib' in Ellen Lewin and William L. Leap (Eds) *Out in Public: Reinventing Lesbian/Gay Anthropology in a Globalizing World*. Wiley-Blackwell, Chichester, West Sussex, pp. 180–201.
West, Kanye and DJ Premier (2010) *Monster* ft. Jay-Z, Nicki Minaj & Rick Ross [Official Music Video], USA.

Abigail Bray[1]

The Pornification of Post-feminism: Why Roddick's $ex Shops Are a Sell Out

A recent example of the relentless pornification of post-feminism is seen in the new venture of Sam Roddick, daughter of the late Dame Anita 'Body Shop' Roddick. Cashed up post-feminist, corporate-minded Sam launched a chain of sex shops in London, Los Angeles and New York called Coco de Mer (<http://www.coco-de-mer.com/>).[2]

Here you can buy "high-end lingerie, sex toys, books and erotic art" with an ethical 'up yours!' post-feminist glow. As an interviewer in *The Guardian* put it, "Smiling, she turns around and says: 'We can stick our fingers up at our parents and go: check this feminism – it comes with a pair of really lacy knickers.'"

Besides the très expensive, oh là là, vive la révolution lingerie, you can also stick your fingers up at the older generation of feminists who banged on about women's poverty, sexual violence, pornography, child abuse, etc., with 'Pearl Anal Beads' for only £215. Or for the well and truly up yours ethical post-feminist consumer there is the 'Crowned Jewels Chancellor Vibrating Butt Plug' which is 'crafted from solid sterling silver' and is yours for the price of £595. (No discounts for pensioners, sorry!)

In an era when women are expected to submit to any sexual practice just to prove that they are sexually liberated, there seems to be something rather apt about this latest corporate pornification of feminism. Or perhaps you would like to buy a naughty little sexually self-empowering mirror? For £1,000, the 'Betony Vernon Sado Chic Masturbation Mirror' liberates your sexuality so that you can "[o]bserve your own pleasure and watch as you reach the heights of sexual ecstasy." Watch out patriarchy!

---

1 First published on Melinda Tankard Reist's blog, <http://melindatankardreist.com/> on 9 June, 2010.

2 This is not to deny that Sam Roddick hasn't done some good things. She has supported campaigns against violence against women and sexual trafficking. But it is difficult to align these activities with an elitist global sex shop chain calling itself feminist. See <http://www.guardian.co.uk/environment/2010/may/23/sam-roddick-coco-de-mer>. See also Bondage for Freedom, the 'activist arm of Coco de Mer': <http://www.coco-de-mer.com/pages/Bondage-for-Freedom/pgid-20236.aspx>.

Also reaching new heights of post-feminist subversion is the 'Ilya Fleet Dog Mask' that comes with a very long pointy snout and alert little ears. Perfect for those protest marches against the new austerity measures that are impacting on disadvantaged women all over the world. Wearing a pointy nosed dog mask will set you back £350. You can also choose from a range of dog collars and leads for when you really want to explore being sexually autonomous. Or, if you're on a budget – or just not a dog person – you could buy the more economical cat mask for £150. If you fancy being ridden like a horse there is a harness or two, or if you want to be treated like a pig you might find a 'Hog Tie' appealing. Dog, cat, horse or pig? Post-feminism has opened up your choices.

Lashings of other bondage gear will help you subvert the dominant paradigm: whips, spanking equipment, and so on, and so forth, etc. You know, things that will "ensure your lover knows who's boss!" Oh, if you say so. But perhaps the most interesting is the "unusual and beautifully crafted leather leg harness [which] accompanies the Marlyn [sic] dildo." Basically, it's a strap-on dildo for the thigh. To be used, I suppose, in those consciousness raising bondage orgies that so terrify those in power.

If you can't quite afford these revolutionary sex toys and would like to settle for a vibrator, rest assured that Coco de Mer offers what might be eco-friendly vibrators. Apparently, Coco de Mer is "the first luxury sex boutique to take responsibility for the materials our designer sex toys are made from." I can't help wondering what this means. Does it mean that the sex toys are eco-friendly, made from recycled rubber, or (and my mind is trying not to go there) that the materials used have some connection to an unspecified 'Third World' economic self-sufficiency program? I do wonder where they got the human hair for the £239 'Bombshell Human Hair Whip'. (Can we have your hair please – we want to turn it into a sex whip.)

Coco de Mer not only wants to liberate the wallets of cashed up Western women, but their minds as well. The shop that sells vibrating silver butt plugs and £1,000 masturbating mirrors is really about "establishing intelligent dialogues ... about what is permissible." The big problem, as Sam sees it, is that 'we' need to sex up feminism, as she told Anushka Asthana:

> Feminism as a word is desexualised. If one claims to be a feminist, one is almost sacrificing her sexuality or her sexiness, right? Because it's not really permissible to be powerful, self-determined, challenging of society and be sexy. So it's very interesting how many women refuse to state they are a feminist. They fear that they are not going to be desired. I think it's something that we've got to tackle.

With obscenely expensive militant lingerie, revolutionary butt plugs and oppositional dildos, apparently. It's all about "reclaiming women's sexuality", you see. Yet, in an era in which "the hard-working hedonist who can afford to spend her income on vibrators and wine" (Power, 2009, p. 21) and does a bit of home porn with her executive lovers for a laugh, invests in botox, fake breasts, and full body-hair removal, has become the aspirational 'it' girl of post-feminist consumer culture, this 'reclaiming of women's sexuality' sounds more like another porn chic sell out. And at the risk of sounding uncool, a huge number of women are probably more focused on keeping a roof over their heads and food on the table than expending their hard-earned cash (assuming they even have a job) on 'empowering' themselves with a vibrating silver butt plug.

In 1980, Florence Rush wrote that "the current concept of sexual liberation has no relationship whatsoever to political freedom" (1980, p. 191) The counter-cultural 60s slogan 'make love, not war' quickly became a slogan for cool capitalism. And it's still largely forgotten that the guru of the sexual revolution, Alfred Kinsey, employed a known paedophile to conduct sexual experiments on 800 girls and boys in order to prove that kids are sexual.[3]

Several decades later, Rush is still right: there is a big gap between sexual liberation and political freedom.

Today, the neo-liberal ideology of Big Porn has colonised just about everything, including what passes for feminism in corporate culture. Yesterday's sexual transgression is today's fast food advert. Big Pharma spams everyone with sexed up drugs. Girls and women are expected to be hot and up for it while also being subjected to new waves of misogyny they are forbidden to name for fear of being slandered as frigid feminists. It's pretty clear what is going on politically. We're not just living with a depthless so-called women's liberation, there is also a big cultural insult at work here: reducing centuries of rigorous and ground-breaking feminist thinking and activism to the right to be hot and have more sex is insulting. It's like reducing the civil rights movement to an Ice Cube rap about sex and drugs.

What would happen if a woman really took the slick ideological con of Coco de Mer seriously and decided to sex up her feminism with these hot new products? To avoid being sexually rejected for defending your rights, you can transform yourself thanks to the new 'up yours!' feminism of Coco de Mer. But inevitably, the products converge into an image of the post-feminist consumer on her knees, with various expensive items inserted into various parts of her body, wearing an animal mask, with a strap on dildo, being spanked, whipped

---

3   <http://www.drjudithreisman.com/archives/2007/02/on_kinseys_germ_1.htm>.

and flogged with another woman's hair, looking into a mirror. All of this would cost, oh say, £4000. That's the price of the pornification of post-feminist sexual self-empowerment.

A more realistic description would be that this expensive sex shop chain is about gentrifying the sex industry with the help of a bit of consumer friendly post-feminist gibberish. Sorry but it's all Coco de *Merde** to me.

*Merde is 'shit' in French.

Bibliography

Asthana, Anushka (2010) 'Sam Roddick: "We have only had a kind of lipstick liberation. Women still have a big battle to fight"', <http://www.guardian.co.uk/environment/2010/may/23/sam-roddick-coco-de-mer> (accessed 17 April, 2011).

Power, Nina (2009) *One Dimensional Woman.* Zero Books, London.

Reisman, Judith (2007) 'On Kinsey's German Nazi paedophile aid; the New York Times asks: "Alfred Kinsey: Liberator or Pervert?"', <http://www.drjudithreisman.com/archives/2007/02/on_kinseys_germ_1.html> (accessed 17 April, 2011).

Rush, Florence (1980) *The Best Kept Secret: Sexual Abuse of Children.* McGraw-Hill, New York and London.

Helen Pringle

A Studied Indifference to Harm: Defending Pornography in *The Porn Report*

Since the 1980s, there has been a steady growth in the number of academics who study pornography and who believe they are being unconventional in their defence, or even celebration, of it (see e.g. Lord, 1997, and Williams, 2004). To treat pornography as a radical or cool political gesture, however, requires its defenders to turn a blind eye to the harms it does. A great deal of pro-pornography academic research in the social sciences is taken up with this task of masking the harms of pornography, in order to defend the lucrative global industry and guarantee a continued supply of cool pleasures to the hip consumer.

This chapter focuses on *The Porn Report* (*TPR*), published by Australian academics Alan McKee, Katherine Albury and Catharine Lumby in 2008 and heralded as "the first piece of serious research" on the state of pornography in Australia (*TPR*, p. xiii).[1] The book promises an up-to-date and evidence-based analysis of production, distribution and consumption, grounded in a survey of pornography users and a content analysis of best-selling X-rated videos. The stated purpose of the authors is not "to challenge any point of view directly or to persuade others to adopt a position that any of the authors currently hold on pornography," but rather to provide "factual information" to enable informed public debate (*TPR*, p. xiii). A central feature of the 'information' provided by the book is the claim that the harm of pornography is negligible and is, in any case, outweighed by the expressed pleasure of its users.

Contrary to the authors' stated purpose, I contend that the heart of *The Porn Report* is not an intellectual inquiry but an ideological mission. That mission is to provide an apologia for the sex industry and, in particular, to shift the terms of public debate to a position consonant with that of the authors which supports the mainstream distribution and use of pornography.

---

1   The Website for the book is at <http://www.thepornreportbook.com>, but it has not been updated since March, 2008.

1 The book and its project: Shifting the terms of public debate

Originally called *Dirty Business*, the book drew on a project entitled 'Understanding Pornography in Australia: Public Discourses and Pornographic Texts' funded by an Australian Research Council [ARC] grant of $174,500 over 3 years, from 2002 to 2004.[2] From the outset, the project was conducted in liaison with, and with support from, the peak Australian sex industry organisation, the Eros Association, and pornography businesses such as Gallery Entertainment and Axis Entertainment (*TPR*, pp. xv, 168, pp. 191–192).

The pattern of funding and support does not of course necessarily dictate the outcomes of any research project. Alan McKee writes that in administering their survey of pornography users, the researchers were 'open-minded' as to its outcomes:

> … we had no preconceptions about what we would find out about consumers of pornography. In particular, we did not assume beforehand that we would discover that pornography had bad effects on people or that those who used it were in any way abnormal, but we were open-minded about the possible effects of the consumption of pornography (McKee, 2007b, p. 36).

The extent of the open-mindedness of the authors is, however, put in question by their own previous work and publicly-announced position on the putative harms of pornography. McKee notes that the researchers did not assume they would find 'bad effects'. And from the project's inception, the researchers assumed that pornography has 'good effects' (see below). In conducting the project, the researchers confirmed those 'good effects' by looking in the obvious place: the self-reporting of a self-selecting group of currently active pornography users.

The Porn Report uses the term pornography in what is sometimes called a 'non-stipulative' manner, meaning that the term is not a *definition* but simply reflects commonly-held views about what falls into the category of pornography. So, for example, in a note attached to the surveys distributed to pornography consumers, the authors explained: "In this survey, we are using the term 'pornography' in its widest sense, from soft porn ('erotica') to fully explicit material. This includes magazines, videos, the Internet and explicit novels" (McKee, 2007b, p. 35). In the book, and in some media discussions, the authors do add a distinction between 'good' and 'bad' pornography. In the Introduction to *The Porn Report*, the authors note, "we are not anti-porn" (*TPR*, p. xv), but conclude the book by

---

2 Information drawn from the ARC Website <http.www.arc.gov.au/pdf/2002_dp_rfcd.pdf> and supplied by the ARC, together with a copy of the funding application, to the Senate Legislation Committee – Questions on Notice, 2003–2004 Budget Estimates Hearings.

saying, "We strongly support good pornography – and we absolutely condemn bad pornography" (*TPR*, p. 186). Throughout the book, the authors shift back and forwards from protestations of dispassionate objectivity to open advocacy of pornography use.

Both Alan McKee and Catharine Lumby have publicly claimed to be users of pornography,[3] and Lumby has argued that "feminists need pornography."[4] While all three authors consider themselves to be "entirely pro-feminist", their idea of sexual equality in pornography is illustrated by the peculiar view that *Girls Gone Wild* is a sign of the *success* of feminism (*TPR*, p. 102). The authors take obvious delight in the material throughout *The Porn Report*. For example, a text-box entitled 'Great Moments in Amateur Porn' judges *One Night in Paris [Hilton]* to be "perhaps the best title ever of a porn movie against stiff competition that includes *Edward Penishands* and *Buttbanged Naughty Nurses*" (*TPR*, p. 134).[5] It is unlikely that many nurses outside of *Carry on Doctor* share their enthusiasm for such a title.

In its early stages, the project was plugged in the Eros Association magazine by Alan McKee, who described its genesis:

> A group of academics, fed up with this studied ignorance[6] have just begun a three-year research project – called 'Understanding pornography in Australia' – to try to get away from the idea that 'ignorance is bliss' and to provide some facts about the subject … Together, Albury, Lumby and McKee hope that this information will help to change the way that we talk about pornography in Australia: to make some facts available, so that we can have a more informed an [sic] intelligent debate about the adult industry in this country (McKee, 2002, p. 21).

The Association appended the comment, "*Eros encourages all of its members to support the researchers in their project* [italics in original]". McKee's statement makes it clear that the very point of the project was to tilt public discourse towards a certain view of pornography, one that is in alignment with that held by the sex industry.

---

3   See respectively McKee (2006a, p. 523) "Alan McKee likes *Big Brother*, pornography, Kylie Minogue, and *New Weekly* magazine", and Harford (1998, p. 1) "[Lumby] watches X-rated videos, and believes that, if exposed to them, women can freely choose the images they wish to see." Katherine Albury has noted that she is "not a huge porn fan" (quoted in Gregg, 2003, p. 14), and her contributions to public debates on pornography are less strident than those of McKee.

4   See Lumby (1997): chapter 5 is entitled 'Why Feminists Need Porn'.

5   This kind of juvenile punning and glib treatment of serious subjects pervades the book, echoing the language of a pulp novel by Catharine Lumby (Scud, 1995). It is odd that the popular video *Hairfree Asian Honeys* is not in the running for 'best title ever'; indeed, the pervasiveness of the theme of racial subordination in pornography is not mentioned at all: see the discussion in Dines (2010, chapter 7).

6   McKee is here referring to the academic, Robert Manne, and radio host, John Laws, as examples of 'studied ignorance'.

He later summed up the project's outcome by saying, "The surprising finding was that pornography is actually good for you in many ways" (quoted in Symons and Mackenzie, 2004, p. 4). Such an outcome was not in the least 'surprising' to the authors, nor to the Eros Association, which enthusiastically welcomed academic support for its position. For example, Yasmin Element wrote in *EROS Magazine* to recommend that McKee's analysis (i.e. McKee, 2005b) of objectification of women in pornography videos "should be used as widely as possible by the industry". Element added:

> I encourage all Eros members to read the report and hand it on to staff, business colleagues and journalists, as it is extremely interesting and informative on many diverse areas of the adult retail industry. It should be passed on to all industry lawyers and lobbyists of all kinds for their reference and could be extremely helpful in all cases from the illegal selling of X rated movies to adult retail planning issues (Element, 2006, p. 7).

The CEO of the pornography firm AdultShop.com, Malcolm Day, apparently concurred that the findings of the project might prove helpful in challenging film and video classification guidelines. In 2007, Day sought a review of a Classification Review Board decision on a film entitled *Viva Erotica*, a pastiche of "real depictions of actual sexual activity between consenting adults." The Board had determined the film to be "offensive to a reasonable adult" and classified it as X18+, which meant it was not available for sale or hire except in the ACT and NT. AdultShop.com challenged the Board's rating in the Federal Court on grounds including how the test of "likely to cause offence to a reasonable adult" should be construed, and whether expert evidence offered in support of Day's claim had been rejected or discounted. The expert evidence at issue was given by McKee, Lumby and Albury, drawing on their research, particularly in regard to the question of the sensibility of 'reasonable adults'.[7]

Catharine Lumby's participation in the AdultShop.com case became the subject of what she later said were "adverse comments" made during the 2008 Senate inquiry into the sexualisation of children. A number of submissions to the Inquiry had argued that Lumby was "publicly pro porn."[8] The Senate committee

---

7 *AdultShop.Com Ltd v Members of the Classification Review Board* [2007] FCA 1871, para. 62, 69–80, 174–178, and *AdultShop.Com Ltd v Members of the Classification Review Board (No.2)* [2007] FCA 1872 (re confidentiality orders). See also Overington (2007, p. 13), citing from the report by McKee for AdultShop.com. Beverland and Lindgreen (2003) provide a useful exploration of the organisation and early history of AdultShop.com.

8 Parliament of Australia, Senate Standing Committee on Environment, Communication and the Arts (2008) Inquiry into the Sexualisation of Children in the Contemporary Media Environment, transcript of 29 April, 2008, p. 18 (Julie Gale), and p. 36 (Lauren Rosewarne). Submissions had also been made to the Senate inquiry by McKee, and by Lumby and Albury.

permitted Lumby to record a formal response to these comments. Her response, addressed to the committee on 9 May, 2008 on University of New South Wales letterhead, denied that she was "pro-porn" or that "my values are seriously out of kilter with current community standards."[9] Lumby argued that she had given evidence in the AdultShop.com case through a contract struck between her then employer (the University of Sydney) and the West Australian law firm of Salter Power.[10] She claimed that she had "never been an advocate for any organisation selling adult sexual material in Australia, and had never represented AdultShop.com in court or otherwise" (Senate Inquiry, Attachment A, p. 104); that she "was not expressing any personal view and certainly not advocating the sale of such material" (Attachment B, p. 105); and that her evidence "simply and dispassionately reported the facts as I have them on what the 'reasonable' or ordinary Australian thinks about the availability of this material to adults" (Attachment B, p. 108). In the face of criticism at the Senate Inquiry, Lumby took on the persona of the objective intellectual, claiming, "I did not publish this research as an advocate of X-rated material but in my capacity as an academic, looking dispassionately at the evidence" (Attachment B, p. 106).

The AdultShop.com case is an example of how the findings published as *The Porn Report* have been used in public forums: to attempt to shift public debate and legal discourse to a position more favourable to the pornography industry. In the AdultShop.com case, the attempt was not successful because the evidence offered did not directly address the criteria at the heart of film and video classification decisions. Judge Jacobson in the case noted that in canvassing the question of how the film *Viva Erotica* would strike "reasonable adults", "Professor McKee's evidence addressed the wrong question because it focussed only on the attitudes of consumers of sexually explicit films,"[11] and not on reasonable adults more generally.

---

9   Senate Inquiry, p. 102. See also Attachment A: Summary of Response to Adverse Comments made in the Senate Inquiry into the Sexualisation of Children, p. 104, "I am not pro-porn".

10 Senate Inquiry, Attachment B: Responses to Adverse Comments in Order They Occur, p. 105. Such 'arms-length' arrangements are common in the proffering of expert evidence; however, the evidence was solicited for AdultShop.com, not by the Classification Review Board or the Federal Court, and not by the University of Sydney. Moreover, people do not usually enter into agreements to present expert evidence in support of positions or organisations to which they are unsympathetic.

11 *AdultShop.Com Ltd v Members of the Classification Review Board* [2007] FCA 1871, para. 177.

2 The construction of expertise on pornography: The gentrified user

Having explored the broad lines of the project and its intended use in debates on pornography, I now turn to the mechanics of the research project, in particular the survey of pornography users and the content analysis of pornographic videos. These aspects of the project represent an attempt to 'gentrify' the consumers of pornography, through a reshaping of the image of the 'average' user from that of a 'dirty old man' to that of an intelligent, educated, reasonable and hip participant in consumer culture, who can offer 'expertise' in the formulation of public policy on such matters. This construction of a previously unrecognised 'expertise' is accompanied by an attempt to conjure away any suggestion of harm in pornographic videos, by a careful selection of the 'typical' material viewed by the 'average' consumer.

The research project is not described in any detail in *The Porn Report* because the authors note that it would prove too academic for readers (*TPR*, pp. 191–192). The scaffolding of the project is instead set out in various journal articles by Alan McKee published since 2005; there is considerable repetition and overlap of the material and argument in the articles.

Prior to beginning their research, the authors of *The Porn Report* made two pivotal assumptions about users of pornography. The first assumption is that the voices of pornography users are not heard. Second, as a consequence, users' "*expertise* on the genre" (McKee, 2006a, p. 524, my emphasis) had not been aired. In a 2003 opinion piece, Alan McKee sarcastically characterised the process of public debate and policy making on pornography as conducted with a malicious indifference to knowledge and expertise:

> When considering the introduction of laws, or setting up government bodies to implement them, it's important that the people involved in public debate, in legislation, and in enforcement, should know nothing about the area in question. Anybody who has even the slightest knowledge of it should be pilloried, insulted and excluded from the process. Obviously (McKee, 12 May, 2003).

The research project elevated the opinions held by pornography users to the status of 'expertise', and characterised their practices as the acquisition of valuable knowledge. This required in turn the construction of pornographic materials as harmless (after all, we do not consult racists in formulating laws against hate speech on the basis that they are involved in and know a lot about racism).

The project accomplished the neutralisation of the harm of pornography through a content analysis of 50 popular X-rated videos which were selected from Gallery Entertainment and Axis Entertainment best seller lists so as to "represent mainstream tastes" (McKee, 2005b, p. 277).[12] Although the hire and sale of videos by mail is of course an appropriate place to look for 'mainstream' pornography, the authors nominated such videos as *representative* of what consumers of pornography use. They claim that it is very difficult to find what they call 'bad porn', and that it is anyway not the most popular type or what the 'average' porn user watches (*TPR*, pp. 172–173). This claim completely ignores the ready availability and widespread usage of pornography on popular Internet sites such as PornHub. Meagan Tyler's disturbing analysis of reviews in the US industry magazine *Adult Video News* also suggests that the pornography industry itself recognises the popularity, and profitability, of increasing violence and dehumanisation in videos (Tyler, 2010).

The unsurprising 'finding' of the content analysis of videos as reported by McKee however was that mainstream pornography is not characterised by objectification, violence, or abuse – and that users of pornography are not thereby participating in such practices. The other major part of the research project comprised a survey designed to discern the effects of pornography on those users. 5000 questionnaires were distributed in August, 2003, one placed in every tenth catalogue of 50,000 Axis Entertainment catalogues, together with a prepaid envelope for return. Only 367 'valid responses' were returned, a low rate explained by Alan McKee as "perhaps to be expected in a public context in which users of pornography are sometimes vilified as being dangerous or criminal" (McKee, 2006b, p. 36).[13] An additional online survey was conducted from 2 June to 29 October, 2003,[14] advertised by the authors in the media and through public debates. This online survey garnered 656 'valid responses'. Out of this total of 1023 survey responses, 329 respondents provided details of their identity for possible interviews. To reflect a variety of backgrounds and hence a diversity of 'expertise', a sample of 46 users was then chosen for face-to-face interviews.[15]

The 'expertise' gathered from the surveys and interviews covered 3 main

12 None of the videos was Australian-made; there is very little professional production of pornography in Australia.
13 This claim is also repeated verbatim in McKee (2007b, p. 35). There are many other explanations that seem just as plausible for the low return rate.
14 The Website was <http.www.understandingpornography.info> which is now only available on Wayback.
15 The survey questions are set out in McKee (2007a, Appendix A, pp. 95–104). The backgrounds of interviewees are set out in McKee (2005a, p. 77, and Appendix 2, pp. 92–94); McKee (2006a, Appendix B, pp. 538–539); and McKee (2006b, Appendix 2, pp. 49–50). The Interview questions are set out in McKee (2005a, Appendix 1, pp. 91–92); McKee (2006a, Appendix A, pp. 536–537); and McKee (2006b, Appendix 1, pp. 48–49).

topics: pornography's aesthetic merits, its effects on users' attitudes to women, and the opinions of users about the regulation and censorship of pornography. Predictably, on the aesthetic merits of pornography, its users joked about poor production values and gratuitous characters (McKee, 2006a, pp. 528–529). Other responses were also not surprising: pornography consumers believe that pornography is good for them and are opposed to censorship. In terms of attitudes to sexual equality, there was some evidence offered that some men liked to see women in control in pornographic scenarios,[16] and that women more than men respond favourably to rough sex in videos.[17]

As I noted above, the survey and interviews were designed to fill a supposed gap in the voicing of expertise by pornography users, enabling those who (allegedly) have been 'othered' (McKee's term) or made to feel like outsiders to finally break their silence and speak for themselves. As the authors admit, the survey relied on self-selected pornography users who were disproportionately well educated.[18] What they do not admit is the possibility of completely different views and practices on the part of several million Australian pornography users who did not complete the research survey. On this score, the authors note, "the ethical constraints imposed by our institutions prevented us from asking people who had not identified themselves as consumers about whether they consumed pornography" (*TPR*, p. 193). Given the emphasis throughout *The Porn Report* on ethical practice, this note about ethical constraints is well-placed. However, one of the authors did ask a person who had publicly identified himself as a non-user of pornography about his use of pornography, in a way that constituted a serious ethical breach even by the understanding of ethics underlying the project and set out in the book.

On 17 January, 2007, Alan McKee wrote, on Queensland University of Technology (QUT) letterhead, to the public intellectual and then Executive Director of the Australia Institute, Clive Hamilton, who is criticised throughout McKee's articles and opinion pieces as having the nerve to speak about or criticise the use of pornography given his own non-use of it (e.g. McKee, 2006b, p. 35).

---

16 As Sarah Maddison commented on the project, however: "It would be naïve, or an extreme form of denial, to think women are not being exploited … Further it's a huge leap to suggest that because a scripted porn production depicts a woman initiating sex, that you can somehow take from that she had a say in the production … It is well known that some men get off on women being assertive and initiating sex, and that will be represented in porn, but it doesn't mean the actress has any agency in that decision" (quoted in Lunn, 2008, p. 11).

17 McKee delightedly exaggerated this 'finding' in an ABC public forum (ABC *Life Matters*, 2008).

18 The researchers also accepted at face value what their subjects said, whether in the survey or interviews, without either challenge or verification.

In the letter, McKee introduced himself in these terms: "I am writing as Chief Investigator on the ARC-funded research project 'Understanding Pornography in Australia'. I work in the Creative Industries Faculty at Queensland University of Technology." McKee continued:

> This project aims to provide an overview of the production, content and consumption of pornographic materials in Australian society.
>
> One issue that we are addressing is the extent to which public figures involved in debates about the censorship of pornography have been exposed to pornography themselves.
>
> I am hoping that you can provide me with some information about your own exposure to the genre?
>
> 1.   How much pornography have you been exposed to?
> 2.   What effects would you say it has had on you?
> 3.   Has this had any effect on your position on the censorship of such materials?[19]

The design of the ARC-funded project at no stage involved asking public figures about their use of pornography. Moreover, the project had been completed 2 years before McKee's letter was sent to Hamilton. After an inquiry and findings by a panel of experts at QUT, McKee wrote to Clive Hamilton on 14 May, 2007, to acknowledge that he should have consulted with the University's Ethics Committee before writing the original letter, and "to apologise for any concerns that have been raised by the request for information." The seriousness of this breach of ethics safeguards, and of principles of ethical research casts a shadow on the ethical bearing of the project more broadly.

Conclusion: Let's do the time warp, again

As noted above, the importance of the survey of pornography users to the research project was based on the claim that "for some reason we [sic] routinely exclude one group of commentators who, one would think, have some expertise on this topic – the people who consume pornography as a part of their everyday lives" (McKee 2006a, p. 523; also McKee, 2005a, p. 72). This exclusion is attributed by McKee and his colleagues to the academic and media framing of pornography only as a problem of addiction. In *The Porn Report*, the authors ask:

> Yet when was the last time that you heard anybody admitting in the media that they use porn themselves? While millions of Australians quietly live their lives and use pornography, the only people we hear from in public debates are church leaders, social scientists, politicians

---

19 The documents in this case were supplied to me in a personal communication by Clive Hamilton. I do not know if similar letters were sent to other critics of pornography, as implied in the letter.

and commentators – people whose claim to expertise on the issue is the very fact that they themselves don't watch porn, aren't friendly with anybody who watches porn, and don't know anything about the everyday use of porn … The only porn users you ever hear from in the media are people who call themselves 'addicts' and are trying to stop using it (*TPR*, p. 25).

In contrast, my own reading of accounts in the media, and not only in the newspaper articles to which the authors refer, suggests that greater prominence is given in them to defenders of pornography like Alan McKee than to pornography 'addicts' (or to the victims of the pornography industry, or partners of pornography users, for that matter). In a search of Australian newspapers on the database *Factiva*, I found only a handful of feature articles characterising pornography users as 'addicts' – and in each of those articles, Alan McKee voices his own view that pornography is good for you.[20]

The authors of *The Porn Report* consider the chief obstacles to the wider acceptance of pornography as such public and scholarly ignorance, together with a religious and political repression that perhaps did flourish in their own youth. The book is framed by anecdotes from the 1950s and 1960s about the silencing and repression of sex and sexuality. Lumby recounts that she was in year 5 when she had her "first brush with the stuff," as schoolboys on her bus read aloud passages of what she calls "pure, delightful filth" from *The Joy of Sex* (*TPR*, p. xi). Kath Albury was seven when she discovered one of her father's *Playboy* magazines (*TPR*, p. xi). And McKee found "an abandoned magazine in the woods behind his house when he was in his early teens" (*TPR*, p. xi). However, the type of hippy nudity that sometimes passed for pornography in the 1950s and 1960s bears little resemblance to the gonzo porn that pervades the Internet of the 2000s (see Dines, 2010). Nor does the sex of pornography and of its users remain repressed, as the industry and its defenders continue with some fervour to complain is still the case.

Like many academic defences of pornography, *The Porn Report* delights in its supposed unconventionality. In fact, its argument is tired and outdated, with little bearing on the brutal reality of popular pornography today. The fact that pornography users are, like McKee himself, "intellectually competent individuals" (McKee, 2005a, p. 81) does not excuse the project's studied indifference to the harm enacted in and by the sexual subordination and cruelty that defines modern pornography.

---

20 This is also the case with the article (Castles, 8 October, 2006) cited in *The Porn Report* to illustrate the media focus on addiction: see *TPR*, chapter 2 'Dirty? Old? Men? The Consumers of Pornography', p. 24.

Bibliography

ABC *Life Matters* (29 September, 2008) Forum: Feminism, Raunch Culture and Porn, <http://www.abc.net.au/rn/lifematters/stories/2008/2375129.htm> (accessed 23 February, 2011).

AdultShop.Com Ltd v Members of the Classification Review Board [2007] FCA 1871.

AdultShop.Com Ltd v Members of the Classification Review Board (No.2) [2007] FCA 1872.

Beverland, Michael and Adam Lindgreen (2003) 'AdultShop.com: Establishing Legitimacy with the "Virgin" Consumer' *Marketing Intelligence & Planning* 21 (6), pp. 379–391.

Castles, Simon (8 October, 2006) 'In the Grip of a Guilty Pleasure' *The Sunday Age*, Melbourne, p. 12.

Dines, Gail (2010) *Pornland: How Porn Has Hijacked our Sexuality.* Beacon Press, Boston; Spinifex Press, North Melbourne.

Element, Yasmin (2006) 'The Objectification of Women in Mainstream Pornographic Videos in Australia' *EROS Magazine* 7 (1), p. 7.

Gregg, Natalie (12 August, 2003) 'Let's Talk about Sex' *Courier-Mail*, Brisbane, p. 14.

Harford, Sonia (21 March, 1998) 'Porn: Taboo Or Not Taboo? That Is The Question' *The Age*, Melbourne, Saturday Extra, p. 1.

Lord, M.G. (1997) 'Porn Utopia: How Feminist Scholars Learned to Love Dirty Pictures' *Lingua Franca*, April/May, <http://linguafranca.mirror.theinfo.org/9704/porn.9704.html> (accessed 23 February, 2011).

Lumby, Catharine (1997) *Bad Girls: Media, Sex and Feminism in the '90s.* Allen & Unwin, Sydney.

Lunn, Stephen (22 February, 2008) 'Bare Facts about Porn' *The Australian*, Sydney, p. 11.

McKee, Alan (2002) 'Understanding Pornography in Australia' *EROS Magazine*, 2 (3), p. 21.

McKee, Alan (12 May, 2003) 'What Do People Like about Porn? Everyone Knows the Answer to That' *On Line Opinion*, <http://www.onlineopinion.com.au/view.asp?article=334> (accessed 23 February, 2011).

McKee, Alan (2005a) 'The Need to Bring the Voices of Pornography Consumers into Public Debates about the Genre and its Effects' *Australian Journal of Communication* 32 (2), pp. 71–94.

McKee, Alan (2005b) 'The Objectification of Women in Mainstream Pornographic Videos in Australia' *Journal of Sex Research* 42 (4), pp. 277–290.

McKee, Alan (2006a) 'The Aesthetics of Pornography: The Insights of Consumers' *Continuum: Journal of Media & Cultural Studies* 20 (4), pp. 523–539.

McKee, Alan (2006b) 'Censorship of Sexually Explicit Materials: What Do Consumers of Pornography Have to Say?' *Media International Australia* no. 120, pp. 35–50.

McKee, Alan (2007a) 'The Positive and Negative Effects of Pornography as Attributed by Consumers' *Australian Journal of Communication* 34 (1), pp. 87–104.

McKee, Alan (2007b) 'The Relationship between Attitudes towards Women, Consumption of Pornography, and other Demographic Variables in a Survey of 1,023 Consumers of Pornography' *International Journal of Sexual Health* 19 (1), pp. 31–45.

McKee, Alan (2009) 'Social Scientists Don't Say "Titwank"' *Sexualities* 12 (5), pp. 629–646.

McKee, Alan, Katherine Albury and Catharine Lumby (2008) *The Porn Report.* Melbourne University Press, Melbourne.

Overington, Caroline (28 February, 2007) 'Porn at X-roads' *The Australian*, p. 13.

Parliament of Australia, Senate Standing Committee on Environment, Communication and the Arts (2008) Inquiry into the Sexualisation of Children in the Contemporary Media Environment.

Parliament of Australia, Senate Legislation Committee – Questions on Notice, 2003–2004 Budget Estimates Hearings.

Scud, Grace (1995) *Dead White Males.* Autopsy, Sydney.

Symons, Emma-Kate and Kate Mackenzie (17 April, 2004) 'Torn on Porn's Net Effect' *The Australian*, Sydney, p. 4.

Thomas, Gerald (Dir) (1967) *Carry on Doctor*, <http://www.imdb.com/title/tt0061450/> (accessed 23 February, 2011).

Tyler, Meagan (2010) "'Now, That's Pornography!'": Violence and Domination in *Adult Video News*' in Karen Boyle (Ed) *Everyday Pornography*. Routledge, London and New York.

Williams, Linda (Ed) (2004) *Porn Studies*. Duke University Press, Durham and London.

Melinda Tankard Reist

Sexpo and the Death of Sex[1]

Billed as the world's biggest health, sexuality and lifestyle exhibition, Sexpo came to Sydney's Hordern Pavilion in October, 2010.

According to its Website (<http://www.sexpo.com.au/>) "[t]his show will increase your attractiveness and sexual drive. It contains beautiful women, hunky men, nudity and crackin' entertainment."

Call me fussy. Say I'm hard to please. But if what I witnessed is supposed to promote a healthy, happy sex life, then I think I just saw the death of sex.

Sexpo sex is formulaic, conveyer belt, plastic, industrialised, peep show porn sex.

The space was filled with pumping, grinding, crotch grabbing and female porn stars 'presenting', as they say in baboon studies. Cosmetically enhanced bodies waxed to within an inch of their lives. A landfill's worth of plastic toys, dildos, whirling vibrators, penis rings and fake vaginas.

There were faux lesbian threesomes in hardcore acts of nastiness. Pole dancers, strippers, bondage mistresses and men in little aprons with their bums showing. Audience members were hypnotised on stage into believing they were receiving oral sex.

Male show goers pulled their pants down on stage and played with their penises. An artist known as Pricasso slathered his in paint, ready to capture your likeness.

Men practised their anal prowess on stage with lifeless blow-up dolls. Others paid a porn star $40 to pose topless with them. Many visited the 'laporium' for paid personalised lap dances. At times it felt like you were walking through one giant erection.

All of it captured by men with video cameras, for a longer lasting Sexpo.

Designed to turn us all on were: a man in a suit covered in fake penises; giant characters depicting male and female sexual parts; a sex sideshow alley including moving clowns with heads as genitals; the gerbil sex train advertised with giant breasts and penis in between.

---

1   An earlier version of this piece was published online on ABC *The Drum Unleashed*, 21 October, 2010, <http://www.abc.net.au/unleashed/40310.html> and on Melinda Tankard Reist's blog, <http://melindatankardreist.com/2010/10/sexpo-and-the-death-of-sex/>.

A celebration of the vandalism of the human body.

Ex-footballer, now porn filmmaker, Warwick Capper, in his *Hustler* t-shirt? Sorry, just not doing it for me. Ex-*Hey Hey it's Saturday*'s Russell Gilbert as 'crackin' entertainer and MC. Define crackin?

Two older long-bearded men sold t-shirts with slogans like 'Wipe ya eyes princess and harden the f*ck up' and offered to sign ladies' underwear. Another t-shirt depicted a woman bound, with a red ball stuffed in her mouth and the slogan 'Silence is golden'. "I look at that and see fun!" said the cheery saleswoman.

I look at that and see the objectification and subordination of women.

My friend and I could 'enhance our assets' for a mere $7,000 each for boobs and 'tush'. Photos of pumped up breasts and tight bums adorned the stand. We were invited to handle the silicone implants.

There were also before-and-after photos of labia subjected to a scalpel for a bit of tidying up. And would we like to know more about the G-spot enhancement? Women are not good enough as they are. We must be sexually modified.

The enthusiastic staff testified to the skill of the boss. He's operated on all of them. One showed me the bandages around her mid-section: pre-wedding liposuction. Hymen repair was also on the menu of services offered. They were seeing one to two Middle Eastern girls a week seeking the procedure to 'prove' their virginity.

Genital repair of another kind was being offered by a charity called Clitoraid. A devastating human rights violation against a woman's bodily integrity is made sexy. They were raising money for female genital mutilation repair in Africa, with slogans such as 'Give a Stranger an Orgasm', 'Help Build a Pleasure Hospital' and 'Adopt a Clitoris'.

There were photos of smiling African women and a baby mid-mutilation. A staffer told me they stopped showing a film of a child being cut as too many men stood around laughing.

I wondered what African women would think of the pornification of their suffering?

And, this, my last encounter as I was leaving.

A shivering young Asian woman in a wet t-shirt, sitting in a cage waiting for someone to strike the 'bang me' target on the image of a woman bent over which would send her plunging into the tub of water below.

Freezing, soaked, alone, disconnected, in an enclosure, to be ogled by men.

In the end, Sexpo is anti-intimacy, anti-connection, anti-warmth. It just leaves you feeling cold.

Sheila Jeffreys

Live Pornography: Strip Clubs in the International Political Economy of Prostitution

It is time for the link between the strip club industry and pornography to be recognised. Feminist research into the harms of the strip club industry and the ways in which it is connected to the international political economy of prostitution has only recently begun. In the last 20 years, stripping has moved from being a small scale, seedy industry, hidden in the sex shop areas of major cities, to a very profitable international industry in which clubs resemble business class airline lounges, and pimping companies supply women from around the world. The new 'gentlemen's clubs' are designed to appeal to a wide range of men from corporate executives to the boy next door, offering stag nights, and even hen's nights. They have been normalised and glamourised. The practice of stripping has been defended, too, by some 'feminist' academics who say that it empowers women and enables them to express their sexuality. In this chapter I will argue that stripping needs to be understood as a harmful part of the sex industry, which is closely integrated with pornography in its personnel and practices.

Academic discussion of stripping rarely examines it as an industry, or as harmful to the women who work in it and to women's equality. Some writers in the field of gender studies even defend the practice of stripping. They euphemise the industry, calling it 'exotic dancing' or 'entertainment'. They argue that stripping should be understood as socially transgressive, an exercise of women's agency, or a form of empowerment for women (Hanna, 1998; Schweitzer, 1999; Liepe-Levinson, 2002). These arguments exemplify the decontextualised individualism which is common to many defences of the sex industry. Katherine Frank who worked as a stripper before researching a PhD on strip clubs and their patrons, says that she had 'increased feelings' of 'self-efficacy' when 'dancing', though she acknowledges in her work that the fact that she was known to be a graduate student and had other options, is likely to have made her personal experience atypical (Frank, 2002). She says that 'sex work cannot be dismissed as a possible form of feminist resistance or an exercise in female agency' (Frank, 2002, p. 16). Feminist critics, however, are arguing that stripping needs to be understood not as resistance to women's subordination, but rather as a most powerful example of it, and harmful both to the women who strip, and to the status of all women (see also Stella, this volume).

Feminist activism on strip clubs

Stripping only became the object of serious attention in the 2000s. Feminists became concerned about the way in which strip clubs form a halfway house between men's pornography use and their becoming buyers of women in prostitution. Whilst pornography constructs the desire to use women as sexual objects, strip clubs provide live pornography in which they can see the women of pornography in the flesh and, often, touch them. The doubling in the percentage of men in the UK in 10 years who now prostitute women has been attributed to the normalisation of the commercial sexual exploitation of women that pornography and strip clubs have enabled (Ward and Day, 2004). Prostitution buyers in one London study spoke of how the strip clubs made them frustrated and made the buying of women in prostitution necessary (Coy et al., 2007). In 2010, Iceland, under the leadership of a lesbian feminist Prime Minister, Johanna Sigurdardottir, became the first country to prohibit strip clubs (in Bindel, 2010).

The strip club industry

The strip club industry is now estimated to be worth more than US$75 billion worldwide (Montgomery, 2005). But very little research has taken place into the economics of the strip club industry. In 2009, a study by the Bureau of Business Research and the Institute on Domestic Violence and Sexual Assault at the University of Texas, demonstrated the socio-economic impact of sexually oriented businesses on the Texas economy. It analysed the impact of the Adult Entertainment Fee imposed by the Legislature and provided recommendations for further regulating the industry. It was unusual in combining the expertise of a business school with concern for violence against women. It asked the question whether the "victimization and perpetration of sexual violence against women" are connected with this industry, and concludes from a review of the literature that they are. It concludes that stripping is, in fact, "a violent and traumatizing line of work that includes sexual, verbal, and physical violence, and exploits female workers" (Bureau of Business Research, 2009, p. 11). The report estimates that the industry has a yearly 'total economic impact' of between $920 million and $1.08 billion. This includes 'direct and indirect effects' of output by 'adult cabarets' and dancer income, adult book and video stores, escort services, and modelling and massage studios. There are 175 'adult cabaret' clubs in Texas which were worth $266.6 million in 2007 i.e. two-thirds as large as the Texas media industry as a whole, which was worth in 2006, $330.1 million. An estimated 8,272 people including 3,181 dancers are employed directly. The average entertainer works four 7-hour shifts per week as an independent contractor. The dancers earn an estimated average of $57,157 per year. In Queensland, Australia, strippers made an average of $1,120 per week, which is more than the average female wage of $804.50 in that state (Jeffries and Lynch, 2007). Stripping enables unskilled women to earn more, but does not provide the riches that pimping Websites promise to 'dancers'. Moreover, they can only engage in it for a few short years.

Domestic and international strip club agencies provide strippers and 'hostesses' not just to clubs but to strip restaurants and a range of corporate and private events (Coalition Against Trafficking in Women, 2010[1]). The newly set up Australian strip club pimping firm, Busama,

> is a premier international exotic dancer, table dancer and hostess recruitment agency and we are based on the Gold Coast in Australia. We provide a FREE dancer, lap dancing jobs and hostess jobs service to our showgirls and bookings into pole dancing clubs all around the world (Busama, n.d.).

Busama will take inexperienced girls and women and train them. They supply 'hostesses' and lap dancers to Macau, Hong Kong and South Africa. The employers will, in some cases, arrange working visas for the women, transportation and accommodation. Busama pimp, Justin, says that stripping and prostitution are not the same, "… exotic dancing is not synonymous to prostitution. It can't be denied that some girls engage themselves into prostitution but it is very wrong to stereotype everyone as prostitutes" (Justin, 2010). But Busama's Website is linked to an escort (prostitution) agency in the Dominican Republic, a well-known sex tourism destination.

Some clubs provide pole dancing classes to induct women into the industry and pole dancing has now become a leisure pursuit for girls and women. Taxi drivers take male buyers to strip clubs. Tailors create the costumes to be worn by women in porn and in strip clubs. Shoemakers design and manufacture cripplingly high heels for use in the industry. Restaurant staff run eateries in the strip clubs. Many technology companies service the pornography and strip industries by offering advertising for the Web, payment and exit services, hosting and so on. Websites act as advertising boards for escorts, brothels, strip clubs, pornography.

---

1   See also <http://melindatankardreist.com/2011/03/not-just-harmless-fun-how-strip-club-harm-women/>.

Strip clubs are now diversifying into the regular provision of sex shops attached to the clubs, either next door or in the foyer. These shops provide clothing for strippers, who are encouraged to take male buyers to the shop so that they can buy the items for the women. An *Adult Video News* (AVN) article on the evolution of the strip club industry says that diversification into linked sex shops is now de rigueur for clubs, which may also offer complimentary valet, premium liquor, gourmet meals, and even 'hand-rolled cigars' (Nelson X, 2008, p. 79). The Penthouse Club's boutique in Las Vegas offers "exotic club fashions, evening wear, novelties and exclusive Penthouse-branded dancewear, lingerie, shoes, jewellery and DVDs (i.e. porn)" (Nelson X, 2008, p. 80). They also sell 'sex toys'. The strippers are the main customers, about 55% of sales. There is a large market since each club has 75–100 strippers. The AVN Website advertises many companies which either service the porn production companies, women who strip, or the women whose partners require sexual servicing in a manner they are used to from their consumption of sex industry products. Products on offer include 'semenex' which makes the taste of semen less distasteful for women, nipple clamps and anal lubricant.

Stripping is a form of prostitution

All of this economic activity is supported by the use of naked women's bodies. Pornography is usually not recognised as a form of prostitution. Defenders of pornography argue that it should be seen as a 'fantasy' or just 'representation' (Kipnis, 2003). In fact, real live women are paid to be penetrated every which way, often for hours, to make pornography, and this practice should be considered a very severe form of prostitution in terms of the forms of violence inflicted upon the women who are used (Jeffreys, 2009; Tyler, 2009). Similarly, stripping is widely promoted as a form of 'dance' or 'erotic dance'. The entangling of stripping with prostitution has not been widely recognised (but see Bray, Farley, this volume). But forms of physical contact between male buyers and naked women seeking to sexually arouse or satisfy them, are very common. In traditional strip clubs, contact has always occurred, with men paying money to thrust their fingers up women's vaginas, for instance (Holsopple, 1998). Now men pay for lap dances in private booths where the women may have to squirm on the semen covered laps of the buyers whilst naked, or they may engage in other sexual acts. The distinction between the regular practices involved in lap dancing, for instance, and other forms of prostitution is hard to make.

Prostitution is often negotiated in the clubs such that male buyers leave with the strippers or make assignations to meet later. Nakita Kash, a stripper in the

US, commenting on the fact that becoming a stripper is now an aspiration of lots of girls when they become 18, says that it is not an easy form of work because, "you have to have your head screwed on straight to not get wrapped up in drugs, prostitution, bad boyfriends – like in porn" (Nelson X, 2008, p. 86). Strip clubs in Queensland arrange outcall 'dates' for men who wish to take women out of the clubs (Jeffries and Lynch, 2007). Strip clubs operate openly and with minimal state interference all over the world (except in Iceland), as if they are genuinely entertainment venues, and not venues for men's sexual abuse of women and girls. In Australia, this has led to the anomaly that legalised brothels are not permitted to serve alcohol, whereas strip clubs are, even when the strip club is on the upper floor of the brothel building and owned by the same person or company. There can be considerable, and deliberate, confusion about the distinctions between brothels and strip clubs. *The Site*, for example, describes itself as "Sydney's No. 1 purpose built 5-Star brothel and gentlemen's club" (*The Site*, 2009). Prostituted women in the brothel are called 'hostesses'.

Connections between the pornography and strip club industries: same owners, same performers

The connections between the pornography and strip club industries are very clear from the fact that strip clubs evolved from the pornography industry, and porn companies and strip clubs frequently feature the same owners and performers. Pornographers extend their empires by setting up strip club chains, and strip club owners branch out into pornography. Harry Mohney is credited with 'pioneering' the first 'upscale' gentlemen's club in 1987 (Nelson X, 2008). He now controls 70 'adult nightclubs' in the Déjà vu chain. He runs the Hustler clubs too, founded by Larry Flynt, which carry the name of the porn magazine Flynt founded. Mohney began his career in the 1960s as a projectionist at an adult movie house. He opened Déjà vu stores in 1970 and now has 30 'love boutiques', many within or adjacent to his strip clubs.

The women in porn and the strippers in clubs are often the same. The 'dancers' in strip clubs are often porn stars who go on tour around the clubs and do feature performances to bring publicity. *Adult Video News* tells us, for instance, that Carmen Hart, who is a Wicked Pictures contract girl, has taken many titles in exotic dancer awards competitions, such as 'Exotic Performer of the Year' in 2007 (Nelson X, 2008, p. 80). Sunny Lane, is a dancer for the Déjà vu chain who tours under the title 'The Girl Next Door Goes Hardcore' and has appeared in porn movies such as *Big Wet Asses 13* (Nelson X, 2008, p. 80). She is now an 'adult feature' on the strip club circuit after starring in an Eminem music video in 2003.

Sometimes strip club chains diversify into porn, when they have not evolved out of the porn industry. Thus the Spearmint Rhino chain, which is now international and has a branch in my city of Melbourne, has its own film studio to produce pornography (Nelson X, 2008, p. 82). John Gray, founder of Spearmint Rhino, has 6 convictions in the US for offences ranging from carrying a concealed weapon to writing dud cheques, for which, collectively, he received a suspended sentence, 68 months probation and periods in jail (Blackhurst and Gatton, 2002). He explains in *Adult Video News* that "[a] lap dance is not a hardcore sexual product like an adult video, they are radically different businesses. But, there's enough synergy between the two that one could gain a lot of ground by dealing in both industries" (Nelson X, 2008, p. 82). He gives, as an example, the showing of the porn star, Jenna Jameson, in club bathrooms with Jameson saying, "Hi, I'm Jenna Jameson with Spearmint Rhino. While you have your dick in your hands, let me tell you about my new movie and some of the upcoming events at the Spearmint Rhino" (Nelson X, 2008).

Cross marketing

Porn and strip clubs are not only frequently created by the same market pimps and players, but they are generally promoted together, with the clubs acting as free billboards for porn. Thus the AVN Website, though it started as a mouthpiece of the porn industry, is now heavily involved in marketing strip clubs. There is, for instance, a strip club review section on the Website. The way the clubs are promoted can provide fascinating glimpses into the way the industry understands the motivations of the buyers. The advertising slogan of the 'upscale' strip club The Lodge in Dallas, for instance, is 'Take back your balls'. The club ran a local TV commercial "in which a timid husband hesitantly tell his wife he's going out with the guys. So she pulls out a key hidden in her blouse, unlocks the wall safe and takes out a box labelled, 'Mike's Balls'. With a disapproving look on her face she reluctantly hands them over" (The Lodge, undated, Website link no longer active). It seems reasonable to assume that this club sees men as wanting revenge or compensation for the fact that the women in their lives are no longer subservient, and may even be critical of their use of the sex industry. I call the practice in which men seek compensation for the better opportunities that women now enjoy in the public world, and the fact that they may rebel against unwanted sexual subservience in the home, *the outsourcing of women's subordination* (Jeffreys, 2009).

Conclusion

The basis of this burgeoning industry is the abuse of the bodies of women and girls. Governments derive taxes from the industry, as do local councils. Tourism, entertainment and fashion industries cross promote their products and make profits. Meanwhile the industry creates harms not just for the women in the porn, in the clubs and in the brothels, but for the status of all women. The sex industry constructs the model of what sex is, i.e. the servicing of aggressive male dominant sexuality. It makes it harder for women to create egalitarian relationships with men. The pornography and strip club industries deliver the subordinate sex class to the male ruling class in the form of bodily orifices to be stuffed, swollen and distended anuses to be stared at, naked bodies to be ogled. This industry of women's subordination and men's revenge stands right in the middle of the road of women's progress towards equality and it is growing and diversifying as we speak.

Bibliography

Bindel, Julie (25 March, 2010) 'Iceland: the world's most feminist country.' *The Guardian*, <http://www.guardian.co.uk/lifeandstyle/2010/mar/25/iceland-most-feminist-country>.

Blackhurst, Chris and Adrian Gatton (16 September, 2002) 'A gangland killing, lap dancers who are said to sell sex and the criminal past of the man behind the Spearmint Rhino empire' *Evening Standard*, London.

Bureau of Business Research, IC2 Institute and the Institute on Domestic Violence and Sexual Assault (2009) 'An Assessment of the Adult Entertainment Industry in Texas'. University of Texas.

Busama (n.d.) 'Busama Entertainment', <http://www.busama.com/> (accessed 9 November, 2010).

Coalition Against Trafficking in Women (CATWA) (December, 2010) 'Not Just Harmless Fun: the strip club industry in Victoria'. Melbourne, Australia.

Coy, Maddy, Miranda Horvath and Liz Kelly (2007) *'It's just like going to the supermarket': Men buying sex in East London*. Report for Safe Exit. Child and Woman Abuse Studies Unit, London Metropolitan University, London.

Eden, Isabel (2007) *Inappropriate Behaviour: Adult venues and licensing in London*. The Lilith Project, Eaves Housing, London.

Frank, Katherine (2002) *G-Strings and Sympathy. Strip Club Regulars and Male Desire*. Duke University Press, Durham and London.

Hanna, Judith Lynne (1998) 'Undressing the First Amendment and corseting the striptease dancer' *The Drama Review* Cambridge, Mass. 42 (2) pp. 38 (32).

Holsopple, Kelly (1998) *Strip Club Testimony*. The Freedom and Justice Center for Prostitution Resources: A Program of the Volunteers of America of Minnesota. 2825 East Lake Street, Minneapolis MN 55406.

Jeffreys, Sheila (2009) *The Industrial Vagina: The political economy of the global sex trade*. Routledge, London.

Jeffries, Samantha and Mark Lynch (2007) 'Female Striptease in the Sunshine State: A Description of Queensland's Live Adult Entertainment Industry and its Regulation' *Queensland University of Technology Law and Justice Journal*, <http://www.austlii.edu.au/au/journals/QUTLJJ/2007/15.html>.

Justin (7 October, 2010) 'The Benefits of Exotic Dancing' Busama Blog, <http://busamagroup.wordpress.com/2010/10/07/the-benefits-of-exotic-dancing/>.

Kipnis, Laura (2003) *Bound and Gagged. Pornography and the Politics of Fantasy in America*. Duke University Press, Durham.

Liepe-Levinson, Katherine (2002) *Strip Show. Performances of Gender and Desire*. Routledge, New York.

Montgomery, Dave (3 October, 2005) 'Industry trying to take its image upscale.' *Fort Worth Star-Telegram* (Texas).

Nelson X (August, 2008) 'The Evolution of the Gentlemen's Club' *Adult Video News*, <http://www.avnmedianetwork.com/magazine/avn/pastissues/August2008.html>.

Schweitzer, Dahlia (1999) 'Striptease: The Art of Spectacle and Transgression' *Journal of Popular Culture* 34 (1) pp. 65–75.

Tyler, Meagan (2009) 'Active Service. The Pornographic and Sexological Construction of Women's Sexuality in the West'. Unpublished Doctoral Thesis, University of Melbourne, Melbourne.

Ward, Helen and Sophie Day (2004) 'Sex work in context' in Sophie Day and Helen Ward (Eds) *Sex Work, Mobility and Health in Europe*. Kegan Paul, London, pp. 15–32.

Stella

Dancing Pornography

It didn't take long to learn how to switch it on, to spin around the brass poles that rose from the centre of the many podiums, to gauge the worth of the crowd, to give it just the right amount of energy. Too much and you wouldn't last the night, too little and you wouldn't pull the cash. It didn't take long to learn to copy the narrow definition of sexuality that made money on the floor, to assemble a costume of fuckability, become a real, living, purchasable manifestation of pornography. It took longer to learn to hustle, to leave aside my humanity and erect that false facade of happy whore, to become that simpering shallow shell of a woman we call a stripper: part air hostess, part sex slave. But it happened, and within a few shifts I was no longer a woman, certainly no lady, but one of 'The Girls'.

The diamond-hard world of glittering disco balls, fluorescent lit podiums, brass poles, booze and the constant thumping bass turned on at 10 am in time to catch the lonely lunch crowd. The regulars, those poor fuckers who we learned to sneer at, to pretend superiority over, to dissemble the reality of their power to purchase us with money earned in a real job in the sunlit world outside. They came to spend their lunch money on a moment's attention from a purchased pussy, while they ate the free meal provided by the club. Sober, these guys were harder to fleece, but being regulars, they would buy a dance if they didn't manage to see enough for free to satisfy them. You had to work efficiently to sort the wheat from the chaff and not waste time with the men who were just there for free food, a free look and to pretend they were living inside one of their well worn porn clips.

Twenty dollars for a song's worth of simulated sex out on the club floor. Fifty dollars for a Fantasy Dance: 3 songs' worth of private stripping in a seedy room downstairs, choose from nurse, schoolgirl or cheerleader. It sounds like easy money – one dance every half an hour and over the course of a 12-hour shift you'd have made some significant money. Some days I walked out with $800, some days I barely made $80. Most shifts I pulled between $150 and $250. Every day was long. Every day was hard. Every day someone forced me in some way – either licked, bit or poked me, sometimes even penetrated me, held me down, hurt me. Then there was the verbal degradation, by the customers and even ourselves. 'Come here bitch and dance on this', 'oh yeah, let me be your little whore'. They cut in, those words, they get inside you. That internalisation of slut slut slut.

Every day I was afraid that I would lose my job. There was no security; if the house said 'Go', you went. Once I gave my house fee to a bar girl who was doing the books, but failed to sign for it as I was being called to the podium to dance. She said she would enter it and I could sign later. When I returned to sign, she said I hadn't given her the money. I protested, but no one would believe me. It was the moment of truth for me: she was believed because she was a real person with a real job. I was just a stripper, a whore, probably a junkie and, no doubt, a thief. I had to pay again or leave the premises. The realisation that I was a stripper now, not a person, was wounding.

People seem to think that strippers work in some kind of protected and controlled environment. That they call the shots, backed up by the authority of the establishment and security staff. That the punters are the underdogs, the manipulated victims of those money-grabbing women who flaunt their sex appeal for cash and never have to pay out. Some strippers themselves perpetuate this myth, I'm not sure whether it is to justify their trade to the world, or to themselves and each other. Sometimes you do feel powerful, twirling around that pole like a dancer in a music box, captivated audience at your feet, but moments later, groped, pinched, and forced, that illusion is quickly broken.

Downstairs we were 'allowed' to open our legs, and we dangled this promise in front of the men like Rolex watches from the inside of a jacket. "Come downstairs where I can dance just for you, three songs and you have me all to yourself in the wildest fantasy dance you've ever wished for ..." The suggestion was always there, the suggestion is always there, when you are buying a woman, that you can script your own porn. Why wouldn't you get confused in the heady euphoria of purchasing a person, a person barely clothed, pretending the opportunity to take those stupid pieces of skimpy clothes off for you was the best thing that had happened to her all night? Minutes later, closed off in a room dimly lit and decorated like a bedroom, with her breasts pressed against your face and her naked vagina hovering above your erection, why wouldn't you think it was okay to force what you wanted on her? Why would you even think you were forcing her?

Downstairs in that carefully constructed porn world of flimsy fantasies, so intent on imitating the kitsch stereotyped scenarios watched on pay TV, in offices on desktop computers, on DVDs smuggled home, in clubs on large screen TVs, seen in newsagents, milkbars, calendars, on billboards ... why wouldn't the delusion deepen and widen to subsume reality? That's the point, isn't it? Aren't we all supposed to want to be porn stars?

Where I worked we took turns to dance on the podiums. It was part of our freelance 'contract' which we had to fulfill in order to operate within the club's rules. Once every couple of hours I would step up onto the podium table and dance around the brass pole, creating that image of free pussy and wanton sexuality that such clubs foster to draw their custom in. For 15 minutes I would rub myself up and down that senseless piece of metal, hoping that someone would pay me to take my g-string or bra off so that I could make some cash. On a crowded night, when men would stand 3-deep around the podiums, this could be a lucrative way to draw in some extra customers. On a bad shift, it was a time when you were just the centre of attention of a bunch of tightwads looking for an opportunity to make themselves look macho in front of their mates. The ugliest and most sexually violent crowds were those men who were there for each other rather than the women, seeking moments to prove their masculinity, their virility, to themselves and each other, fuelled by alcohol, fear and testosterone. On those nights, even inside the club it felt lawless, intimidating, and unsafe.

I really don't know how I found myself, at 23, dressed up as a schoolgirl, smacking my naked buttocks with a wooden ruler and chewing gum. It wasn't where I imagined I'd be. I also hadn't imagined taking the school dress off in a very small room, the chairs around the walls filled with charged-up, drunken men, pumped up with the insane belief that buying a dance from a stripper means that you own her, you can do what you like with her, and that she should shut the fuck up and take it. I hadn't seen in my future a time when I would be passed around that room, dry fucked and felt up, hit with the ruler, frightened and fragile like a rabbit in a petting zoo. It wasn't supposed to be like that, my future. I was smarter than that, but there I was, becoming further enmeshed in this foreign world, a long way from the offices and restaurants I'd previously worked in, and further still from the tertiary qualifications I knew I could achieve.

I guess it started a couple of years before when, after leaving a violent relationship with nothing, I'd answered an ad in the paper for 'glamour' modelling, or soft porn photography, and been published in a couple of those tacky porn mags for some easy cash. Stripping didn't seem so far from that – it was just the image of your body that was consumed, not the body itself, yes?

So while out drinking with male friends we found some flyers in a pub and they wanted to go and have a dance. I was curious, so we went. In my memory it seemed exotic – the lights and costumes made the women look beautiful, raunchy – pornographic. Stilettos and wigs, fake tans, wide white smiles and knowing looks echoed the images many of us have seen in porn flicks. One of the girls came and asked me if I was interested in working there. She talked up the working conditions and the money she made and before I knew what I was doing, I had taken the number, spurred on by the encouragement of my male friends. A couple of the blokes had dances and then we went home. I thought about it for a month or so and when my personal circumstances began to pinch harder, I rang and organised to go in. I mean, if I didn't like it, I could just stop and go back to waitressing, right?

I scored speed to cope with the stress of my first shift. While speeding, and while it was all optional, I can almost say I enjoyed it. I liked being looked at, I liked feeling sexy, and the provocative flirting came easily. An experienced girl took me in and introduced me around the floor, using my newness and my naivety as fresh bait to secure herself more cash, dancing doubles with me, the 'new girl'. I made a couple of hundred bucks that first night and felt powerful. I agreed to come back. I quit my day job. I was a showgirl.

The euphoria didn't last long. The tiredness, the agony of dancing for so many long hours on those ridiculous heels, the sheer length of the shifts, took their toll and I quickly grew weary of the vacuous world of the club. Some of my earnings went straight back into my costumes as the right look pulled more cash. A long, blonde wig could add $50–100 a night to your earnings; thigh-high PVC stiletto boots, another $50–100; new costumes, imported stripper shoes, proper stripper bikinis for sexy disrobing; acrylic nails, tans; all that Barbiefied junk popularised by those mindless porn flicks. For the career showgirls this included surgical procedures like boob jobs, often funded in part by the club, offered to promising girls who lacked that silicone contour that pornography has taught men to desire. The cost of keeping up was high. My days became caught up with grooming and sleeping, my nights with performing at the Club.

My relationships suffered; I was becoming more and more isolated. I started using heroin to soothe the pain, all of the pain: the physical pain of my deteriorating knees and back; the emotional pain of being nothing, negative space, dirt, slut, whore, stripper, junkie. The fear and desperation rose. I just couldn't afford to lose my job. I couldn't afford my heroin habit without it, and I couldn't face dancing without the heroin to buffer the ugliness and pain. My life became one tiny circle that revolved around dancing and scoring. But I never caught up with those debts. In fact, they grew as my life shrank. I was depressed, and desperately miserable.

There was very little socialising or support among the women in the club. Everyone tended to keep to themselves, but I did make friends with one other girl – she called herself Kelly. She had been a prostitute before she stripped and I was drawn to her positive attitude and upbeat persona on the floor and we sometimes worked together in double acts on slow nights. It was nice to know one other person there by her real name; that little intimacy meant a lot. Listening to her stories made me realise how thin the veil was between the stripping and prostitution worlds, with many of the women moving between the two. We were instructed by the management to refer men who were looking for prostitutes on, down the chain, to a brothel not far from the club. I wondered if there was a connection, as many men seemed to come to the club to 'warm up' before moving on to a brothel (see also Jeffreys, this volume).

It was against the club rules to go home with a customer, and any dancer caught doing so was fired. I could easily imagine how it would happen, and before long I had also left with a customer and, while not formally arranged, I accepted payment for my time afterwards. It happened more than once. I couldn't then, and I still struggle now, to call what I did prostitution, but by any definition it was … I suppose denial helped me keep going.

It is easy to imagine where my life may have gone if I had continued to follow this well trodden, spiralling path downwards. It was my body that tripped me up and forced me to change direction. My knees, which had gradually been failing me, finally became too sore and swollen to dance on, and my back, too laced with pain. I rang my father who reached out a loving hand and pulled me as far as he could out of the mire. After I had suffered through the withdrawal from my heroin addiction and my head had cleared, I put in a late application to university and, miraculously, was accepted. Within a few weeks I was studying.

It took me four and a half years to complete the degree. My body suffered from the damage I had done to it from dancing, making full-time study difficult, and my heart and mind suffered from their own slowly healing scars. I relapsed many times with heroin, and it took more than half a decade to overcome the burning need for some chemical amnesia. My personal grief was immense – the time wasted, the damage done, the lack of self-love, all stung me deeply and I struggled to heal. Writing this today, 12 years later, my eyes still prick with tears, and the fear that my own 3 daughters might suffer the same experiences and the fact that I may be incapable of stopping them, truly stills my heart.

I didn't think that stripping would have the profound and long reaching effect on my life that it did. I didn't realise that when I left it, it might not leave me, that each time I sold myself, each time I danced pornography, I altered myself, redefined myself, demeaned myself, erased myself on a fundamental level. The trauma from dancing came in many guises and has taken a long time to recover from. I left with my self-esteem in shreds, my pockets empty, my body damaged, and my heart filled with shame, both self-imposed and compounded by the social stigma of being a junkie stripper. It was a hair-raising ride to the bottom. I often wonder where life would have taken me if I hadn't been pressed by circumstance to become a stripper, if I had lived in a world without strip clubs, brothels, and other institutions built on the trade of flesh and so heavily reliant on people in compromised positions to feed them. I passionately hope that my daughters might inhabit such a world.

Melissa Farley

Pornography Is Infinite Prostitution[1]

Pornography is an act of prostitution

The first time I heard Evelina Giobbe[2] explain that "pornography is pictures of prostitution," a light bulb went on in my mind. Of course. How had the two gotten separated in the first place?

Prostitution is sexual violence that results in massive economic profit for some of its perpetrators. It is a gendered survival strategy based on the assumption of terrible risks by the woman in prostitution. Sexual violence and physical assault are the norm for women in all types of prostitution, regardless of its legal status or physical location.[3]

Although the real lives of those in prostitution and pornography are often indistinguishable from the experience of incest, intimate partner violence, and rape – human rights violations are obscured when pornography is falsely differentiated from other kinds of prostitution, as if they're not at all connected. Pornographers and their public relations people will fight to the death to deny the overlapping parallels of prostitution and pornography, but johns (punters) and comedians know there's little difference. Jay Leno joked, "Did you hear about the porn convention that is going on right now in Las Vegas? They say that you can mingle with porn stars at the convention. Yes, and they act just like everyday normal whores" (NBC Tonight Show, 17 January, 2007).

People laughed at the joke, but what made it funny for them, I wondered? The misogyny? Because he winked at what johns were getting away with: pretending to be just porn viewers when in fact they were really just good old johns? Did the audience experience complicity with Leno in his dehumanization

---

1 Many thanks to Harvey L. Schwartz and Eleanor Kenelly Gaetan for helpful edits.
2 Evelina Giobbe is a US feminist, and founder of WHISPER, Women Hurt in Systems of Prostitution Engaged in Revolt. WHISPER was one of the first organizations to offer survivors of prostitution support for exiting prostitution along with a feminist understanding of prostitution as domestic violence.
3 For resources and articles documenting the human rights violations of prostitution see the Coalition Against Trafficking in Women Website <www.catwinternational.org> or the Prostitution Research & Education Website <www.prostitutionresearch.com>.

of women? Did the listeners feel some kind of guilt or shame that made them laugh uncomfortably?

A john interviewed for a study of men who buy sex explained, "Yes, the woman in pornography is a prostitute. They're prostituting before the cameras. They're getting money from a film company rather than individuals" (Farley, 2007b, p. 147).

A survivor of prostitution further explained, 'Pornography is prostitution that is legalized as long as someone gets to take pictures ..." (Simonton and Smith, 2004, p. 355).

The same kinds of violence against women are perpetrated in both pornography and prostitution: verbal abuse, including racist verbal abuse, contempt, degradation, physical and sexual assault, and acts that are identical to torture as defined by international legal conventions.

A survivor of pornography and prostitution described their sameness, explaining that she had been physically hurt, raped on camera, and pressured to do more extreme sex acts on film, such as anal sex, just as women in prostitution are pressured by johns to perform more extreme sex acts (Simonton and Smith, 2004).

The conditions leading to entry into pornography are much the same as the conditions leading to entry into prostitution

The same factors that compel women into prostitution, compel women into pornography. These include:

➤ Poverty
➤ Vulnerability to deceptive job offers
➤ Racism
➤ Lack of educational and job training opportunities
➤ Childhood physical and sexual abuse
➤ Childhood neglect
➤ Sexual harassment
➤ Abandonment
➤ Culturally mainstreamed contempt for women and girls
➤ Seductive manipulation by sexual exploiters who are businessmen

Most women in the sex industry were sexually abused as children (Silbert and Pines, 1983; Nadon et al., 1998; Widom and Kuhns, 1996). The pornography replicates the sexual abuse, with psychological as well as physical coercion as the perp's means of control.

As in prostitution, women are coerced into pornography by threat, deception, or the threat of violence. After an agreement to perform one specific act of prostitution for the camera, many women tell us they are physically coerced into performing another and often more dangerous sex act.

The pornographer/pimp uses the camera as his tool of intrusive degradation. For example, she may be secretly filmed while using the toilet, with that footage used as pornography (Morita, 2004).

Women's economic desperation serves as a means of coercion into pornography. One woman explained that she was about to be evicted from her apartment when she saw an advertisement for nude photos. "The owner of the 'nude photo agency' offered me a place to live and a lot of other work if I did film. At that point in my life, I really didn't have any other options" (Simonton and Smith, 2004, p. 352).

A 20-year-old woman was employed at a Ukrainian 'modeling agency' that sent her to beauty pageants throughout Europe where she had the chance to meet rich men. The modeling agencies functioned as pimps and traffickers. Buyers from United Arab Emirates, France, Italy, Japan and Russia inspected the women in beauty pageants, chose those they wanted to buy, and then rented the young models for up to a month at a time. The young woman herself may not have known that the modeling job was actually prostitution (often including pornography) until she arrived in another country (Plekhanova, 2006).

A Nevada legal pimp specialized in hiring women who had previously made pornography videos. He then used their videos to promote his brothel, advertising 'pornstars for rent' (Mead, 2001). At this pimp's brothel, women told a research team that it was not possible to make much money *unless* they permitted the pimp to film their prostitution. Women new to prostitution reported intense pressure from this particular pimp to be filmed by him, even though they often preferred not to have that documentation made of their prostitution (Farley, 2007a).

Once their prostitution was documented via pornography, women felt that it defined and shamed them. In the long run, the pornography made it more difficult to escape the sex industry since it was a permanent record of their prostitution circulating on the Internet or in stores selling pornography.

The sold and re-sold film of prostitution that is pornography generates massive profits for pimps. But for her, it is infinite prostitution, a document of her sexual exploitation, her body exploited and masturbated over endlessly into the future as long as it generates profits. One session of paid sex in prostitution goes global on the Internet when she is turned into pornography.

Pornographers are specialty pimps

Pimps typically recruit women into prostitution by using pornography to glamorize the sex industry. Survivors at a public hearing on the harm of pornography testified that they had all been introduced to prostitution by pimps who showed them pornography (MacKinnon and Dworkin, 1997, p. 114). Once in prostitution, pimps use pornography to teach women and girls what sex acts to perform (Silbert and Pines, 1987, pp. 865–866).

Survivor Miki Garcia testified under oath that Hugh Hefner, pornographer and founder of *Playboy* magazine, was a pimp who controlled an international prostitution ring, and that Playmates under contract to *Playboy* were prostituting (MacKinnon, 2001, pp. 1539–1543).

In many cases, pornographers are indistinguishable from other pimps (see Nozaka, 1970). These predatory people exploit women's economic and psychological vulnerabilities, coercing them to get into and stay in the sex industry. Pornographers and pimps both take pictures to advertise the people they are selling. One pornographer proclaimed that he was in the business of "degrading whores for your viewing pleasure," clearly eliminating the alleged boundary between pornography and prostitution (in Jensen, 2006).

British torture pornographer Peter Acworth purchased a 14 million dollar building in San Francisco for his business in 2007. Acworth maintains he's just a pornographer, not a pimp. He's a fetishist with a camera who gets off by paying women to be terrorized, stuffed into boilers, hogtied, beaten, near-drowned, hung from ceilings.

Just as some prostitution is more violent than other prostitution, some pornography is more violent than other pornography. Calling it 'kink' not torture and calling the women he films 'models' not prostitutes, Acworth uses the same price structure used in prostitution: the more invasive and the more violent, the higher the price. In a newspaper interview, Acworth recruited women by publicizing the following rates for his pornography: "$700 for vaginal dildo and finger penetration; $800 for vaginal/anal dildo play *and* finger penetration; $900 for vaginal and/or oral sex; $1,000 for vaginal and oral sex plus anal dildos; $1,100 for vaginal and anal sex; and $1,300 for double penetration." Acworth offered more pay for "forced finger fucking" (Harper, 2007).[4]

Sometimes the violence is perpetrated by johns, pimps, and pornographers simply because they can and because women in prostitution, whether it's filmed

---

4   If you go to Acworth's Website, be forewarned that it contains disturbing photographs of women being tortured. <www.kink.com>

or not, are not considered worthy of safety, protection, or of being offered real alternatives. As one woman testified about the making of pornography:

'I got the shit kicked out of me,' … 'I was told before the video – and they said this very proudly, mind you – that in this line most of the girls start crying because they're hurting so bad … I couldn't breathe. I was being hit and choked. I was really upset, and they didn't stop. They kept filming. You can hear me say, "Turn the fucking camera off," and they kept going' (in Amis, 2001).

Research provides evidence for harmful effects of pornography

There is now research evidence for the harms generated by pornography. Some of the traumatic stress (PTSD) suffered by women in prostitution results from the ways that men use pornography of them and against them.[5] Having pictures taken of one's prostitution causes more distress than if the prostitution was not filmed. When their prostitution is filmed, the pornography haunts them for the rest of their lives, causing the women distress and anxiety about it being viewed by family, friends, or future employers. Women in prostitution whose buyers or pimps made pornography of them in prostitution had more severe symptoms of PTSD than did women who did not have pornography made of them (Farley, 2007b, p. 146).

Women explain that the harms of pornography are worse than prostitution alone. A survivor explained,

[P]ornography is much worse than prostitution because it affects me for the rest of my life. It's not like I just … had sex with a john, collected my money, and went home … I'm still exploited all over the Internet ten years later. People recognize me. I'm harassed because of it. My kids are being harassed (in Simonton and Smith, 2004, p. 355).

In other research, pornography has been shown to affect men's sexual aggression against women. Malamuth and colleagues have shown that in combination with other factors, pornography contributes to men's increased sexual aggression against women. These factors include impersonal sex, hostile masculine identification, a history of family violence, adolescent delinquency, and attitudes supportive of aggression (Malamuth and Pitpitan, 2007).

In findings that are consistent with Malamuth's, a research study of 110 sex buyers in Scotland compared high frequency prostitute-users to low frequency

---

5   The psychiatric diagnosis of posttraumatic stress disorder (PTSD) describes mental and physical avoidance behaviors, psychological numbing, social distancing, flashbacks, and anxious physiologic hyperarousal that result from extreme emotional distress. Two-thirds of women, men, and transgendered people in prostitution in 9 countries suffered PTSD at the same level as rape survivors, combat veterans, and state-sponsored torture survivors. See Farley et al. (2003).

users. The most frequent prostitution users were also the most frequent pornography users. The most frequent prostitution users were also more likely to have committed sexually aggressive acts against non-prostituting women (Farley et al., in press).

Other research studies have found similar statistical associations between pornography and prostitution. Monto and McRee (2005) compared the pornography use of 1,672 US men who had been arrested for soliciting women in prostitution with samples of US men who had not used women in prostitution. Men who had purchased sex were far more likely to use pornography on a regular basis than men who had not purchased sex. Men who were repeat users of women in prostitution were more likely than first time users of prostituted women to use pornography, and first time users of women in prostitution were more likely than men who had not bought sex to have used pornography.

It is possible that more frequent use of pornography supports and stimulates men in their use of women in prostitution. Three studies support the feminist understanding of prostitution as a form of violence against women: the Scottish sex buyer study described above, the Monto and McRee study in 2005, and a meta-analysis from Hald, Malamuth and Yuen in 2010 that found a significant association between pornography use and attitudes supporting violence against women.

In the real world, pornography, prostitution, and sex trafficking are indistinguishable

Human rights violations are obscured when trafficking is falsely differentiated from prostitution and pornography. The pimps' and johns' spin is that trafficking is bad but prostitution is a good-enough job for poor women. Some even say that *forced trafficking* is bad but *voluntary migration for sex work* is OK when the experience of the women is the same in both situations. Or that non-consenting prostitution is a problem but if there's a camera in the room, pornography is then assumed to be consenting.

There is an endless stream of words that cover up the interconnections of the sex trafficking industry.[6] Like other global businesses, it has domestic and international sectors, marketing sectors, a range of physical locations out of which it operates in each community, many different owners and managers, and it is constantly expanding as technology, law, and public opinion permit. Pornography today is used as advertising for prostitution and as a way to traffic

---

6   Many thanks to Annie Lobert, Las Vegas, for the words 'sex trafficking industry'.

women (MacKinnon, 2005). Creating disconnections when in reality all sectors of the hydra-headed sex trafficking industry are deeply connected – leaves the door open for ideological arguments that permit pimps and johns to defend harmful practices. Manipulating these false distinctions can result in deep confusion about the nature of sexual harm and sexual freedom. When pornography is conceptually morphed into sex work, then brutal exploitation by pornographers becomes an employer–employee relationship. When prostitution is defined as labor, the predatory purchase of a human being by a john becomes an everyday business transaction.

Defining pornography as a choice can be confusing to women in it as well as to the public. She accepts the pornographers' propaganda that it's her choice, so she blames herself for the harm done to her, even though she often has no other options.

False distinctions confuse people who are trying to abolish these human rights violations. Endless elaboration on the differences rather than a focus on the essential similarities between pornography, prostitution and trafficking makes it challenging to end these sexual exploitation businesses.

In some scenarios, pimps and johns create a false distinction between modeling and prostitution. It's called modeling for the viewer/john of an Italian beauty pageant who can afford "dates with available, beautiful women" but it's experienced as trafficking for the 'contestant' who comes from desperate circumstances in the Ukraine and who accepted an offer to come to Italy to meet interesting, affluent men.

Although described as separate entities, Web-based, video, and print pornography are integral to the sex industry, including prostitution and trafficking. Legal brothel owners have attempted to "cross fertilize" prostitution with legal adult businesses such as strip clubs, Internet sex sites and pornography (Hausbeck and Brents, 2000). *The Girls of Cheetah's* is pornography made at a Las Vegas strip club where prostitution happens (Jordan, 2004, p. 107). Connecting stripping and pornography, a strip club Website advertised, "Breeding pornstars: one showgirl at a time!!!" (<http://tour.stripclubnetwork.com/>).

The overlap between different arms of the sex industry is illustrated by a law enforcement investigation that took place in Las Vegas. Appearing to be an office complex from the street, a sex business operation blended pornography production with escort and web cam prostitution.[7] The pimp/pornographer

---

7   On a web cam site, the john pays to chat with women who perform prostitution on streaming video, performing in real time what masturbating johns pay them to do.

rented six offices that functioned as Internet pornography businesses, cyber-peepshow prostitution with a web cam, as well as a location out of which women were illegally pimped to hotels and to a brothel (confidential Nevada law enforcement source).

As the Leno joke indicates, the adult industry trade shows are promotion for prostitution. The sex trafficking industry is named an 'adult industry' not only to conceal the fact that it's prostitution but to manipulate people into seeing the sex industry as grown-up, mature. In Australia and in the United States, sex trade shows shout out the message that prostitution is a fun, consensual, lifestyle choice accompanied by HIV-free health and the right to privacy. Despite these claims, at their core these sex trade shows have been described as "19th century freak shows"[8] where "the industry rejects no act of exploitation demanded by customers" (O'Connor and Healy, 2006, p. 18). The robotic, mocking and at times sadistic enactments of 'erotic play' at sex trade shows are especially harmful because of the pretense of genuine pleasure.

Pornography is a document of a woman's humiliation (Clarke, 2004, p. 205). It's a record of what men's extreme domination of women looks like – in all its violently racist and classist specificity. But there are a few positive signs of real social change. Here's some good news: Glenn Marcus, like Peter Acworth of kink.com, ran a torture pornography Website. A woman who was psychologically coerced by Marcus to permit pornography of her to be sold on Slavespace.com brought charges against Marcus who was her pimp/pornographer/trafficker. At one point he stuffed a ball gag in her mouth, sewed her mouth shut with surgical needles and hung her on a wall.

Her attorneys, as I understand it, used the following definition: *Sex trafficking is coercing or selling a person into a situation of sexual exploitation, such as prostitution or pornography.*

On 5 March, 2007, pornographer Marcus was convicted of sex trafficking (Bartow, 2007). This United States legal decision reflects a deepening understanding of how pornography harms women and the ways in which pornography and prostitution are the same for the person who is being sexually exploited for profit.

---

8   Andrew Masterson, the *Age*, 1998, p. 2 cited in Sullivan (2007) p. 181.

Bibliography

Amis, Martin (17 March, 2001) 'A Rough Trade' *The Guardian* <http://www.guardian.co.uk/books/2001/mar/17/society.martinamis1> (accessed 20 March, 2001).

Bartow, Ann (24 May, 2007) 'Bondage Webmaster Likely Going to Jail. Feminist Law Professors' <http://feministlawprofs.law.sc.edu/?p=1833> (accessed June, 2008).

Clarke, D.A. (2004) 'Prostitution for everyone: Feminism, globalization, and the "sex" industry' in Christine Stark and Rebecca Whisnant (Eds) *Not For Sale: Feminists Resisting Prostitution and Pornography*. Spinifex Press, North Melbourne.

Farley, Melissa (2007a) *Prostitution and Trafficking in Nevada: Making the Connections*. Prostitution Research & Education, San Francisco.

Farley, Melissa (2007b) '"Renting an Organ for 10 Minutes:" What Tricks Tell Us About Prostitution, Pornography, and Trafficking' in David E. Guinn and Julie DiCaro (Eds) *Pornography: Driving the Demand for International Sex Trafficking*. Captive Daughters Media. Los Angeles, pp. 144–152.

Farley, Melissa, Ann Cotton, Lynne Jacqueline, Sybil Zumbeck, Frida Spiwak, Maria E. Reyes, Dinorah Alvarez, Ufuk Sezgin (2003) 'Prostitution and Trafficking in 9 Countries: Update on Violence and Posttraumatic Stress Disorder' *Journal of Trauma Practice* 2 (3/4), pp. 33–74.

Farley, Melissa, Jan Macleod, Lynn Anderson and Jacqueline M. Golding (in press) 'Attitudes and Social Characteristics of Men Who Buy Sex in Scotland' *Psychological Trauma: Theory, Research, Practice, and Policy.*

Hald, Gert Martin, Neil Malamuth and C. Yuen (2010) 'Pornography and Attitudes Supporting Violence Against Women: Revisiting the Relationship in Nonexperimental Studies' *Aggressive Behavior* 36 (1), pp.14–20.

Harper, Will (21 February, 2007) 'Kinky Town' *San Francisco Weekly* <http://www.sfweekly.com/content/printVersion/459991/> (accessed 22 February, 2007).

Hausbeck, Kathryn and Barbara G. Brents (2000) 'Inside Nevada's Brothel System' in Ron Weitzer (Ed) *Sex for Sale: Prostitution, Pornography and the Sex Industry*. Routledge, New York, pp. 217–243.

Jensen, Robert (2006) 'The Paradox of Pornography' *Op Ed News* <http://www.opednews.com/articles/opedne_robert_j_060201_the_paradox_of_porno.htm> (accessed 1 February, 2006)

Jordan, Brent K. (2004) *Stripped: Twenty years of secrets from inside the strip club*. Morris Publishing, Kearney, Nebraska.

MacKinnon, Catharine A. (2001) 'Testimony of Miki Garcia' *Sex Equality*. pp. 1539–1543. Foundation Press, New York.

MacKinnon, Catharine A. (2005) 'Pornography as Trafficking' *Michigan Journal of International Law* 26 (4) pp. 993–1012.

MacKinnon, Catharine A. and Andrea Dworkin (1997) *In Harm's Way: The Pornography Civil Rights Hearings*. Harvard University Press, Cambridge, MA.

Malamuth, Neil M. and Eileen V. Pitpitan (2007) 'The effects of pornography are moderated by men's sexual aggression risk' in David E. Guinn and Julie DiCaro (Eds) *Pornography: Driving the Demand in International Sex Trafficking*. Captive Daughters Media, Los Angeles, pp. 125–143.

Mead, Rebecca (23 April, 2001) 'American Pimp' *New Yorker* <http://www.rebeccamead.com/2001/2001_04_23_art_reno.htm> (accessed 9 July, 2003).

Monto, Martin A. and N. McRee (2005) 'A comparison of the male customers of female street prostitutes with national samples of men' *International Journal of Offender Therapy and Comparative Criminology* 49, pp. 505–529.

Morita, Seiya (2004) 'Pornography, prostitution, and women's human rights in Japan' in Christine Stark and Rebecca Whisnant (Eds) *Not for Sale: Feminists Resisting Prostitution and Pornography*. Spinifex Press, North Melbourne, pp. 64–83.

Nadon, Susan M., Catherine Koverola and Eduard H. Schludermann (1998) 'Antecedents to Prostitution: Childhood Victimization' *Journal of Interpersonal Violence* 13, pp. 206–221.

Nozaka, Akiyuki (1968/1970) *The Pornographers* (translated by Michael Gallagher, 1970). Charles Tuttle Publishing, Tokyo.

O'Connor, Monica and Grainne Healy (2006) 'The Links between Prostitution and Sex Trafficking: a Briefing Handbook' Coalition Against Trafficking in Women <www.catwinternational.org>

Plekhanova, Lena (10 August, 2006) 'Prostitution remains issue for Ukrainian modeling industry' *Kyiv Post* <http://www.kyivpost.com/business/general/24915/> (accessed 11 December, 2006).

Silbert, Mimi H. and Ayala M. Pines (1983) 'Early Sexual Exploitation as an Influence in Prostitution' *Social Work* 28, pp. 285–289.

Silbert, Mimi H. and Ayala M. Pines (1987) 'Pornography and Sexual Abuse of Women' *Sex Roles* 10, p. 857.

Simonton, Ann and Carol Smith (2004) 'Who are Women in Pornography?: A conversation' in Christine Stark and Rebecca Whisnant (Eds) (2004) *Not for Sale: Feminists Resisting Prostitution and Pornography*. Spinifex Press, North Melbourne, pp. 352–361.

Sullivan, Mary (2007) *Making Sex Work. A Failed Experiment with Legalised Prostitution*. Spinifex Press, North Melbourne.

Widom, Cathy Spatz and Joseph B. Kuhns (1996) 'Childhood victimization and subsequent risk for promiscuity, prostitution, and teenage pregnancy: A prospective study' *American Journal of Public Health* 86 (11), pp. 1607–1612.

Abigail Bray

Capitalism and Pornography: the Internet as a Global Prostitution Factory

She is sold and bought minute by minute, breath by breath
In the slave markets of the earth – Kotzia is near here
Wake up early.
Wake up to see it.
She is a whore in the rotten-houses
The german drill for conscripts
And the last
Endless miles of the national highway towards the centre
In the suspended meats from Bulgaria.
And when her blood clots and she can take no more
Of her kind being sold so cheaply
She dances barefoot on the tables a zeibekiko
Holding in her bruised blue hands
A well sharpened axe.
Loneliness,
Our loneliness I say. Its our loneliness I am speaking about,
Is a axe in our hands
That over your heads is revolving revolving revolving revolving

– 'Three Clicks Left', Katerina Gogou (1940–1993)[1]

To those who think critically about pornography, it is clear that "[p]ornography *is* prostitution" (Whisnant, 2004, p. 20).[2] The bodies within pornography have been bought and sold for sex. Kathleen Barry writes that the "producers and distributors can be defined as pimps as they are living off the earnings of prostitutes" (Barry, 1979, p. 99). The pornographer buys the living sexual labour of human beings and then pimps their prostitution to 'johns' across the Net. Porn has become so normalised as liberating adult sexual entertainment that it is difficult to think of pornographers as pimps, the global porn industry as a form of human trafficking, porn consumers as 'john' or 'buyers', or the people in pornography as prostituted women. Instead, we are encouraged to use a language that masks the prostitution pornography is founded on, and that

---

1   This is from the translation offered by Taxikipoli, <http://libcom.org/history/katerina-gogou-athens-anarchist-poetess-1940-1993>.
2   See also Sheila Jeffreys (2008), Diana Russell (1993).

disconnects us from the living bodies who are prostituted. Women and men whose bodies are bought and sold by pornographers are celebrated as 'actors' or sexually self-empowered 'pornstars'. Pornographers are described as 'film makers' or 'producers in the adult entertainment business', while men who pay pornographers or porn-hosting ISPs, are called 'consumers' or 'porn users', if they are named at all.

Internet pornography is a complex form of prostitution: the social and economic relations within pornography go beyond our commonsense under-standings of prostitution. By commonsense understanding of prostitution I mean a commercial transaction between a living prostitute, a buyer/john, and a pimp or brothel owner, that occurs for a specific period of time at a specific location. Within Internet pornography prostitution these kinds of social and economic relations – between a living prostitute, a pimp and/or john – and these kinds of historical constraints – time and place – are radically transformed. To put it simply, her living labour is prostituted for a day or so by a pornographer so that her prostitution can be sold for an unlimited amount of time. She is prostituted in a porn studio in North America so that her prostitution can be circulated globally. She is purchased once by a john so that an unlimited number of anonymous johns and pimps can sell and buy her prostitution. Through the production process of pornography, one act of prostituted sexual labour is reproduced indefinitely and put to work 24 hours a day, for an infinite number of years, across the world, *without pay*. Understood this way, pornography prostitution is closer to sexual slavery than it is to commonsense understandings of prostitution.

Within pornographic prostitution, the living labour of a prostituted woman is transformed into dead labour through the process of mass production. What she has produced with her living body does not belong to her, her prostitution is taken from her and turned into a commodity, a thing, dead, yet potent. To paraphrase Marx, pornography is dead labour, that, vampire-like, only lives by sucking living labour, and lives the more, the more labour it sucks.[3] Her living labour is transformed by Net porn into an indestructible commodity. It is impossible to completely remove pornography from the Net. As soon as her prostitution enters the Net, her prostitution remains there forever as an endlessly circulating commodity. In this way, her prostitution lives on after she is dead. Her

---

3   See Karl Marx, *Capital: A Critique of Political Economy* Vol. 1 where he writes "[c]apital is dead labour, that, vampire-like, only lives by sucking living labour, and lives the more, the more labour it sucks" (1976, p. 342).

prostitution, in other words, will be put to work by the pornography industry after her body has died. *Ultimately, all pornography becomes the prostitution of the dead.*

It is worth recognising that, already, quite a few of the prostituted men and women within pornography are no longer alive. Many pornography prostitutes die young. In 2011, 23-year-old Caroline Berger died from brain damage caused by cosmetic surgeons who injected 800g (28oz) of silicone into her breasts. "She's a hero," comments a john, "[s]he died doing something awesome to the extent that most people wouldn't dream of."[4] 'The Dead Porn Stars Archive – Frances Farmer's Revenge' contains a lengthy list of deceased porn prostitutes with details of their cause of death that include suicide, murder, drug overdose, and AIDS.[5] 'The dead porn stars memorial' also features a similar list.[6] 'A tribute to dead pornstars' reads glowingly:

> These dead pornstars were trailblazers and many paid a heavy price for their adventures in the adult entertainment arena. Whether thru suicide, accident, drug overdose or illness due to a crazy lifestyle, these dead pornstars still touched more that our peckers. They touched our lives and gave us a visual remembrance that we will never forget.[7]

For 'adventures in the adult entertainment industry' read: prostituted by the pornography industry; for 'heavy price' read: death. Destructive prostitution is masked as a gift 'they gave us' (the johns) that extends beyond the grave.

Pornography prostitution can be described as a kind of virtual slavery: once in the Net, her prostitution is caught up in an endless system of exchange that feeds off her living labour without paying her for it. The perversion increases once we recognise that this virtual slavery continues after she has died. In this way, all pornography becomes the virtual sexual slavery of the dead. The pornography industry feeds off the bodies of the living and the dead: it is a system of virtual sexual slavery that makes no distinction between profit made from the living, or profit made from the dead.

The technology involved in pornography prostitution not only transforms her living labour into an infinite form of prostitution (see Farley, this volume), but the production process also refashions her living body. The dead labour of pornography technology, to use a Marxist term, dominates her living labour, her very body, her life activity. High definition communication technology,

---

4   See Melinda Tankard Reist's blog on <http://melindatankardreist.com/2011/02/one-wanted-a-bigger-bum-one-wanted-bigger-breasts-both-are-dead/>.

5   See: <http://www.francesfarmersrevenge.com/stuff/archive/oldnews/deadpornstars.htm>.

6   See: <http://www.youtube.com/watch?v=r0q_VGacfNk>. The video mentions that one girl, Taylor Summers, was murdered during a bondage scene. Her death was filmed as pornography.

7   See: <http://www.pornstarcraze.com>.

for example, transformed the living bodies of pornography prostitutes. In his homage to the technological innovations created by Big Porn, Patchen Barss reports that with the emergence of Blu-ray and HD, the bodies of pornography prostitutes begin to change:

> [H]itherto invisible 'flaws' – from moles and wrinkles to razor burn and surgery scars – were suddenly visible to audiences. This forced actors and producers to take all manner of compensatory action, including changing camera angles, increasing makeup, changing diet and exercise habits and even undergoing cosmetic surgery to remove the smallest imperfection. The technology has created too much clarity for the fuzzy fantasies that are the heart of pornography' (2010, p. 274).

This is a clear example of the way that the dead labour of the pornographic production process changes the living bodies of prostitutes. The new HD communication technology contains an implicit command to prostitutes to transform their bodies. To become a viable commodity, she must now spend extra time and money refashioning her body with diet, exercise and cosmetic surgery. This intensifies her economic exploitation, for it is unlikely that a pornographer will pay her for breast implants or cosmetic surgery for her vagina and face. The new HD pornography technology expands her exploitation into her everyday life, taking her time and money just as it demands that she transform her body at her own expense. Capitalist technologies begin to converge on her body, extracting profit from an already exploited human being. Her body becomes a thing she must pay for so that she can prostitute herself. Her relationship to her own body becomes distorted in the mirror of pornography – her body is transformed into a sexual object she must pimp.

The new surgically altered HD porn body is not confined to the Net. With the mass marketing of pornography, and the pornification of everyday life, the image of the HD porn body moves into the mainstream: Brazilian waxes, breast implants, cosmetic surgery for women's genitals, weight-loss drugs, make-up, hair products, Botox. A complex capitalist system of body modification is opened up and expanded by the new demands of HD pornography technology. Looking like a 'porn star' becomes confused with sexual self-empowerment, as though relating to her own body like a pimp were an act of freedom. Yet the money she invests in transforming herself into a sexually competitive commodity is rarely returned.

As Dunia Montenegro says, "[i]n porn, the money is a big cake and the [large] companies eat it all. The porn actress gets nothing" (in Barss, 2010, p. 279). Montenegro's solution is to create her own pornography Website and copyright her prostitution. Without this she "would get paid a couple of hundred dollars for a day of having sex on camera, and would never see another dime of profit" (Barss, 2010, p. 279). That Montenegro has pimped her own body is often celebrated as an example of self-empowerment and a role model for prostituted women. Attempts at reforming the sex industry, for example, the creation of better working conditions for prostituted women, women-owned porn companies and so on, are opportunistic. There is nothing to celebrate about the increased wages of a pornography prostitute; it is merely the temporary lengthening and lightening of a chain and nothing more. The point is to break the socio-economic chains that have constrained women's and girls' work options to the barbaric point where a society offers women prostitution as a way of economic survival. Indeed, Montenegro's example merely calls attention to the extreme levels of exploitation in the pornography industry. Unable to copyright their own prostitution, women are selling themselves for next to nothing. Pornography becomes, in effect, a form of sexual slavery.

The aggressive presence of the pornography industry within social networking sites, and across the Net as a whole, has normalised this trend. It is cool and fun to act like a sexy hot porn star. "We're all prostitutes!" shouts the Facebook status of a teenager who is posed half naked on her bed. Within MSN, for example, there are peer-to-peer networks where women share pornographic pictures of themselves and perform pornographic acts on web cam without being paid. Adult social networking Websites also encourage women to web cam themselves to peers without pay. So-called homemade porn has a large circulation, seeping outside peer groups into territories women cannot predict. This new phenomenon cannot be called prostitution because women are not being paid for producing pornography. But what it reveals is that pornography prostitution has become so wedded to neoliberal ideas of sexual liberation that women are pimping themselves for free.

Although 'free' pornography might not generate money (and today the majority of pornography on the Net is free, which is not to say that ISPs do not benefit from it) it does generate powerful social or symbolic capital. In other words, the explosion of 'free porn' and peer-to-peer porn does not mean, as the porn industry often argues, the death of the porn industry as such. What it does reveal is that the idea of pornography has moved up from being part of a system of embodied economic exchange to becoming a form of symbolic exchange. Now pornography has become a form of social capital and has attached itself to the reproduction of social status. The pornification of everyday life has been achieved by the elevation of pornography prostitution to the level of social status.

Pornography prostitution has been re-branded by capitalism as the new 'cool':

porn is cool, pimps and hos are cool, the Playboy logo is cool, DIY porn is cool, getting off on watching a prostituted woman gag and struggle under a quadruple penetration is *cool*. Once, pornography was associated with sexually frustrated old men; now pornography is associated with sexually successful, hip young men, women, and teens. Pornography is so cool that the global anti-capitalist movement have yet to really notice or fight it.

Combating the new cool social status of pornography is challenging. When people question their sexual and emotional investments in pornography they risk losing their 'cool' social status. However, this social status is a collective mask that hides the real face of global pornography. The sexual exploitation of living prostitutes to the point of death and beyond, the relentless violent degradation of the living bodies of women, children and men is nothing to gain cool social status from (see also Bray, 2011). And while pornography has been elevated to the level of social status and social capital, the global prostitution factory of pornography continues to thrive.

Time and time again, it has been proven that prostitution is both a symptom of women's oppression and the foundation of a socio-economic system which treats women as sexual objects to be traded, abused, and discarded. As the shock and awe tactics of disaster capitalism smash through decades of workers' rights across the world, plunging millions into poverty, more women will be forced to turn to pornography prostitution in order to survive. Women and children are always the poorest of the poor. These women cannot copyright their prostitution like Montenegro; they will not be in a position to negotiate for better pay with pimps. Many, like women immigrants and their children, will become sexual slaves in networks of human trafficking, their bodies turned into pornography. Pornography is a feminist issue, a social justice issue, a human rights issue and a socialist issue that requires urgent attention.

Are the women in the porn you are watching still alive?

Bibliography

'A Tribute to Dead Porn Stars', <http://www.pornstarcraze.com/> (accessed 9 March, 2011).

Barry, Kathleen (1979) *Female Sexual Slavery*. New York University Press, New York.

Barss, Patchen (2010) *The Erotic Engine: How Pornography Has Powered Mass Communication from Gutenberg to Google*. University of Queensland Press, St. Lucia.

Bray, Abigail (2011) 'Merciless Doctrines: Child Pornography, Censorship, and Late Capitalism', *Signs* (Autumn, in press).

Dead Porn Stars Memorial, <http://www.youtube.com/watch?v=r0q_VGacfNk> (accessed 9 March, 2011).

Frances Farmer's Revenge, <http://www.francesfarmersrevenge.com/stuff/archive/oldnews/deadpornstars.htm> (accessed 9 March, 2011).

Gogou, Katerina: Athens' Anarchist Poetess, 1940–1993, <http://libcom.org/history/katerina-gogou-athens-anarchist-poetess-1940-1993>.

Jeffreys, Sheila (2008) *The Idea of Prostitution*. Spinifex Press, North Melbourne.

Marx, Karl (1976) *Capital: A Critique of Political Economy, Volume 1* Trans. Ben Fawkes, Penguin, Harmondsworth. Originally published in 1867.

Russell, Diana (1993) *Against Pornography: The Evidence of Harm*. Russell Publications, Berkeley, California.

Tankard Reist, Melinda (2011) 'One Wanted a Bigger Bum, One Wanted Bigger Breasts, Both Are Dead', <http://melindatankardreist.com/2011/02/one-wanted-a-bigger-bum-one-wanted-bigger-breasts-both-are-dead/>.

Whisnant, Rebecca (2004) 'Confronting Pornography: Some Conceptual Basics' in *Not For Sale: Feminists Resisting Prostitution and Pornography* edited by Rebecca Whisnant and Christine Stark, Spinifex Press, North Melbourne, pp. 15–27.

Hiroshi Nakasatomi[1]

When Rape Becomes a Game: *RapeLay* and the Pornification of Crime[2]

The animated computer game *RapeLay*[3] contains content based on brutally misogynistic attitudes towards women and the normalisation of the sexual enslavement of women and girls. The game features scenes that depict women and girls being subjected to commuter train groping, stalking, forceful confinement, rape and gang rape until they succumb to the assaults, even up to the point where a victim is shown begging her rapist to abuse her.

The concern of critics of pornography has been that men who watch rape scenes in pornography might emulate them like a game and perpetrate rape in real life. Ironically, *RapeLay* has now made rape an actual 'game'. In fact, *RapeLay* stands for 'rape play', and the game has turned rape into a recreational activity. *RapeLay*'s aim is to turn women into sexual slaves by taming them through sexual assault. *RapeLay* portrays the male player as a tamer who is in a position of power and control over women. It is important to note that inflicting rape and controlling the women in the game gives a sense of pleasure and entertainment to the male player and instils in him a rapist mind-set.

RapeLay inflicts a severe blow on the reproductive autonomy of women

One of the notable aspects of *RapeLay* is its brutal attack on, and attempt to control, the reproductive functioning of women. One of the main scenes of *RapeLay* depicts a mother and her two daughters being raped and made pregnant and then forced to have abortions. Failing to make the victims get abortions

---

1 Translated by Caroline Norma and R. Sanjeewa Weerasinghe.
2 This is an edited excerpt of an article about the Japanese animated computer game *RapeLay* (see Hiroshi Nakasatomi, 2009).
3 Women's groups around the world protested this game's release in 2009, and a complaint to the Australian Communications and Media Authority by Melinda Tankard Reist in that year prompted the Australian government to prohibit the downloading of the game, in spite of opposition from groups like Electronic Frontiers Australia (Moses, 2010). In the USA and the UK, Equality Now led the protest campaign, and received "vitriolic rape and death threats" as a result (Equality Now, 2009).

results in the game player being stabbed to death by one of the victims. Pregnant women are depicted as demons in this segment which also confirms the misogyny of the game.

Another criminal aspect of *RapeLay* is its plot which contains a scene in which a mother and her two daughters are raped out of revenge to punish an older sister who, after witnessing a rapist sexually assaulting a woman on a commuter train, reported the incident to police. *RapeLay* conveys the idea that reporting sexual assault to authorities is a betrayal of men and men's sexual privilege. Reporting is portrayed as a treacherous act, and this is a further indication of the male-dominant ideals that permeate the game.

RapeLay as a form of child pornography

The Komeito Party and parts of Japan's media see *RapeLay* as a problem confined to the issue of child pornography. Indeed, *RapeLay* does contain child pornography – of the 3 female victims depicted in the game, 2 are children below the age of 18. However, it is common knowledge that under Japan's *Act on Punishment of Activities Relating to Child Prostitution and Child Pornography and the Protection of Children*, only materials containing images of *real* children are legally defined as child pornography. Under this definition, computer games such as *RapeLay* which use graphically animated images do not count as child pornography. At present, there are 2 laws in Japan that govern the sexual depiction of a person. The first is Article 175 of the Penal Code: 'Distribution of Obscene Objects'. The article applies to any person who distributes, sells or displays in public an obscene document, drawing, or other item. The second is the *Child Prostitution and Child Pornography Act*, which regulates the sexually explicit depiction of persons under 18 years. The scope of Article 175 is limited because the law applies only to the public display of genitals and sexual intercourse. On the other hand, the *Child Prostitution and Child Pornography Act* can be more widely applied. However, while images in comic, animation and computer graphics are subject to regulation under Article 175, they are not covered in the *Child Prostitution and Child Pornography Act*, and this makes the *Act* even more limited with regard to child pornography offences than Article 175.

As a result, children are endlessly subjected to abuse, torture, and exploitation in a sexually explicit way in the animated world in a fairly open manner in Japan. These materials circulate more or less freely on the Internet. Animated depictions portray children in a sexually explicit way which makes the material child pornography. Nonetheless, people in Japan argue that animated depictions cannot constitute child pornography because, they say, in the animated world children cannot have their rights violated. As a result, the animated depiction of sexually explicit images of children continues in an unregulated state in Japan. The legal regulation of pornography, including rape simulation computer games, is strongly opposed by many factions in Japan. Opposition to the regulation of pornographic computer games is stronger than opposition to the regulation of child pornography, but only because the number of gaming enthusiasts – including the majority of male left-wing intellectuals – is larger than the number of child pornography users.

RapeLay as a rape simulator

The main reason *RapeLay* has attracted international criticism is not because of its computer generated graphics or video imagery, but because it is a computer game. If *RapeLay* had been an animated movie containing pornography, its pornographic content might not have generated such international outrage, given the relatively common circulation of animated films containing this kind of content. International uproar over *RapeLay* arose because of the understanding that violent and pornographic computer games have a stronger impact on users than pornographic comics or animated films. People in Japan came to understand this dangerous effect of rape simulation games only once international campaigns emerged over *RapeLay*. There is a clear correlation between men using violent pornography to seek sexual gratification and the perpetration of rape against women. Graphically animated violent pornography is not currently banned in Japan because of the argument that a rights violation does not occur due to the absence of a victim. However, it can be clearly demonstrated that violent computer games do violate children's rights.

In rape simulation computer games like *RapeLay*, the player can simulate rape which makes the impact of the violent pornography stronger. The impact is stronger because the player uses his hands (through a console) to move the on-screen victim in any direction he wants. He is able to manipulate the victim a full 360 degrees as if the victim were a puppet on a string. The game player is able to use the characters as objects for his sexual gratification, as things he can play around with. As a result, the player feels a sense of dominance and conquest over the female characters in the game.

The extent of the harmful impact of games like *RapeLay*, if the player acts out his experience in real life, is immeasurable. Accordingly, in the campaign to enact legislation to ban all forms of child pornography in Japan it is important that the harmful effect of animated pornography is recognised. With the spread of animated child pornography throughout the world via the Internet, more and more countries will come to prohibit such material. This will increase pressure on countries like Japan that do not maintain a ban, and on countries like Japan from where the material originates.[4]

Bibliography

Equality Now (2009) Information on Japan for consideration by the Committee on the Elimination of Discrimination against Women at its 44th Session, <http://www2.ohchr.org/english/bodies/cedaw/docs/ngos/Equality_Now_Japan_cedaw44.pdf> (accessed 18 March, 2011).

Moses, Asher (10 March, 2010) 'Rape simulator game goes viral amid calls for censorship' *Sydney Morning Herald*, <http://www.smh.com.au/digital-life/games/rape-simulator-game-goes-viral-amid-calls-for-censorship-20100331-rcpz.html> (accessed 19 March, 2011).

Nakasatomi, Hiroshi (2009) 'Reipurei mondai no keii to hou kaisei no kadai' *Poruno/baishun mondai kenkyuu kai: Ronbun/shiryou shuu* Vol 9, pp. 21–43.

---

4   The Yokohama-based company, Illusion, also produces the games *Battle-raper* and *Oppai slider*, which include pornified and violent content.

Chyng Sun

Investigating Pornography: The Journey of a Filmmaker and Researcher

I grew up in Taiwan and did not see a hardcore pornographic film until I was 31 years old, when I came to the United States as a graduate student in Boston in 1990. Unlike many women who are pushed to watch pornography by their boyfriends, mine was a shy one, and I was the one who sometimes rented porn videos. I would stand on my toes to reach the top shelf at the Video Smith in Brookline, a suburb of Boston, and then I went through the tortuous ritual of ignoring men peering at me out of the corner of their eyes, holding the extra-large video box with vivid pictures while I stood in a long check-out line, and then waiting for the clerk to slowly take the video out of its box and put it in a black box which everyone knew was for porn. There was something thrilling and daring about renting a porn video. I thought I was acting against the prohibition by both Chinese and American patriarchies of women pursuing sexual pleasure. I figured that if not being allowed to watch porn was part of sexual repression, then rebelling against it must be liberating and even feminist.

However, the act of renting the videos was for me more exciting than watching them. On-screen porn women seemed to be coy, infantilized, not caring who had sex with them, enjoying whatever was done to them, and wanting to be dominated. I asked myself: If these types of images appeared in a beer ad, wouldn't I call them sexist? On the other hand, it was just so cool to be a girlfriend who was taboo-breaking and adventurous. Did I really want to ruin the fun? Although I felt unsettled, I did not have the knowledge and conceptual tools, or the willingness, to think it all through clearly.

I picked up my tangled thoughts 15 years later when I started making my documentary, *The Price of Pleasure: Pornography, Sexuality and Relationships.*

1 Approaches to the film

My film was aimed at exploring pornography as a media genre and an industry, through the examination of the 3 aspects of production, content and consumption.

I interviewed 130 people, including porn performers, producers, critics, social workers, therapists, sex columnists, physicians, and users. My genuine curiosity, nonjudgmental attitude, and my respect for the interviewees, I believe, were felt by most of them. When I started making the film, I was most curious about pornographers: who are they, and what are their views of women, men, and sexuality? How do they justify the mistreatment of women?

Mark Kernes, editor of *Adult Video News*, the so-called bible of the pornography industry, provided me with contacts, including Ernest Greene, editor of *Hustler's Taboo Magazine*, a prominent pornographer active in the BDSM community. Greene was eloquent and knowledgeable, with a tendency to exhibit his intellectual and cultural sophistication. After I asked him a few questions, such as "Why do male performers ejaculate on a woman's face or in her eyes? Would it hurt?," he became defensive and said: "I never experience a single moment of guilt or shame or anxiety over the prospect that the pictures that I make might inspire people to do things that would be evil. I believe evildoers do evil things and don't need pictures to tell them how." When asked if there were a certain trend in pornography, Greene replied:

> There's all kinds of porn, there's everything for everybody who likes any kind of erotic depiction … It's very easy for outsiders, particularly those who have a hostile agenda towards porn of some kind [it was clear he included me in this group], to seize on ugly porn or mean porn, or porn where the object seems to … where the purpose seems to be to inflict some kind of abusive sexuality on one or another party involved.

Greene led me to ask the question of exactly what is the pornography that I was analyzing and how I could justify my choice.

I decided to focus on mainstream pornography for heterosexual audiences, the type of material that comprises the bulk of the market, has the widest viewership, and has the biggest potential impact. Not finding literature on what kind of pornography content people are really watching, my associate producer, Robert Wosnitzer, and I decided to design and conduct our own study, together with Erica Scharrer, Ana Bridges, and Rachael Liberman. With the support of Robert Jensen, we directed 3 female students to code films according to the scheme we developed, our focus being on sexual acts and sexual aggression. We randomly selected 50 out of 275 pornographic movies from *Adult Video News*'s best-selling and most-rented lists.

The full report has been published in the journal *Violence Against Women* (Bridges et al., 2010), so I only summarize the findings here. The popular pornographic movies depicted a world that mixed sexual excitement with aggression. Verbal aggression occurred in almost half of the scenes and almost all the expressions involved name-calling (e.g. 'bitch', 'slut'). Physical aggression appeared in almost

90% of the scenes, with spanking being the most frequently observed physically aggressive act. Here there were drastic gender differences: women were spanked on 953 occasions, while men were spanked only 26 times, less than 3% of the total. Gagging, where male performers' penises were inserted deeply inside a woman's throat until they induced a gag reflex, had not been noted in previous content studies, but appeared in 28% of the scenes. Other types of aggression included open-hand slapping, hair-pulling, and choking. Most targets of the aggression were women who usually responded with expressions of pleasure (encouragement, sexual moans etc) or with no change at all in facial expression or interruption of action.

Apart from aggression, sexual acts causing pain or discomfort or those that may be interpreted as degrading, were frequently noted. For example, external male ejaculation (the 'money shot') occurred on women's mouths or faces in over 60% of the scenes. Anal sex, rarely reported in previous studies, occurred in more than half of the scenes. Extreme sexual acts such as double penetration, where two men penetrate a woman anally and vaginally at the same time, occurred in 20% of the scenes. The ass-to-mouth (ATM) sequence, in which a man inserts his penis first in a woman's anus and then in a woman's mouth, was never recorded in previous content analyses. But this act was seen frequently in our study, occurring in about 40% of scenes. Compared to studies conducted in the 1980s and 1990s, our study revealed that pornography has become much more aggressive in both frequency and type of act.

2 What I've learned from pornographers

Scholars have observed 2 paradoxical trends in current pornography: on the one hand, it has become more acceptable, and on the other hand, its content has become more violent and degrading (Jensen, 2007; Dines, 2010). These researchers refer to the popularity of gonzo pornography where there are non-stop, aggressive sexual acts, in scenarios meant to degrade female characters. Max Hardcore – some call him 'the father of Gonzo' – wrote on his Website:

> Everyone knows that Max Hardcore is the undisputed KING of Filthy Fucking! He takes these luscious ladies and turns them into cum drooling, anal gaping sluts just begging for his piss! Max really knows how to turn tight assholes into massive, gaping fuck tubes. Using speculums he stretches these holes nice and wide so he can get a full load of piss squirted in without missing a drop. Then watch them slurp up every drop through a tube!

Some pornographers, like Jeff Stewart, have described Max Hardcore as their inspiration, and Stewart has in turn inspired others. Stewart said:

> Before the scene starts, [Hardcore] does basically violent, throat-fucking before he does ass-fucking. I used to approach him and tell him, 'Look, you know, you should probably just do – just a movie with just the gagging.' And he wasn't interested. So after six months, I decided to do it myself. We've won Best Oral Series [*Adult Video News* Awards] three years in a row. There's like, twenty-five other companies that are copying our *Gag Factor* series.

Stewart is the creator of *Gag Factor*, in which the women choke and cry because men's penises are inserted in their throat deeply, thrusting in very fast and aggressive movements. Stewart stated, "We also started the American Bukkake craze. American Bukkake is … a group of men that ejaculate on a woman's face. There's no sex. It's just like just gallons of cum being drenched on a girl."

Sex has been endlessly explored in art, literature, and film, but what makes those depictions stand out are the emotions the characters experience when they connect with one another in different circumstances. Pornography has much less variability. As one pornographer said bluntly: "There's only so many ways to have sex. They've all been shot. All you can try to do is make it a little more sensational, but it's been so sensationalized, what can you – how many dicks can you stick in a girl at one time?" He answered himself: "At one time, three. Well, I guess you could make it four, one in her mouth, two in her ass, one in her pussy, maybe." So where else can pornographers go to make pornography more exciting? Sam Benjamin, the author of *Confessions of an Ivy League Pornographer*, reflected on his experiences as a gonzo pornographer:

> While my overt task at hand was to make sure that the girls got naked, my true responsibility as the director was to make sure the girls got punished. Scenes that stuck out, and hence made more money, were those in which the female 'targets' were verbally degraded and sometimes physically humiliated.

The pornographers who punish girls in these ways are not marginalized outsiders. For example, Stewart has won awards sponsored by *Adult Video News*, the leading trade journal. The AVN Awards Show, the porn Oscars, has been broadcast on Showtime to an audience of millions since 2008. Titles such as *All New Beaver Hunt, Innocent Until Proven Filthy, Fresh Meat, Daddy's Lil' Whore, Teens for Cash*, and *Deep Anal Drilling* also enter the lexicon to be articulated to the masses. Gonzo pornographers such as Max Hardcore, Jeff Stewart and John Stagliano are rich men, who have made their money from verbal degradation and physical humiliation.

Even pornographer Joe Gallant said: "I hate to say, but I think the future of American porn is violence. I see the signs of it already … the culture will become much more accepting of gang rape movies and abuse movies." What illustrates his sentiment most vividly is the popular S/M Website kink.com, where women are tied up, chained, gagged, whipped, electrified, immersed in water, and penetrated by machines. Even though my film concerns mainstream pornography, and does not include BDSM materials, I included clips from kink.com because this type of image has become popular, even mainstream. Kink.com has been featured in *The New York Times* as innovative, technologically savvy, and profitable, and is touted as a company just like any other company, but in some ways better (it gives its employees good benefits and retirement plans).

3 Porn performers: Beyond choice

When discussing issues related to *Gag Factor* or kink.com, the conversation often drifts into the question of choice: did the woman who was gagged or whipped freely choose to go into the industry? Such questions concern the autonomy and agency of women in pornography. Christine Stark, a writer and anti-porn activist who has worked with hundreds of women in porn and prostitution, problematized the focus on choice to me:

> What difference does it make how someone gets into pornography? Why do you have to have this extreme amount of violence incurred in getting into pornography in order to make it matter, to make you matter? It's like you have to prove that you're a good victim. Do we sit and have endless conversations about domestic violence victims? 'Did you choose to walk down the aisle with that man, because if you did, I'm not sure if this is really a form of sexual violence.'

Stark raises an important point regarding the need to shift the focus from the conditions that shape porn performers' decisions to enter the porn industry and towards the conditions created by both the pornographers and the consumers, under which those performers work.

Diane Defoe, a black woman from Hawaii, entered the porn industry in 1999, first as a performer and then later as a director. She has seen many performers come and go:

> This industry definitely attracts a certain mindset. You normally have to be a little bit liberal ... but you also have to be very young ... eighteen, nineteen, twenty years old with little education, little business sense, little financial skills and they're making ten, twenty times more than that seven dollars an hour they were making at Jack in the Box ...

"Making ten, twenty times more" than in a low-wage job is indeed a strong allure for young women getting into the porn industry. For example, Annie Cruz started in pornography when she was 19; at the time of our interview she had worked for a year and already had appeared in 150 movies. She constantly receives emails from women seeking employment in the industry, who write, "I only got eight dollars in the bank account – to my name. I really want to get in bad." Both Cruz and Defoe observe that there are many women who do pornography for emergency reasons, such as paying off credit card debts or back-up rent, and then get out. Defoe also reports:

> People are entranced by the idea that you can go and make an entire month's salary in a day, and they think that they're going to be able to do it everyday, and you're not going to be able to do it everyday. You may not be able to do it, you know, next week. No matter how smart you are, beautiful you are, how many people you know, if there's a girl coming behind you … that's better than you, you're going to be out … It just has to do with who's … going to do something cheaper than you.

4 Not Easy Money

In mainstream porn, men perform acts on women, while women have acts done to them, so it is mostly women who bear the brunt of pain and discomfort, physically and psychologically. Annie Cruz matter-of-factly gives the price list for each sexual act:

> For blow jobs, regular blow jobs, I get three hundred for those, for a girl on girl scene with me and another girl, that's usually six hundred … me and a girl, anal, which means, you know, penetration in the butt, that's usually eight hundred. Me and one guy, that's nine hundred. Me and one guy, anal, that's a thousand. Me and two guys, whether or not it be anal or regular, is eleven hundred. Double penetration, which is one in vagina, one in the butt, that's twelve hundred, and gang bangs … I start at thirteen hundred for three guys and then add a hundred for each additional guy, so you know, it's like two thousand for six guys [it should be 10 guys] … double anal, fifteen hundred, and double anal would be two in the butt …

This pricelist was verified to me as the standard pay for the industry's more established film companies. For a low-budget, small company, or in amateur movies, the price could be significantly lower. Anal sex is prevalent, but based on my interviews with both men and women, it is not something many women are eager to do. P.T., a female 20-year-old porn performer, a pre-med dropout, explained why she was reluctant to do anal sex: "In porn, they tend to be rougher than in real life, and it tears the capillaries, and it can spread some diseases."

Sharon Mitchell, a porn performer in the 1970s and 1980s, founded the Adult Industry Medical Health Care Foundation (AIM) to provide medical and testing services for the porn industry. Mitchell has been very vocal in criticizing the industry, particularly the extreme and brutal gonzo genre. Mitchell stated that in the film *Porn Shut Down*, for example, "I sat there everyday and I saw anal tear and anal prolapses. The physical condition people put their body through is getting very far away from the sexuality as we know it." AIM's Website also lists some of the health risks of standard sexual acts in pornography – from tears in the vagina, throat, and anus, to HIV, hepatitis, and rectal chlamydia and gonorrhea of the throat.

But beyond each individual woman's experiences, the crucial question is why an economic system would pay a woman 50 times more money to be gagged than for her to take a McDonald's job? As Sarah Katherine Lewis, a former stripper and porn performer, said: "When your best choice is taking off your clothes and sticking toys in your cunt for money, I think there's a real problem with the labor system."

Conclusion

In my conversations with male porn users, many of them expressed some ambivalence or even guilt. Pornographers attribute this 'guilt' to sexual repression or religion. But that is not its only source. I ended my film with a quotation from a 20-year-old college student, Gregg, who said:

> When you're watching porn, you're in the heat of the moment, you're in the passion of it, you're aroused, you're actively masturbating or whatever, sex can seem very, very fun. It can seem like, 'Oh, maybe someday I want to lube up a woman and flip her over, and you know, fuck her from behind.' But, honestly, the second I have an orgasm and that passion kind of sinks out of my body and you're still watching the movie, you start to really see what's going on and it's kind of just foul, you know? ... and you're left in the end, you're done masturbating, you've had your orgasm, you're not really feeling passionate anymore, onscreen is this woman who's naked, get down on her knees, has cum all over her, and the man's just standing there in his power position and he's loving it, and you just kind of wonder like, this is not sexy, this is not sex, this is not how I want to experience sex.

Most of the men I talked to knew that it was wrong to treat another human being the way women were treated in pornography. It was empathy that induced Gregg's guilt, as he so eloquently articulated.

What has driven me through this long journey of 7 years, from making my documentary to engaging in various research projects on different aspects of pornography, is a genuine curiosity about human sexuality, identity, and relationships. What propels me to continue is my optimism in our ability to care, connect, and love ourselves and another human being. My question is whether making and consuming pornography may hurt those capacities. So far, my evidence suggests it does.

Bibliography

Bridges, Ana, Robert Wosnitzer, Erica Scharrer, Chyng Sun and Rachael Liberman (2010) 'Aggression and Sexual Behavior in Best-Selling Pornography Videos: A Content Analysis Update'. *Violence Against Women* 16 (10) pp. 1065–1085.

Dines, Gail (2010) *Pornland: How Porn Has Hijacked our Sexuality*. Beacon Press, Boston; Spinifex Press, North Melbourne.

Hardcore, Max (n.d.) 'Max Hardcore Porn', <http://maxhardcoreporn.net/front.php?s=MHP&r=6688b&t=no&refer_url=http://www.google.com/search?client=safari&rls=en&q=max+hardcore+website&ie=UTF-8&oe=UTF-8&ip=128.122.78.144&ip=128.122.78.144> (accessed 18 March, 2011).

Jensen, Robert (2007) *Getting Off: Pornography and the End of Masculinity*. South End Press, Cambridge, MA.

PART THREE

Harming Children

"All the while, there was a part of me that was disgusted with what I was watching ... but the self-hatred part was so strong that I couldn't get past the idea that this violence and degradation was okay, and even right. I felt like it was the kind of treatment I deserved and, by extension, the treatment that all women deserve. It was about my feelings of worthlessness being reinforced in me by watching other women being treated as worthless objects." – Ellen

"It's not just the trauma ... I live with the constant fear the photos taken of me being raped as a boy by older men will surface somewhere someday ... I have children of my own now and would give my life for them; I love them so much ... [M]y childhood is like another world I try to forget; there is this terror that is always there that my photos are out there somewhere circulating amongst filthy perverts ..." – Richard

"He'd make me sit and watch porn videos with him and I'd feel sick. He'd then make me do to him what they had done and he took photos of me naked on the bed and he wanted me to look at the photos and you can see my face frozen and twisted with fear and I have no idea where the photos are ... I live with this terror that they are going to surface or that he will die and the photos will be found and everyone will know then what happened and I think that would kill me." – Natasha

"The damage to my self-image and confidence has been huge – I used to be so confident but found myself feeling completely unattractive and unlovable. I fear for my gorgeous baby girl – if porn is so permissible now, how much worse is it going to be when she is older?" – Linda

Diana E.H. Russell

Russell's Theory: Exposure to Child Pornography as a Cause of Child Sexual Victimization[1]

Many people believe that exposure to pornography is cathartic, providing "a release of wishes, desires or drives such that they do not have to be acted on in reality" (Kelly et al., 1995, p. 23). The exposure is frequently described as a 'safety valve'. According to the 'safety valve' theory, viewers of child pornography should be less likely to sexually victimize children, therefore child pornography should be legalized. I argue, in contrast, that exposure of men[2] to child pornography can *cause* some of them to sexually abuse children when 3 causal factors (detailed below) co-occur. Each of these causal factors is necessary but not sufficient, and they do not have to occur in any particular order.

While some clinicians (e.g. Wyre, 1990), law enforcement officers, and the public at large believe that perpetrators of child sexual abuse are always pedophiles, I do not subscribe to this view. I agree with Philip Jenkins that "a sexual interest in children is not confined to a tiny segment of hardcore ... 'pedophiles'" (2001, p. 25). I also reject the view that there are fundamental differences between perpetrators of child sex abuse who are *not* pedophiles, and 'normal' males. Jenkins refers to the sizable legal market in pseudo-child pornography in which adult women are made to look like young teens and argues that "the popularity of such materials indicates a mass popular market for teen sexuality" in the United States (2001, p. 28). For example, in a recent study, 92% of child sexual abuse offenders were in possession of images of minors that emphasized their sexuality or portrayed them as involved in explicit sexual activities (in M'jid Maalla, 2009, p. 10).

As I will show, the existing research supports Jenkins's contention and reveals

---

1 This article is a much shortened version of a chapter I co-authored with Natalie Purcell (in Dowd et al., 2006, pp. 59–83). I would like to thank Alix Johnson for her conceptual and editorial assistance.
2 Use of the term 'men' includes juvenile males in this chapter. While acknowledging that women too sexually abuse children, *Russell's Theory* focuses on males because they are the overwhelming majority of child pornography consumers and perpetrators of child sexual victimization.

that child pornography can help cultivate, normalize, and legitimize male sexual interest in children.[3]

The theoretical foundation of this model, which I call *Russell's Theory*, comes from the work in which I have been engaged over 3 decades.[4]

Causal Factor 1a
Viewing child pornography predisposes some males, not previously so disposed, to sexually desire children

It is commonly believed that exposure to child pornography cannot create a desire for sexual contact with children in men for whom it did not previously exist. I disagree. There are 4 main ways in which exposure to child pornography *can* cause sexual arousal in these men.

First, child pornography sexualizes or sexually objectifies children. Pornographers often instruct girls to get into sexual poses or to engage in masturbation or sexual intercourse by imitating women so engaged in adult pornography. One pornographer declared that "Girls, say between the ages of 8 and 13, are the very salable objects ... young girls without overdevelopment [sic] and preferably with little or no pubic hair on their body" (cited in Campagna and Poffenberger, 1988, p. 133). By sexualizing children, child pornography sends the message that they are appropriate and desirable objects of sexual interest (American Psychological Association, 2007). Here, child pornography works in concert with other widely accessible media and products that depict young girls as 'sexy' and/or potentially interested in sex with adults (Durham, 2008; Oppliger, 2008; Levin and Kilbourne, 2009; Levy, 2005; Tankard Reist, 2009). The American Psychological Association (2007) has shown that the widespread sexualization of young girls in mainstream media and consumer culture can dehumanize girls and lead viewers/consumers to equate them with sexual objects (see also Frederickson and Roberts, 1997).

Second, pseudo-child pornography is an increasingly popular genre that merges sexual images of girls and women, thereby confounding the distinctions between them. This genre, which is exceedingly prevalent online in the 21st century, portrays young-looking adult women as if they were young girls, using props (e.g. teddy bears and lollipops) and captions or text to describe the depicted

---

3 I include References to research findings from the 1960s onwards to demonstrate what an epic, long-standing, and ongoing struggle it has been to expose the pernicious activities of child pornography consumers.

4 I wrote my first feminist analysis of pornography in an article published in 1977, and started my anti-pornography activism in 1976. This included being a founding member of Women Against Violence in Pornography and Media (WAVPM) in 1976, which was the first feminist activist group in the world to focus on combating pornography.

women as children (Dines, 2010; see also Dines, this volume). The *childification* of women in pseudo-child pornography is also accomplished by dressing them in childish clothes and hairstyles, positioning them in childlike poses with childlike expressions and surrounding them with children's toys. The transition of a male's arousal to child pornography can be achieved through a step-by-step process of exposure to gradually younger sexualized teenagers and then prepubescent girls – a process described by the child-porn users who Pamela Paul (2005) interviewed. *Adultification*, on the other hand, involves depicting girls as mini-adults with the use of makeup, seductive clothes, sexy adult-like poses, and/or accompanying text. Like pseudo-child pornography, adultified child images can sexualize girls for some male viewers who never before experienced sexual interest in young girls.

Third, there is learning by association. A classic experiment by Rachman and Hodgson (1968) found that male subjects can learn to become sexually aroused by seeing a picture of a woman's boot after repeatedly seeing women's boots in association with sexually arousing slides of nude females. Masturbation to these images reinforces this association, which was conceptualized by McGuire, Carlisle, and Young as "masturbatory conditioning" (1965, p. 185). The pleasurable experience of orgasm is a potent reinforcer. Several of the pornography consumers interviewed by Paul (2005) said that their initial disinterest in, or even disgust with, child pornography gradually diminished after repeated exposure, especially in the context of masturbation.

The fourth way concerns males who have become habituated to adult pornography and who seek out more extreme forms of pornography. Margaret Healy argues that continued exposure to generally available so-called nonviolent pornography arouses an interest in, and creates a taste for, pornography that portrays less commonly practiced sexual activities, including those involving the infliction of pain:

> With the emergence of the use of computers to traffic in child pornography, a new and growing segment of producers and consumers is being identified. They are individuals who may not have a sexual preference for children, but who have seen the gamut of adult pornography and who are searching for more bizarre material (2002, p. 4).

Gail Dines (2010) interviewed several incarcerated men who used child pornography and found that "not one of them fitted the definition of the pedophile" (p. 161).

> All seven told [Dines] that they preferred sex with an adult woman, but had become bored with regular pornography. Five of them had looked at PCP [pseudo-child pornography] sites first and then moved into actual child porn (p. 161).

Causal Factor 1b
Viewing child pornography intensifies the desire of some males who are already sexually aroused by children

When pedophiles and other males who desire sex with children are exposed to child pornography which corresponds to their specific preferences (e.g. the gender and age of the child), their sexual arousal intensifies. For example, John Ferguson, an 18-year-old pedophile, described his reaction to seeing hardcore child pornography for the first time:

> One of the guys brought in three or four hardcore porno magazines that aroused me so intensely that I could barely control myself. Never in my life had I ever seen or heard of anything like this. Sex … oral sex …, everything … close up and in color. I fed on these magazines like a man possessed. Never in my life had I ever been aroused like this (Ferguson, 1985, p. 285; ellipses in original).

Many males with a sexual interest in children deliberately use child pornography to intensify their sexual desire as a prelude to masturbation or the sexual abuse of children. Silbert and Pines report that a father in their study used to show "his friends pornographic movies to get them sexually aroused before they would rape" his 9-year-old daughter (1993, pp. 117–118). Masturbation reinforces the fantasies accompanying this activity which intensifies the desire to sexually abuse children.

Child pornography also provides new ideas for sexually abusing children. Jenkins suggests that

> [a] common theme on pedophile Internet boards is requests for material that is not readily available: A few themes recur often and arouse real enthusiasm. By far the most common include calls for 'Black loli', African or African American subjects … Also in demand are incest pictures" (2001, p. 85).

Most child pornography portrays the victims as enjoying the sexual abuse. Such depictions undermine any guilt the viewers may feel, as well as facilitate imitation by males who need or prefer to believe that the sex acts depicted are not abusive. Sadistic perpetrators are more aroused by pictures of terrified, crying, or traumatized child victims. For example, a young girl testified as follows to the 1985 Government Commission on Pornography (AGCP):

> My father had an easel that he put by the bed. He'd pin a picture on the easel and like a teacher he would tell me this is what you're going to learn today. He would then act out the pictures on me (AGCP, 1986, p. 782).

Similarly, Pamela Paul (2005) found that the child pornography users she interviewed often wanted (and sometimes tried) to enact the sexual scenarios they watched with actual children. In addition, there is now widespread use of live web cams on the Internet to provide made-to-order child sexual abuse, that also constitutes child pornography. A father, for example, asks his online web cam buddies what sex acts they would like him to enact on his child. He then acts out the sexual abuse that they request, after which his buddies pay him for his live show.

Habituation is an intrinsic feature in the escalation described by child pornography viewers, resulting in the desire to see more callous and sadistic images showing children upset, traumatized, or tortured. On the sadistic end of the range are Websites like russianrape.com (link no longer active) which invited viewers to "see the poor young girls swallow what they don't want, but have to do … see the horror in the eyes of the young girls and see them wild scream [sic] in brutally [sic] rape and pain!" Another Website called rapedasians.com (link no longer active) promised "the very best collection of very young Asian girls brutally raped." Gail Dines (2010) offers other examples of sexually sadistic materials that are easily accessible online. As explained below, some users visit these sites only after they have become habituated to non-violent material that portrays children 'enjoying' their abuse.

Causal Factor 2
Viewing child pornography undermines some males' *internal* inhibitions against sexually victimizing children

Each component identified in Causal Factor 2 undermines beliefs and feelings that inhibit the acting out of sexual desires.

The first involves sexualizing, sexually objectifying, and/or depersonalizing girls. Many types of child pornography that portray girls in sexually provocative poses or happily engaged in sexual acts with other children or with adult men or women, can convince those exposed to it that some children want and enjoy sex with adult males. For example, a sexual offender who enjoyed viewing child pornography showing "girls actually having sex" said that the girls "had to look happy … I mean I wasn't looking for rape or anything" (Taylor and Quayle, 2003, p. 82). The 2009 UN report on child pornography comments that "[n]etworks for the exchange of child pornography display photographs in which the children have been forced to smile in order to prove that they 'are having fun'…" (in M'jid Maalla, 2009, p. 12).

Secondly, child pornography undermines the prohibition against sex with children. Hiromasa Nakai, a spokesman for the Japan Committee for Unicef, said that to a degree, it has become socially accepted to lust over young girls in Japan. As Mr Nakai commented, "Condoning these works has meant more people have access to them and develop an interest in young girls" (Tabuchi, 9 February, 2011; see also Norma, this volume).

There are also large numbers of child pornography Websites that promote adult–child sexual victimization through photographs, videos, or written stories. For example, an incest Website titled 'Golden Incest Sites!' listed 50 titles (www. incest-gold.com/indes.php, 6 June, 2002; link no longer active). The prevalence of child pornography sites, their content, and their positive portrayals of adult–child sexual abuse all serve to diminish recognition of the harm of incestuous and extra-familial child sexual abuse (see also Taylor, this volume). The Internet boards allow people to form their own subcultural communities in which such behaviors or desires are not considered wrongful and where pedophiles and others interested in child pornography can feel 'normal' (see Whisnant, 2010).

Third, child pornography minimizes or trivializes the harm of adult–child sex by masking the pain and trauma of child victims. For example, a pedophile called Stewart describes how he masked victims' pain when he photographed young girls:

> They couldn't show fear or doubt in the pictures. They had to show happiness or love … To get that look, I'd give them something, from tricycles to stereos. It depended on what they wanted. You have to be able to express [evoke] excitement in the pictures (in Campagna and Poffenberger, 1988, p. 126).

British journalist Davies (1994) describes "a video of a girl with her wrists and ankles chained to an iron bar in the ceiling and a grotesque dildo hanging out of her" (cited by Itzin 1996, p. 185). As Catherine Itzin comments, "The pornographer who was showing the video pointed to the girl's smile as evidence of her consent" (1996, p. 185). Linz and Imrich note:

> Potential molesters who watch child sex depictions that supposedly had positive consequences for the victim may come to think that the victim does not suffer and may believe that a larger percentage of children would find forced sex pleasurable (2001, p. 91).

Masking the pain and trauma of child pornography victims can thus undermine inhibitions against sexual abuse.

Fourth, child pornography creates and/or reinforces myths about child sexuality and child abuse. Joseph LoPiccolo has emphasized that most sex offenders have "distorted cognitive beliefs that are intimately related to their deviant behavior" (LoPiccolo, personal communication, 16 September, 2005; LoPiccolo, 1994). These 'false belief-systems' (in Itzin 1996, p. 170) can be created and reinforced when males view child pornography. For example, child pornography can convince some males "that the feelings and desires they have towards children are not wrong" (Tate, 1990, p. 110). Jenkins notes that many pedophiles justify their sexual behavior with children by claiming that children "consented to the actions" or directly sought sexual contact with their perpetrators (2001, p. 117). These pedophiles consider such experiences to be consensual: "Even if the child is three or five, she was still asking for it" (Jenkins, 2001, p. 117). Jenkins also maintains that "[l]inked to this is the denial of injury, since the sexual activity is seen as rewarding and even educational for the child, rather than selfish or exploitative" (2001, p. 117). As Kelly, Wingfield, and Regan observe, child pornography "enables them [perpetrators] to construct a different version of reality" (1995, p. 34) in which it is possible for them to believe that their needs and the needs of the child are being met.

The fifth factor concerns the desensitization of some viewers of child pornography "to the pathology of sexual abuse or exploitation of children," causing them to perceive the acting out of such sex acts as acceptable (in Linz and Imrich, 2001, p. 51). According to the US Congress:

> One likely source of desensitization to the degrading and abusive aspects of child pornography may be repeated exposure to 'adult' pornography wherein the models, although over the age of 18, are described and depicted as underage [pseudo-child pornography] (p. 94).

Desensitization can also result in a preference for increasingly deviant and ever more abusive forms of child pornography.

Sixth, the legitimatizing and normalizing of adults' sexual victimization of children in child pornography are among the most frequently cited ways in which this material undermines inhibitions. As Tate points out:

> All paedophiles need to reassure themselves that what they are doing or want to do is OK. It [child pornography] validates their feelings, lowers their inhibitions and makes them feel that their behaviour is pretty normal ... they see other people doing it in the videos or the magazines and it reassures them (1990, p. 24).

For example, a woman who was abused as a girl testified before the US Congress that she had been told: "See, it's okay to do because it's published in magazines" (AGCP, 1986, p. 786). Like other pornography users (see Whisnant, 2010), pedophiles "use porn to convince themselves that their behavior is not abnormal, but is shared by others" (Calcetas-Santos, 2001, p. 59).

Seventh, child pornography provides specific instructions on how to sexually victimize a child (see also Taylor, this volume). Some men who have never acted on their desire to have sex with a child may be ignorant or anxious about how to proceed. Child pornography can remove this impediment by providing instructions for the sexual abuse of children. Tyler, a detective sergeant in a California Sheriff's Department, testified in hearings on child pornography and pedophilia about a child pornography magazine that detailed "how to have sex with prepubescent children" (Child Pornography and Pedophilia, 1984, p. 33). The 1984 hearings also considered a book titled *How to Have Sex With Kids* that described "how to meet children, how to entice them, how to develop a relationship with them, and how to have sex with them" (1984, 30). Gail Dines, Robert Jensen, and Ann Russo have analyzed a scene in the best-selling pseudo-child pornography video titled *Cherry Poppers Vol. 10* that included "realistic detailed instructions on how to initiate a child into sex" (1998, p. 88; see also Dines, 2010, chapter 8). According to law enforcement officials, the Bulletin of the North American Man Boy Love Association (NAMBLA) "has step-by-step 'how to' instructions for locating, seducing, sexually assaulting, and preventing the disclosure of their crime by their child victims" (in Linz and Imrich, 2001, p. 92). In 2010, a similar publication, *The Pedophile's Guide to Love and Pleasure* (Greaves, 2010), was the subject of considerable controversy in the United States and around the world. Protests ultimately succeeded in pressuring Amazon. com to remove it from its online retail store (Heussner, 2010). Shockingly, but revealingly, this despicable book was rated #96 on Amazon's Top 100 list at the time of its removal.

As the next section explains, social inhibitions also have to be overcome before potential abusers are likely to become actual abusers.

Causal Factor 3
Viewing child pornography undermines some males' *social* inhibitions against acting out their desires to sexually victimize children

Child pornography undermines viewers' social inhibitions against sexually victimizing children in several ways. First, it diminishes fear of disapproval. The enormous number of child pornography Websites, DVDs, and Internet forums reveal to viewers that they are not alone in their deviant interests (Jenkins, 2001, p. 106). This revelation suggests that the boards are safe spaces that they can visit and find like-minded friends (p. 108). In addition, Jenkins argues that "[t]he more pedophiles and pornographers are attacked by law enforcement agencies [and] mass media … the greater the sense of community [they feel] against common enemies" (2001, p. 114). The knowledge that they have a support group of like-minded colleagues also contributes to undermining the fear of disapproval for sexually victimizing children.

Second, fear of legal and social sanctions is the most important factor in inhibiting potential and active child molesters from sexually abusing children. For example, a pedophile called Duncan said that his fear of getting caught "was what stopped me progressing to buggery with the boys" (Tate, 1990, p. 120).

However, viewing child pornography communicates that those who sexually violate children are in no danger of being apprehended or of facing other negative consequences. Child pornography is unlikely to show a sexual predator being apprehended by the police or ending up in prison. The same applies to written child pornography stories, fantasies, lists of Websites and DVDs, as well as child pornography in men's magazines. The outcomes of real or portrayed child sexual abuse in pornographic materials are always positive for the perpetrators. Hence, exposure to child pornography conveys a false sense of immunity to legal sanctions, thereby undermining the social inhibitions of potential and active abusers.

Third, child pornography provides users with a means of making money. According to a child pornographer, "the most money is made in child pornography because it's hard to get and willing children are hard to come by" (in Campagna and Poffenberger 1988, p. 133). Frequent exposure to child pornography on the Internet promotes the perception that many child pornography producers are 'getting away with it' and profiting from it. The stronger the need or motivation to make money, the more this motivation is likely to overwhelm social inhibitions (see also M'jid Maalla, 2009, UN report on profits from child pornography).

Contributory Factor 4
Viewing pornography undermines some children's abilities to avoid, resist, or escape sexual victimization[5]

Some perpetrators use physical force to accomplish their acts of child sexual victimization. In these cases, children's efforts to avoid, resist, or escape sexual victimization are ineffective. There are, however, cases where children's exposure to pornography undermines their efforts and permits sexual abuse to occur where it otherwise would not.

First, child pornography is used to arouse children's sexual curiosity. Showing pornography to boys and girls is a common abuse grooming strategy.

Pedophiles posing as young teenagers in Internet teen chat groups often send pornographic pictures or email messages containing pornographic language to

---

5   Factor 4 is not necessary to *Russell's Theory*, but it can be a significant facilitator of child sexual victimization.

child participants in order to arouse their curiosity and to manipulate them into meeting in person.

Research on adults reveals that many females became upset or disturbed when exposed to pornographic pictures during their childhoods (Check, 1995; Check and Maxwell, 1992a, 1992b; Senn, 1993; Stock, 1995). Since many boys, in contrast, become sexually aroused by pornographic pictures, showing them this material is typically far more successful at undermining their abilities to avoid, resist or escape being subjugated to sexual abuse by adult pedophiles, non-pedophilic abusers, and incest perpetrators. Children's arousal in response to pornography can be used to keep them in positions of abuse.

Second, showing pornography to children legitimizes and/or normalizes child sexual abuse in the eyes of victims. Many pedophiles and child molesters show pornography to children "in order to persuade them that they would enjoy certain sexual acts" (Kelly, 1992, p. 119). Another motive is "to convince them that what they are being asked to do is alright." Showing them a picture "legitimizes the abuser's requests" (Kelly, 1992, p. 119). The following testimony of a woman illustrates a father's attempts to use pornography to normalize and legitimize sexually abusing his daughter:

> The incest started at the age of eight. I did not understand any of it and did not feel that it was right. My dad would try to convince me that it was ok. He would find magazines, articles or pictures that would show fathers and daughters or mothers, brothers and sisters having sexual intercourse. [Mostly fathers and daughters.] He would say that if it was published in magazines that it had to be all right because magazines could not publish lies ... He would ask me later if I had read them and what they said or if I looked real close at the pictures. He would say, 'See it's okay to do because it's published in magazines' (AGCP, 1986, p. 1786).

Child molesters also send pornography to the children they have targeted for sexual victimization to convince them "that other children are sexually active" (Hughes, 1999, p. 28).

Third, showing pornography to children desensitizes or disinhibits children. A child molester's step-by-step 'grooming' of a child serves to gradually desensitize her or him to the sexual abuse that is his goal. He moves from befriending a child, to touching her or him, to introducing her or him to an X-rated video, slowly showing more of it "until the child is able to sit and watch the videos without becoming too uncomfortable" (Whetsell-Mitchell 1995, p. 201). Showing adult pornography to children can be "used in the same way [as child pornography] to lower the inhibitions of children" (Tate 1992, p. 213).

Fourth, exposure to pornography can create feelings of guilt and complicity for child victims, thereby silencing them. Children exposed to pornography often feel guilty. According to Scotland Yard investigations, one of the 5 major ways in which pedophiles use pornography is to "ensure the secrecy of any sexual activity with a child who has already been seduced [sexually abused]" (Tate, 1990, p. 24). Child molesters can often silence their victims by telling them that their parents would be very upset to learn that they had watched pornography. Children who are sexually abused following the exposure may feel complicit in the abuse and thus become even more motivated to remain silent. This reduces the likelihood that abused children will disclose the sexual abuse to their parents or report it to others.

Conclusion

Russell's Theory explains how the exposure of males to child pornography can generate the sexual desire for children in some males who previously had no such interest. In an age where the Internet has greatly increased the volume of child pornography and pseudo-child pornography available to, and viewed by, ever greater numbers of males, there is reason for great and urgent alarm. The epidemic proportions of child pornography, and the increasing accessibility of other media that sexualize children will lead to a corresponding increase in sexual abuse and millions more devastated young victims.

"Child pornography is the theory, molestation is the practice ..." This succinct statement by Philip Jenkins (2001, p. 4) which is consistent with my theory, has staggering implications, especially as massive numbers of individuals worldwide now have access to child pornography on the Internet. Furthermore, the sexual abuse and rape of children will keep escalating if nothing is done to stop it.

In an effort to rid our countries of child pornography, I propose the organization of an International Tribunal on Child Pornography. I was one of the major organizers of the first feminist International Tribunal on Crimes Against Women in Brussells, Belgium, in 1976 which was extremely successful in combating some forms of violence and discrimination against women, particularly in Western Europe. A mere handful of international feminists with virtually no funding, managed to organize this global speak-out attended by about 2,000 women.[6]

Finally, besides the causal relationship that exists between some males' viewing of child pornography and their sexual abuse of children, we must never forget that the *making* of most child pornography is itself evidence of child sexual abuse.

---

6   The book describing how this International Tribunal was organized is still in print. See Russell and Van de Ven (1976/2000).

Bibliography

American Psychological Association (2007) *Report of the APA Task Force on the Sexualization of Girls.* American Psychological Association. Washington, D.C.

Attorney General's Commission on Pornography (AGCP) (1986) *Final Report* Vol. 1. United States Department of Justice, Washington, DC.

Calcetas-Santos, Ofelia (2001) 'Child pornography on the Internet' in Carlos Arnaldo (Ed) *Child abuse on the Internet.* Berghahn Books, New York, pp. 57–60.

Campagna, Daniel S. and Donald L. Poffenberger. (1988) *The sexual trafficking in children: An investigation of the child sex trade.* Auburn House, Dover, Massachusetts.

Check, James (1995) 'Teenage training: The effects of pornography on adolescent males' in Laura Lederer and Richard Delgado (Eds) *The price we pay: The case against racist speech, hate propaganda, and pornography.* Hill and Wang, New York, pp. 89–91.

Check, James and Kristin Maxwell (June, 1992a) 'Adolescents' rape myth attitudes and acceptance of forced sexual intercourse'. Paper presented at the Canadian Psychological Association Meetings, Quebec.

Check, James and Kristin Maxwell (June, 1992b) 'Children's consumption of pornography and their attitudes regarding sexual violence'. Paper presented at the Canadian Psychological Association Meetings, Quebec.

Davies, N. (November 26, 1994) 'Dirty business' *The Guardian*, pp. 12–17.

Dines, Gail (2010) *Pornland: How Porn Has Hijacked Our Sexuality.* Beacon Press, Boston, MA; Spinifex Press, North Melbourne.

Dines, Gail, Robert Jensen and Ann Russo (1998) *Pornography: The production and consumption of inequality.* Routledge, New York.

Dowd, Nancy E., Dorothy G. Singer and Robin Fretwell Wilson (Eds) (2006) *Handbook of Children, Culture, and Violence.* Sage Publications, Thousand Oaks, California.

Durham, Meenakshi Gigi (2008) *The Lolita Effect: The Media Sexualization of Young Girls and What We Can Do About It.* Overlook Press, Woodstock, New York.

Ferguson, J. (1985) 'Effect of pornography on women and children' (prepared statement). Subcommittee on Juvenile Justice of the Committee on the Judiciary (98th Congress, Second Session on Oversight on Pornography, Magazines of a Variety of Courses, Inquiring into the Subject of Their Impact on Child Abuse, Child Molestation, and Problems of Conduct Against Women). US Government Printing Office, Washington, DC, pp. 281–288.

Fredrickson, Barbara L. and Tomi-Ann Roberts (1997) 'Objectification Theory: Toward Understanding Women's Lived Experiences and Mental Health Risks' *Psychology of Women Quarterly* 21, pp. 173–206.

Greaves II, Phillip Ray (October, 2010) *The Pedophile's Guide to Love and Pleasure: A Child-Lover's Code of Conduct.* Self-published e-book.

Healy, Margaret (February 27, 2002) 'Child pornography: An international perspective' Paper presented at the Second World Congress Against Commercial Sexual Exploitation of Children, Yokohama, Japan.

Heussner, Ki Mae (11 November, 2010) 'Amazon Removes Pedophilia Book From Store' *ABC News Online*, <http://abcnews.go.com/Technology/amazon-removes-pedophilia-book-store/story?id=12119035>.

Hughes, Donna M. (1999) *Pimps and predators on the Internet: Globalizing the sexual exploitation of women and children.* The Coalition Against Trafficking in Women, Kingston, Rhode Island.

Itzin, Catherine (1996) 'Pornography and the organisation of child sexual abuse' in P.C. Bibby (Ed) *Organized abuse: The current debate.* Aldershot, Hampshire, UK, pp. 167–196.

Jenkins, Philip (2001) *Beyond tolerance: Child pornography on the Internet.* New York University Press, New York.

Kelly, Liz (1992) 'Pornography and child sexual abuse' in Catherine Itzin (Ed) *Pornography: Women, violence, and civil liberties.* Oxford University Press, Oxford and New York, pp. 113–123.

Kelly, Liz, Wingfield, Rachel and Linda Regan (1995) *Splintered lives: Sexual exploitation of children in the context of children's rights and child protection.* Barnardos, Ilford, Essex, UK.

Levin, Diane E. and Jean Kilbourne (2009) *So Sexy So Soon: The New Sexualized Childhood and What Parents Can Do to Protect Their Kids.* Ballantine Books/Random House, New York.

Levy, Ariel (2005) *Female Chauvinist Pigs: Women and the Rise of Raunch Culture.* Free Press, New York.

Linz, Daniel and Dorothy Imrich (2001) 'Child pornography' in Susan O. White (Ed) *Handbook of Youth and Justice.* Kluwer Academic/Plenum, New York, pp. 79–111.

LoPiccolo, Joseph (1994) 'Acceptance and broad spectrum treatment of paraphilias' in Steven C. Hayes, Neil Jacobson, Victoria M. Follette and Michael Dougher (Eds) *Acceptance and change: Content and context in psychotherapy.* Context Press, Reno, Nevada, pp. 149–170.

M'jid Maalla, Najat (2009) 'Report of the Special Rapporteur on the sale of children, child prostitution and child pornography' A/HRC/12/23 Human Rights Council, Geneva.

McGuire, R.J., J.M. Carlisle, and B.G. Young (1965) 'Sexual deviation as a conditioned behavior: A hypothesis' *Behavioral Research and Therapy* 2, pp. 185–190.

Oppliger, Patrice A. (2008) *Girls Gone Skank: The Sexualization of Girls in American Culture.* MacFarland & Company, Jefferson, North Carolina.

Paul, Pamela (2005) *Pornified: How Pornography is Damaging Our Lives, Our Relationships, and Our Families.* Times Books, New York.

Rachman, S. and R. Hodgson (1968) 'Experimentally-induced "sexual fetishism": Replication and development' *Psychological Record* 18, pp. 25–27.

Russell, Diana E.H. (1977) 'On Pornography' *Chrysalis* 4, pp. 11–15.

Russell, Diana E.H. (1986) *The Secret Trauma: Incest in the Lives of Girls and Women.* Basic Books/Perseus, New York.

Russell, Diana E.H. (1993) *Making Violence Sexy: Feminist Views on Pornography.* Teachers College Press, New York.

Russell, Diana E.H. (1994) *Against Pornography: The Evidence of Harm.* Russell Publications, Berkeley, California.

Russell, Diana E.H. and Natalie Purcell (2006) 'Exposure to Pornography as a cause of child sexual victimization' in Nancy E. Dowd, Dorothy G. Singer and Robin Fretwell Wilson (Eds) *Handbook of Children, Culture and Violence.* Sage Publications, Thousand Oaks, California.

Russell, Diana E.H. and Nicole Van de Ven, (1976/2000) *Crimes Against Women: The Proceedings of the International Tribunal.* Russell Publications, Berkeley, CA.

Senn, Charlene (1993) 'Women's responses to pornography' in Diana E.H. Russell (Ed) *Making violence sexy: Feminist views on pornography.* Teachers College Press, New York, pp. 179–193.

Silbert, Mimi and Ayala Pines (1993) 'Pornography and sexual abuse of women' in Diana E. H. Russell (Ed) *Making violence sexy: Feminist views on pornography.* Teachers College Press, New York, pp. 113–119.

Stock, Wendy (1995) 'The effects of pornography on women' in Laura Lederer and Richard Delgado (Eds) *The price we pay: The case against racist speech, hate propaganda, and pornography.* Hill and Wang, New York, pp. 80–88.

Tabuchi, Hiroko (9 February, 2011) 'In Tokyo, a crackdown of sexual images of minors' *New York Times,* <http://www.nytimes.com/2011/02/10/business/global/10manga.html?_r=1>

Tankard Reist, Melinda (Ed) (2009) *Getting Real. Challenging the Sexualisation of Girls.* Spinifex Press, North Melbourne.

Tate, Tim (1990) *Child pornography: An investigation.* Methuen, London, UK

Tate, Tim (1992) 'The child pornography industry: International trade in child sexual abuse' in Catherine Itzin (Ed) *Pornography: Women, violence, and civil liberties.* Oxford University Press, Oxford and New York, p. 213.

Taylor, Maxwell and Ethel Quayle (2003) *Child pornography: An Internet crime.* Brunner-Routledge, New York.

United States Senate (1984) *Child Pornography and Pedophilia.* 98th Congress, second session, pp. 30–37.

Whetsell-Mitchell, Juliann (1995) *Rape of the innocent: Understanding and preventing child sexual abuse.* Accelerated Development, Washington, DC.

Whisnant, Rebecca (2010) 'From Jekyll to Hyde: The Grooming of Male Pornography Consumers' in Karen Boyle (Ed) *Everyday Pornography.* Routledge, London and New York, pp. 114–33.

Wyre, Ray (1990) 'Why do men sexually abuse children?' in Tim Tate (Ed) *Child pornography: An investigation.* Methuen, London, pp. 281–288.

S. Caroline Taylor

The Pornification of Intrafamilial Rape[1]

The topic of my chapter is the pornification of intrafamilial rape – commonly termed 'incest'. I have elsewhere argued at length why I do not use the term 'incest' when describing the rape and sexual assault of children, adolescents or young adults within a family setting (Taylor, 2001a, 2004a, 2004b). It is a misogynist's word. It is a word that is used to denigrate children and young people who are raped by their father or other relatives. As the majority of offenders are fathers and the majority of victims are daughters (though males are abused also),[2] intrafamilial rape and sexual assault is considered a gendered crime. The word 'incest' is derived from Latin and means impure, unchaste, soiled, and unclean. More generally, the word invokes illicit but consensual sex. Anthropologists have used the term to describe inbreeding practices among close relatives and other forms of tabooed consensual sexual behaviour among lineal relatives. But men raping their girl or boy children are not doing so in order to breed, and they are not engaging in 'consensual' sex. What they are doing is committing sexual, physical and emotional violence against their children.

Lawyers prefer the word 'incest' because it continues to embed ideas of 'consent' in the minds of the public. It masks the reality of what is actually happening, that a child or young person is being systematically raped by their relative. Use of the term 'incest' arouses all manner of stigma towards the victim – so the use of the word helps to protect perpetrators. The term is proactive in that its use immediately conjures up a prohibited 'sexual relationship', making the term even more inappropriate to describe the systematic rape and sexual abuse of children by their parent or other relative. The media too is guilty of pornographising the term 'incest' and I have highlighted this trend elsewhere (see Taylor, 2002). In a 2010 news story, in print and on TV, about a perpetrator

---

1   I wish to acknowledge and thank Dr Abigail Bray for assisting me with editing, research assistance and researching online material from pornography sites. Personally I found the experience of writing this chapter deeply distressing and traumatic because of the material content I needed to access. I am very grateful to Abigail for assisting me with this chapter and providing collegial support to complete this task.
2   A discussion of brothers abusing younger siblings falls outside the scope of this chapter.

who was found guilty of sexually abusing his young daughter, he was called a man who "had sex with his daughter."[3] Many survivors report feelings of intense distress, shame and humiliation when they encounter this continued intimation of victims as proactive partners to their own rape.[4] Such language continues to fuel a public discourse of intrafamilial sexual abuse as 'incest' and as such, an illicit but consensual, even if only partially, act involving the victim.

The word 'incest' has become so eroticised that it fuels the staple diet of pornography users, readers and pornography makers. International research highlights the significant degree to which pornography is dedicated to 'incest' themes (e.g. Finkelhor, 1984; Itzin, 1996; Jenkins, 2001; Russell and Purcell, 2006). But not just any theme – pornography makers know their market well – and they know what men want to see. Nearly always the theme is of father and daughter. Reflecting patriarchal psychological theories of 'incest', pornography depicts the girl child as seducing her father. The mother is portrayed as sexually unavailable or sexually unattractive – either way, in a pornographic script, the mother fails to sexually service her husband's needs – just as she does in much of the literature on child sex abuse. The child is portrayed as nymph-like. Most importantly, she 'loves' being penetrated vaginally, orally and anally by her own father. Being penetrated is great fun for girls of all ages according to porno makers. Even in popularised pornography such as *Playboy* and *Penthouse*, a lot of energy is directed toward fathers raping their daughters (see Russell, this volume). 'Rape' is what every child and woman wants. Female bodies are designed for penetration and it is considered a male right to access women's and children's bodies any time they wish to do so. Pornography provides and enforces such an ideology – an ideology of rape.

Gail Dines argues that much of 'incest porn' is pseudo child pornography, a popular genre within the increasingly violent billion-dollar gonzo pornography market that is now mainstream (2010, p. 154). Many 'incest' porn Websites urge fathers to rape their daughters, often providing them with advice about how to 'seduce' their daughters. As 'Family Seduction' puts it: "you won't get this advice anywhere. Family Seduction is here to help. Don't wait anymore. Go tell the family member that you want sex right now!" This incitement to child rape is described as a "step-by-step guide to sexual heaven!" Questions such as "how can I seduce my own daughter?" rotate relentlessly in a pop-up window on the Website along with gratuitous prompting: "always get an erection when

---

3   <http://news.ninemsn.com.au/national/8143268/father-in-court-for-sex-offences>
4   This information is gleaned from personal interviews as part of previous and current research undertaken by the author.

she's around" which then rapidly segues to numerous pornographic images of old, greying, overweight men penetrating childish-looking females. Other sites show younger-looking men and pre-pubescent girls with small hands, flat chests, hair in pigtails and ankle socks with lace around the edge and button-flat shoes, like a 5-year-old might wear. Her hands look tiny against the erect penis of the father with the text next to it saying, "daddy's little girl knows what she wants" or "daddy's little girl loves to suck his cock." Short stories accompanying these images tell of little girls with 'hairless pussies' seducing their daddy and begging for sex. The father is simply gratifying his highly sexualised and nymphomaniac child. Just satisfying her wish.

Promoting mother–son 'incest' is also a feature of pornography. Clearly the trendy but repugnant term of MILF (mothers I'd like to fuck) is promoted on some of these sites as sons fulfilling a type of Oedipal fantasy, and mothers, as some sites say, simply 'gagging' for it.[5]

'Incest' pornography Websites often mock and trivialise the criminalisation of child rape. As YoungDaughter puts it:

> The disapproval of incest, especially between father and daughter, is a classic example of 'projection'. The alleged reason for disapproval [sic] is that incest is the same as sexual abuse, aggression and violence. These are all rational argument [sic] but they are used to justify an irrational opinion. In fact, most cases of incest have little to do with violence.

'First Time With Daddy' flatters the ego of fathers who want to rape their daughters: "when a dad is so handsome incest is natural. Don't think it's filthy. After all, father will always be the paragon man for their daughter. Just set your mind free and get in! Tons of XXX love stories inside!"

Raping dependent children is transformed by pornography into a natural, open-minded, love story. "[F]eel the overwhelming incest passion flowing through your body and mind – and get ready to enjoy!" boasts '3D incest videos'.

Narratives about seductive children saturate the 'incest' genre. In *Daddy's Whore* viewers can watch "sexy naughty girls seducing their own fathers". In *My Sexy Daughter* children are "sweet, irresistible angels teasing and tempting their own daddies." Websites such as 'First Time with Daddy' are common. Girl children are depicted as devious and sexually rapacious, even resorting to drugging fathers in order to seduce them. In many of the written pornographic stories, daughters are eager, willing and cooperative and are turned on rather than traumatised. This

---

5   See for example: 'MILF Episodes' of mother–son incest at <http://www.luchstories.com/ stories/incest/the milf-episode-3.aspx>; <http://incestreviews.com/?advic=5668>; <http// www.hardsextube.com/video/8846/mature-sex-incest>.

fantasy of the child willing, wanting and loving it, reflects men's desires and the patriarchal rule of the father.

Unfortunately, one doesn't even need to access 'incest' pornography to find these scenarios. Read Family Dysfunction literature from the discipline of psychology and social sciences and you will find research-based scenarios that explain 'incest' as illicit sexual desires girls harbour for their fathers. And of families where the mother is sexually unattractive or sexually unavailable to the husband and so the daughter 'substitutes', most often with the full knowledge and support of the mother.

Family Dysfunction theory is replete with proactive language describing the 'incest' as a father–daughter 'affair'; a 'sexual relationship'; 'consensual' sex and 'seduction'. Some of the research case studies read like pornographic vignettes, a point I have made explicit in previous published work. Read some legal judgements in 'incest' trials: far from understanding that a girl or young woman has been raped by her father or other male relative, some judges are prone to talk down trauma and talk up the 'sexual relationship' between the offender and victim. In some cases, the 'culpability' of the victim has been discussed on the basis that 'incest' is consensual and simply cannot be regarded as rape (for sources see Taylor, 2001a 2001b, 2004a and b).

In *Court Licensed Abuse* (2004a) I discuss a court judgement where a 12-year-old girl was merely a "sexual substitute to replace the dissatisfying sex the man was having with his wife." Under the rubric of 'incest' laws, the victim can be co-charged with the offender as they are considered complicit in the commission of the crime (Taylor, 2001a). Indeed, some disturbing studies have shown the very real propensity for health and welfare professionals to view child abuse identified as 'incest' as less serious than other forms of child abuse with the child held accountable for the abuse to varying degrees (see Taylor, 1997; 2001a and b; 2004a). And several studies on juror attitudes have shown that the longer a child is subjected to abuse within the family unit, the more likely those jurors were to blame the child (Taylor, 2001a and 2004a).

Male pornography consumers can 'choose' between porn that perpetuates the self-serving fantasy that fathers and daughters are engaged in consensual sex, or pornography which celebrates fathers violently raping their daughters. MySexyDaughter.com states that "We know you enjoy *rough and bewildering incest action*, so we have a very special thing for you" (my emphasis). 'UseMyDaughter.com' has a banner that reads, "Want to Fuck My Daughter?" and then states "Watch this slut take cocks for cash in my pockets." The word 'rape' is a key word in the advertisement for these popular 'incest' Websites. In 'How I Became My

Daddy's Whore' a father repeatedly rapes his daughter in her bedroom one night: "I flipped my daughter over and shoved my cock back into her sopping wet pussy and pounded the shit out of my little girl! I pulled her hair, and made her scream into her pillow and said 'Be yer daddy's little whore tonight, baby' … I raped my little girl on all fours on the floor." A disclaimer at the end of this child rape story states: "The author does not condone child abuse, this story is meant as an erotic fantasy not real life." I ask: For whom is the raping of children an erotic fantasy?

Another large 'incest' site is described as "a unique site offering reality videos from a real *incest-addicted* family" (my emphasis). Here viewers can watch videos called *brother rapes little sister, dad fucks his little daughter in ass, old dad fucks his little daughter, little daughter raped in the bath*, and *innocent daughter raped by daddy*. The normalisation of 'incest', rape and abuse are, as Gail Dines (2010) argues, achieved by desensitising the users of pornography through repetitions and gradual escalations of violence.

Smiling or providing the necessary groans and/or self-derogatory language that will excite the unknown eyes that view her flesh are common in 'incest' pornography. Because she is only flesh that is there for men to penetrate and control and denigrate.

But children's expressions of terror and horror are also a source of sexual excitement for men. In 2004, I was informed about a case in Australia when police swooped on a child sex abuse and pornography ring. One lot of pornographic images showed an infant girl the police believed to be approximately 2 years old. The photographs show her being held down by at least two adult men while she is being fully penetrated. The child's face is twisted in pain and terror. Police also uncovered a video of the same horrendous crime. During an interview, the man who had penetrated the toddler told a female detective that there was "nothing quite like hearing the 'crack' of an infant's pelvis while you are penetrating them." This 'crack' was the breaking of the child's pelvic bone.

Pornography debases women – every woman and every girl child. Those who view pornography are not partaking in a morally neutral activity. They are acting as 'patrons'. Their patronage fuels pornography, commissions further pornography and leads to ever more degrading ways of depicting women and children. Furthermore, those who view pornography are more likely to then act out what they see. In my previous and current research on intrafamilial sexual abuse, many survivors have relayed to me how they were forced to view pornography by the offender and how the offender then wanted them to replicate the sex acts portrayed on the screen. In several cases I know of victim/survivors who were abused well into adolescence were forced to take part in sexual acts that were filmed. Many live with the sheer terror that one day these photos will surface. This greatly exacerbates their trauma. A 2009 US media article identified a serious case of long-term, repeated rape and sexual abuse of children and adolescents by family relatives, with the case only coming to light when the wife of one of the men found 'incest porn' in the family home. The case has revealed years of horrendous rapes and sexual assaults on children and adolescents including the production of pornography. Authorities identified the accused men as being in possession of significant amounts of 'incest porn' and as the authorities noted, while 'incest' is illegal, pornography depicting incest is often not illegal (CBS News, 2009).

Here is my question for you: Does pornography reflect fantasy or reality? We often hear the arguments that pornography affords a 'release' and an 'escape' from reality and that it delivers just harmless sexual fantasies. But we know that far from providing fantasies, pornography reflects only too sharply the lived reality of so many women and girl children. Yet given the theoretical and legal placement of victims in much of psychological and legal discourse, is it any wonder that pornography is defended as a 'right' of men to purchase, produce, commission and view?

Ostensibly, the law prohibits rape and sexual assault, including intrafamilial sexual abuse. Reality shows us that too often the legal process sustains the rights of child rapists via the construction of children as liars and fantasisers, vengeful colluders or seducers (Taylor 2001a and 2004a). Pornography too 'legalises' rape because it shows men that women and children are bodies that are there for the taking. Pornography is the training ground of future and current rapists. It is the training ground for society to understand that women and girl children are groups of sub-human citizens and how to respond accordingly. It is the training ground for social stereotypes that make the work I and others do all the more difficult. For all the excellent research into the extent, nature and trauma of sexual violence, pornography is out there depicting the opposite. Its harm to women and children generally is immeasurable.

Pornography is not just about dirty pictures and books sold in sex shops and restricted bookshelves in newsagents. Pornography – and in particular intrafamiliar pornography – is the ideology that regards women and girl children as repositories for men's sexual needs; it is the mindset that excuses and sanctions sexual offending and refuses to acknowledge the harm of sexual violence.

Bibliography

CBS News (19 November, 2009) 'Mohler Family Sex Crimes Case: Wife Found Incest Porno, Say Cops', <http://www.cbsnews.com/8301-504083_162-5708939-504083.html> (accessed 23 January, 2011).

Dines, Gail (2010) *Pornland: How Porn Has Hijacked Our Sexuality.* Beacon Press, Boston; Spinifex Press, North Melbourne.

Finkelhor, David (1984) *Child Sexual Abuse: New Theory and Research.* The Free Press, New York.

Itzin, Catherine (1996) 'Pornography and the organisation of child sexual abuse' in P. C. Bibby (Ed) *Organized Abuse: The Current Debate,* Aldershot, Hampshire, pp. 167–196.

Jenkins, Philip (2001) *Beyond Tolerance: Child Pornography on the Internet.* New York University Press, New York.

Russell, Diana and Natalie J. Purcell (2006) 'Exposure to Pornography as a cause of child sexual victimization' in Nancy E. Dowd, Dorothy G. Singer, Robin Fretwell Wils (Eds) *Handbook of Children, Culture, and Violence.* Sage Publications, London.

Taylor, S. Caroline (1997) 'Betrayal of the Innocents.' *Australian Journal of Women Against Violence.* Issue 3, November, pp. 31–37.

Taylor, S. Caroline (2001a) *The Legal Construction of Victim/Survivors in Parent-Child Intrafamilial Sexual Abuse Trials in the Victorian Country Court of Australia in 1995.* PhD, University of Ballarat.

Taylor, S. Caroline (2001b) 'A Name By Any Other Word Does Not Necessarily Make It Merely Another Rose' in Alice Mills and Jeremy Smith (Eds) *Utter Silence: Voicing the Unspeakable.* Peter Lang, New York, pp. 211–228.

Taylor, S. Caroline (11 October, 2002) 'Correct Language Necessary for Victims of Family Violence' *The Courier,* Ballarat, p. 9.

Taylor, S. Caroline (2004a) *Court Licensed Abuse.* Peter Lang, New York.

Taylor, S. Caroline (2004b) *Surviving the Legal System.* Coulomb Communications, Port Melbourne.

Caroline Norma

Teaching Tools and Recipe Books: Pornography and the Sexual Assault of Children

At a 1984 US Senate Subcommittee hearing on juvenile justice, Katherine Brady testified that her father used pornography to sexually abuse her as a child in 3 different ways. Firstly, "he would use it as a teaching tool – as a way of instructing me about sex and what he wanted me to do with him." Secondly, he "used the pictures to justify his abuse and to convince me that what we were doing was normal." Thirdly, "he used the pornography to break down my resistance ... [because] [t]he pornography made the statement that females are nothing more than objects for men's sexual gratification" (in Russell, 1993, pp. 43–44). One year earlier, in 1983, psychologist Sue Schafer testified at the Minneapolis City Council pornography ordinance hearings about a fourth way in which men use pornography to aid their sexual assault of children. She saw them using it as a source of inspiration for their crimes. Schafer said she had counselled a number of children who had been abused in situations where "the perpetrator has read the manuals and manuscripts at night and used these as recipe books by day" (Schafer, 1988, p. 126).

Twenty-five years later, these 4 different ways in which Brady and Schafer describe men using pornography in their abuse of children are not generally discussed in mainstream academic studies of 'grooming', which is the umbrella term that now popularly describes the tricks and techniques of child sexual abuse. When comment on grooming does occasionally broach the topic of pornography, concern coalesces around 3 things. Academics are mainly concerned about offenders' use of pornography to pique sexual feelings or curiosity in children, their use of pornography to blackmail children into keeping quiet about abuse, and their use of pornography to create a sexualised environment conducive to abuse. Legal theorist Anne-Marie McAlinden's following comments from 2006 are typical of how narrowly pornography is discussed in contemporary studies on grooming:

The offender will often use 'forbidden fruit' type activities such as cursing, telling 'dirty jokes' or showing the child pornography to introduce sexual themes into their conversations. This latter stage not only begins to normalize sexual behaviour but may also be used to entrap the child further. The use of pornography in particular may encourage feelings of shame and guilt which the offender may exploit by persuading the child that they were willing accomplices in their activities (McAlinden, 2006, p. 347).

The ways in which McAlinden observes men using pornography in their sexual abuse of children are certainly important and worrying. There have also been a number of good outcomes of this kind of research. In Australia, and around the world, in the last 10 years governments have amended their criminal codes to include 'anti-grooming' provisions (Australian Institute of Criminology, 2008), even if these provisions mostly target online offenders. The 1995 Australian *Criminal Code Act*, for example, now includes provisions against "[u]sing a postal or similar service to 'groom' persons under 16" and "[u]sing a carriage service to 'groom' persons under 16 years of age", as well as a clause against " '[g]rooming' a child to engage in sexual activity outside Australia."

Despite increased levels of public awareness of the tricks and techniques of child sexual abuse, pornography continues to be marginalised in the academic conversation on grooming. This is in spite of accounts as far back as the 1980s from women like Brady and Schafer that establish pornography as a 'teaching tool' and a 'recipe book' that facilitates child sexual abuse, as well as inspires the abuses men inflict. These accounts show that one of the harms of pornography can be seen in the way men use it, and this harm derives from its instrumental use as a tool of child sexual assault.

The understatement of the problem of pornography in contemporary discussions of grooming continues in spite of plentiful evidence of men using pornography as a 'teaching tool' to sexually abuse children. The records of criminal cases are an easily accessible source of evidence, and contain precise accounts of pornography being used as an instrument of child sexual assault. In a 2010 New Zealand case, for example, a father was sentenced to a term of imprisonment after sexually abusing his daughter for 13 years, including when she was in hospital for injuries sustained after a serious accident (R *v H* HC AK CRI 2009-092-02). In sentencing, the judge noted that 'Mr H' had "used pornographic films extensively" in his offending. The judge commented that "you cynically took advantage of her when you first detected the possibility of growing sexual awareness on her part at a time when she was still very young." Mr H's daughter had asked him about reproduction when she was 5 years old and, in response to this, he had "showed her a pornographic movie as a method of instruction." Mr H himself acknowledged that "things simply developed from there." He introduced pornography very literally to his daughter as a 'teaching tool' when she was 5 years old in order to initiate the abuse he inflicted on her for the next 13 years.

Mr H also used pornography to expand the range of his sexual abuse to the young friends his daughter brought home to stay overnight. The judge noted that, in the case of one friend who intermittently slept over at the house for a number of years, "whenever she went to your house, you showed pornographic movies and would ask [your daughter] and [her friend] to act out what was being screened." The judge further commented that this "led to explicit touching and to masturbation on your part." Using pornography, Mr H was able to not only expand the range of his own assaults, but also teach his daughter to offend against her young friend for his gratification.

It is worth noting the severe effects of Mr H's crimes on his victims, in which pornography was recognised by the court as playing a large part. In a victim impact statement, Mr H's daughter said she had been "unable to sleep during the night" during her childhood, and would "remain awake watching the bedroom door which she kept locked." She would catch up on sleep during the day. In her teenage years she had "turned to cannabis and alcohol, but found that things just became worse", and this led her to attempt suicide in the year before the court case.

The Melbourne case of *R v FVK* (2002) further shows a man using pornography to commission his sexual abuse of a girl. A father was charged with twelve counts of sexual and physical assault of his daughter. As a 15-year-old, the girl testified in court that, when she was 10, her father showed her

> … pictures of naked women and guys having sex and then he showed me this lady sucking this other guy's dick. And I went to have a bath and he came in as well and started undressing and he got in, and he said, "Why don't you suck my dick like you saw in the picture?"

The girl recalled that, "I had to put his dick in my mouth[,] … but I didn't suck it ... [h]e kept on urging me to suck it but I didn't." The incomplete success of pornography as a 'teaching tool' in this instance was only due to the girl's exceptional bravery. At the same time her father was using pornography as a 'teaching tool' against her, he was also enforcing its 'lessons' through brutal violence. In one instance he "made her bend over a chair and whipped her," and in court the girl testified that "sometimes I fall to the ground and he keeps on kicking me ... he's kicked me in the ribs and legs and he has given me a black eye before …"

Not surprisingly, this physical violence consolidating the father's pornographic 'teachings' generally secured the girl's acquiescence to sexual abuse. In relation to a later instance, she recalled that,

[w]hile he was sucking my private part, he was asking me, "Does it feel good?" and that I didn't respond 'cos it didn't feel good and I didn't want to say that 'cos then he might have hit me or something.

In this girl's case, obedience secured through physical violence gradually came to replace the use of pornography as a 'teaching tool', but pornography nonetheless featured prominently in her initial victimisation.

Even with this kind of direct and recent evidence of men relying on pornography to orchestrate child sexual assault, the Australian government recognises this particular harm of pornography in only the most limited of terms. In 2008, it legislated against the carriage of pornography into a number of "vulnerable [Aboriginal] communities" (Emergency Response Consolidation Bill, 2008) on the basis of the publication of the *'Little Children are Sacred' Report* (Northern Territory Government, 2007), which contained discussion of pornography being used in the sexual abuse of children in Aboriginal communities. The report prompted the government to legislate against pornography as an instrument of child sexual abuse, but only in very narrow and racially-defined terms. The government chose to ignore evidence, like that circulating in Australia's criminal courts, of men from a range of backgrounds using pornography in a similar way. It also chose to overlook the sex industry businesses that had been profiting from the trafficking of pornography into Aboriginal communities for many years, as Melinda Tankard Reist points out:

The government needs not only to ban pornography in the Northern Territory but to stop it being shipped out of Canberra. If the ACT Government will not take responsibility for its porn trade, it is time for the Federal Government to show even greater resolve and override the territory's laws (Tankard Reist, 2007).

In limiting its pornography suppression order to only a small number of remote Aboriginal communities, the government also ignored concerns raised by Aboriginal women leaders outside of the Northern Territory that pornography was escalating rates of child sexual abuse in their communities (see Queensland Government, 1999, p. 100). One of these leaders, Gracelyn Smallwood, spoke out 18 years before the enactment of the legislation, in 1990, about her experience as a nurse in a remote Queensland community in Cape York. She told a newspaper reporter at the time that:

... videos are being sold by the same unscrupulous individuals who make a fortune out of peddling sly grog on communities. The people who watch them think, if it's in the movie, it must be all right to go out and do it ... [As a result,] [l]ittle kids are brought into hospital with heavy sweating and other symptoms ... [a]t first it was baffling until syphilis and gonorrhoea were diagnosed (in Roberts, 1990).

Feminist insights like this from the 1990s, and those from earlier in the 1980s, articulating the fact that men rely on pornography as a 'teaching tool' and 'recipe book' to sexually assault children do not feature within the conceptual frame of 'grooming' that currently conveys mainstream public concern about male sexual behaviour. However, as a publicly palatable way of naming and problematising this behaviour, the discourse of grooming currently presents feminists with an opportunity to have one of pornography's harms more widely recognised. Through highlighting the central role of pornography in all of the tricks and techniques men use to groom their victims, whether online or in real life, feminists can capitalise on the grooming discourse to show pornography to be a product of compounding sexual violence for women and girls who are harmed first in its production, and then its application.

Bibliography

Australian Institute of Criminology (2008) 'Online grooming laws', <http://www.aic.gov.au/publications/current%20series/htcb/1-20/htcb017.aspx>. (accessed 30 January, 2011).

Brady, Katherine (1993) 'Testimony on pornography and incest' in Diana Russell (Ed) *Making violence sexy: feminist views on pornography*. Teachers College Press, New York, pp. 43–44.

Commonwealth of Australia, *Criminal Code Act*, 1995.

Families, Housing, Community Services and Indigenous Affairs and Other Legislation Amendment (Emergency Response Consolidation) Bill (2008) *Explanatory Memorandum*.

McAlinden, Anne-Marie (2006) '"Setting 'em up": Personal, familial and institutional grooming in the sexual abuse of children' *Social Legal Studies* 15 (3) pp. 339–362.

Northern Territory Government (2007) *'Little Children are Sacred': Report of the Northern Territory Board of Inquiry into the protection of Aboriginal children from sexual abuse*.

Queensland Government (1999) *Report of the Aboriginal and Torres Strait Islander Women's Task Force on Violence*.

Roberts, Greg (11 August, 1990) 'Damned children on the islands of despair', *Sydney Morning Herald* p. 69.

R v FVK [2002] Supreme Court of Victoria, Court of appeal, <http://www.austlii.edu.au/au/cases/vic/VSCA/2002/225.html>.

R V H [2010] HC AK CRI 2009-092-02 High Court of New Zealand, <http://www.nzlii.org/nz/cases/NZHC/2010/1150.html>.

Schafer, Sue (1988) 'Pornography as instruction manual for abuse' in Everywoman (Ed) *Pornography and sexual violence: evidence of the links* (p. 126). Everywoman, London.

Tankard Reist, Melinda (2007) 'An invasion of pornography', <http://www.onlineopinion.com.au/view.asp?article=6114&page=2> (accessed 19 March, 2011).

Helen Pringle

Civil Justice for Victims of Child Pornography

Child sexual abuse materials are trafficked through exchange or sale at an increasing rate, with the Internet making access much easier, faster and more private. The United Nations Convention on the Rights of the Child places a comprehensive legal duty on states to protect children from sexual abuse and exploitation. In most countries, those who produce and traffic images, videos and other child abuse materials face prison sentences if they are caught and successfully prosecuted, just as do those who sexually assault children. The Optional Protocol to the Convention on the Sale of Children, Child Prostitution and Child Pornography requires states to bring under their criminal or penal law the "[p]roducing, distributing, disseminating, importing, exporting, offering, selling or possessing" of child pornography. Of 196 nations, however, 122 do not criminalise the knowing *possession* of child pornography (ICMEC, 2010).

It is sometimes claimed that the chief harm of child pornography lies in its production, and that by the time the images are downloaded, the harm has already been done – the conclusion being that 'mere possession' is like a 'victimless crime' and should not be penalised heavily. This claim and this conclusion fly in the face of how child pornography works.

Once in circulation on the Internet, child abuse materials constitute a continuing victimisation of children which goes beyond the wrong, damage, and injury done in their original production. Not all child abuse materials involve the sexual assault of children in their production,[1] but where they do, these children are victimised again *every time* their image is viewed or downloaded. These children, as well as adults who were abused in their childhood for the purpose of producing pornography, can also be subject to further victimisation when people

---

1   For example, cartoons and digitally altered material, and manuals of child abuse, do not necessarily involve the direct abuse of children in their *production* (see Pringle, 2011).

recognise them on the street, or even try to contact them to do further harm (see examples in *McDaniel*, 28 January, 2011, and *Falso*, 6 February, 2009).[2]

Where pornography is so ubiquitous, and its effects are so far-reaching, it is easy to fall for the idea that not much can be done in these cases. In such circumstances, despair can easily take over, and hope can easily be lost. But there are some hopeful signs that promise redress for victims of child pornography.

One of these is the development of innovative approaches to civil justice now being widely used in the United States. These approaches involve recovering damages and making restitution for the children (or the adults they have become) from those who participated in, or recorded, the original abuse, and from the 'end-users' of pornography. By 'end-users', I mean those who view, download, circulate or possess those images, even long after they were first made.

An important step here was the passing by the United States Congress of a provision known as Masha's Law. Masha's Law forms part of the Adam Walsh Child Protection and Safety Act, which became law with bipartisan support in July, 2006 (now 18 USC § 2255). This law increased the minimum *mandatory* penalty for downloading (including viewing) child pornography to US$150,000, up from US$50,000 (which was at that time one-third of the penalty for unlawfully downloading songs). Masha's Law also allows people over 18 to continue to sue those who download or possess images of them made when they were children.

The law was named after Masha Allen who was adopted from a Russian orphanage in 1998 at the age of 5 by Matthew Mancuso, a wealthy engineer. Masha's account of what happened over the following 5 years was given as testimony in committee hearings at the US Congress in 2006 (Allen, 2006a; see also US Congress, 2006). Mancuso sexually assaulted Masha from the first day she arrived at his home, and straight away began posting her images to the Internet. He had also previously abused his two older daughters. Mancuso was found guilty of the sexual abuse of Masha, and gaoled. However, Masha's images are still being trafficked on the Internet, and in a Victim Impact Statement, Masha said that the circulation of her pictures is actually even more disturbing to her than Mancuso's actions:

> The absolute worst thing about everything that happened to me was that Matthew put my pictures on the internet. He traded them with other people like baseball cards. What kind of people want to see pictures of a little girl being sexually abused? I was told that my pictures

---

2   I would like to thank James Marsh of the Marsh Law Firm PLLC for his generosity in providing me with materials as well as invaluable suggestions and comments for this chapter. I would also like to commend his grace and courage, and that of the children, young and old, whom he supports and defends.

are the most popular on the internet. How can so many people enjoy the horrible things that happened to me? Now every day and everywhere I go I have to worry about who has seen the awful things that happened to me. And what do they think about me now? Do they want to hurt me? Or rape me? Or do they think I am bad, dirty, and ugly. I know that these pictures will never end and that the abuse from them will go on forever ...

I want every single person who downloads my picture to go to jail and really be punished as much as possible. They are as bad as Matthew. They want to see me suffer. They want to see me starved and hurt and sad and abused. Child pornography is not a victimless crime. I am a victim and I still suffer every day and every time someone sees me being abused (Allen, 2006b).

Because of the long period during which Masha was assaulted by Mancuso, police found it wrenching to watch her growing up as a victim of sexual assault, as she aged in the pictures that they traced. The Internet circulation of the pictures prolongs her abuse to infinity, as each person who downloads her pictures participates in her abuse. For a time, Amazon.com sold a book by a convicted child pornography user, Peter Sotos, called *Show Adult*, which was advertised as featuring "the child porn star Masha Allen" (Marsh, 2007).[3]

Those who download child pornography often know exactly what harm they are doing. For example, a young US college student arraigned on child pornography charges who saw Masha on TV and realized that he had seen her pictures online, said, "It made me feel like an evil monster – as if I had helped in hurting her" (Koch, 2006). The young man was right; he had helped to hurt her.

The possibility of gaining justice for those hurt by child pornography has been explored in the United States in other ways as well. A section of the US Code enacted in 1994 provides for Mandatory Restitution in cases involving certain crimes, including child pornography and sexual exploitation (18 USC § 2259). Under this statute, US federal courts have a duty to order defendants to pay "the full amount of the victim's losses" following successful criminal prosecutions, including those for possession of child pornography.

The case of Amy (a pseudonym) involved a little girl sexually assaulted by her uncle who then uploaded images of the abuse. Amy tells her story in the next chapter of this book. The man was arrested and convicted, but the images (known as the 'Misty Series') continue to circulate on the Internet. The 'Misty Series' of images was viewed by at least 8,800 Internet users in 2009 alone; unfortunately, this figure is likely to be only a fraction of the total number of viewers. Amy first became aware of the circulation of her images when she received victim notifications from the US government, as mandated by the Crime Victims Rights Act. Amy's lawyer, James Marsh, is asking that *each* person found

---

3 James Marsh kindly provided me with a copy of chapters from this book.

guilty of possessing even a single image of Amy's abuse pay restitution until her total claim of over US$3.4 million is paid. This amount includes her losses, costs for future psychological care, future lost income, and attorney's fees (see Schwartz, 2010).

James Marsh contends that each person found guilty of Amy's violation through pornography should be ordered to pay the full amount of restitution, under the legal doctrine of 'joint and several liability'.[4] This approach entails that a victim would stop collecting restitution once the full amount of damages claimed is paid; those held responsible for the acts could then sue others who are found culpable so as to recoup any over-payments of their proportionate contribution. Amy's court filings have been emailed to US Attorneys in over 500 child pornography cases, many of whom have filed restitution claims for Amy.

For example, in February 2009, in the state of Connecticut, the US District Court Judge Warren W. Eginton indicated that Alan Hesketh should pay a total of US$200,000 to Amy. Hesketh was a British citizen and a vice-president and global patent director of the pharmaceutical firm Pfizer (*Hesketh*, 2009). Hesketh was held responsible even though he had played no direct part in the *originating* production or initial uploading of Amy's images; he had traded the images while posing online as a 28-year-old woman named 'Suzybibaby'. Amy received US$130,000 in a settlement reached with Hesketh (see also Rothman, 2011, pp. 349–350), the first time the *possession* of child pornography images involved payment of restitution to the victim.

Later in 2009, in 2 separate Florida cases (*Freeman*, 2009, and *Staples*, 2009), men convicted on child pornography charges were ordered to pay almost US$3.3 million and US$3.7 million respectively to Amy (also see Rothman 2011, p. 335). The former case involved an international network of child pornography which was uncovered in part through the efforts of Australian police (Department of Justice, 2009). By mid-2010, Amy had received about US$236,100 from 10 defendants (Edwards, 2010).

Amy's claims have met some setbacks however. For example, in a Texas court in 2009, a Request for Restitution of around US$3.4 million was made from a man called Doyle Paroline who had pleaded guilty to child pornography charges. The Request was denied with the judge finding that the argument had not been successfully made for the 'proximate causation' of injury resulting from possession of Amy's images by Paroline, as distinct from other viewers of her pictures (*Paroline*, 2009, and *In re Amy*, 2009; see also Rothman 2011, p. 335,

---

4   The responsibility in this context of Internet service providers (ISP) for material hosted is as yet unclear. See on this question more broadly, Akdeniz (2008, Part Three).

pp. 351–353). In March 2011, however, that decision was overturned by the Texas Court of Appeals, and the case was sent back for Amy's damages to be determined on the basis that Paroline could be held financially responsible for injury to Amy (*In re Amy Unknown*, 2011).

Through the efforts of Amy and her lawyers, a valuable body of case law and argumentation has been built up. Even temporary setbacks like the 2009 *Paroline* decision have in turn provided opportunities to clarify different aspects of the law on restitution. In that sense, the courage and perseverance of Amy and her defenders provide a basis on which other countries might work out and implement similar approaches to civil justice for victims of child pornography.

Another group of attorneys in the United States has begun to open up further opportunities for claiming civil damages for the victims of child pornography. For example, in 2010 the firm of Jeff Anderson & Associates filed suit in a Minnesota District Court on behalf of a man who was 9 years old when images of his sexual abuse were originally produced. The defendants in the case include Gregg Alan Larsen, a schoolteacher and foster care provider, and 100 unnamed 'downloaders' who received and/or viewed the boy's images (Forliti, 2010). Larsen was sentenced in November, 2010, for producing and possessing child pornography. Four civil claims have been filed against Larsen on behalf of children who were in his care.[5]

The approaches in search of justice for child pornography victims mentioned in this chapter differ in important ways. But the striking common feature of all these approaches is that the viewers and possessors, and not merely the original producers, of abuse materials can be held accountable in financial as well as penal terms for the damage that their actions do. Importantly also, such claims for damages and restitution shift the financial burden of the crimes onto convicted criminals, and away from the victims of crime and away from the public more broadly. In that sense, what can be seen here is the emergence of a 'civil rights' approach to child pornography, capable of being used in other countries to address the global trade in abuse.

I conclude by noting that such an approach, whatever its variations in form, is not without controversy. Some academic writers like Amy Adler have criticised the approach, asserting that a problem with cases involving claimants like Amy is that those convicted of possession of images seem to be penalised as much or even more than those who physically assault the child and originally produce

---

5   I would like to thank Patrick Noaker of the firm of Jeff Anderson & Associates for his helpful comments (personal communication, March, 2011).

the images. Adler notes, for example, "Not to excuse what the downloaders do and their complicity, but the actual abuser, the person who took the picture is worse. He actually harmed the child" (quoted in James, 2010; see more broadly Adler, 2001).

Adler draws attention to what she sees as a loss of perspective in such cases, with the possibility of people being prosecuted for possessing pictures of a child in a bathtub. James Marsh replies:

> There's a real disconnect on what the true nature of child porn is ... 99.9999 percent of the material I deal with features pre-pubescent children being raped ... the most graphic hardcore images you can imagine. People think downloading a picture of a baby in a bathtub is going to send them to prison. That's not what we're talking about (quoted in James, 2010).

Marsh noted that "[i]n one notorious set of images, the father used to put a studded collar around his 6-year-old and wrote on her in what looked like blood, 'I am Daddy's little girl, rape me.' He locked her in a dog cage" (quoted in James, 2010).

In a child pornography case involving a student at my own university in Sydney, the materials at issue included "videos of a baby bound and sexually assaulted, a two year old girl subjected to anal intercourse, numerous images of young girls apparently heavily sedated being sexually assaulted and a girl under ten bound and subjected to an act of anal intercourse while crying with the pain" (*Puhakka*, 2009). On appeal, the student's gaol term was reduced, in part because of his young age.

Among some academics like Amy Adler, there is not only a disconnect with the actual character of the material that is globally trafficked. There is also a disconnect with how child pornography does its work of harm and injury. Each viewer who delights in such images *participates* in the abuse of the child in the image. Amy's Victim Impact Statement, reprinted in the next chapter, emphasises this point: "Every day of my life I live in constant fear that someone will see my pictures and recognize me and that I will be humiliated all over again. It hurts me to know someone is looking at them – at me – when I was just a little girl being abused for the camera." And each viewer who gets off on that abuse should pay the price of making that little girl whole again.[6]

---

6   I am persuaded by the argument of Amar and Widawsky (1992) that we should treat child abuse as slavery; the implications of that argument for child abuse materials is a topic for further exploration.

Bibliography

Adam Walsh Child Protection and Safety Act, Public Law 109–248, § 707, <www.justice.gov/criminal/ceos/Adam%20Walsh.pdf> (accessed 6 April, 2011).

Adler, Amy (2001) 'The Perverse Law of Child Pornography' *Columbia Law Review* 101 (2), pp. 209–273.

Akdeniz, Yaman (2008) *Internet Child Pornography and the Law: National and International Responses.* Ashgate Publishing, Aldershot.

Allen, Masha (3 May, 2006a) Testimony submitted to the [US Congress] House Energy and Commerce Committee Subcommittee on Oversight and Investigations, 'Sexual Exploitation of Children over the Internet: What Parents, Kids and Congress Need to Know about Child Predators', <http://archives.energycommerce.house.gov/reparchives/108/Hearings/05032006 hearing1852/Allen.pdf> (accessed 6 April, 2011).

Allen, Masha (2006b) Victim Impact Statement, <http://poundpuplegacy.org/files/victim_statement.pdf> (accessed 6 April, 2011).

Amar, Akhil Reed and Daniel Widawsky (1992) 'Child Abuse as Slavery: A Thirteenth Amendment Response to *DeShaney*', *Harvard Law Review* 105, pp. 1359–1385.

Crime Victims Rights Act [US], <http://www.law.cornell.edu/uscode/42/usc_sup_01_42_10_112.html> (accessed 6 April, 2011).

Department of Justice [US] (9 July, 2009) Press Release 'Man Ordered to Pay Restitution to Victim in International Child Exploitation Case', <http://jacksonville.fbi.gov/dojpressrel/pressrel09/ja070909.htm> (accessed 6 April, 2011).

Edwards, Amy L. (29 June, 2010) 'Prosecutors Pursue Restitution for Child-exploitation Victims'. *Orlando Sentinel*, <http://articles.orlandosentinel.com/2010-06-29/news/os-child-exploit-pay-20100629_1_child-pornography-case-child-pornography-restitution> (accessed 6 April, 2011).

[*Falso*] Letter Brief, Plaintiff's Application to Proceed under a Pseudonym, re *An Individual Known to the Defendant as 08MIST096.jpg and 08MIST067.jpg v Falso* 2009 WL 4807537 (NDNY).

Forliti, Amy (26 May, 2010) 'Minn. Lawyer Aims to Track, Sue Child Porn Users', <http://abcnews.go.com/US/wireStory?id=10749941> (accessed 6 April, 2011).

[*Freeman*] US *v Freeman* No 3:08CR22-002/LAC (ND Fla. 9 July, 2009).

[*Hesketh*] US *v Hesketh* No 3:08-CR-00165-WWE (D.Conn. 23 February, 2009).

[ICMEC] International Center for Missing & Exploited Children (2010) *Child Pornography: Model Legislation & Global Review*, 6th Edition, <http://polis.osce.org/library/view?item_id=3721&attach_id=2989> (accessed 6 April, 2011).

In re Amy 2009 WL 4928376 (CA5 (Tex)), <http://caselaw.findlaw.com/us-5th-circuit/1499195.html> (accessed 6 April, 2011).

In re Amy Unknown, No 09-41238 (5th Cir, 22 March, 2011), <www.ca5.uscourts.gov/opinions/pub/09/09-41238-CV0.wpd.pdf> (accessed 6 April, 2011).

James, Susan Donaldson (8 February, 2010) ' "Misty Series" Haunts Girl Long After Rape', <http://abcnews.go.com/Health/internet-porn-misty-series-traumatizes-child-victim-pedophiles/story?id=9773590> (accessed 6 April, 2011).

Koch, Wendy (2006) 'Kids Can Be Victims or Violators', *USA Today*, 17 October, 2006, p. A13.

Marsh, James (2007) Statement Regarding Masha Allen and Peter Sotos: *Show Adult*, <http://poundpuplegacy.org/node/19771> (accessed 6 April, 2011).

[*McDaniel*] US *v Ricky Lee McDaniel* No 09-15038 (11th Cir, 28 January, 2011), <www.ca11.uscourts.gov/opinions/ops/200915038.pdf> (accessed 6 April, 2011).

Optional Protocol to the Convention on the Rights of the Child on the Sale of Children, Child Prostitution and Child Pornography, adopted 25 May, 2000, UN Doc A/RES/54/263 (2000), 2171 UNTS 227 (entered into force 18 January, 2002), <http://www2.ohchr.org/english/law/crc-sale.htm> (accessed 6 April, 2011).

[*Paroline*] *US v Paroline* 2009 WL 4572786 (ED Tex), <http://sentencing.typepad.com/files/paroline-memorandum-opinion-and-order.pdf> (accessed 6 April, 2011).

Pringle, Helen (2011) 'Cartoon Wars: The Interpretation of Drawn Images', paper presented to International Conference of the Indian Association for the Study of Australia (Eastern Region), Kolkata.

[*Puhakka*] *Puhakka v R* [2009] NSWCCA 290, <http://www.austlii.edu.au/cgi-bin/sinodisp/au/cases/nsw/NSWCCA/2009/290.html> (accessed 6 April, 2011).

Rothman, Jennifer (2011) 'Getting What They Are Owed: Restitution Fees for Victims of Child Pornography' *Cardozo Journal of Law and Gender* 17 (2), pp. 333–357.

Schwartz, John (2 February, 2010) 'Child Pornography, and an Issue of Restitution', *New York Times* <http://www.nytimes.com/2010/02/03/us/03offender.html> (accessed 6 April, 2011).

[*Staples*] *US v Staples* 2009 WL 2827204 (SD Fla. 2 September, 2009).

US Congress (2006) *Sexual Exploitation of Children over the Internet: Follow-Up Issues to the Masha Allen Adoption*, Hearing before the Subcommittee on Oversight and Investigations of the Committee on Energy and Commerce, House of Representatives, 109th Congress, Serial No 109–145 <http://frwebgate.access.gpo.gov/cgi-bin/getdoc.cgi?dbname=109_house_hearings&docid=f:31471.pdf> (accessed 6 April, 2011).

[USC] US Code <http://www.law.cornell.edu/uscode/> (accessed 4 April, 2011).

Amy

The Victimisation of Children by Pornography: Victim Impact Statement of Amy

Introductory note by Helen Pringle

In this Statement, Amy (a pseudonym) tells her story. Amy was a victim of sexual abuse by her uncle. He later uploaded images of the abuse, picturing a little child being forced to perform sexual acts with an adult man, including oral and anal penetration, and masturbation. Amy's images became known as the 'Misty Series', which have been globally trafficked since the late 1990s. Amy's uncle was convicted of sexual abuse and sentenced to a prison term. She is now seeking restitution for the further victimisation by those who trade in the images of her abuse on the Internet. This Statement was written in 2008, and has been put forward in Amy's claims for Restitution in US courts since then. It is reprinted here with kind permission of James Marsh, Esq. of the Marsh Law Firm PLLC, Amy's counsel.

Amy's Victim Impact Statement

I am a 19-year-old girl and I am a victim of child sex abuse and child pornography. I am still discovering all the ways that the abuse and exploitation I suffer has hurt me, has set my life on the wrong course, and destroyed the normal childhood, teenage years, and early adulthood that everyone deserves.

My uncle started to abuse me when I was only 4 years old. He used what I now know are the common ways that abusers get their victims ready for abuse and keep them silent: he told me that I was special, that he loved me, and that we had our own 'special secrets'. Since he lived close to our house, my mother and father didn't suspect anything when I walked over there to spend time with him.

At first he showed me pornographic movies and then he started doing things to me. I remember that he put his finger in my vagina and that it hurt a lot. I remember that he tried to have sex with me and that it hurt even more. I remember telling him that it hurt. I remember that much of the time I was with him I did not have clothes on and that sometimes he made me dress up in lingerie. And I remember the pictures.

After the abuse he would take me to buy my favorite snack which was beef jerky. Even now when I eat beef jerky I get feelings of panic, guilt, and humiliation. It's like I can never get away from what happened to me.

At the time I was confused and knew it was wrong and that I didn't like it, but I also thought it was wrong for me to tell anything bad about my uncle who said he loved me and bought me things I liked. He even let me ride on his motorcycle. Now I will never ride on a motorcycle again. The memories are too upsetting.

There is a lot I don't remember, but now I can't forget because the disgusting images of what he did to me are still out there on the Internet. For a long time I practiced putting the terrible memories away in my mind. Thinking about it is still really painful. Sometimes I just go into staring spells when I am caught thinking about what happened and not paying any attention to my surroundings.

Every day of my life I live in constant fear that someone will see my pictures and recognize me and that I will be humiliated all over again. It hurts me to know someone is looking at them – at me – when I was just a little girl being abused for the camera. I did not choose to be there, but now I am there forever in pictures that people are using to do sick things. I want it all erased. I want it all stopped. But I am powerless to stop it just like I was powerless to stop my uncle.

When they first discovered what my uncle did, I went to therapy and thought I was getting over this. I was very wrong. My full understanding of what happened to me has only gotten clearer as I have gotten older. My life and my feelings are worse now because the crime has never really stopped and will never really stop.

It is hard to describe what it feels like to know that at any moment, anywhere, someone is looking at pictures of me as a little girl being abused by my uncle and is getting some kind of sick enjoyment from it. It's like I am being abused over and over and over again.

I find myself unable to do the simple things that other teenagers handle easily. I do not have a driver's license. Every time I say I am going to do it, I don't. I can't plan well. My mind skips out on me when I think about moving forward with my life. I have been trying to get a job, but I just keep avoiding things. Forgetting is the thing I do best since I was forced as a little girl to live a double life and 'forget' what was happening to me. Before I realize it, I miss interviews or other things that will help me get a job.

Sometimes things remind me of the abuse and I don't even realize it until it is too late. For example, I failed anatomy in high school. I simply could not think about the body because of what happened to me. The same thing happened in college. I went to a psychology class where we watched a video about child abuse. Without even realizing why, I just stopped going to class. I failed my freshman year of college and moved back home.

It's easy for me to block out my feelings and avoid things that make me uncomfortable. I don't know when I will be ready to go back to college because I have huge problems with avoiding anything that makes me uncomfortable or reminds me of my abuse.

I am always scared that people can look at me and tell that I am a victim of sex abuse because my abuse is a public fact. I am worried that when my friends are on the Internet they are going to come across my pictures and it fills me with shame and embarrassment.

I am humiliated and ashamed that there are pictures of me doing horrible things with my uncle. Everywhere I go I feel judged. Am I the kind of person who does this? Is there something wrong with me? Is there something sickening and disgusting about who I am?

I am embarrassed to tell anyone what happened to me because I'm afraid they will judge me and blame me for it. I live in a small town and I think that if one person knows then everyone will know. I am just living in fear of the day someone sees those awful pictures of me and then 'the secret' about me will be out. It's like my life is on hold for that day and I am frozen in time waiting. I know those disgusting pictures of me are stuck in time and are there forever for everyone to see.

I had terrible nightmares for a long long time. I would wake up sweating and crying and go to my parents for comfort. Now I still get flashbacks sometimes. There are thoughts in my head that are memories of the things that my uncle did to me. My heart will start racing and I will feel sweaty and then a stronger picture will pop up in my head and I have to leave the situation I am in. I have heard the voice of my uncle in my mind still talking to me saying, "don't tell, don't tell, don't tell." Thinking and knowing that the pictures of all this are still out there just makes it worse. It's like I can't escape from the abuse, now or ever.

Because I've had so many bad dreams, I find it hard to sleep when it's dark. I like to keep the lights on thinking that will protect me from bad dreams. I hate scary movies and sometimes have nightmares for days.

Sometimes I have unreasonable fears that prevent me from doing the normal things that other kids do. My friend once asked me to go with her and her uncle to an amusement park. I could not get it out of my head that I would be abused. In the end I just couldn't go. I kept wondering if my friend's uncle had seen my pictures. Did he know me? Did he know what I did? Is that why he invited me to the amusement park?

Trust is a very hard thing for me and often people just make me uncomfortable. I had to quit a job I had as a waitress because there was a guy who I thought was always staring at me. I couldn't stop thinking, did he recognize me? Did he see my pictures somewhere? I was simply too uncomfortable to keep working there.

I have trouble saying 'no' to people since I learned at a young age that I really don't have control over what's happening to me. I am trying to learn to get better at this because I know that not saying 'no' makes it easier for someone to hurt me again.

Because of the way my uncle bribed me to perform sex acts on camera, I have trouble taking gifts from anyone. I always feel that people will expect something from me if they give me a present. This makes it difficult in my relationship with friends.

I want to have children someday, but it frightens me terribly to think about how I could keep them safe. Who could I possibly trust? Their teacher? Their coach? I don't know if I could ever trust anyone with my children. And what if my children and their friends see my pictures on the Internet? How could I ever explain to them what happened to me?

I am very confused about what love is. My uncle said he loved me and I wanted that love. But I know now that what he did to me is not love. But how will I be able to tell in the future if it is real love or just another person trying to exploit and use me?

The truth is, I am being exploited and used every day and every night somewhere in the world by someone. How can I ever get over this when the crime that is happening to me will never end? How can I get over this when the shameful abuse I suffered is out there forever and being enjoyed by sick people?

I am horrified by the thought that other children will probably be abused because of my pictures. Will someone show my pictures to other kids, like my uncle did to me, then tell them what to do? Will they see me and think it's okay for them to do the same thing? Will some sick person see my picture and then get the idea to do the same thing to another little girl? These thoughts make me sad and scared. I blame myself a lot for what happened. I know I was so little, but why didn't I know better? Why didn't I stop my uncle? Maybe if I had stopped it there wouldn't be so many pictures out there that I can never take back or erase. I feel like now I have to live with it forever and that it's all my fault.

I feel like I am unworthy of anything and a failure. What have I been good for except to be used by others over and over again. That's one of the reasons

I haven't been able to get a job or stay in school. I'm tired of disappointing myself. I've already had enough disappointment for a lifetime and just don't want any more failure. To me this brings back all the terrible feelings and shame of abuse and exploitation.

Sometimes I deal with my feelings by trying to forget everything by drinking too much. I know this isn't good, but my humiliation and angry feelings are there with me all the time and sometimes I just need a way to make them go away for awhile.

I feel like I have always had to live a double life. First I had to lie about what my uncle was doing to me. Then I had to act like it didn't happen because it was too embarrassing. Now I always know that there is another 'little me' being seen on the Internet by other abusers. I don't want to be there, but I am. I wish I could go back in time and stop my uncle from taking those pictures, but I can't.

Even though I am scared that I will be abused or hurt again because I am making this victim impact statement, I want the court and judge to know about me and what I have suffered and what my life is like. What happened to me hasn't gone away. It will never go away. I am a real victim of child pornography and it effects me every day and everywhere I go.

Please think about me and think about my life when you sentence this person to prison. Why should this person, who is continuing my abuse, be free when I am not free?

PART FOUR

___

Pornography and the State

"I could make our home environment porn free, but as soon as we stepped outside into a shopping centre, past a bus stop, or to get petrol, there was a reminder. While my husband was trying to leave this part of his life behind, and we were trying to strengthen our marriage, we could not avoid it." – Cate

"I have struggled with pornography for a long time and I hate it. I hate what it does to my mind and my perception of women. I hate how it can consume my thoughts. I hate the fact that I constantly fight to keep my mind free and I will have to fight for the rest of my life." – Oliver

"I fear for future generations when 'intelligent' men are slaves to the need for ever increasing degrees of excitement rather than deepening intimate connection." – Ginger

"I don't want to view, read or encounter pornographic materials. Why is this so hard for so many people to understand … Why are the sexual desires of those who wish to use porn more important than those who don't? Why should I have to change so many aspects of my life in order to avoid feeling violated, to protect my mind, to protect my child?" – Nicole

Anne Mayne

The Power of Pornography – A South African Case Study[1]

There is verbal evidence from survivors of incest and childhood sexual abuse that pornography circulated in the dark, dank corridors of underground networks under apartheid in South Africa. When Diana Russell conducted a study on incest in South Africa in the 1990s, she found that as far back as 40 years ago, pornography was used to groom and intimidate children into lives of abuse. Survivors remembered being forced to watch movies and look at magazines, then forced to act out the sexual scenes (Russell, 1997). In those days anyone found in possession of pornography faced criminal charges and serious penalties.

With the end of apartheid and the release of Mandela in 1990, South Africa began to reassemble itself into a constitutional democracy under the African National Congress (ANC) government. While the Interim Constitution was being drafted in 1996, Frene Ginwala, a well-known leader in the liberation struggle, was asked to find an expert to draft a policy on pornography for the ANC. Ginwala invited Diana Russell, the internationally renowned feminist sociologist, activist and author of books on pornography and violence against women and girls, to undertake this task. Russell drafted a paper in which she cited evidence of the severe harm done to females who are victimised in the production of pornography, as well as those who are sexually abused by males acting out sex acts that they had been exposed to in pornography (Russell, 1998a). Ginwala's response to Russell's paper was total silence.

In August 1994, the then Minister of Home Affairs, Dr M. Buthelezi, appointed a Task Group to draft a new act to replace the existing Publications Act of 1974, the scope of which included the production and dissemination of pornography (van Rooyen, 1996, p. 172). This group began by researching and

---

1   With grateful thanks to Robyn Fudge for generously sharing her huge fund of information; Doreen Meissner, Clive and Michele Human of S.T.O.P, for information on their campaign and constructive advice and help with editing; Diana Russell, for sending copies of her articles and helpful suggestions; Alix Johnson for her excellent editorial assistance; Rheina Epstein, Jessica Samson, Leah Abramsohn, Carol Bower and Pat and Horace van Rensburg for constructive advice and help with editing.

consulting internationally, and concluded that a mere amendment of the Act would not remedy the situation, and that the current approach to pornographic material needed to reflect that there was a clear movement away from morality to whether it could cause harm (van Rooyen, 1996, p. 172).

At the same time that van Rooyen was conducting his research, a nationally circulated petition against the legalisation of pornography, drawn up by Pat and Horace van Rensburg's organisation STOP Pornography, which drew 250,000 signatures, was presented to the then Minister of Home Affairs and later 1800 submissions were presented at the Portfolio Committee Hearings, 95% of which called for the government not to legalise pornography (pers. comm. retired MP Horace van Rensburg). These appeals from the public appear to have been ignored.

It took a mere 6 weeks for this research to be completed and the new Act to be drafted. The research of internationally recognised anti-pornography feminists, sociologists, legal experts and psychologists – plus a large sector of the South African public – was totally ignored in favour of the opinion of international patriarchal 'legal experts'. Russell's published revision of the recommendations she had previously sent to Ginwala was once again not responded to. (This legislation was passed in 1995 and enacted in 1996; pers. comm. Pat van Rensburg, February, 2011.)

The fact that the vast majority of the South African population was in a state of crisis – impoverished; denied adequate education; their communities destroyed by the slave-like migrant labour system, forced removals and a devastating HIV/AIDS pandemic – did not appear to concern those drafting this legislation which eventually allowed pornography to be sold in South Africa. It did not seem to occur to them that the proliferation of extremely misogynistic pornographic material would be harmful to masses of already vulnerable women barely surviving in an oppressive, male-dominated society.

From 1996, a number of anti-pornography groups began to be established. STOP Pornography inspired another effective and long-lasting campaigning group Standing Together to Oppose Pornography (S.T.O.P). By various means this group has achieved great success over the past 15 years – initially by getting pornography removed from convenience stores, gaining co-operation from local school principals and backing up the African Christian Action group who had succeeded in removing pornography nation-wide from supermarket shelves. They organised marches to raise public awareness, poster demonstrations at Council meetings, a community meeting and a widely attended conference. From worldwide sources they collected and edited information which was then printed and handed to the chairperson of the newly created Film and Publications Board (FPB). S.T.O.P initiated workshops for the police and presentations at schools and continue to deliver them today. Importantly, their actions have resulted in credibility with Government. They now also run support groups for growing numbers of men addicted to pornography – increasingly younger in age – who are trying to break free. Throughout the years, their letters have been published in the main daily newspapers and S.T.O.P is frequently featured in the media (pers. comm. Doreen Meissner, Michele and Clive Human of S.T.O.P, 25 January, 2011).

The liberalisation of the previous legislation coincided with the emergence of a multifaceted sex industry which had not existed in the country before 1994. Sex shops, strip/lap-dancing clubs, escort agencies, massage parlors, brothels and visible evidence of mostly black women being prostituted on the streets appeared in cities all over the country. The normalisation of images of women and girls being sexually exploited in pornography – which led to the prevalence of images of women being sexually exploited in advertising – appears to have been the impetus for the sudden explosion of the local sex industry. This new women-selling industry now exploits a large number of poverty-stricken South African women and girls. In so doing, it has created yet another industry new to the country: sex trafficking. Those who drafted the legislation ignored the fact that the pornography industry, dependent on the commercial sexual exploitation of young and vulnerable members of society, is extremely lucrative for those who manufacture and control it.

Paradoxically, prostitution and associated activities, such as brothel keeping, lap dancing, selling of 'indecent acts', living off the proceeds of prostitution and procuring, has remained criminalised and, in fact, was strengthened by the criminalisation of the buyer in the Sexual Offences Amendment Act 2007. However, the policing of the sex industry appears to be a low priority with the South African Police Service.

Sheila Jeffreys (2009, p. 62) states that according to research by Ward and Day, the percentage of men prostituting women doubled in 10 years in the UK when hardcore pornography became mainstream in the early 1980s. Though the prevalence of prostitution in South Africa after the passage of this law is not known, a study by the Institute for Child and Family Development at the University of the Western Cape shows its devastating effects (Barnes-September et al., 2000). The findings of this research were that all the respondents, i.e. the prostituted girls, came from poor, abusive, dysfunctional backgrounds and some had been trafficked from rural areas, believing that they were going into domestic work. One told of being videoed while having sex, clearly for pornography. She was an illiterate rural girl, and could not understand why they were videoing her.

Pornography has been visibly present in South Africa for 17 years and we are now a country that has one of the highest police-reported rape statistics in the world. Diana Russell noted in 1998 that "some people have argued that because the rape rate in South Africa is so high, and because pornography has only recently become much easier to obtain ... this proves how insignificant pornography is as a cause of rape." Her response was that "it proves no such thing ... It merely means that the rape rate will become even higher" (Russell, 1998b). Her prediction, unfortunately, has come true: current rape rates in South Africa are exceedingly high.

The following illustrates how invasive the pornography business is. As soon as the news filtered out of South Africa that Mandela was going to be released and the ANC unbanned, the big pornography-producing companies in the US moved in to set up their offices in Johannesburg. *Hustler* was the first to establish itself in 1993 and *Penthouse* set up its office in Johannesburg in 1994 (Krouse, 2010). *Penthouse* had secured the right to publish a South African edition, with the explicit pornography left out, in 1991. The first South African edition of *Playboy*, along the same lines as *Penthouse*, came out in 1993 (see Russell, 1994). The new Film and Publication Bill (FPB) had not yet been drafted, they knew that the country was in a state of flux, and clearly the pornographers wanted to capture their market as soon as possible. As the US-funded industry was establishing itself, an Australian, Arthur Calamaris, moved in with the capital and stock to set up the Adult World chain of sex shops, which have now become established in all the major cities along with the sex shops of the chain Private that came later. Many smaller shops now sell pornography and even street sellers illegally display their usually pirated wares on the pavements at bus and taxi terminuses.

In the beginning, when pornographic magazines flooded into supermarkets and convenience stores, one heard distressed and angry women calling in to radio talk shows complaining that they and their children were being traumatized by sexual images in the magazines displayed in check-out areas and that pornographic publications were sometimes being placed adjacent to children's magazines. Angry women called in saying that their husbands/partners were buying these magazines and leaving them around the house, and that they were disgusted and sexually turned off because their men wanted them to act the same way as the women in the magazines. These have been removed now as a result of pressure brought to bear by S.T.O.P.

But no one would have guessed then that, 17 years later, the very legislation that was designed to protect children from exposure to pornographic images would have failed completely. Children have now become so pornified and so desensitised to sexual abuse that they are making pornographic videos of each other on their cell phones and even selling them! Nobody could even envisage then what is happening today. Children could well be prosecuted for making and distributing child pornography made by themselves (see also Funnell, this volume).

The legislation administered by the FPB does not allow an explicit sex act, as depicted in pornography, to be viewed by anyone under the age of 18 (X18), and these magazines, videos and DVDs can only be legally bought at sex shops by adults. However, the FPB did not anticipate the casual way adults would treat this material or the flood of hardcore pornography that children would be accessing accidently and/or knowingly on the Internet in the course of their school research or on their cell phones. A recent national survey of school children conducted by the FPB found that 81% of children between the ages of 13 to 17 had been exposed to pornography (Film and Publications Board of South Africa, 2008).

The proportion of the population who buy pornographic magazines, videos and DVDs from the sex shops is relatively small. This is the reason why *Playboy* folded after a few years, but the publishers intend to make a come back in March 2011. Pornography is expensive and out of the reach of the average working-class man, black or white; it filters into the low socio-economic communities in the form of second-hand copies and pirated videos. These are usually bought by individuals who accumulate this material and charge for viewing it, or men with a pimping agenda who use it to groom young girls into prostitution. Social workers and teachers have reported that there are certain houses in the townships where young people gather to view this material.

Recently there has been media excitement about the first locally-made black pornographic movie, *Mapona*, as well as about Tau Morene the movie-maker. He gave himself this name, which means 'Lion King' in Sesotho. His Website Sondeza (which means 'come closer') was given a lot of free publicity in the media. The gonzo pornographic material on this Website appears to contravene the law regarding the unlawful distribution of X18 material. A complaint is languishing at the FPB which appears to be beset with operational problems.

According to Patrick Meyer, general manager of Joe Theron Publishing, the company that warehouses and distributes *Mapona*, just days after its release the video had sold well over 3,000 copies at approximately R200 (US$30) a disc. Recent local films have been made in 3 to 5 days at a cost of about R150,000 (US$21,000), making it a lucrative proposition. Joe Theron Publishing is the company that first brought *Hustler* magazine to the country. His company includes the Sting Music Company and a number of Afrikaans pornography magazines; he has built a pornography empire from his offices in Johannesburg (in Krouse, 2010).

Tau Morene has received thousands of Rands of free publicity from a popular national radio station, an e-TV political comedy show, and a double-page spread in what is regarded as a highly respected weekly newspaper, the *Mail & Guardian*. This newspaper, though claiming to champion a value system concerned with social justice and equality, under its previous name *The Weekly Mail* twice published articles publicising and promoting *Penthouse* (in Russell, 1994). Morene has been applauded for his ground-breaking enterprise: the first local, black, full-length pornographic movie made by the first local, black pornographer. His Website is also the first one created by a black pornographer. The journalist Matthew Krouse, who wrote the feature, claims that the story behind local black pornography,

> ... is really the story of the new South Africa. Urban Africans have gained the means of production – even owning the pornographic image is ostensibly empowering (Krouse, 2010).

So now industrialising black women's vaginas is 'empowering'! Krouse continues:

> Stephen McDermott, who buys stock on behalf of Adult World's national chain of 65 stores, says he's had to re-order the video three times for placement in his stores in the month since its release.

To conclude: pornography has entered the mainstream of the new South Africa and entrenched itself despite an initial significant attempt by the public to stop it, and the effort to control its impact through the excellent campaigning of a small group of valiant citizens in S.T.O.P and other organisations. The Constitution includes the development of a non-sexist society as one of its goals and women's right to dignity and equality are considered paramount. But the Constitution's Gender Commission and its Human Rights Commission, tasked with driving the imperatives of our Constitution and seeing that the Equality Act is implemented, have not fulfilled their mandate. The NGOs concerned with women's and children's rights have been silent on the subject of pornography. And there has been a complete lack of engagement by political parties.

South Africa has signed the Convention on the Elimination of Discrimination Against Women (CEDAW), the Beijing Platform for Action, and the Protocol to the African Charter on Human and Peoples' Rights on the Rights of Women in Africa (the last being the only one that mentions pornography). And yet we have allowed ourselves to be overwhelmed by violent, racist, sexist pornography which has tragically impacted on the status of South African women.

In the removal of the old forms of censorship around matters pertaining to sex, the legislators' inability to recognise the violence against women intrinsic in the making and the consuming of pornography has made a mockery of the aims of the Constitution, and is responsible for the growth of a sex industry with interests totally inimical to women's right to dignity and equality.

Bibliography

Barnes-September, Roseline, Ingrid Brown-Adam, Anne Mayne, Danielle Kowen, and Geraldine Dyason (2000) *Child Victims of Prostitution in the Western Cape.* Institute for Child and Family Development, University of the Western Cape.

Film and Publications Board of South Africa (2008) *Internet Usage and the Exposure of Pornography to Learners in South Africa.* Johannesburg.

Jeffreys, Sheila (2009) *The Industrial Vagina. The Political Economy of the Global Sex Trade.* Routledge, London and New York.

Krouse, Matthew (22–28 October, 2010) 'The money shot: Getting a rise out of the local porn industry' *Mail & Guardian*, South Africa.

Russell, Diana E.H. (1994) *U.S. pornography invades South Africa: A content analysis of* Playboy *and* Penthouse. Human Sciences Research Council, South Africa.

Russell, Diana E.H. (1997) *Behind Closed Doors in White South Africa. Incest Survivors Tell their Stories.* Macmillan Press Ltd, London.

Russell, Diana E.H. (16 April, 1998a) 'Pornography: Towards a non-sexist policy' *Agenda – Open Forum*. Durban, South Africa.

Russell, Diana E.H. (1998b) 'A Comparison of South Africa and Other Nations' *Women's Studies* 10 (1) pp. 30–39.

van Rooyen, Kobus (1996) 'Drafting a New Film and Publication Bill for South Africa' in Jane Duncan (Ed) *Between Speech and Silence. Hate Speech, Pornography and the New South Africa.* Freedom of Expression Institute and Institute for Democracy in South Africa.

Asja Armanda and Natalie Nenadic

Genocide, Pornography, and the Law[1]

The role of rape and other sexual atrocities in genocide came to international attention for the first time in the 1990s during the conflict in what was then Yugoslavia. We played a central role in a landmark civil lawsuit in New York against Radovan Karadžić, head of the Bosnian Serbs. For the first time in history sexual atrocities were recognized under international law as acts of genocide.[2] It then became easier to identify sexual atrocities in other genocides like Rwanda and Darfur and in conflicts such as Congo.

In uncovering this gendered dimension of genocide, we also uncovered pornography's role in it. In this chapter, we provide a summary of our work in highlighting the role of sexual atrocities in genocide, and focus on showing how pornography is intertwined with them. We conclude with suggestions about how law might help in making the pornographic dimensions of genocide more visible which might then affect the way that pornography is understood in what is called peacetime.

1 Background: Genocide and Sexual Atrocities

The difficult work of gaining international recognition of the genocidal purpose of sexual atrocities began in the summer of 1991. Serbia had just launched a campaign of 'ethnic cleansing' against civilians in Croatia, which soon expanded to include Bosnia-Herzegovina, and finally Kosovo. The term 'ethnic cleansing' is a euphemism for the destruction of non-Serbian peoples in the region, characterized by a system of camps for torture, mass killings, and mutilations.

Asja Armanda, a Croatian-Jewish feminist in Zagreb, began hearing from women fleeing the Serbian-occupied parts of Croatia about the mass rape and killing of women. Soon she discovered that the mass rape, torture, murder, and

---

1   A version of this paper was presented by Natalie Nenadic at the *International Stop Porn Culture Conference* in Boston, Wheelock College, 13 June, 2010. Thank you to Rebecca Whisnant for the opportunity to present this work and to Lierre Keith, Gail Dines, Melinda Tankard Reist and Abigail Bray. The help of R. Demirovic is also gratefully acknowledged.
2   *Kadic v Karadzic*, 70 F.3d 232, 236–237 (2d Cir. 1995).

mutilation of women, both in and out of camps, were distinctive features of this campaign. *In some cases these atrocities were filmed as pornography.*

Armanda had grown up under state repression in which her own family was politically suspect and victimized by the secret police. Just a year earlier she had co-founded Croatia's first feminist group, something that became possible with the advent of democratic elections in the region. Armanda tried to convince international human rights groups to investigate, but initially had little success. At first, she also had little success with the international women's community. One reason is that Yugoslavia's communist-era women's representatives already had a relationship with this community and denied the atrocities and discredited those who were trying to get word out about them.[3]

Armanda contacted Natalie Nenadic, an American whom she met during a trip Nenadic took to Europe. Nenadic graduated from Stanford University and was on her way to the University of Michigan Law School to study with Catharine MacKinnon, the leading US legal authority on issues of sexual violence and pornography, and now Special Gender Adviser to the Prosecutor of the International Criminal Court. Armanda took Nenadic to visit survivors so that she could see and hear for herself what was happening.

2 Genocide and Pornography

We termed the distinctive crime taking place *genocidal sexual atrocities* or *genocidal rape.* Here, we describe that part of this crime tied specifically to pornography. Our information comes from our years of work with survivors.[4] Sexual atrocities were filmed in the camps and elsewhere. Rozalija, a Croatian survivor of the Bučje camp near the town of Pakrac, Croatia, told us how pornography was made of her rape: "In front of the camera, one beats you and the other – excuse me – fucks you, he puts his truncheon in you, and he films all that." One survivor of a camp near Kozarac, Bosnia-Herzegovina, said the mat on which the soldiers were raping her had a spotlight trained on it. Other men watched the rapes as if it were a kind of theatre, sometimes putting out cigarette butts on the women's bodies.

Pornography was also made to serve as an incitement to commit genocide. An elderly Croatian woman from the Bučje camp told us how she was filmed being gang-raped and tortured by electric shocks by soldiers of the Yugoslav People's Army (JNA). During the rapes, the soldiers were dressed in generic camouflage uniforms

3   Asja Armanda and Natalie Nenadic (1994). See also Nenadic (2010).
4   We provided Catharine MacKinnon with these findings which she presented in MacKinnon (1993), p. 24.

and forced her to say on film that the rapes were committed by Croatians, and that she was in fact a Serb. This film could then be used by the perpetrators to spread misinformation about events and to incite Serbs viewing such films to acts of 'ethnic cleansing'. Armanda saw such footage on the evening news of Banja Luka, a town in Bosnia-Herzegovina, just over the border from Croatia. In September, 1992, Armanda saw news broadcasts of actual rapes in which the ethnicities of victim and perpetrator were switched. One of the aired rapes showed a naked, visibly bruised, middle-aged woman with a Serbian Orthodox cross around her neck. The speech on the video was dubbed to make it seem as if the rapist and speaker were Muslim or Croat and the victim a Serb, whose ethnicity the rapist was cursing. A few days later, Armanda saw another actual rape on Banja Luka television. Here, however, the dubbing stopped for about four to five seconds due to a technical lapse which allowed the actual voice to be heard. The soldier was laughing and asking the woman, "Do you like a Serbian stud?" while spewing at her ethnic epithets used against Croats and Muslims.

A woman from the destroyed Croatian city of Vukovar who was repeatedly raped and tortured in other ways in the Begejci camp in the Vojvodina autonomous region of Serbia, told us how she was forced to read 'confessions' for TV Novi Sad. A camp guard later told her that he recognized her from seeing her 'confession' on television. In January 2011, Serbia, with Republika Srpska (a Serbian governed region of Bosnia-Herzegovina that came into existence through genocide), began using such false 'confessions' as part of issuing international arrest warrants against survivors, thereby manipulating the instruments of international law to re-attack survivors through *legal* means.[5] The 2009 conviction by the Court of Bosnia and Herzegovina of Serbian paramilitary leader, Predrag Kujundžić, for crimes in the municipality of Doboj makes a reference to such false 'confessions'. Among his crimes was the rape in June, 1992 of a Muslim minor whom he held in sexual slavery through December, 1992. Kujundžić forced her to identify herself as a Serb and gave her a Serbian name, making her read a statement on Radio Doboj claiming that "Muslims were guilty of the war, that Muslims had killed her brother."[6]

Osman, a Bosnian Muslim from Croatia, spoke to Nenadic about witnessing sexual atrocities which he believes were taped, and seeing Serbian forces regularly carry cameras with them to film the atrocities they were committing. As a citizen of Croatia, he came to the aid of its civilians when they were attacked, joining

5 Balkaninsight (28 January, 2011)
6 Court of Bosnia & Herzegovina (2009).

a defense unit there, and then did the same when Bosnia-Herzegovina was attacked. So he was able to witness Serbian paramilitary and Yugoslav People's Army (JNA) forces, from occupied Croatia to occupied Bosnia-Herzegovina, "slaughter, kill, set on fire" everything that is Muslim or Croatian and the filming of these crimes.

He described witnessing a gang-rape committed on orders in Ličko Petrovo Selo in what was Serb-occupied Croatia. They tied the woman to 4 stakes in the ground. She was lying down but was still suspended, and they took turns raping her, laughing at her, asking her if she enjoyed it, saying that they were doing it for 'Greater Serbia'. In April, 1992, hiding in a tree and spying on what occupying forces were doing, he observed a small concentration camp in this region, with emaciated, tortured, bloody, and beaten people. He saw a woman who looked 7 to 8 months pregnant, and a man who appeared to be her husband, taken from the camp into the woods. The woman was tied vertically to a cross. They cut her belly with a knife, after which she soon died. They attempted to make the man eat the baby's arm, and then they cut him until he bled to death. As they were doing this, they were laughing and saying "We're going to slaughter all of you. This is our Serbia."

Survivors told us of pornography's pervasiveness in the camps. A woman from Vukovar who was repeatedly raped by members of the Yugoslav People's Army (JNA) in a Belgrade military prison, described pornography magazines being passed around among the soldiers. They showed naked women in vulnerable, sexually accessible poses, and pornography of men with animals and women with animals. She described pornography that showed women hanging from ceilings, women chained to wooden boards, with masks over their eyes, and women being beaten by a whip of the kind with which she and other concentration camp inmates had been whipped. The guards' sleeping room had pornography on the walls; she said that it was "those usual pictures from *Start*," a Yugoslav pornography publication. Pornography was even plastered on some Yugoslav Army tanks of the Banja Luka Corps that were rolling in to 'cleanse' Bosnia-Herzegovina, as Armanda saw on the regular news coverage of events.

3 Pornography and Genocide Denial: *A Serbian Film*

In 2010, a pornography film entitled *A Serbian Film* debuted on the international art film circuit. The movie has been banned in some countries for having some of the most disturbing, sexually sadistic scenes ever filmed. A court in Spain banned the film from festivals there while Australia refused to classify it, effectively banning it.[7] Some British festival venues refused to show it though a British distributor recently released a cut version, and rights have been bought in other countries.[8] German and Hungarian film print companies refused to process it.[9]

The film sets out to shock, and takes delight in the cruelty it shows. But the film also functions as a vehicle for denying the reality of the sexual atrocities committed as part of Serbia's genocidal campaign, and for denying the reality of sexual atrocities in general. The film's director, Srdjan Spasojević, recasts sexual atrocities as 'art' and paints the perpetrators as 'victims', claiming that the film is a political allegory about the 'molestation' "of the Serbian people by the Serbian government." For Spasojević, the film is a cinematic victim statement as to the trauma of the *perpetrators*.[10] An example is a graphic depiction of a man helping a woman give birth to a baby girl whom he then rapes to death in what the director calls 'newborn porn', which for the director conveys Serbia's loss of innocence.[11] A woman handcuffed to a bed is raped and then decapitated with a machete; the man continues to rape her as her body goes into rigor mortis, which is presented as a particular pleasure.[12]

Horror Website reviewers, accustomed to gruesome and pornographic films, likened viewing the film to "having [one's] soul raped" and commented that they would never watch it again.[13] It has been described as evil, depraved, and vile; as soul-killing, pure exploitation, and "simply beyond rational certification."[14] However, *A Serbian Film* has also been hailed as 'subversive' and 'transgressive' in some film circles, being called 'intelligent', 'fantastic', 'brilliant', and one of the best films of 2010.[15] It has been celebrated as 'art on display', as substance and therefore justifiably depraved.

The film premiered at the Novi Sad Film Festival in June 2010, held at the Serbian National Theatre. This venue is near the concentration camps where many Serbs *really* did commit such atrocities, and whose audience likely has perpetrators in it, perhaps reliving their glory days, as rapists and murderers are

---

7   Diana Lodderhose and John Hopewell (6 November, 2010); Australian Government (4 December, 2010).

8   Diana Lodderhose and John Hopewell (6 November, 2010); Fiona Bailey (26 November, 2010).

9   Anton Bitel; Tim Anderson.

10   Anton Bitel; *Guardian* Film Blog (13 December, 2010); *Sun* (7 September, 2011).

11   Xan Brooks (27 August, 2010).

12   *Movies Online* (3 December, 2010); Wikipedia; Transgressive Cinema.

13   Tara Brady (9 December, 2010); Tim Anderson.

14   Pete Cashmore (28 August, 2010).

15   Harry Knowles (9 April, 2010); Harry Knowles (5 January, 2011). See also Pete Cashmore (28 August, 2010).

known to do. The film has won other awards, such as Best Screenplay at a 2010 Serbian film festival at Vrnjačka Banja, and is defended as free speech.[16]

Think about what is taking place here. A film portrays, as graphic entertainment, the distinctive manner in which genocide was carried out by this country, through sexual atrocities. The film is feted and praised. And these festivities are taking place near the very sites and mass graves of those crimes. In this rewriting of history, the only thing that the film *does* consider real about the sexual atrocities it portrays is how they represent the suffering of the perpetrators. In the film, it is not their victims who were raped to death but the rapists and those who, in various ways, covered up for them.

An analogy may perhaps help one to appreciate the genocide denial at work in this pornography. Imagine a German film made not long after the Holocaust that depicts, as graphic entertainment, atrocities in gas chambers and crematoria, the distinctive way the Nazi genocide was carried out. Then imagine the film being screened and celebrated near the death camps where these atrocities *actually* took place. What the film conveys as real is how its atrocities represent the suffering of the German people. They are metaphorically gassed to death and not their victims who *really* were gassed to death.

In August, 2010, *A Serbian Film* won awards at the Montreal Fantasia Film Festival where it was presented as part of a 'Subversive Serbia' series which also included the recent Serbian hit *The Life and Death of a Porno Gang* and another co-written by the writer of *A Serbian Film*.[17] Presented in the genre of fantasy, the film accomplishes even more effectively its *real* work of erasing the reality of the genocide and supplanting it with a fiction. And what the film world now mainly registers about the film is what it calls 'freedom' and 'daring'. Nikola Pantelić, *A Serbian Film's* producer, states that "Montreal Fantasia [Festival] is one of the few places left on this earth where artistic freedom and unorthodox cinema thinking still mean something ... a Mecca for gutsy and vital cinema today."[18] A court ruling prevented its screening at Spain's San Sebastián Film Festival, but the film still won the Special Audience Award for 'Becoming a Symbol of Freedom of Speech'.[19]

---

16 Jinga Films.
17 Jinga Films.
18 Todd Brown (10 March, 2010).
19 Wikipedia; Wikinoticia (5 November, 2010).

Law

In 1992, Natalie Nenadic returned to the University of Michigan Law School where she approached Catharine MacKinnon about representing survivors pro bono for our legal action. In early March, 1993, when Radovan Karadžić, head of the Bosnian Serbs, came to the UN in New York to participate in 'peace talks', US Marshalls handed him our lawsuit, charging him with sexual atrocities as acts of genocide, including mass rape, serial rape, sexual murder, forced prostitution, sexual torture and mutilation, and forced pregnancy. Karadžić fled from the US and eventually went into hiding, but he is now on trial at the International Criminal Tribunal for the Former Yugoslavia (ICTY). Our case went through the courts until we finally went to jury-trial in Manhattan in August, 2000, where survivors testified about the sexual and other atrocities they experienced. A judgment found for compensatory and punitive damages and an injunction to stop the genocide.[20] There was some indirect testimony at trial about pornography's role in the genocide, but that role is not yet as explicitly recognized in international law as other sexual atrocities are.

We have some suggestions about how possibly to accomplish such a recognition which in turn could bring more recognition to the harms of pornography in peacetime. In July, 2008, around the time of Karadžić's transfer to the ICTY at The Hague, there were reports from Bosnia-Herzegovina about the discovery of pornography in relation to him, including pornography that features him in it. However, it has been interpreted as a collection that is part of his *private* domain.[21] In other words, a traditional way of denying the reality of pornography's harms to women as something private and harmless has also been used to dismiss pornography's significance in this context.

We had faced a similar problem when word first started coming out about sexual atrocities as genocide in the 1990s. There too, traditional ways of denying sexual violence against women were imported to do their work of denial. So, for instance, mass rapes were referred to as 'excesses' and the rape concentration camps as 'bordellos' or 'brothels' and the like. Feminism gave us a way to break out of this euphemistic and obfuscating language and to name the reality of what

---

20 The judgment was for US$745 million, though it is potentially misleading to refer to that sum without qualification as survivors have yet to see any of that money. For details of the case see MacKinnon (2006).

21 This information was first reported by the Sarajevo daily *Dnevni Avaz* in July, 2008. See also *Slobodna Dalmacija* (29 July, 2008); Arhiva Net (29 July, 2008); Dalje (29 July, 2008); *Croatian Times* (30 July, 2008).

was taking place as genocidal sexual atrocities. This in turn made it possible for us to pursue a legal initiative that established an international precedent.

Feminism can also help us come up with a more adequate understanding of the pornography aspect of genocide. This breaks the traditional approach which hides pornography's harms to women by miscasting those harms as private and benign. With this better conceptual framework in hand, we may bring pornography that is connected to genocide to bear on international legal proceedings, perhaps at The Hague War Crimes Tribunal, or at a case that could be brought at the International Criminal Court or in a civil suit of the kind we initiated in New York. We might thereby get pornography's role in genocide recognized as it needs to be.

Bibliography

Anderson, Tim, <http://www.bloody-disgusting.com/review/4501> (accessed 4 February, 2011).

Arhiva Net (29 July, 2008) 'Pronašli Karadžićevu pornografsku snimku', <http://arhiva.net.hr/vjesti/europa/page/2008/07/29/0279006.html> (accessed 13 August, 2009).

Armanda, Asja and Natalie Nenadic (November, 1994) 'Activists Warn Not to be Fooled by Genocide/Rape Revisionists' *Northwest Ethnic News Seattle*, p. 2.

Australian Government Classification Website, <http://www.classification.gov.au/www/cob/find.nsf/d853f429dd038ae1ca25759b0003557c/243d814a377ff75fca2577ea0058041c?OpenDocument> (accessed 21 February, 2011).

Bailey, Fiona (26 November, 2010) '*A Serbian Film* is "most cut" movie in 16 years', <http://www.bbc.co.uk/news/entertainment-arts-11846906> (accessed 2 February, 2011).

Balkaninsight (28 January, 2011) 'Croatia Rejects Call to Withdraw Envoy to Serbia', <http://www.balkaninsight.com/en/article/croatia-rejects-call-to-withdraw-envoy-to-serbia> (accessed 29 January, 2011).

Bitel, Anton 'Srdjan Spasojevic (uncensored)', <http://www.eyeforfilm.co.uk/feature.php?id=848> (accessed 2 February, 2011).

Brady, Tara (9 December, 2010) 'It is hell. It is not entertainment', <http://www.irishtimes.com/newspaper/features/2010/1209/1224285096711.html?via=mr> (accessed 2 February, 2011).

Brooks, Xan (27 August, 2010) 'A Serbian Film pulled from FrightFest', <http://www.guardian.co.uk/film/2010/aug/27/a-serbian-film-frightfest> (accessed 4 February, 2011).

Brown, Todd (10 March, 2010) 'Fantasia 2010 Announces Subversive Serbia!', <http://twitchfilm.com/news/2010/03/fantasia-2010-announces-subversive-serbia.php> (accessed 7 February, 2011).

Brown, Todd (21 December, 2010) 'A Dozen Discoveries from 2010: New Faces to Watch', <http://twitchfilm.com/news/2010/12/a-dozen-discoveries-from-2010.php> (accessed 4 February, 2011).

Cashmore, Pete (28 August, 2010) 'Will this new movie kill off torture porn for good?', <http://www.guardian.co.uk/film/2010/aug/28/torture-porn-frightfest-quiz> (accessed 1 February, 2010).

Court of Bosnia & Herzegovina (2009) 'Predrag Kujundzic found guilty of Crimes against Humanity' 30 October, 2009, <http://www.sudbih.gov.ba/komponente/print_vijesti.php?id=1420&jezik=e> (accessed 29 January, 2011).

Croatian Times (30 July, 2008) 'Karadzic starred in his own porn movie', <http://croatiantimes.com/news/Around_the_World/2008-07 30/639/Karadzic%20starred%20in%20his%20own%20porn%20movie> (accessed 1 February, 2010).

Dalje (29 July, 2008) 'Karadzic Made Porn Video', <http://dalje.com/en-world/karadzic-made-porn-video/167828> (accessed 1 February, 2010).

Guardian Film Blog (13 December, 2010) '*A Serbian Film*: when allegory gets nasty', <http://www.guardian.co.uk/film/filmblog/2010/dec/13/a-serbian-film-allegorical-political> (accessed 4 February, 2011).

Jinga Films, <http://jingafilms.com/film_details.asp?film_id=38> (accessed 2 February, 2011).

Kadic v. Karadzic, 70 F.3d 232, 236–237 (2d Cir. 1995).

Knowles, Harry (9 April, 2010) 'Harry says SERBIAN FILM will be the best film you won't likely see in Theaters this year!', <http://www.aintitcool.com/node/44577> (accessed 2 February, 2011).

Knowles, Harry (5 January, 2011) 'Harry's Top Ten films of 2010!!!', <http://www.aintitcool.com/node/47938> (accessed 2 February, 2011).

Lodderhose, Diana and John Hopewell (6 November, 2010) 'Spanish court bans "A Serbian Film"', <http://www.variety.com/article/VR1118027037?refCatId=13> (accessed 4 February 2011).

MacKinnon, Catharine A. (1993) 'Turning Rape into Pornography: Post-Modern Genocide' *Ms Magazine* July/August, pp. 24–30.

MacKinnon, Catharine A. (2006) *Are Women Human? And Other International Dialogues.* Harvard University Press, Cambridge, MA.

Movies Online (3 December, 2010) 'Torture Porn Redefined: Dressing Down *A Serbian Film*', <http://www.moviesonline.ca/2010/12/torture-porn-redefined-dressing-serbian-film/> (accessed 1 February, 2011).

Nenadic, Natalie (2010) 'Feminist Philosophical Intervention in Genocide' in James R. Watson (Ed) *Metacide in the Pursuit of Perfection.* Rodopi, New York/Amsterdam.

Slobodna Dalmacija (29 July, 2008) 'Žalba nije stigla do suda; Dnevni avaz: Karadžić ima pornić'.

Sun (7 September, 2011) 'Sick Serbian film hits London', <http://www.thesun.co.uk/sol/homepage/showbiz/film/3128497/Sick-Serbian-film-hits-London.html> (accessed 4 February, 2011).

Transgressive Cinema, <http://transgressivecinema.com/>.

Wikipedia, <http://en.wikipedia.org/wiki/A_Serbian_Film> (accessed 2 February, 2011).

Wikinoticia (5 November, 2010), <http://en.wikinoticia.com/entertainment/Movies/64928-qa-serbian-filmq-prohibited-and-rewarded-equally> (accessed 2 February, 2011).

Ruchira Gupta

Pornography in India

"I put my dick on the mouth of her pussy and pushed my dick into it quickly. She screamed louder ahhhhhhhh ohhhhhhh and I quickly put a pillow on to her mouth so that her family member will not hear her scream" (Indiansexstories. net).

Indiansexstories.net is only one among 15 million Indian porn blogs and Websites; Savitabhabhi.com, BollywoodHardcore.net, IndianPornTube.net, IndianAngels.net, IndianSeduction.com and SanskritPorn.com are some others.

A recent survey shows that Indians contribute most of the traffic to these porn Websites. Take for example, Debonairblog.com. A random survey shows that around 0.2% of global Internet users browsed through this site daily, and 68.8% of this traffic came from India. Before it was banned (see below), Savitabhabhi.com got about 60 million visitors every month with 70% of the traffic originating from India. On average, the visitors spent 10 minutes on the site.

All these sites feature hardcore porn videos, movies, and animated comic strips. Many are written in Indian languages and feature the kind of storylines below:

Story 1 My Girlfriend's Virgin Pussy[1]

I kept my cock on her pussy entrance and tried to push it in. Her hole was wet but very tight. I knew that I will pain her a lot first time so I took her lips in my mouth and started kissing her and put my cock on her entrance and gave a hard push, my cock was in pain and I can also feel her pain as she bit my lips while kissing, I continued kissing her and also pressed her boobs and she was relaxed after that then I slowly pushed my cock in her pussy and started movement of too [sic] and fro, her eyes were wet with tears.

Story 2 (Hindi story) *Riya Ki Seal Tori* (The Breaking of Riya's Seal)

Kosis ki wo phisal ke bahar aagaya fir maine dubara dalla aur mera lund ka agala hisa uski choot mein ghus gaya aur wo dard se chila rahi please gaurav jaldi nikalo nahi toh mein maar jauge. Aur uski choot se khoon nikalne laga meine apna lund nahi nikala aur mae uske hotho ko chusne laga . (I put my penis into her anus and she started screaming with pain, please Gaurav, pull it out or I will die. She started bleeding but I did not pull out and started sucking her lips.)

---

1   These stories are so ubiquitous that I will not provide Websites.

239

Story 3 Savita is the Best Secretary Mishraji Has

Savita has taken up a job and is fucking the boss, Mishraji, to get a promotion. Before every intercourse she insists on giving a full blowjob to her boss who insists on coming in her mouth. Then he usually pulls her by her long hair and fucks her in the 'bitch' position.

On all of the sites, forceful sex with infliction of pain on the girl or woman is the norm. Her hair is pulled, her nipples are pinched, she is penetrated any-which way – into her mouth, anus or vagina – sometimes simultaneously. Verbal abuse is showered on her by the man (or men) as they penetrate her. Subjugation and humiliation of girls and women are depicted repeatedly. In fact, some sites blatantly advertise the abuse of girls as their drawcard and openly call themselves, for example, Galleries.exploitedindiangirls.com.

In June 2009, using the 2000 Information Technology Act,[2] the Indian Government banned porn cartoons featuring the Internet porn star Savita Bhabhi as a result of a complaint received from a women's group in Maharashtra who used the *Protection Against Sexual Harassment of Women Bill* (2005) as the basis of their complaint.[3] But the Government has been unable to rein in the growing pornography industry in India with new sites mushrooming daily. In 2010, India alarmingly moved into 2nd position of Internet porn users in the world, from 5th in 2005.[4]

A search of the Alexa list of the Top 100 Websites of India on the 'Web, Advertising and Technology Blog' (WATBlog.com) in April, 2011, revealed that Websites like Rapidshare and MegaUpload which have links to download porn clips, are the 11th and 16th most popular Websites in India. Also ranked in the Top 100 are: at 21, Xboard – a huge majority of its user activity (90%+) comes from its Masala Videos section; 25, MasalaTalk – a forum similar to Xboard; 37, MegaShare; 41, FreeSexyIndians; 47, DaDesiForum; 74, IndianSexStories; 83,

---

2   According to Section 67 of the Information Technology Act (2000):
    "Whoever publishes or transmits or causes to be published in the electronic form, any material which is lascivious or appeals to the prurient interest or if its effect is such as to tend to deprave and corrupt persons who are likely, having regard to all relevant circumstances, to read, see or hear the matter contained or embodied in it, shall be punished on first conviction with imprisonment of either description for a term which may extend to five years and with fine which may extend to one lakh rupees (approx. US$2,233) and in the event of a second or subsequent conviction with imprisonment of either description for a term which may extend to ten years and also with fine which may extend to two lakh rupees."
3   The *Protection Against Sexual Harassment of Women Bill* (2005) states that sexual harassment "includes such unwelcome sexually determined behaviour as physical contact and advances, sexually coloured remarks, showing pornography and sexual demand, whether by words or actions …"
4   In April, 2011, it is back to position #4, see <http://google.com/trends?q=porn&ctab=1&geo=all&date=ytd&sort=0>.

AdultFriendFinder; 92, DesiTorrents – nearly 90% of this site's activity is seen in the porn video section; 96, Masala4India; and at 99, ChitChatters. At number 14, DebonairBlog is perhaps the most popular blog in the country. States like Rajasthan, Delhi, Kerala and Maharashtra top the list of Internet porn users.[5] Already in 2007, WATBlogger Ekalavya Bhattacharya proclaimed: "Boasting of nearly 50 million online users, India will surely be a porn capital in the online world to come" (Bhattacharya, 2007).

Not satisfied with capturing the Internet market, the porn industry has also begun to target the mobile phone market. Rohit Srivastawa, founder of clubhack, claims that 13% of Indians sent or received X-rated material on the phone. Forty per cent of default Websites available at present on mobile phone browsers directly or indirectly take users to porn sites (in Tejaswi, 2011). Service providers are currently in the process of cultivating an appetite for pornography among very young customers so they can reap the benefits later (Tejaswi, 2011). Agreements and business contracts between telecommunication operators with porn portals and porn content providers are generating large profits in the USA and Europe. Playboy licenses pictures and content to mobile phones in Europe, while in France telecom operator Orange provides porn video clips on mobile phones from their wireless portal.

It is tragic that these new markets are targeted at teenage boys whose first introduction to sex is through pornography. In India today, 1 in 5 teenagers watch porn before the age of 13.[6] Violent 3-D animation sex video games are especially created for this young market. They start with a pop-up site in which a woman prompts the user to undress her. That act then leads to violent sex games.

Gopal, 13, of Chennai, got sucked into this world of pornography. It all started with a pop-up. It flashed a woman and prompted him to undress her. He did, and got trapped via unending windows into a Website of violent, sex-filled games. It became a habit until, one day, his father accidentally clicked the Internet history button and discovered a long list of Websites with names such as Playboy, Leisure Suit Lady, Guy Game and PC Rape. The cyber crime unit of the police traced them to the narrow lanes of Burma Bazaar and the Internet browsing centre that was beaming these Websites. K. Srinivasan, co-founder of the Cyber Crime Society of India, says: "More than 50% of the victims are young children from affluent families" (in Datta, 2011).

Boys between the ages of 8 and 16 are particularly lured to the porn sites

---

5   <http://google.com/trends?q=porn&ctab=1&geo=all&date=ytd&sort=0>
6   Udaan Online Survey, quoted in Bollywood Hungama News Network (6 July, 2010).

through 'porn-napped' and 'typosquatted'[7] Websites. Figures reveal that nearly 90% of boys aged 8 to 16 who have access to the Internet, have viewed pornographic sites while doing their homework (Jayachandran, 2003). In fact, the easy accessibility of pornographic content has led to a growing interest in pornography among school-age children and urban youth who have now moved beyond simply watching pornography to shooting their own porn videos and uploading them online.

This trend becomes even clearer as mainstream news media in India keep breaking shocking stories about Multimedia Messaging Service (MMS) scandals involving school children and pornographic rings being busted by police after they engaged in the filming and distribution of 'reality' sex videos shot with hidden cameras.

- In December 2004, the country was rocked when the news of the now infamous Delhi Public School MMS sex scandal broke. A 17-year-old schoolboy filmed his girlfriend in a sex act and made the footage into a pornographic film. The video was circulated widely online and by roadside DVD vendors.
- A girl in Siliguri committed suicide in October, 2010, after an obscene MMS clip which captured her in a compromising position was made and circulated by Anindya Garai, a fellow student at the Siliguri Polytechnic Institute.
- In October 2010, 4 students of a school in Salt Lake, Kolkata, and West Bengal sent porn MMS clips to one of their teachers – just for the fun of it.
- In November 2010, 38-year-old Sarvjit Singh, an architect, was arrested for making a MMS clip of a girl in the Dalanwala area. The girl complained to the police after being blackmailed by Singh.
- In December 2010, a woman in Murshidabad, West Bengal, had her own husband arrested for allegedly shooting their intimate moments on a cell phone and circulating it online.
- Also in 2010, the 'North Karnataka MMS' featured a former beauty queen from Dharwad. The clip was uploaded by her ex-boyfriend after she had dumped him.

These uncovered cases reveal a deep link between pornography and real life sexual violence. Those who frequent pornography sites are more likely to view sex as a purely physical function and to regard women as sex objects. They are

---

7   'Typosquatting', also called URL hijacking, is a form of cybersquatting which relies on mistakes such as typographical errors made by Internet users when inputting a Website address into a Web browser. Should a user accidentally enter an incorrect Website address, they may be led to an alternative Website owned by a cybersquatter. Wikipedia (<http://en.wikipedia.org/wiki/Typosquatting>, accessed April, 2011).

also more likely to hold such views permanently if they perceive the material as more realistic. A survey by Jochen Peter and Patti M. Valkenburg about Dutch teenagers, published in *The Journal of Communication* in 2006, has found that there is a relationship between porn use and the feeling that it is not necessary to have affection for people to have sex with them. Boys were much more likely to hold such views than girls.

The Mizoram police also found a link between the increased incidence of sexual assaults including rape and paedophilia, and the watching of pornographic tapes and videos. The Aizawl superintendent of police, Lalbiakthanga Khaingte, commented that convicted rapists and others caught for assaulting young girls and minors confessed to having watched porn videos before committing such crimes (Karmakar, 2010).

For those who cannot access the Internet, the Indian pornography industry produces 'blue' movies mostly in Hindi, Bengali, Malayalam and Tamil languages. Local cable networks show these pornographic films in the middle of the night. They are also sold as DVDs. Some hardcore Indian porn is available illegally in Indian markets through high-speed Solid State Drive (SSD) productions.

Earlier scripts in Indian pornography often included lengthy bathroom scenes featuring the lead actress who is later raped by 2 or 3 men simultaneously and penetrated in the mouth, vagina and anus. In more recent pornography, most of the girls depicted as 'porn stars' in the films seem to be in their early teens. The preference is for very young girls, especially real clips of schools students, or girls in school uniforms or frocks. A new trend is to depict the rape of tribal girls, especially from hill tribes:

- In January 2011, a porn clip of a young tribal girl being forced to disrobe and walk naked for 8 km and being molested by 100 men hit the markets as DVDs and videotapes.
- In West Bengal in July, 2010, a private tutor in Burdwan was lynched to death by a mob after a porn DVD featuring one of his students hit the market.
- In a film called *Deepa India*, a teenage girl, Deepa, is seen stripping in front of a camera before she is sexually abused. This seems to be a real life video shot of a college girl coaxed into being filmed, or filmed unknowingly.
- In *Sonia Mauled by Three Studs*, a girl dressed in a frock is forced to have violent penetrative sex with 3 youths. She is down on her knees sucking on three large Indian penises, at the same time as these boys take turns to penetrate her. They also use dildos and cucumbers whilst screaming abuse at her.
- To satisfy the demand for depicting the rape of girls from Indigenous hill tribes, pornographic films are made in Nepal's homes. "Watch these nepali's

244 Pornography and the State

[sic] bang hard in desi style", says the cover of a DVD readily available in Kathmandu. "Exclusive Nepali sex" boasts another.

The greatest number of child pornography videos are shot in Nepal and this has attracted a large number of paedophiles from Britain, Germany and USA who now prefer Nepal over their traditional hunting grounds of Thailand and Cambodia (Mukherjee, and Basu, 2007). The most talked about scandal that attracted public notice and condemnation was the case of Irish poet, Cathal O'Searcaigh, who abused street kids and young boys in Nepal (Sarkar, 2010).

In India and Nepal, pornography filmmakers are increasing the exploitation of women as well as coercing and forcing young children into making homemade cheap pornographic videos for sale. The police suspected that Moninder Singh Pandher, accused in the Noida serial killings case, might be part of an international child pornography racket (Sinha, 2007). They seized photographs of nude children from his residence as well as pornographic literature, a laptop computer and a web cam.

In India, Section 292 of the Indian Penal Code (1860) provides protection from child pornography.[8] But Section 292 does not per se deal with obscenity online. This difficulty was solved by the insertion of Section 29A which included electronic documents also within the purview of documents thus making the law applicable to electronic media as well (see Indian Child, 2010).

Growing concerns over the pernicious effect of porn on children and adults alike, and the rise in abductions, coercion and shooting of illicit porn films without the knowledge of the victims, have finally led the Indian Government in December 2008 to pass RAID or *The Information Technology (Amendment) Bill* with 45 amendments. The law now treats both purveyors and recipients of pornography in the same manner and provides a full section subtitled "punishment for publishing or transmitting of material depicting children in sexually explicit acts, etc. in electronic format" (in Gilani, 2008).

Most pornographic 'tableaus' depict women as being submissive and passive. A woman undresses, assumes a number of sexual positions, the male protagonist(s) achieve(s) orgasm – this is the typical formula that the majority of porn scripts follow. Pornographers use every aspect of a woman's body, sexualise it and find a way to dehumanise it.

Books, postcards, magazines, painting, animation, drawing, videos, films, video games, sound recording, photos, sculpture ... pornography uses all these

---

8   It is important to note that in India, pornography is legally defined as obscenity. See Rana (1990).

mediums to present sexually graphic content. Books and magazines published in different Indian languages have a long history from early *Bat tala* publications to modern magazines like *Meri Kahaniyan* (Hindi), *Satya Kahaniyan* (Hindi), *Alokpaat* (Bengali).

The north Indian regional pulp fiction industry was mostly centered around Meerut and Daryagunj in Delhi. In the 1960s and 1970s, these magazines and books were selling in the hundreds of thousands. Some popular writers were Pyareylal Awaaraa, Kushvaahaa Kant, Gulshan Nanda, Ved Prakash Sharma, Rajhans, Ibn-e-Safi, Akram Ellahabadi, Ranu and Surendra Mohan Pathak, some of whom had written over 1500 novels each. In the 1980s, many of these novels were easily selling 500,000 to 600,000 copies without any pre- or post-launch publicity (Pande, 2008).

A dash of crime romance laced with a heavy dose of pornography where women were stereotyped as passive and brutalised by 'macho' men was the main content. Ved Prakash Sharma's *Vardi Wala Gunda* (1996; translated as *The Criminal in Uniform*) is a story based on Rajiv Gandhi's assassination and is laced with a liberal dose of black magic and tantric potions induced to make the women wild, though ultimately subjugated by brutal men. It sold a million copies.

These books are a long way away from the *Kama Sutra* by Vatsyayana, the *Sougandhikaparinay*, the *Shritawanidhi* or the Basholi, Kangra and Rajasthani style of miniature paintings with erotic illustrations. These earlier texts contained practical descriptions about the art of sex and did not depict the degradation or domination of women, violence or paedophilia.

The sex industry has confused and manipulated the minds of many who believe in sexual equality by normalising pornography (see Suraiya, 2004). Due to this there has been little resistance to the flooding of the Indian markets with explicit, sexually violent and degrading material.

This normalisation has even led to top government officials using pornography and the judiciary defending them. In 2008, the Bombay High Court Judge Justice Vijaya Kapse-Tahilramani, crushed the case against top customs officers arrested for watching porn flicks. He stated that merely watching an obscene film in the privacy of one's home is not a punishable act under the Indian penal code.

In May 2010, following a tip-off from police in Germany, a serving lieutenant colonel of the Indian Army was arrested by the Crime Branch in Mumbai for uploading child pornography on Websites. The police are investigating whether the officer, Jagmohan Balbir Singh, 42, was also involved in producing these videos (Sharma and Singh, 2010).

Religious men too are not out of the purview as pornography makers and distributors. In January, 2011, a 'godman' from Mathura near Lucknow, called Vrindavan 'Porn Swamy' Rajendra, was arrested for making sex clips with children for his foreign disciples, who helped him market these through some Websites. Police confiscated a movie camera, DVDs, and hours of footage with children, his wife and some foreigners. Mathura police said he had been booked under Section 377 (unnatural sex) of the Indian Penal Code and 67B of the IT Act.[9]

A 2007 report suggests that the surge of foreign tourists in India is mainly due to the rampant child pornography industry in India. According to the data issued by the Ministry of Tourism, the number of tourists visiting India has gone up from 3.92 million in 2005 to 4.43 million in 2006. This is a sharp increase of 13%. Jeff Avina, director of operations at the UN Office on Drugs and Crime (UNODC) in Vienna, speculates that the paedophilia industry might be one of the causes of the sharp increase in foreign tourism in India (Pratyush, 2007). In 2009, a Dutch national, 56-year-old William Heum, was arrested on child pornography charges in Chennai on a tip-off by Interpol.[10]

Feminist anti-pornography resistance does not match the might and money of the sex industry. Saheli Women's Resource in Delhi has been running a continuous campaign against pornography since 2004 on the basis that it commodifies women's sexuality and depicts women as sex objects (Saheli, 2004). In July 2009, at a conference 'Daughters of Fire: India Courts of Women', organised by Vimochana in Bangalore, feminist anti-porn activists drew links between pornography and violence, the oppression of women and girls, and negative impacts on the sexual behaviour of people in general (<http://www.vimochana.in/blog/>). As mentioned earlier, in 2009, cartoons featuring the Internet porn star, Savita Bhabhi, were banned as a result of a complaint by a women's group in Maharashtra. And in 2011, the Vrindavan 'Porn Swamy' was arrested based on a widespread campaign by women's groups against him.

These victories seem small at a time when news magazines are writing cover stories that glorify the sexual emancipation of Indian women. But they are significant for highlighting the fact that there are a whole lot of men in India who are not very emancipated and have a hard time accepting women's sexual emancipation. They are having such a hard time that they must secretly film nude girls and women having sex, and then disperse the results to thousands of others in the global world of online pornography.

---

9   <http://hawkstix.blogspot.com/2011/01/vrindavans-porn-swamy-arrested-cds.html>
10 <http://news.rediff.com/report/2010/feb/09/chennai-dutch-gets-bail-in-child-pornography-case.htm>

Bibliography

Bhattacharya, Ekalavya (15 May, 2007) 'Online Status of PORN in India', <http://www.watblog.com/2007/05/15/online-status-porn-india/>.

Bollywood Hungama News Network (6 July, 2010) 'UTV conducts online survey among teenagers as part of marketing plan for Udaan', <http://www.bollywoodhungama.com/news/2010/07/06/14329/index.html>.

Datta, Damayanti (25 February, 2011) 'Secret Life of Indian Teens' *India Today*, <http://m.indiatoday.in/itwapsite/story?sid=130880&secid=134>.

Gilani, Iftikhar (28 December, 2008) 'Internet pornography becomes serious crime in India', <http://www.dailytimes.com.pk/default.asp?page=2008\12\28\story_28-12-2008_pg7_34>.

Government of India (2000) *Information Technology Act*, <http://www.mit.gov.in/content/information-technologyact>.

Government of India (2005) *Protection Against Sexual Harassment of Women Bill*, <wcd.nic.in/protshbill2007.htm>.

Indian Child (2010) 'Child Pornography Laws in India', <http://www.indianchild.com/childlaws/child-pornograhy-laws-in-india.htm>.

Jayachandran, C.R. (26 September, 2003) 'World Wide Porn: 260 mn, growing' *The Times of India.com*, <http://timesofindia.indiatimes.com/World-wide-porn-260-mn-growing/articleshow/203486.cms>.

Karmakar, Rahul (15 November, 2010) 'Mizoram Police Blames Sex Tapes for Sexual Assault, Rape Incidents', <http://www.sinlung.com/2010/11/mizoram-police-blames-sex-tapes-for.html>.

Mukherjee, Dyutimoy and Anunoy Basu (2007) 'Child Pornography: A Comparative Study of India, USA and EU' *Calcutta Criminology Law Journal*, <http://works.bepress.com/dyutimoy_mukherjee/3>.

Pande, Mrinal (20 October, 2008) 'The life and death of Hindi pulp fiction', <http://www.livemint.com/2008/10/20225113/The-life-and-death-of-Hindi-pu.html>.

Peter, Jochen and Patti M. Valkenburg (2006) 'Adolescents' Exposure to Sexually Explicit Online Material and Recreational Attitudes Toward Sex' *The Journal of Communication* 56 (4) pp. 639–660, <http://www.ingentaconnect.com/content/bpl/jcom/2006/00000056/00000004/art00001>.

Pratyush (15 October, 2007) 'Is Child Sex Industry behind increasing foreign tourists in India?', <http://www.indiadaily.org/entry/is-child-sex-industry-behind-the-growing-tourism-in-india/>.

Rana, Inder S. (1990) *Law of obscenity in India, USA & UK*. Mittal Publications, New Delhi.

Saheli Women's Resource Centre (2004) 'The Decency Debates: Censorship and the Journey of a Women's Group', <https://sites.google.com/site/saheliorgsite/gender-sexuality/the-decency-debates>.

Sarkar, Sudeshna (3 December, 2010) 'Nepal's porn industry spreads its net', <http://nayanepalikura.blogspot.com/2010/12/nepals-porn-industry-spreads-its-net.html>.

Sharma, Somendra and Divyesh Singh (8 May, 2010) 'Indian Army officer caught uploading child porn on websites', <http://www.dnaindia.com/mumbai/report_indian-army-officer-caught-uploading-child-porn-on-websites_1380415>.

Sinha, Varun (2007) 'Found in horror house: photos of nude children, foreigners, porn', <http://www.indianexpress.com/news/found-in-horror-house-photos-of-nude-children-foreigners-porn/20259/>.

Suraiya, Jug (15 August, 2004) 'Don't Confuse Porn with Erotica' *The Times of India*, <http://articles.timesofindia.indiatimes.com/2004-08-15/india/27171546_1_pornography-rushdie-reductio-ad-absurdum>.

Tejaswi, Mini Joseph (2 January, 2011) 'Smartphone Porn in Latest Buzz' *The Times of India*, <http://articles.timesofindia.indiatimes.com/2011-01-02/bangalore/28374616_1_video-clips-smartphone-pavan-duggal>.

Betty McLellan

Pornography as Free Speech: But is it Fair?

For its legitimation and continued existence in Western societies, pornography depends on a narrow interpretation of the principle of Freedom of Speech, and while the right to free speech is guarded jealously by all who live under a democratic system of government, an interpretation which privileges the rights of one individual over another is not sustainable. In such circumstances, it is inevitable that speech will be available in much greater measure to those individuals with power and influence than to those with little or no power.

In Western democracies, politicians, business and community leaders as well as the media have ready access to speech, which means that the views of the powerful and those who agree with them are freely available to all, while the views of others rarely see the light of day. It is evident, too, that the current system gives men more access to speech than women, non-Indigenous more access than Indigenous, the wealthy more access than those who live in relative poverty.

Such a situation leads me to ask: Can there be freedom of speech in a truly democratic sense unless it is freely available to all? Can there be free speech when it is not also fair speech? How can pornography be described as a free speech issue when it is clearly not fair to those performing in it and to women in general? Following a brief discussion of the inconsistencies surrounding the principle of Freedom of Speech using recent high-profile examples, I point to the feminist maxim 'the personal is political' to shed light on the relationship of women to pornography and to support the view that pornography is not fair speech.

Freedom of Speech

There are many arguments in academic literature supporting the democratic principle of freedom of speech.[1] The most popular argument and the one used most often in the general community is called 'the Argument for Self-Determination'. Freedom of Speech, sometimes referred to as Freedom of

---

1   For a list of the various arguments, see Campbell (1994) p. 17.

Expression, encompasses more than just speech. It includes freedom to say, to read, to do and to go.[2] Those who choose to interpret Freedom of Speech in absolute terms see it as their own individual right to do and say and read and view whatever they like regardless of how their speech and actions may affect others. It is this absolute focus on the individual that is unsustainable due to the fact that it takes little account of the rights of others. When one person demands the right to do whatever he/she likes, it follows that others will be affected and, in many cases, have their own rights to freedom of speech curtailed.

In the Preface to *Only Words*, Catharine A. MacKinnon alerts readers to the fact that her book "attempts to move people to face the reality of harm done through what is called speech ..." The aim of her book, she explains, is "to stop the harm and open a space for subordinated voices, those shut down and shut out through the expressive forms inequality takes" (1994, p. x).

Those who live under a democratic form of government hold democracy up as superior to all other forms of government precisely because it advocates freedom and equality for all its citizens. One would expect, therefore, that an analysis of the inequalities inherent in the way freedom of speech is interpreted would be carried out as a matter of urgency. But no democratic nation has yet had the courage to confront the power elite's unquestioned right to free speech. It is obvious that those with more power in society have much greater access to speech than those with less power, and that the powerful can subordinate and exploit the powerless with impunity in the name of free speech.

In *Unspeakable: A feminist ethic of speech*, I introduced the concept of Fair Speech and set up an oppositional relationship between free speech and fair speech, similar to the relationship between free trade and fair trade. My aim was to draw attention to the fact that 'free' is not always 'fair' and that, for the principle of freedom of speech to mean anything at all, it must incorporate fairness. There is an illusion in Western societies, perpetuated from time to time by government propaganda, that anything called 'free' is necessarily good. Free trade, free speech, free choice must all be good because they are 'free'. Individual freedoms are prized and any hint that governments may attempt to reduce the freedoms enjoyed by mainstream citizens to allow for greater freedom for those on the margins usually brings howls of protest from many in the mainstream.

---

2   Defining pornography as "graphic sexually explicit materials that subordinate women through pictures and words" Catharine A. MacKinnon and Andrea Dworkin attempted to highlight the fact that pornography harms women by what it says and what it does (see MacKinnon, 1994, pp. 15–16).

Consequently, fairness is pushed aside and inequality and injustice are allowed to continue in the name of free speech.

Such a situation of inequality and injustice has led me to the conclusion that for free speech to have any legitimacy at all, it must also be fair speech. If justice and fairness are to be served, then any activity which invokes the defence of freedom of speech must be scrutinised on two counts: the power dynamics involved, and the potential for harm to others.

When Free Speech is not Fair Speech

The controversy around the WikiLeaks saga reveals that freedom of speech is not a simple matter. Indeed, there is evidence to show that the legal right to free speech is used by some, including the United States government, as a matter of convenience.

The release in October and November, 2010 of secret United States documents and cables, previously leaked to WikiLeaks by named and unnamed sources, saw the US government and its allies loudly condemning the action, with some calling for the group's spokesperson, Julian Assange, to be arrested and charged with treason. This prompted left-wing libertarians around the world to ask with one voice: Where is the United States government's commitment to freedom of information and freedom of speech? Defending WikiLeaks's action, they reminded politicians that, under a democratic rule of law, people have a right to know and a right to speak and that Julian Assange was doing nothing illegal.[3]

The United States Administration had a very difficult situation on its hands. While the constitutional amendment granting individuals the right to freedom of speech is always held up as the primary and central freedom enjoyed by US citizens, on this particular issue they were prepared to make an exception based on the possible harms that could come from the leaking of their sensitive documents.

My aim in raising the dilemma the United States finds itself in over the WikiLeaks controversy is not to analyse the controversy and present an opinion here but, rather, to show that the defence of freedom of speech is not always the simple matter it is made out to be when politicians, community leaders, libertarians and others use it to dismiss feminist arguments against pornography

---

3 The fact that Julian Assange has been charged with sexual molestation under Swedish law is a separate matter altogether. While his supporters have sought to confuse the 2 issues, saying that the allegations of rape are simply a mechanism for having him extradited to Sweden and then on to the United States, the charge of sexual misconduct is real and ought to be dealt with independently from the WikiLeaks issues.

with the accusation of 'censorship'. As with the WikiLeaks controversy, it is more complex, and deserving of more thoughtful analysis. Indeed, every activity, including pornography which uses the defence of free speech ought to be subjected to the test of fairness. It must be asked: Will this particular speech, this particular activity, cause harm or offence to anyone else?

While the charge of inconsistency can be aimed squarely at the US government on the WikiLeaks issue, left-wing libertarians and others who call for absolute freedom of speech also reveal their inconsistency on issues involving free speech which they deem to be unfair. Two recent examples involve religious vilification and paedophilia.

Free Speech versus Religious Vilification

On 9 September, 2010, Florida Pastor, Terry Jones, announced that he would burn copies of the Koran on 11 September in protest against the attacks on the World Trade Centre by Muslim extremists in 2001. His announcement sparked outrage around the world and was openly condemned by President Barack Obama and Secretary of State Hillary Clinton, by the Vatican, by Muslim clerics, and Muslim and Christian people alike. When Pastor Jones's Internet service provider cancelled his Website, he complained that his freedom of speech rights had been violated (<http://www.abc.net.au/lateline/content/2010/s3007729.htm>).

This is a clear example of free speech which was not fair speech and many people around the world – including free-speech advocates across the whole spectrum from right to left – spoke out loudly against Pastor Jones's intended action and in favour of the Internet provider's action. In doing so, they revealed their belief that speech which does harm to others is to be condemned.[4]

Free Speech versus the Promotion of Paedophilia

In November, 2010, Amazon.com was forced by public protest to remove from its Kindle reader an e-book by Phillip R. Greaves titled *The Pedophile's Guide to Love and Pleasure: A Child-Lover's Code of Conduct*. In this book, the author gives advice on how to use children for one's own sexual pleasure, how to break the law and avoid being caught.

---

4   Subsequently, on 20 March, 2011, Pastor Jones did carry out his threat to burn the Koran in the name of freedom of speech and, as a direct consequence of his action, 7 members of the United Nations staff in Afghanistan were murdered on 2 April by protesters incensed at the desecration of Islam's holy book. Pastor Jones remarked that he had no regrets about his action.

Initially, Amazon.com responded to the storm of criticism and protest by relying on the defence of freedom of speech. "Amazon.com believes it is censorship not to sell certain titles simply because we or others believe their message is objectionable" (<http://www.presstv.ir/detail/150560.html>). Using the Marketplace of Ideas argument for freedom of speech, they went on to state that they support the right of every individual to make their own decisions about what books they purchase.

Melinda Tankard Reist, in her 12 November, 2010 opinion piece, asked the question which was on every protester's lips: "Should 'freedom of speech' trump a child's right to be safe and not be harmed?" (<http://www.abc.net.au/unleashed/41030.html>).

The storm of protest via online opinion pieces, comments and blogs from people concerned about the harm this book could do to children, caused Amazon.com eventually to remove the title from Kindle. In this case, the perceived right to absolute freedom of speech was overridden by the urgency in the minds of the protesters to protect children.

While governments and free speech advocates may differ in their judgement about which issues require a less than absolute reliance on the defence of freedom of speech, there is one issue on which they all agree: Pornography. As if with one voice, they proclaim that pornography is a freedom of speech issue and any suggestion, even when backed up by solid evidence, that it does ongoing harm to women and irreparable damage to relationships, is met with disdain and labeled 'censorship'. In the case of pornography, it seems that freedom of speech is more important than a woman's right to equality, dignity and respect.

A Word about Censorship

There seems to be an irrational fear on the part of Western governments, lawyers and other devotees of absolute freedom of speech, that to censor anything at all will result in the eventual loss of all human rights. While such a fear is unfounded, the 'slippery slope' argument against censorship is vigorously supported in the case of pornography, regardless of all the evidence of the harm it does to women and children. It is remarkable, in my mind, that supposedly intelligent people are blind to the inconsistencies inherent in their opposition to censorship. Vehemently opposed to the censoring of pornography, they happily live in a society which has all manner of laws governing behaviour, including defamation laws, classification laws, road rules, and laws against physical and sexual violence. In order for people to live together in fairness and equality, any individual behaviour that has the potential to cause harm to others ought to be subject to laws governing behaviour.

Pornography: Free Speech which is not Fair Speech

If 'the personal is political' as early Second Wave feminists argued, then pornography as freedom of speech, as individual choice, as harmless fun, is called into question. Anything which happens to women at a personal level is also political and, as with religious vilification and paedophilia, pornography clearly fails the test of fairness. When pornography is scrutinised on the basis of the 2 counts mentioned earlier: power dynamics and the potential for harm, it fails on both counts.

Power dynamics

The power differential in pornography involving children is clear: adult men exploiting children, both girls and boys. The power differential in pornography involving adults is also clear to many, but discounted as unimportant by producers and consumers of pornography: mostly men (supported by a male-dominated society, by a global multi-billion dollar industry and by politicians and high-profile free speech advocates) exploiting women. The power differential is overwhelming.

Potential for harm

It is unfortunate that repeated and long-term discussion and research about the harms caused by pornography has not been able to change legal reliance in the United States on the defence of freedom of speech. As I see it, the evidence is indisputable that pornography does cause harm to women, to men and to relationships.

Harm to Women: Women are dehumanised, humiliated and reduced to body parts by pornography (MacKinnon, 1987, p. 176). It is "hate propaganda" against women, "violence and contempt openly expressed" (Whisnant, 2004, p. 18). Women are depicted as subordinate to men, as enjoying hurt and pain, as existing only to give sexual stimulation to those men who find pleasure in the humiliation and pain of women (McLellan, 2010, pp. 68–73; see also Jensen this volume).

For as long as pornography exists, the harms to all women will continue: a lowered self-esteem; a confused and embarrassed self-image; a struggle to rise above the image of women perpetuated in pornography; a losing battle to reach and maintain equality with men; the desire to be treated with respect and dignity by one's male colleagues in the workplace only to be disappointed again and again by those whose image of women is affected by their reliance on pornography.

Harm to Men: Men, too, are harmed by pornography. The sex they are presented with in pornography is:

... debased, dehumanised, formulaic, and generic, a kind of sex based not on individual fantasy, play, or imagination, but one that is the result of an industrial product created by those who get excited not by bodily contact but by market penetration and profits (Dines, 2010, p. x).

It is lonely sex. With no actual partner, "... there is no before and after, sex occurs in isolation ... There is no communication ... no emotional resonance to sex ..." (Walter, 2010, p. 109). While a man may wish for a satisfying sexual relationship in real life, once he starts using pornography, it often happens that sex with his partner never quite measures up to his fantasies. Dolf Zillman, a leading researcher in the field, found that long-term use of pornography "... breeds discontent with the physical appearance and the sexual performance of intimate partners" (Zillman, 1989, pp. 127–58).

Harm to Relationships: The lack of respect for women which is the basis of pornography makes equality in relationships impossible. Many men fool themselves into believing that the pornography they consume will stay in the realm of fantasy, thereby keeping it separate from their real-life relationships with women, but "... the more men watch porn, the more the stories become part of their social construction of reality" (Dines, 2010, p. 67). Whether in intimate relationships, in social situations or in the workplace, women will always be seen by men who use pornography as less than equal. The subordinate status given to women in pornographic depictions carries over into every other part of life.

Conclusion

If equality between women and men is ever to be a reality, then pornography has to go. Any activity which encourages men to enjoy, and be sexually turned on by, images of women being hurt and demeaned and humiliated, any activity which subordinates women to men in such an obvious way, will never result in equality and fairness. In free speech terms, pornography robs all women of their free speech rights. In feminist terms, it is not simply a matter of personal choice. It is a highly political activity. The power dynamics involved and the harms done to women show pornography to be an activity privileging men's desires over women's rights.

Recent examples, cited earlier, of the United States government and free speech advocates suspending their absolute dependence on freedom of speech in the interests of fairness show that it can be done. Pornography does harm to half the world's population in the name of free speech. The question must be asked: Is free speech really free if it is not free and fair for all?

Bibliography

Campbell, Tom (1994) 'Rationales for Freedom of Communication' in Tom Campbell and Wojciech Sadurski (Eds) *Freedom of Communication.* Dartmouth Publishing, Aldershot, pp. 17–44.

Dines, Gail (2010) *Pornland: How Porn Has Hijacked Our Sexuality.* Beacon Press, Boston; Spinifex Press, North Melbourne.

MacKinnon, Catharine A. (1987) *Feminism Unmodified: Discourses on Life and Law.* Harvard University Press, Cambridge, MA.

MacKinnon, Catharine A. (1994) *Only Words.* HarperCollins, London.

McLellan, Betty (2010) *Unspeakable: A feminist ethic of speech.* OtherWise Publications, Townsville.

Tankard Reist, Melinda (12 November, 2010) 'Why is Amazon promoting sexual abuse of children?' *The Drum Unleashed,* <http://www.abc.net.au/unleashed/41030.html>.

Walter, Natasha (2010) *Living Dolls: The Return of Sexism.* Virago, London.

Whisnant, Rebecca (2004) 'Confronting Pornography: Some Conceptual Basics' in Christine Stark and Rebecca Whisnant (Eds) *Not For Sale: Feminists Resisting Prostitution and Pornography.* Spinifex Press, North Melbourne, pp. 15–27.

Zillman, Dolf (1989) 'Effects of Prolonged Consumption of Pornography' in Dolf Zillman and Jennings Bryant (Eds) *Pornography: Research Advances and Policy Considerations.* Erlbaum, Hillsdale, NJ.

PART FIVE

Resisting Big Porn Inc

Julia Long

Resisting Pornography, Building a Movement: Feminist Anti-porn Activism in the UK[1]

It is an exciting and important time to be a feminist activist. As inequality remains massive, misogyny and violence against women remains rife and the backlash against the struggle for equality intensifies – with women being objectified and sexualised by the mainstreaming of the sex and porn industries – women and men across the country are increasingly standing up to object.
(Publicity for 'Activism Training' workshop, Feminism in London Conference, 2009)

The first decade of the 21st century has seen a remarkable resurgence of grassroots feminist activism in the UK. Lively online feminist blogs and discussion groups have appeared. Feminist networks have proliferated across the country, the first and largest of which, the London Feminist Network, has grown from just a handful of members in 2004 to a membership of around 1,600 by December, 2010. The decade saw the revival of 'Reclaim the Night' and the instigation of 'Million Women Rise' marches against male violence, several large-scale feminist activist conferences, numerous actions and campaigns, and the emergence of a national information and resource organisation – UK Feminista – which aims to help co-ordinate and support UK grassroots feminist activism.

Anti-porn campaigns

A striking feature of this flourishing activism is the centrality of pornography and the sex industry as mobilising issues. Whilst the re-emergent movement is far from homogenous, anti-porn feminism is nonetheless a significant and high-profile element within the new activism. In particular, the *mainstreaming* of pornography and the sex industry has galvanised many new activists to engage in various forms of resistance, including: Web-based discussions, petitioning and blogging; challenging sexist attitudes expressed by friends, family and colleagues; requesting local newsagents to not stock 'lads' mags', or to place them on the

---

[1] This article draws on research findings from my doctoral research, which involved carrying out ethnographic studies of two UK groups involved in feminist anti-porn activism, along with 24 in-depth, qualitative interviews with anti-porn activists from across the UK.
I would like to thank all the courageous and inspiring women who participated in this research.

top shelf; writing to Members of Parliament or complaining to the Advertising Standards Association; stickering lads' mags or sexist posters and advertisements, or disrupting displays of lads' mags in shops.

Some activism has developed into more formal campaigns. Such campaigns have targeted high street stores, encouraging them not to stock Playboy-branded goods or lads' mags (or at least not to display such publications at eye-level); in at least 2 cities, Sheffield and Bristol, campaigns have been run against the opening of branches of the American 'Hooters' franchise.[2] Most activism to date has concentrated on pornification and sex object culture rather than campaigning around hardcore and Internet pornography, although some groups have used the anti-porn slideshows developed in the US by 'Stop Porn Culture'[3] as part of training and in awareness-raising exercises.

Three of the most successful and high-profile UK campaigns are *Bin the Bunny, Stripping the Illusion,* and *Feminist Fridays. Bin the Bunny* (see Fig.1) was a campaign organised by Anti-Porn London, a group emerging out of the London Feminist Network, which took the form of a series of protests outside the newly-opened Playboy concept store in London's Oxford Street. The campaign focused on raising awareness about the nature and business of the Playboy corporation,

Fig. 1 *Bin the Bunny* protest   Fig. 2 *Feminist Friday* protest

---

2   'Hooters' is an international restaurant franchise that originated in Atlanta, USA. The company states that "the element of sex appeal is prevalent in the restaurants" and that "Hooters hires women who best fit the image of a Hooters girl to work in this capacity", <http://www.hooters.com/About.aspx> (accessed 25 April, 2010).

3   'Stop Porn Culture' produces a wealth of resources for feminist anti-porn activists. See <www.stoppornculture.org>.

through producing a DVD, giving out leaflets, talking to passers-by and wearing campaign t-shirts and badges.

Stripping the Illusion and *Feminist Fridays* (see Fig. 2) are campaigns run by OBJECT,[4] an organisation which campaigns against 'sex-object culture'. The former is a highly strategic campaign which challenged the proliferation of lap dancing clubs through successfully lobbying for changes in licensing arrangements. The latter involves direct action protests calling for lads' mags to be recognised as part of the porn industry, and, if sold, to be covered up, placed on the top shelf and age-restricted. *Feminist Fridays*, held monthly on Friday evenings, take the form of direct intervention in public space, transforming displays of lads' mags through placing the publications into brown paper bags upon which feminist slogans have been written, sometimes followed by exuberant chanting, singing and dancing.[5] The format of these protests is therefore highly effective at bringing a feminist message into the public realm, and providing an alternative message to that intended by the publishers.

Activist motivation and involvement

Activists I spoke to were highly motivated to challenge porn culture, seeing pornography as part of the backlash against gains made by feminism, and a means by which women are objectified and dehumanised, and violence against women is normalised. Activists spoke of emotions such as anger and distress as a motivation for getting involved in activism. The distress experienced came about for a number of reasons, including male partners' use of porn, workplace sexual harassment relating to porn, and the undermining effects of the presence of porn within mainstream culture:

> I was surrounded by a lot of misogynist men, and other people in my life had similar attitudes, and ... I just felt so unhappy and I felt, I can't handle [porn] being everywhere, I don't want to be in a world that's like this (Sheryl, 30).

Prior to getting involved with activism, women often felt isolated and alone in their objections to pornography. They found friends, colleagues and acquaintances hostile or unsympathetic to anti-porn sentiments, and spoke of their opinions being consistently trivialised or ridiculed. Such hostile responses tended to have a powerful silencing effect, and the need to break this silence and isolation was a strong motivating factor:

---

4   See <www.object.org.uk>.
5   For a flavour of the assertive and extrovert style of *Feminist Fridays* protests, see a video of the July, 2010 action, available at <http://www.youtube.com/watch?v=iA7aAizybG8> (accessed 28 March, 2011).

> I remember the first time I clicked on the link for the OBJECT website and I was just so pleased that there were like-minded people out there! (Nadia, 32).

Once involved, the activism was overwhelmingly experienced as affirming and empowering, and the sense of participating in struggle and making a difference was a key factor in maintaining activist involvement:

> [t]he protest outside the lap dancing club was fantastic ... Cos for me, before I found OBJECT I just felt really, um, impotent ... So it just feels really good to feel you've done something ... I do get a lot out of it (Nadia, 32).

However, taking a public stand against porn is far from easy, and challenges inevitably arise. Anti-porn work carries a number of specific stress factors and emotional challenges, including the stress of taking an oppositional stance in the context of a 'pornified' society; dealing with pornographic material; public perceptions and negative stereotypes of anti-porn feminists, and the reactions of friends, families and partners. The activists I interviewed were involved in a variety of anti-porn activities ranging from campaigns, petitioning, lobbying, protests and actions to delivering workshops and training, and working within professional settings. Sometimes the work was carried out in the context of paid employment; more often it was undertaken on a purely voluntary basis. The different contexts and kinds of work tended to have different implications in terms of the nature of the stress involved and kinds of support needed, though some challenges were common to all forms of activism. In the final section, I will set out some of the challenges that can arise and outline strategies that activists have developed in order to deal with these.

Protective measures and support strategies

> [T]he support! I tell you what ... the support of feminists, the feminist friends that I've made, I feel so much more supported by them mentally and when we're out in a group doing an action, I know they've all got my back (Rita, 53).

The importance of support structures was evident in how groups dealt with the challenges of doing anti-porn work. This support took different forms depending on the nature of the activism, as outlined below.

Protests and actions

Group co-ordinators and members developed a range of practical strategies to ensure that activists felt supported and able to cope with the challenges of a public demonstration. These included:

- Ensuring thorough planning and preparation prior to the action

- Meeting up beforehand to make sure new people were welcomed
- Using resources such as 'comeback sheets' to build confidence in dealing with members of the public
- Building group spirit through chant practice, banner-making sessions and sharing practical tasks
- Working as a team and 'looking out' for each other
- Providing training for dealing with the media
- Dividing up tasks and agreeing roles (e.g. one person to deal with media interest whilst on a demo)
- De-brief sessions after the actions
- Building informal support networks, including through phone, email and online discussion
- Socialising and celebrating

Knowledge is power

A key part of being involved in activism was the opportunity for activists to build knowledge and become more informed about the issues. Activists spoke of how this opportunity helped them to develop confidence in dealing with hostile or uninformed attitudes from work colleagues, family and acquaintances. The importance of being part of a supportive group was emphasised, as this provided a context for developing networks and gaining knowledge.

Dealing with pornographic material

Trainers responsible for delivering anti-porn awareness raising sessions developed practical strategies for dealing with pornographic content and its potentially distressing and 'triggering' effects. These strategies included delivering the training in pairs, providing details of support agencies dealing with sexual violence and offering participants the chance to opt out at any point. While most of the women I interviewed were not generally involved in this kind of work, all groups tended to recognise the need for women to share and discuss feelings and experiences regarding porn in a safe space. In one group, this was built into meeting structures, with time set aside for confidential discussion and sharing, separate from the 'business' parts of the meeting.

Managing emotions and group dynamics

Various practical supports, often informal, were developed for managing emotions and group dynamics. For example, Lydia spoke of 'having to have de-brief sessions' after group actions:

264 Resisting Big Porn Inc

I always made sure I sent round emails afterwards that were positive and upbeat. Often, even when an action had gone well, there would always be a confrontation, obviously usually with a man, or there would be an incredible adrenalin crash because you really had to build yourself up to these things (Lydia, 34).

In other groups, there was a desire to create a structure where emotions could be explored and women could support each other. However, time pressures and limited resources meant that these kinds of structures did not always get beyond the ideas stage. In the meantime, activists developed personal friendships and informal support networks within groups. It was evident that great attention was given to recognising and valuing the contribution of individual activists, perhaps in recognition that their activist work was not always valued by friends and family outside the group.

Combating isolation

For most of the women I spoke to, isolation was a problem that they had encountered prior to getting involved in activism, rather than an issue once they had become active. However, for some anti-porn activists isolation can be a significant and ongoing problem. For women in small communities or rural settings, feelings of isolation and the stigmatisation of the 'anti-porn' label can be acute. Measures taken to combat this included online communication with other feminists, and reading online blogs and feminist books. Sharing the company of other women at feminist events such as 'Reclaim the Night' marches and conferences was especially valued, particularly if this was a rare opportunity.

Conclusion

Feminist resistance to pornography is re-emerging in the 21st century as a significant and important development in the trajectory of the UK feminist movement. A new generation of activists are embracing radical feminist analyses of pornography, and developing dynamic, creative and strategic campaigns to resist pornification and the expansion of the sex industry. They are also developing support strategies in order to help build and sustain an anti-porn resistance movement: strategies which emerged strikingly as a vital element of the activism.

The global scale, technological reach and economic power of the porn industry are huge challenges for feminists, as is negotiating the dominant discourse of 'choice', 'free speech' and 'empowerment' that serve to legitimise its existence. However, in a short space of time and with extremely limited resources, a new generation of UK anti-porn feminists have achieved some notable successes, particularly in attracting media attention and driving through important legislative changes. Through their involvement in activism, this new generation of feminists are breaking the silence around porn and gaining strength, confidence and assuredness in their arguments, and discovering a sense of solidarity and shared purpose. In the UK in the 21st century, anti-porn feminism is once again emerging as a vital and urgent political force.

Gail Dines

Stop Porn Culture!

Stop Porn Culture! is dedicated to challenging the pornography industry and an increasingly pornographic pop culture. Our work toward ending industries of sexual exploitation is grounded in a feminist analysis of sexist, racist, and economic oppression. We affirm sexuality that is rooted in equality and free of exploitation, coercion, and violence.

The founders of SPC are long time anti-pornography activists who have been organizing against the porn industry since the 1980s. In March, 2007 we held a conference called 'Pornography and Pop Culture: Reframing Theory, Re-thinking Activism' at Wheelock College in Boston. This was the first feminist anti-porn conference in the US in 15 years and the response was overwhelming. Within a day of going live with our Website, we had over 200 registrations. About 550 people came to Boston for the conference and it was the beginning of a new era in anti-porn activism. Stop Porn Culture! was founded that weekend and we have been active ever since.

One of our goals was to create a movement to fight the hypersexualization of culture and the increasingly violent nature of mainstream Internet porn. As the porn industry continues to grow and creep into all areas of our lives, it is more important than ever to organize a movement that resists the misogyny of porn. On our Website we ask:

Do you ever feel overwhelmed by pornography? … Are you ever concerned that mass media reduce women, and increasingly girls, to sexual objects while encouraging men and boys to be sexually callous? Is it getting more difficult for you to protect your kids from the porn culture?

You aren't alone. Stop Porn Culture! is a group for those willing to ask these questions – activists and academics, young people and parents, organizers and ordinary people. We are no longer willing to accept the ways the pornography industry has pushed its way into our lives, distorting our conceptions of sex and sexuality. We are ready to fight back.

The central organizing tool of SPC is a series of slide shows that explore the nature and effects of contemporary porn. The first slide show, written by Gail Dines, Rebecca Whisnant and Robert Jensen, is called 'Who Wants to be a Porn Star?' It can be downloaded free of charge from the SPC Website and it is now being used across the USA as well as in Canada, Europe, Russia, and even parts of Africa. With a script and over 100 slides, the show is an excellent resource for people who want to raise awareness about the harms of porn. It is being used by educators, anti-violence professionals, community activists and citizens who are concerned about the increasing pornification of our society.

The second slide show, written by Rebecca Whisnant, is called 'It's Easy Out Here for a Pimp: How a Porn Culture Grooms Kids for Sexual Exploitation.' This show focuses on how a pornified popular culture (including pornography itself) shapes the identities of children and adolescents, while increasingly portraying them as sexual objects for adults. Our goal is to produce more slide shows that look at the different ways porn infiltrates our daily lives.

Every year Stop Porn Culture! holds training sessions for people who want to become anti-porn activists. These two-day seminars introduce participants to the literature on the effects of porn and provide a general introduction into the history of feminist anti-porn activism. Central to the training is a day of mock question and answer sessions where we train people in how to answer the various questions that audience members typically have after seeing the slide show. This helps people develop the confidence necessary to give public lectures on porn.

The SPC Website has an array of resources for people seeking more information on the effects of porn, on how to deal with a partner who is a habitual user, as well as videos and articles on issues relating to the sex industry. Over the years SPC has become a visible movement in fighting the porn industry and we are now developing international links with other groups who are trying to raise consciousness as to the harms of porn.

<http://stoppornculture.org>

Linda Thompson

Challenging the Demand

Imagine standing up in a room full of strangers. Imagine standing up talking to them about pornography. Imagine going into that knowing that a good few will be hostile to everything you say and extend that personally to you. Imagine hearing young women talk of practising faked orgasm sounds and faces to meet partners' expectations. Imagine talking with parents supporting their teenagers as they deal with their naked images being shared online.

And yet, I love my job challenging demand for commercial sexual exploitation, including prostitution and pornography. I don't love what I see, read and hear, but every day I am proud to be involved in challenging one of the most destructive forces in our culture. Saying "I am anti-porn" is definitively stating a position which some are surprised even exists. There is disbelief that anyone does such a job and that I would confess to being like *that*. Sometimes there is a nervous laugh, slight defensiveness or even an envious "Wow, I'd love to look at porn and get paid for it!" Clearly, I am part of a minority, holding an alternative position outside the dominant view of pornography as acceptable, liberal and progressive.

Years ago, this anti-porn position would have seemed incompatible with my work with young people in sexual health projects in Belfast. Now, my work as the Development Officer with the Women's Support Project[1] includes reading porn industry journals,[2] viewing the latest uploads on Youporn or scanning the highest-rated pornography on British Bukakke Babes. The idea that this regular

---

1   <www.womenssupportproject.co.uk> This work is funded through the Equality Unit Violence Against Women fund in Scotland with the overall aim to challenge the demand for commercial sexual exploitation, which includes prostitution, pornography, and so-called adult entertainment (e.g. stripping/lap dancing). This is delivered through awareness raising, public education, training, multi-agency working and developing new resources. The Women's Support Project is a Scottish feminist charity, which has been operational for over 26 years working against violence against women and children. This work has highlighted the links between different forms of male violence and promoted interagency responses to the abuse of women and children.

2   The porn industry, similar to other large commercial sectors, has its own trade journals. Included in these are *Adult Video News* (AVN), <http://business.avn.com/>, XBIZ <http://www.xbiz.com/> and in the UK, *Adult Industry Trade Association* (AITA). <http://admin.gdbtv.com/aita/about.php>.

exposure to the pornography industry would radically change my views was something I never expected.

In the 1990s, I was a woman who knew about pornography, knew its language but thought if someone wanted to use it to get off – what was the problem? Back in that era of videos, DVDs and magazines, I reassured female friends that all guys look at this stuff and blew the whistle on the usual hiding places. I said, "Where is the harm?" This seemed to fit with my sexual health work and with the ostensible need to be sex-positive.

So, what changed? Simply, I took a step back, found out more and had to accept that pornography was not unproblematic.

I thought I had a good working knowledge of the sex industry but I was not prepared for what I discovered. Finding out about the US activists' group Stop Porn Culture! and watching their slide show started the steep learning curve. After I decided to develop their 'Who wants to be a porn star?' slideshow[3] for the Scottish context, I read all the research, checked out the evidence and looked at examples down to local levels.

As all elements of the sex trade are inextricably linked, so is my work. I not only watched pornography but read opinion pieces, talked to women involved and became au fait with punters'/consumers' review sites. I had to be informed which meant, in turn, being shocked, angry and upset. I heard the experiences of women in the sex trade, saw the language used to market them as commodities and consumers' total disconnect with them as individuals. I had to then find a way to get all this across with a feminist underpinning. When I delivered this information to wide audiences, I also got feedback on their own real, lived experiences with pornography. This showed me how far we have gone with letting porn become mainstream.

I have yet to talk with any groups of women, men and young people without hearing real concerns about porn in people's lives. Research undoubtedly guides and informs, but the whole process from funding to peer reviewed articles takes a long time. Meanwhile there is growing lived evidence around us. People's experiences may not be currently captured in research results but activism provides the bridge.

This activism offers understanding outside of the myths and justifications of men's need for porn as they are peddled in the mainstream. It uncovers people's concerns, the emerging trends, and so, paying heed to what you hear 'out there'

---

3   Stop Porn Culture! through Gail Dines, Rebecca Whisnant and Robert Jensen developed a slide
    show for activists to use, <www.stoppornculture/resources.com>.

can form a comprehensive agenda about how pornography is affecting us. Sexual health clinicians, health advisors, relationship counsellors and help-lines are *increasingly* dealing with pornography's adverse effects. Why do we ignore them for cutting across the idea that porn is a positive, liberating influence?

Attendees at our seminars frequently have preconceived, and sometimes outdated, ideas of what pornography is and does. What I offer is often the first unequivocal challenge to these assumptions. I am conscious of what I show people and maintain a sense of responsibility. Things seen cannot be unseen. It is necessary to have safeguards in place; people decide to attend after being informed about my approach including looking at images drawn from pornography, from its move into the mainstream, from advertisements, videos, DVDs and the Internet. I remind them at the start of my talk, and then, before they see any images, they are reminded again.

I have found that using references from the everyday media can have more impact than current mainstream pornography. Some of the hardest days at work are not spent immersed in porn land but in supposed 'entertainment'. A memorable occasion was ZOO online lads' mag[4] showing a series of images, purportedly uploaded by a young woman who was penetrated by bottles in her bedroom with framed family photos on the wall, soft toys on a bed ... It takes only a few steps to access young people's social networking sites on the Internet, and it becomes immediately clear how internalised the porn messages have become, with 13-year-olds posting semi-naked pouting images in the hope of being rated a 'sexy hot babe' by self-appointed panels of older male peers.

Some in our audiences perceive anti-porn activism as personal challenges and sometimes retaliate in vicious ways, launching personal attacks. Their 'helpful' advice ranges from the "Just watch more porn – then you will understand," to the more threatening suggestion that a porn-style f*cking, notionally delivered by the commentator will ensure we 'get' the benefits of pornography. Anti-porn activism is under constant scrutiny and unless we are experts on media, philosophy, economics, ethics, the law, and human rights, to name just a few, then our work is undermined. People are all too eager to attack, vilify, dismiss and trample you underfoot in their rush to defend this global industry at any costs. But it is precisely at the point when it feels you are pushing against an ever-expanding frontier directed by the sex industry, that we must celebrate and share our successes. These connections motivate and keep the energy going.

---

4   ZOO *magazine* is a high-street lads' mag with an accompanying Website, <http://www.zootoday.com>.

It is hearing from women who now have, for the first time, words to express and validate how they have been feeling. It is a young woman writing that she is taking a break from sex while she works out what she wants sexually, without pornography's influence. It is reading a young man's blog who is now pushing pornography back from his life and making personal changes. It is men opening up about their experiences with porn and struggling to counterbalance its messages on their kids' understanding of sex and relationships. It is hearing from a father of teenage girls now challenging his friends' acceptance and sharing of 'hot schoolgirl sluts' porn. It is hearing about women discussing pornography in new ways with their friends. When others are showing enough commitment to question, discuss and take action – then the balance can be redressed. Imagine the potential for change if more people spoke up. Then imagine if *you* did something.

You have to make it personal – take a stance and make decisions. With growing economic hardship, women are facing even more reduced opportunities while the sex industry is ever more acceptable, accessible and affordable. There are fewer resources to fund support services and run campaigns so we *need* a groundswell of activism. This is crucial if we really want to change assumptions, confront the apologists, and challenge the demand.

My work across Scotland would not be possible without the foundations laid down by women in the 1980s and 1990s, especially in the field of violence against women. Activism worked to allow victims and survivors of rape and sexual assault to be the ones who defined what was violent. A growing number of women with experience in domestic abuse and sexual assault work moved into positions of influence in party politics and community development. This forged the links between the real lived experiences of women and policy-making (Macleod et al., 1994). Much effort and energy went into furthering understanding of the dynamics and realities of domestic abuse and sexual violence, against the backdrop of deeply rooted male attitudes about entitlement and power. Thirty years later, it is sobering to see the same discussions and processes repeated with commercial sexual exploitation, which is now specifically identified in the national approach to violence against women, Safer Lives, Changed Lives (2009).

The birth of my daughter also prompted me to take fresh stock of our culture. Did I want her coming of age in a world where coming on her face would be the marker of manhood for her male peers (Clark-Flory, 2009). Did I want her value to be judged against how 'porn-ready' she is (Sawyer, 2010)? Did I want her sexuality to be directed and dictated by certain industry moguls? Most of all, did I want my daughter to ask why I hadn't done anything?

People can remain in denial that sexual exploitation doesn't affect them, but through anti-porn work you are really asking them to consider where they are positioned with the industry. Do they collude with the exploitation of women's social and economic status? Do they consume sexualised inequality and sustain the market? Do they turn a blind eye to the consequences of what they and their partners and friends are demanding? Or do they become informed and honestly appraise how it all relates to them? Do they then take action?

The global growth of the sex trade, pornography included, counters so much of what I believe in. But I believe that if we are given factual information, are supported when we process this information, and understand what it really means personally and for others around us, we can make informed decisions. We need skills to weigh the consequences of our decisions and follow them through with a sense of respect. With the growth of the sex trade and its seepage into everyday life, the notion of 'informed choice' has changed. Sexual health promotion is almost rendered valueless given the affordability, accessibility and anonymity of the pornography industry (in Cooper, 2000). When high numbers of young people identify porn as their main sex education, we have allowed the pornography industry to write the script (Flood, 2009).

If *I don't* challenge this, I am helping open the floodgates to allow this take over of our public spaces, our online world, our media and our entertainment as well as the co-opting of our personal lives. As Alasdair Robertson, a Scottish activist against violence against women said, "If you think that it doesn't affect you – you must be living on another planet."[5]

---

5   See <http://www.womenssupportproject.co.uk/content/challengingdemand/180/> for copies of the Money and Power resource packs and <http://www.youtube.com/watch?v=fCYIJCGO 2Gw> for a short film clip developed to raise awareness of commercial sexual exploitation in Scotland which quotes Robertson.

Bibliography

Cooper, Al (Ed) (2000) 'Cybersex: The Dark Side of the Force' Special Issue *Journal of Sexual Addiction and Compulsion*. Brunner-Routledge, Philadelphia, PA and Hove, Sussex.

Clark-Flory, Tracy (18 August, 2009) 'Generation XXX: Having sex like porn stars. How is smut changing teen sexuality? One word: Facials', <www.salon.com/life/broadsheet/feature/2009/08/18/gen_porn/index.html> (accessed 18 August, 2009).

Flood, Michael (2009) 'Boys, Sex, and Porn: New technologies and old dangers', <http://www.xyonline.net/sites/default/files/Flood,%20Boys,%20sex%20and%20porn%202007.pdf>.

Macleod Jan, Patricia Bell and Janette Foreman (1994) 'Bridging the gap: feminist development work in Glasgow' in Miranda Davis (Ed) *Women and Violence*. Zed Books, London.

Safer Lives Changed Lives (2009) Section 4.1, <http://www.scotland.gov.uk/Publications/2009/06/02153519/0>.

Sawyer, Miranda (2010) 'Shag bands, porn on mobile phones … kids need more help to understand sex', http://www.guardian.co.uk/commentisfree/2010/oct/03/sex-education-porn-twitter.

Stop Porn Culture! <http://stoppornculture.org/slide-show-home/>.

ZOO Today! <http://www.zootoday.com/>.

Anna van Heeswijk

OBJECT: Challenging 'Sex-object Culture'[1]

My name is Anna van Heeswijk. I'm 29 and the Campaigns Manager for OBJECT – the award winning pressure group set up in 2003 to challenge the sexual objectification of women and the mainstreaming of the multi-billion pound sex industries. OBJECT has no office and little money, yet with the help and support of trade and student unions, survivors of the sex industry, feminist policy makers, sister organisations, and committed activists across the country, in 5 years we have changed 2 laws and helped revitalise grassroots anti-pornography feminism in the UK.

In partnership with the Fawcett Society,[2] a leading campaigning group for equality between women and men, OBJECT stemmed the proliferation of lap dancing clubs and stripped the illusion that lap dancing is a harmless part of the leisure industry. We have exposed the exploitative industry of lap dancing for what it is and lobbied successfully for a change in the law to allow for better regulation and for limits to be placed on the number of clubs in any vicinity – which can now be set at zero by local councils. We have provided a feminist analysis to underpin our campaign and put the issue of sexism and sexual objectification at the heart of the licensing debate.

In partnership with Eaves,[3] a feminist front-line service provider for women exploited in the sex industry, we secured the first piece of legislation in the UK to directly tackle the demand for prostitution, bringing the buyers out of the shadows and making it a crime to purchase sex from a person who has been exploited. This shifts the criminal gaze away from the person exploited in prostitution on to the person who directly contributes to this exploitation by paying for sex. We have raised awareness of the harmful nature of the sex industry and successfully lobbied for government-run job centres to ban advertising vacancies in the sex industry.

---

1   This is an excerpt from a longer article; for the full version contact the author at anna@object.org.uk Do not quote from this article without permission from the author.
2   <www.fawcettsociety.org.uk>
3   <www.eaves4women.co.uk>

As well as legislative change, OBJECT campaigns for a shift in cultural attitudes. We make explicit the links between the explosion of the sex industries, the ever-increasing portrayal of women as sexual objects, and the misogynistic attitudes which underpin and legitimise violence and discrimination against women. In order to raise awareness and to develop grassroots activism on these issues, OBJECT spearheads national days of action against 'sex-object culture' including *Feminist Fridays* which initiate direct action against 'lads' mags'. *Feminist Fridays* have served to empower individuals and groups to take action and have led to major retailers agreeing to cover up lads' mags and put them on the top shelf.

An important time to be an anti-porn feminist activist

Women in the Western world are told that feminism is outdated and that sexism is a thing of the past. And yet, wherever you look, sexism and inequality remain rife. In the UK, approximately 80% of Parliament is male;[4] nearly 1 in 4 women over 16 has experienced sexual violence;[5] 2 women are murdered each week by male partners (Povey, 2005); and the gender pay gap means that in effect women stop being paid in October whilst men continue to be paid until the end of the year.[6]

The explosion of the sex industries represents a backlash against the struggle for equality between women and men. Increased levels of objectification and the sexualisation of women's bodies promotes the idea that no matter how intelligent or capable women are, and how far we progress as a group, our worth is still dependent on how attractive we are to men.

The role of the sex industries in fuelling and maintaining patriarchy is highlighted by research into male motivations for going to lap dancing clubs (Frank, 2003). When men were asked why they frequent strip clubs, common responses included that they wanted to meet women who were not 'feminist' and that, with a growing fear of sexual harassment lawsuits at work, they wanted to 'let out frustration' and be in an environment in which they could revert back to traditional male–female roles and relationships.

Patriarchal relations are most blatant in relation to prostitution – an industry based on the premise that men can buy access to women's bodies. The effect on those exploited in prostitution (the majority of whom are women and girls) is

---

4   <http://www.parliament.uk/education/online-resources/parliament-explained/women-in-politics/>
5   Prevalence of intimate violence by category among adults aged 16 to 59, Homicides, Firearm Offences and Intimate Violence 2005/2006.
6   <http://www.fawcettsociety.org.uk>

devastating, with statistics showing that prostituted women are more likely than not to experience serious sexual and/or physical abuse at the hands of pimps and punters (Home Office 2004b), and that 68% of women in prostitution suffer Post Traumatic Stress Disorder at the same level as torture victims (Farley et al, 2003). The prostitution industry further undermines broader struggles for women's equality. What is the meaning of our efforts to combat sexual harassment and male violence in the home, in the workplace, and on the streets if men can buy the right to perpetrate these very same acts against women and girls in prostitution?

Prostitution represents an extreme end of commercial sexual exploitation. But sexual objectification exists on a continuum, with images and messages stemming from pornography increasingly seeping into all aspects of popular culture. Feminist language of 'choice' and 'empowerment' has been co-opted to legitimise sex-object culture and promote the sex industry as liberating. In fact, treating women like sexual objects dehumanises women and this is a core element of sexism. The more acceptable it becomes to view women as a sum of body parts, the easier it becomes to disrespect, mistreat and act out violence towards women as a group. This makes anti-porn activism crucial in challenging the industries that promote the attitudes and beliefs which underpin sex discrimination and male violence.

'Activists Rise Up'

It is an exciting time to be an anti-porn feminist. Women and men across the country are increasingly speaking out against the oppression of women. This spirit of resistance has been mobilised by the Million Women Rise marches which galvanise thousands of women to call for an end to male violence; by the Reclaim the Night marches organised annually by the London Feminist Network and other groups nationally to take back our streets; by the Feminism in London conferences, and the UK Feminista Activist Summer Schools; by the success of the OBJECT-Fawcett campaign to challenge the mainstreaming and proliferation of lap dancing clubs; the student union-led campaign against sexist beauty pageants being reintroduced into universities; monthly OBJECT *Feminist Fridays* to campaign against sexist lads' mags (see Long, this volume); and the *Demand Change!* OBJECT-Eaves coalition to tackle the demand for prostitution.

Lessons learned in challenging sex-object culture

• Big vision, achievable goals

OBJECT mobilises activism around campaign goals which are achievable while providing a broad analysis of sexual objectification and sexism.

In relation to lap dancing, the legislative goal of the *Stripping the Illusion* campaign was relatively straightforward – to change the way that lap dancing clubs are licensed. Lap dancing clubs promote the idea of women as sexual objects who are always sexually available and who exist to fulfil the sexual fantasies of men (see Stella, this volume). They represent sites of commercial sexual exploitation, with performers paying to work and structural conditions of competition leading to women often ending shifts in debt to the club. They make sexual harassment seem normal, and they create no-go zones for women who feel unsafe walking past them at night. Yet, until 2010, lap dancing clubs were licensed in the same way as ordinary leisure venues. This rendered it virtually impossible for licenses to be refused, and acted as a green light to the industry which doubled in size over 5 years.

The 2010 change in the law allows local councils to license lap dancing clubs as Sexual Entertainment Venues. This allows councils to consider the gender impact of clubs and set a limit on the number of licences they grant, which can be set at zero. This is a powerful tool to clamp down on the lap dancing club industry and OBJECT are in the process of supporting local communities to lobby their councils to apply this legislation to its fullest.

As well as pushing through legislative change, the *Stripping the Illusion* campaign exposed the reality of the lap dancing industry and located arguments about licensing within the broader context of sexism and sexual objectification of women and girls.

• Making women's voices central

A central goal of OBJECT's work is to provide a platform for women who have been exploited in the sex industry to speak out about the reality of their experiences. This is crucial to counteract the glamourised portrayal of lap dancing, prostitution and pornography peddled by the mainstream media. Perhaps the most effective campaigning tool developed with survivors of the sex industry has been 2 short films in which actors read out the testimonies of women involved in prostitution and lap dancing. OBJECT and Eaves screened the *Demand Change!* film in Parliament on the eve of the vote to criminalise the purchase of sex from a person who has been exploited. Survivors of prostitution from the film were quoted in the House of Lords debate and their testimonies marked a crucial turning point in discussions. It was powerful to inform these women that their words were pivotal in changing the law.

Testimonies have also helped to create a sense of solidarity amongst women who have been exploited in the sex industry who often feel isolated in their experiences. Throughout the lap dancing campaign we were approached by former lap dancers who expressed relief at seeing the other side of the story being put forward and who wanted to share their experiences about what they consistently described as an exploitative and soul-destroying industry. After identifying a clear need for support, OBJECT has been awarded funding to work in partnership with a women's service provider to establish provision for women who have experienced harm in the lap dancing industry.

• Partnership work

Partnering with Eaves and the Fawcett Society and building coalitions with NGOs, unions, politicians, activist groups and survivors of the sex industry has allowed us to share expertise, divide the workload and effectively reach audiences less accessible to us as a single organisation. It has also provided an inspiring model for joint working and helped establish a unified force committed to ending the sexual objectification of women.

• The importance of activism

Grassroots activism has been pivotal to OBJECT's success as a campaigning organisation. As well as influencing policy, activism empowers the individuals and groups who take part. It ameliorates feelings of isolation and powerlessness and provides opportunities to unite and make change.

In spreading anti-porn activism, it has been important for OBJECT to set a tone that is bold and unflinching in our demands whilst providing a welcoming and uplifting experience for those involved. Creativity, visual stunts and the use of songs and chants have been instrumental in terms of making noise, taking up space, and creating a sense of solidarity which has characterised our protests and inspired ordinary people to take action.

Examples of our activism include a protest outside the lap dancing industry awards ceremony in which placard-holding OBJECT activists descended upon the red carpet queue of men in suits, banging tambourines and chanting 'Women, Not Sex Objects!', then enacting and filming our own awards ceremony outside the venue. We awarded the lap dancing lobby for, amongst other things, 'promoting sexist attitudes', and 'the biggest misuse of the word *gentlemen*' in reference to 'Gentlemen's Clubs'!

OBJECT's monthly *Feminist Fridays* involve targeting high street retailers, writing anti-sexist slogans on brown paper bags, and covering whole displays of lads' mags with messages such as 'love women, hate sexism' and 'FHM – For Horrible Misogyny' (see Long, Thompson, this volume). The displays are followed by songs, sit-ins, and congas as we hand out leaflets and collect signatures.

Monthly activist meetings give opportunities for activists to brainstorm ideas and take ownership of campaigns whilst providing guidance to ensure that campaign messages remain consistent.

As well as organising protests and stunts, OBJECT develops diverse ways for people to get involved in campaigns. This includes devising 'Lobby Your MP Weekends', organising 'National Days of Action' to collect signatures, and producing template letters, consultation responses, toolkits and 'Joint Statements of Support' to facilitate individuals and NGOs to take action. Politicians and policy makers often refer to campaign actions they read about in the media, or to the number of letters they have received urging them to support our campaigns.

The power of persistent lobbying, campaigning and activism should never be underestimated!

• Use of the media

OBJECT press-releases our actions and regularly uses the media as a tool to spread awareness, garner support and help put issues on the political agenda. We have built a media contact list and made relationships with key journalists who support our work. However, when campaigning against the multi-billion pound sex industry the playing field is uneven in terms of access to media coverage. This makes utilising alternative media outlets such as online discussion groups, social networking sites, email newsletters and YouTube videos a crucial part of anti-porn activism.

Challenges

Challenging the sex industries which groom society into accepting the object-ification and commercial sexual exploitation of women as normal, is threatening to those who profit and/or benefit from this multi-billion pound system and the sex-object culture that it promotes. It is therefore not surprising that there is widespread and structural opposition to feminist activism on this issue. An important part of the OBJECT campaign has been to provide arguments to counter the claims and accusations used by those who defend sex-object culture and seek to silence anti-porn activists.

This involves exposing the truth about the sex industry to challenge claims that it is 'harmless fun' or glamorous. It involves moving beyond arguments centred on 'individual choice' to provide analysis of the power imbalances and structural inequalities which influence our choices; refuting accusations of being 'anti-sex' by demonstrating that sex-object culture is more related to sexism than sex; challenging charges of censorship by making it clear that objecting to an industry which normalises sexual violence and discrimination against women is taking a political stand against sexism; and revealing the harms of representing women as sexual objects who are always sexually available in a society in which sexual violence is endemic and inequality between women and men is rife.

Grassroots anti-porn activism provides a powerful vehicle with which to take on and win these arguments.

Conclusion

Feminist activism means challenging the institutions, mechanisms and attitudes which promote, legitimise, and keep sexist practices and beliefs in place. The intensification of the sex industries represents a vicious backlash against gains made by the women's movement. As anti-porn activists, we refuse to stay silent whilst women are objectified, sexualised and dehumanised.

There are important battles to be won, but our experience is that the tide is turning in favour of feminist activism. Standing united as women is vital to achieving the changes we are fighting for. This unity requires facing and challenging the oppressions which can divide us so that our diversity, as women, becomes our strength. It will be our ability as a movement to continue to grow in strength, diversity, and numbers as we continue to speak out and take action against sexism that will resoundingly put to rest the notion that feminism is dead. Our wins demonstrate the power of collective action. They show that treating women like sexual objects is neither inevitable nor unstoppable, and that there are growing numbers of women and men who are willing to stand up and object.

Get involved!

Bibliography

British Crime Survey (2005/2006). *Prevalence of intimate violence by category among adults aged 16 to 59, Homicides, Firearm Offences and Intimate Violence.* Supplementary Volume 1 to Crime in England and Wales.

Farley, Melissa, Ann Cotton, Lynne Jacqueline, Sybil Zumbeck, Frida Spiwak, Maria E. Reyes, Dinorah Alvarez, Ufuk Sezgin (2003) 'Prostitution and Trafficking in 9 Countries: Update on Violence and Posttraumatic Stress Disorder' *Journal of Trauma Practice* 2 (3/4), pp. 33–74.

Frank, Katherine (2003) 'Just Trying to Relax: Masculinity, Masculinizing Practices, and Strip Club Regulars' *The Journal of Sex Research* 40 (1) pp. 61–75.

Home Office (2004b) *Solutions and Strategies: Drug Problems and Street Sex Markets.* UK Government, London.

Povey, D. (Ed) (2005) *Crime in England and Wales 2003/2004: Supplementary Volume 1: Homicide and Gun Crime.* Home Office Statistical Bulletin No. 02/05. Home Office, London.

Melinda Liszewski

A Collective Shout for Women and Girls

What started as an idea in the minds of a group of women who had only just met, has evolved into a dynamic grassroots campaign movement challenging the sexploitation of women and girls.

In late 2009, 7 women met to discuss an idea for a new national movement in Australia that would challenge the sexual objectification of women and girls in popular culture. Melinda Tankard Reist had just launched her collection, *Getting Real: Challenging the Sexualisation of Girls*. It was part of a growing body of research into the harms of an increasingly pornified culture and many women were asking 'So what can we do?' The name 'Collective Shout: for a world free of sexploitation' (<www.collectiveshout.org>) came from one of the book's contributors, Tania Andrusiak, who described it as a "collective shout against the pornification of culture." It was time to turn the growing community concern surrounding the sexual objectification of women and girls into grassroots action.

In 2009, the word 'sexualisation' was relatively new to the Australian discourse on the health and well-being of young people. Research papers from the USA, Australia and the UK all documented the ways in which children – especially girls – were sexualised (e.g. Rush and La Nauze, 2006 a, 2006 b; Zurbriggen et al., 2007; Papadopoulos, 2010). Yet despite the demonstrable harm to girls' health, and an Australian Senate Inquiry into sexualisation, there had been little to no response from government and regulatory bodies.[1] The industries significantly responsible for sexualisation – advertisers, marketers, the fashion and beauty industries – had not been made accountable for the harm they were doing.

We began by establishing an online presence with a Website, Facebook page and Twitter account.[2] Interest in our movement was so great that even before the site was finished, concerned individuals began to sign up to Collective Shout. The

---

1 <http://www.aph.gov.au/senate/committee/eca_ctte/sexualisation_of_children/index.htm>

2 <http://www.collectiveshout.org>
<http://www.facebook.com/collectiveshout>
<http://www.twitter.com/collectiveshout>

Website was designed to act as an online meeting point for supporters. Members were invited to alert us to sexist and objectifying advertising and products by using the forum and blog facility. This allowed others in the Collective Shout community to join those members in protesting or boycotting offending products or services.

In our first 12 months, Collective Shout has racked up a significant number of wins against major corporations.

- The Australian Football League forced AFL Queensland and a Gold Coast football club to withdraw from a sponsorship deal between the sexist restaurant chain, Hooters, and an under 16s football team.[3]
- Major Australian underwear retailer Bonds withdrew their range of bras for girls as young as 6.[4]
- Complaints against Calvin Klein's simulated sexual assault billboard were upheld by the Advertising Standards Board following our campaign against the portrayal of violence against women to sell jeans. This attracted significant worldwide media attention.[5]
- Collective Shout helped to stop a Gold Coast racecourse's plans to hold a 'bikini track sprint.'[6]
- National grocery retailer Woolworths pulled out of a joint 'Lynx' promotion which offered winners a visit to the sexist Playboy Mansion-styled 'Lynx Lodge'.[7]

We have been part of global campaigns against: Amazon, for selling a guide to child sexual assault; Etsy, for selling rape greeting cards; and rapper Kanye West's *Monster* video clip, in partnership with Adios Barbie, the Coalition Against Trafficking in Women (Australia), and Media Watch. We have a current campaign

---

3   <http://community.collectiveshout.org/profiles/blogs/afl-withdraws-from-under-16s>
    <http://melindatankardreist.com.au/2010/05/boys-babes-and-balls-hooters-mascots-for-u16-boys-footy/>
4   <http://collectiveshout.org/2010/09/win-bonds-withdraws-little-girls-bras/>
    <http://www.heraldsun.com.au/news/national/bonds-stops-sale-of-bras-for-kids/story-e6frf7l6-1225932238263>
5   <http://collectiveshout.org/2010/10/win-calvin-klein-gang-rape-billboards-removed/>
    <http://news.ninemsn.com.au/national/8109416/calvin-klein-gang-rape-billboard-removed>
6   <http://collectiveshout.org/2010/09/win-racing-qld-bans-bikini-track-sprint/>
7   <http://collectiveshout.org/2010/10/win-woolies-withdraws-from-lynx-promotion/>

against the importation of toxic US-style child beauty (sexualisation) pageants to Australia.[8]

None of these wins would have been possible without the active participation of Collective Shout supporters who are growing in number and strength. Individual members have told us that they had previously felt alone in their concern about the sexual objectification of women and children. But now, with the knowledge that they are part of a bigger movement, they feel empowered to speak out and take action. They are challenging retailers about sexualised clothing for children, are bold enough to confront shop managers for their open display of pornography, and willing to persist with writing to the Advertising Standards Board about sexist advertising. At times, opposition to Collective Shout has been fierce, but when we support and encourage one another we stand strong for a world free of sexploitation. We invite you to join us.

Bibliography

Papadopoulos, Linda (2010) 'Sexualisation of Young People: Review', UK Home Office. Available at <http://webarchive.nationalarchives.gov.uk/20100413151441/homeoffice.gov.uk/about-us/news/sexualisation-young-people.html>.

Rush, Emma and Andrea La Nauze (2006a) 'Corporate Paedophilia: Sexualisation of children in Australia'. *Discussion Paper*, Number 90, The Australia Institute, Canberra, <https://www.tai.org.au/documents/downloads/DP90.pdf>.

Rush, Emma and Andrea La Nauze (2006b) 'Letting Children be Children: Stopping the sexualisation of children in Australia'. *Discussion Paper*, Number 93, The Australia Institute, Canberra.

Tankard Reist, Melinda (Ed) (2009) *Getting Real: Challenging the Sexualisation of Girls*. Spinifex Press, North Melbourne.

Zurbriggen, Eileen L., Rebecca L. Collins, Sharon Lamb, Tomi-Ann Roberts, Deborah L. Tolman, Monique L. Ward, Jeanne Blake (2007) Report of the APA Task Force on the Sexualization of Girls. American Psychological Association. Available at <http://www.apa.org/pi/women/programs/girls/report.aspx>.

---

8   <http://collectiveshout.org/2010/11/amazon-delists-pedophiles-guide-to-love-and-pleasure/>
    <http://melindatankardreist.com/2011/01/congratulations-you%E2%80%99ve-been-raped/>
    <http://www.thepetitionsite.com/1/prevent-official-release-of-kanye-wests-women-hating-monster-video/>
    <http://www.thepetitionsite.com/1/Stop-Child-Beauty-Pageants-in-Australia/>

Matt McCormack Evans

Men Opposing Pornography in the UK

The
AntiPornMenProject

It was at university in 2008 that I experienced firsthand how pornography affected my perception of women as I caught myself constantly sexualising them in an increasingly demeaning way. I believed I could keep the time I spent using pornography partitioned away from the rest of my life, and my attitudes, values and behaviour. But it became more and more obvious that this 'partitioning' was not possible; that porn continued to negatively influence the way I viewed women and could not be separated from who I was and how I behaved.

Along with this realisation came a new awareness of how pervasive porn use was among my male peers. I became more receptive to male friends revealing the influence pornography had on how they saw and thought about women. This led to a heightened awareness of references to porn in mainstream media, and it became obvious to me that pornography is a huge part of modern culture, promoting a relentlessly misogynistic kind of propaganda. With the content of mainstream porn being so sexist, violent and degrading to women, and with an increasing number of men watching it for an increasing amount of time, pornography is one of the primary issues facing men who believe in gender equality and ending violence against women.

The year 2010 saw a huge resurgence in UK feminist activism and involvement (see Long, van Heeswijk, this volume). However, despite this renewal, there was little being done to specifically target men. Many men experience a conflict between their intellectual values and the nature of the pornography they use, finding it incredibly difficult to reconcile their use of sexist, violent and degrading material and their beliefs in equality and respect for women. However, few men openly admit such a conflict and it is difficult to find sources. There was little online that addressed this phenomenon and provided a space where men could read posts by other men talking about these issues.

In response to this, The Anti Porn Men Project was created to provide an online forum for (mainly) men to speak, discuss, and learn about porn, porn culture and the anti-porn movement. We wanted to create a space where those who were coming to anti-porn thoughts for the first time could read material that would confirm and legitimise these concerns and help them feel like part of a wider community as well as for those further along the path who wanted to develop and discuss their anti-porn perspective. The Anti Porn Men Project was launched in September, 2010 to a huge response. The Website had over 10,000 visits in its first 3 weeks and received media interest spanning 6 continents in the next 2 months. It had certainly struck a nerve.

The Project's approach has been one of combining a user-authored blog with more traditional educational material. The Project's mission is to raise awareness of the harms of pornography and encourage men to speak out against it with the aim of bringing about a greater level of debate and questioning of pornography in our culture. Our strategy for consciousness raising and increasing the level of questioning of pornography essentially lies in the maintenance of a growing online presence through the regularly updated multi-contributor blog and an active comment and debate section.

In accommodating both newcomers to anti-porn thought as well as more seasoned activists, we publish a wide variety of material including general opinion pieces, personal experiences, reviews, academic-style studies, comment on current affairs, news and events updates, along with a 'Featured Posts' section. The comment and debate section plays a significant part in the Website's activity, and is central to the community that has built itself around the site which largely takes care of itself in answering the queries of newcomers and maintaining a healthy level of debate amongst the site's subscribers.

The Project also hosts online educational resources and acts as a signpost for links to other organisations and Websites in the anti-porn movement. The Website (<www.antipornmen.org>) has a wealth of videos, audio files, pdf files, academic papers, news articles, and links. We try to cater for researchers by providing an extensive backlist of news articles on porn as well as various interviews, speeches and articles by leading anti-porn academics and campaigners. We also produce leaflets that are circulated at anti-porn events and are currently designing workshops that we intend to run at various conferences and festivals across the UK.

Despite the early success and attention enjoyed by The Project, we have become very aware of the obstacles that exist when attempting to get men to talk critically about pornography. Before The Project, those anti-porn organisations that were aimed at men were largely driven by religious concerns, or concerns about sex, family or addiction. People who speak out against porn are routinely thought to be prudish and/or deeply conservative or religious. We demonstrate that this is not the case. We are clear about the basis for our objection to porn and this is central when communicating our message.

The concept of a 'real' man represents another serious problem. Men who object to porn are often thought to not be 'real' men in some way. The accepted view of masculinity is largely built on dominance and control over women. This not only plays a huge role in shaping the aggressive nature of pornographic content but also acts as a powerful barrier to men's openness about their usage of and concerns about porn. Challenging the macho posturing and rhetoric, so integral to porn usage and culture, is essential to engaging men in serious discussion about pornography. Aside from having the vast majority of our articles authored by men, The Project has an 'anti-porn men' page which features leading male anti-porn scholars and activists, as well as popular figures who have raised objections to porn. The Website also has a page devoted to 'men and masculinity' which seeks to challenge established concepts of masculinity.

Finally, when challenging pornography, the pervasiveness of its use and influence on our culture is a huge obstacle. The normalisation process that comes with the widespread use of pornography and the mainstreaming of pornographic imagery in the music, magazine, and advertising industries has led to a society which is accustomed to seeing women presented in provocative poses, as being essentially associated with sex and only valued for how they look. This desensitisation to the 'pornographic norm' renders the sexism and degradation in porn invisible and unnoticed. Remarkably, while pornography is so obviously present in the private lives of a huge number of men it remains largely absent from both private and public discussion about serious issues of gender equality and violence. For many men it is already an incredibly uncomfortable task to challenge one's own behaviour when it comes to pornography use and this is only compounded by the normalisation of both the industry and pornographic imagery.

However, despite the difficulty many men experience when challenging their own behaviour, a visible presence of men who are openly anti-porn can only encourage more men to question it. It is for this reason that activism is essential and why activism that is conducted by men and which targets men, has such great potential. It is vital for men to get involved in the rejection of pornography and porn culture. Porn is overwhelmingly produced and consumed by men and if it is going to be effectively challenged it must be done so with the inclusion of men.

In the wider context of the struggle for gender equality and the eradication of violence against women, pornography represents the primary barrier to men's mass engagement in the cause for women's equality. The cultural and social impact of porn on the way in which men think about and treat women is profound. Pornography has become the principal machine of patriarchal propaganda and its use is fundamentally incompatible with genuine engagement with and respect for women, I believe that the inclusion of men in the anti-porn feminist movement is vital to its success.

The anti-porn movement in the UK is largely activist-led. This gives it the energy and freshness required to stay motivated and ready for the ever more insidious ways in which porn culture is normalised and justified. The Anti Porn Men Project hopes both its membership and contributor base will continue to grow through the use of this dynamic activist-led approach. We have plans to develop workshops for men and boys, pursue greater support for the anti-porn movement in both feminist and left-wing political circles, and push ever further for it to be socially acceptable for a man to be anti porn. The Project, unique in its focus on men and its presence online, at events, and in the media, will continue to give a voice to the growing number of men who are speaking out against pornography.

Caroline Norma

Challenging Pornography in Japan: the Anti-Pornography and Prostitution Research Group (APP)

Over the organisation's 10-year history, members of the Tokyo-based Anti-Pornography and Prostitution Research Group (APP) have initiated a wide range of research projects and campaigns against pornography and prostitution in Japan. These activities are described in the organisation's yearly journal (*Poruno/ kaishun mondai kenkyuukai: Ronbun/shiryoushuu*) and Webpage (http://www.app-jp. org/), as well in a number of books. The Group's activities mostly focus on the harm of pornography for women and children in its production, distribution, and consumption in Japan.

The harms of pornography production are documented in the Group's investigation into a Japanese pornography production company called Bakkii Visual Planning. This research has involved APP members monitoring a chat forum run by the company for consumers of a particular film series in which women are dragged around by the hair, pushed face first into bathtubs of water, set alight, and beaten up. In the chat forum, pornography users discussed with the series producer what sex acts and abuses they wanted to see women undergo in the next release of the series. APP members documented the harms that were requested by pornography consumers, and then matched them to the abuses that were perpetrated in the next release of the film series. These findings were published in a 2004 article that discussed producer/consumer collaboration in the abuse of women in pornography (*Poruno/kaishun mondai kenkyuukai*, 2004, pp. 6–9).[1]

In another major project to document the harm of the distribution of pornography in Japan, APP members received funding to survey counsellors and lawyers working with women's support organisations in Tokyo about their experience of assisting sexual assault victims whose abuses featured pornography or prostitution. The APP collected a large volume of qualitative data on this

---

1 An English translation of this article will be published in a volume edited by Caroline Norma in 2012.

issue, which was presented in an article published in 2003. The Group identified 7 different ways in which pornography is used by sex offenders to victimise women. These include women being: 1) forced to watch pornography, 2) forced to re-enact scenes in pornography, 3) forced to appear in pornography by boyfriends or husbands, 4) raped by men provoked by consuming pornography, 5) blackmailed by pornography made of them, 6) having pornography made of them distributed on the Internet, and 7) women having their faces superimposed onto pornographic pictures distributed on the Internet (*Poruno/kaishun mondai kenkyuukai*, 2003, pp. 5–73).

The APP has also led a campaign to mobilise support for an amendment to be made to the Tokyo metropolitan youth development regulations to regulate the selling to minors of graphically animated pornography that glorifies rape or incest. In this campaign, the Group has faced strong opposition from gamers, manga authors and publishers, gaming industry associations, lawyers associations, and the heads and other leaders of the Socialist Party of Japan and the Japan Communist Party.

Another one of the Group's activities includes a campaign against 'upskirting', and the secret filming of women in public places like bathhouses, fitness clubs, public toilets, and 'love' hotels. The Group believes this kind of activity is not just a sex crime of individual men, but is closely linked with the sex industry in Japan, because the footage is often compiled and edited into films that are sold as pornography. The small cameras that are used to secretly film women and girls are sold in Akihabara, which is a shopping district where pornography is sold in Tokyo. The APP campaigns for a national law to be enacted against this filming activity, as well as a ban on the small cameras being sold or possessed when used for unlawful purposes.

The Group also campaigns against the producers of DVDs and Websites dedicated to pictures of underage girls wearing bathers and other revealing clothing. This genre of pornography is openly sold in districts like Akihabara, and is recognisable from shelf labels that indicate the age-range of the children in the different films (e.g. 'second year primary school'). These films evade Japan's child pornography law because they are perceived not to be arousing or provocative enough because children's genitals are not shown. Nonetheless, the APP has audited chat forums of online sites selling the films, and has documented sexualised discussion among consumers. On the basis of this research, the Group campaigns against the films as a form of child pornography.

Other research projects by the APP have included content analysis of 32 different violent pornographic films with findings published in the Group's 2000 edition journal, and sponsorship of Catharine MacKinnon to speak in Tokyo in 2002. Group members publicise their availability to speak at forums against pornography, and run workshops to promote abolitionist activity in Japanese society against pornography and prostitution. In its daily activity, the group further aims to foster support networks for women harmed in the production of pornography in Japan.

Bibliography

Poruno/kaishun mondai kenkyuukai (2003) 'Ankeeto chousa kekka no bunseki' pp. 5–73.
Yamamoto, Yukino (2004) 'Seisaku genba ni okeru henka', *Poruno/kaishun mondai kenkyuukai* pp. 6–19.

Susan Hawthorne

Quit Porn Manifesto

Just as lung cancer and other illnesses were identified as having links to tobacco consumption, pornography is linked to an increase in harm to women. The tobacco industry, like the pornography industry, pumped billions of dollars into advertising and sponsorship around the world. Particular targets of that marketing were young people at a point in their lives where they are especially vulnerable to peer group pressure and to the idea of looking and being cool. Advertising towards men emphasised manliness (think 'Marlboro Man').[1] Advertising towards women emphasised beauty and sexiness (think Virginia Slims). Cigarette placement in films was the norm, and holidays in Europe were associated with Peter Stuyvesant cigarettes.

Pornographers use all the same tricks to get their message across to consumers. But this time it is not a product, but a person. By and large, that person is female and young. The purchasers, on the whole, are male. Boys are groomed through masculine culture to become purchasers, responding to pornography as propaganda (Jensen, 2007). Propaganda for a particular kind of social structure that fosters the exploitation of women by men, that is, patriarchy. The message for men is about manliness, about power and pleasure. Just as in tobacco advertising, the message for women is different: it's about presenting an aura of sexiness and of being appealing to men.

The first reports of the dangers of cigarette smoking appeared in 1964 when the *Surgeon General's Advisory Committee Report on Smoking and Health* was released in the USA. Tobacco advertising is banned in many countries and sponsorships of sport almost unheard of 45 years after the *Surgeon General's Report*. While feminists have been providing evidence for the harm of pornography for many years (Dworkin and MacKinnon, 1988; McKinnon and Dworkin, 1997) the Surgeon General has not appointed an Advisory Committee to report on Pornography and Health.

---

1   'Marlboro Man', Wayne McLaren, died of lung cancer in 1992.

Pornography increases suffering

Pornography influences the kinds of intimate relationships people have. Pornography has deleterious effects not only on the individuals in those relationships but also on the extended family and on later generations. Trauma is not restricted to the generation in which it occurs (Atkinson, 2002).

The making of pornography is itself harmful to those involved in its production: to the women portrayed in porn shoots and the men making those films. While the upshot may not be lung cancer, it does have detrimental effects on health and it is highly likely that the impact of pornography results in the death of some of its players.

Some say that pornography is freedom of expression. Whose expression is free? The women with cum on their faces? The young girls and boys penetrated anally? Get real. This is not about freedom of expression, it is about endorsing men's violence against the feminised other: women, children and animals as well as men who are poor, gay or from a despised ethnic group.

Pornography is an industry, just like tobacco is an industry. It is intended to make large profits for a small number of individuals and corporations. There is no greater social good to be found in pornography. Instead, it has negative effects on the developing brains of young men exposed to endless streams of porn culture (Doidge, 2009, pp. 102–112). Those young men (from age 11 according to Dines, 2010) are not engaging in instinctual behaviour, but a learned behaviour that requires ever more stimulation. It leads to an escalation of 'learned need' on the part of men, and suggests that the more pornography there is, the greater the damage (Doidge, 2009, pp. 104–106). And further, that porn causes erectile dysfunction in men (Murphy, 2010). Rather than enhancing the sexual experience, pornography requires a bigger and bigger fix to the point where only the most gratuitously violent images have any effect.

"Porn is bad for your health" says Linda Thompson (2010). It's bad for women's health because of the increase in sexually transmitted diseases and physical injury by those engaged in the production of pornography. Add to that the post-traumatic stress disorders and psychological effects of abuse. These, however, are not restricted to the makers of porn, but also to the watchers of pornography. They lose their capacity to form intimate relationships with others. "The consumers become the consumed" (Murphy, 2010).

Pornography has many defenders including those on the left who want to dismantle capitalism but leave the pornography industry intact. But if we want a society in which justice is at the centre, then we cannot justify supporting pornography. Porn is about injustice and hatred.

Who is porn good for? It's good for capitalists. It's good for organised crime. It's good for the purveyors of violence, such as those in the military who give porn to soldiers in training (Caputi, 1992). It's good for those engaged in genocide who film the rape and torture of prisoners and then distribute this as porn (Clarke, 2004). It's good for a handful of corporate exploiters. It's good for patriarchy.

Strategies to Quit Porn

Identify the reasons why you want to Quit Porn. Reflect on when you first used porn. Your age, the social setting in which it occurred. Think about whether the things that were important to you then are now. Ask yourself whether you were pressured to use porn? What made you continue after the pressure ceased? Do any of those things still matter? Reflect on what you thought was good about porn. Did that good feeling always continue? Did you experience any negative feelings? Try to identify them. How did using porn affect your partner? Did you ask? What affect did porn have on your relationship? Are any of them strong enough reasons to help you Quit Porn?

Reflect on your politics. Are you in favour of social justice? Do you think racism is a bad thing? Do you put ecological issues high on your list of priorities? Do you think women should be treated with respect? Do you think that people in poverty should get more equitable access to resources? Do you think it's a good thing that slavery is illegal? If you answer yes to any of these and you use porn, how do you justify that to yourself? How do you justify it to others? What do you think of your justifications after pondering these issues?

Create a plan to Quit Porn. It might include changing some social settings that make it hard for you to refuse using porn. Work out how you might change these. It might include changing habits and routines. Try to replace these with something active, something that will give your mind and body energy. It might involve some quite strong emotions. Finding a supportive person or group might be helpful in dealing with your emotions.

In the plan you create to Quit Porn, try to work out whether you feel more comfortable with your politics now? Does that help you to Quit Porn?

Put your plan into action. Just as smokers have relapses, it's possible that circumstances and a range of other events might create obstacles to giving up porn. It's worth continuing through these difficult patches. If you need to make several attempts before you Quit Porn, think of your previous attempts as practice runs. Reflect on what helped you to stop and what encouraged you to use again. Think about the things you might do to get you through the next time.

Using porn is learned behaviour. If you learned it, it is possible to unlearn it. While the plasticity of the brain means that using porn affects the brain, it also means that by not using porn, you are creating new ways for the brain to operate. You are changing your behaviour. People have changed their behaviour over millennia. Feminism helped women changed their behaviour, and most reasonable people in this society have worked to stop themselves from expressing racist views. It is possible to change the way you live in the world. It is possible to change how you relate to others.

Reasons to Quit Porn

Why bother to Quit Porn? Just as smoking affects a person's quality of life, using pornography does too. It reduces social interactions and the quality of that interaction. Relationships become disengaged and people are dehumanised.

Who do you support? The profiteers and purveyors of violence? Or those harmed by pornography?

Porn is bad for you. It's bad for boys. It's bad for girls. It's bad for women. It's bad for men. It's bad for our relationships with one another.

It's time to Quit Porn.

Bibliography

Atkinson, Judy (2002) *Trauma Trails, Recreating Song Lines: The Transgenerational Effects of Trauma in Indigenous Australia*. Spinifex Press, North Melbourne.

Caputi, Jane (1992) *The Age of Sex Crime*. The Women's Press, London.

Clarke, D. A. (2004) 'Prostitution for everyone: Feminism, globalisation and the "sex" industry' in Starke, Christine and Rebecca Whisnant (Eds) *Not For Sale: Feminists Resisting Prostitution and Pornography*. Spinifex Press, North Melbourne, pp. 149–205.

Dines, Gail (2010) *Pornland: How Porn Has Hijacked Our Sexuality*. Beacon Press, Boston; Spinifex Press, North Melbourne.

Doidge, Norman (2009) *The Brain That Changes Itself*. Scribe, Melbourne.

Dworkin, Andrea and Catharine A. MacKinnon (1988) *Pornography and Civil Rights: A New Day for Women's Equality*. Organizing Against Pornography, Minneapolis.

Hamilton, Maggie (2010) *What's Happening to Our Boys?* Viking, Camberwell.

Jensen, Robert (2007) *Getting Off: Pornography and the End of Masculinity*. South End Press, Cambridge, MA.

MacKinnon, Catharine A. and Andrea Dworkin (1997) *In Harm's Way: The Pornography Civil Rights Hearings*. Harvard University Press, Cambridge, MA.

Murphy, Cameron (11 June, 2010) 'Working with Men to Stop Pornography' Workshop presentation given at Stop Porn Culture Conference, Wheelock College, Boston.

Stark, Christine and Rebecca Whisnant (Eds) (2004) *Not For Sale: Feminists Resisting Prostitution and Pornography*. Spinifex Press, North Melbourne.

Tankard Reist, Melinda (2009) *Getting Real: Challenging the Sexualisation of Girls*. Spinifex Press, North Melbourne.

Thompson, Linda (12 June, 2010) 'International Organizing against the Sex Industry' Workshop presentation given at Stop Porn Culture Conference, Wheelock College, Boston.

Author Biographical Notes

Asja Armanda is an ethnologist and philosopher. She is co-founder of the *Kareta Feminist Group*, the first feminist group in Croatia. She broke the story of the sexual atrocity dimension of genocide as a feminist issue. With Natalie Nenadic, she initiated the *Kadic v. Karadzic* case in New York against the head of the Bosnian Serbs which pioneered the claim for sexual atrocities as acts of genocide under international law.

Dr **Abigail Bray** is a Research Fellow at the Social Justice Research Centre at Edith Cowan University. She has published widely in leading international academic journals on anorexia, child sexual abuse, moral panics, and child pornography. She is the author of *Hélène Cixous: Writing and Sexual Difference* (2004) and *Body Talk: A Power Guide for Girls* with Elizabeth Reid Boyd (2005). She was an inaugural inductee into the Western Australian Women's Hall of Fame in 2011. Her forthcoming book *Misogyny Re-Loaded* will be published by Spinifex. She is a member of Socialist Alliance and the Marxist collective Das Argument.

Caroline is a health educator in Scotland who requested anonymity.

Gail Dines is a Professor of Sociology and Women's Studies at Wheelock College in Boston. A long time radical feminist activist, Dines is a founding member of Stop Porn Culture. Her latest book is *Pornland: How Porn Has Hijacked Our Sexuality* (2010).

At non-profit Prostitution Research & Education in San Francisco, Dr **Melissa Farley** addresses the connections between prostitution, racism, sexism and poverty. The PRE Website is a widely used resource <www.prostitutionresearch.com>. PRE is affiliated with the Center for World Indigenous Studies and Pacific Graduate School of Psychology. Melissa Farley has written 25 peer-reviewed articles on prostitution and trafficking, and 2 books, *Prostitution, Trafficking & Traumatic Stress* (2004) and *Legal Prostitution and Trafficking in Nevada: Making the Connections* (2007).

Nina Funnell is a sexual ethics researcher and opinion writer who has written extensively on issues connected with violence against women. Nina also works as a victim's rights advocate and was awarded the Australian Human Rights Commission Community (Individual) Award in 2010 for this work. Nina is currently completing her first book on sexting and sexual ethics education.

Ruchira Gupta was inspired to found Apne Aap (<http://www.apneaap.org/>) after working with courageous young women in the brothels of Mumbai, and make her award-winning documentary, *The Selling of Innocents*. Well known for highlighting the link between trafficking and prostitution, Ruchira brought groups of survivors to speak before the UN General Assembly in 2008 and 2009. She has been honoured with the Clinton Global Citizen Award in 2009, the UK House of Lords' Abolitionist Award in 2007, an Emmy in 1995, and was featured in Nicholas Kristof and Sheryl WuDunn's 2009 *New York Times* bestseller, *Half the Sky*.

Writer and social researcher **Maggie Hamilton** gives frequent talks and lectures, is a regular media commentator and a keen observer of social trends. Her many books include *What Men Don't Talk About*, as well as *What's Happening to Our Girls?* and *What's Happening to Our Boys?* which look at the 21st century challenges that our boys and girls are facing.

Dr **Susan Hawthorne** has been involved in the Women's Liberation Movement for around 40 years and writes fiction, non-fiction and poetry. She is Adjunct Professor in the School of Arts and Social Sciences at James Cook University, Townsville. She received her PhD in Political Science and Women's Studies at the University of Melbourne and is the author of numerous books including *Wild Politics* (2002) and *Cow* (2011).

Professor **Sheila Jeffreys** is a lesbian feminist who has been an activist against violence against women and the sex industry since the early 1970s in London. She is a founding member of the Coalition Against Trafficking in Women Australia. Dr Jeffreys teaches sexual politics and international feminist politics at the University of Melbourne. *The Idea of Prostitution* (1997/2008) is one of her 7 books on the history and politics of sexuality, with *The Industrial Vagina: The political economy of the global sex trade* the most recent (2009*)*. Her next books are *Man's Dominion: The rise of religion and the eclipse of women's rights* and a new edition of *Anticlimax: A Feminist Perspective on the Sexual Revolution* (both 2011).

Robert Jensen is a Journalism Professor at the University of Texas at Austin, USA. He is the author of *All My Bones Shake: Seeking a Progressive Path to the Prophetic Voice* (Soft Skull Press, 2009); *Getting Off: Pornography and the End of Masculinity* (South End Press, 2007), *The Heart of Whiteness: Confronting Race, Racism and White Privilege* (City Lights, 2005); *Citizens of the Empire: The Struggle to Claim Our Humanity* (City Lights, 2004); and *Writing Dissent: Taking Radical Ideas from the Margins to the Mainstream* (Peter Lang, 2002).

Originally from Canada, **Christopher N. Kendall** now practices as a Barrister at John Toohey Chambers in Perth, Western Australia. Formerly he was the Dean of Law at Murdoch University. Chris has published and lectured throughout North America and Australia on the harms of gay male pornography, sexual violence and gay male domestic abuse. In 2004, he published *Gay Male Pornography: An Issue of Sex Discrimination* (University of British Columbia Press, Vancouver).

Dr **Renate Klein** is a long-term women's health researcher and has written extensively on reproductive technologies and feminist theory. A biologist and social scientist, she was Associate Professor in Women's Studies at Deakin University in Melbourne until 2006 and a founder of FINRRAGE (Feminist International Network of Resistance to Reproductive and Genetic Engineering). She wrote on the dangers of premature medicalisation of girls in Melinda Tankard Reist's *Getting Real: Challenging the Sexualisation of Girls* (2009).

Melinda Liszewski is a co-founder of Collective Shout and manages its Websites and campaigns.

Dr **Julia Long** is a radical feminist activist and campaigner, particularly involved with the London Feminist Network and OBJECT. She recently completed her PhD on the re-emergence of feminist anti-porn activism at London South Bank University. Julia is a firm advocate of women-only organising, and prefers marching and chanting to emails and online activism! Her professional background is in education, the voluntary sector and gender equality policy. Julia's book on the resurgence of anti-porn feminism will be published by Zed Books in 2012.

Catharine A. MacKinnon, who worked closely with Andrea Dworkin until her death in 2005, including in originating the human rights approach to pornography, is Elizabeth A. Long Professor of Law at the University of Michigan, The James Barr Ames Visiting Professor of Law (long term) at Harvard Law School, and Special Gender Adviser to the Prosecutor of the International Criminal Court (The Hague).

Jeffrey Moussaieff Masson is the author of 26 books, among them: *The Assault on Truth; A Dark Science: Women, Sexuality and Psychiatry in the 19th Century; Final Analysis; Against Therapy; When Elephants Weep; The Pig Who Sang to the Moon; The Face on Your Plate;* and *The Dog Who Couldn't Stop Loving.* He lives on a beach in Auckland with his golden lab Benjy, 3 cats, 2 sons, Manu and Ilan, and his wife Leila, a pediatrician.

Anne Mayne is a long-time activist against violence against women. She was the co-founder of Cape Town Feminists (1973) and Rape Crisis Cape Town (1976). Anne is the current vice-chairperson of Embrace Dignity, an organisation that campaigns against trafficking in women and girls.

Matt McCormack Evans was born in 1988 and is a feminist campaigner and activist. He is the co-founder and Project Coordinator of The Anti Porn Men Project. He has also worked for OBJECT, a leading human rights organisation that challenges the sexual objectification of women, and volunteered for UK Feminista, a new feminist activist organisation. He is currently in postgraduate education studying Philosophy at Durham University in the UK.

Dr **Betty McLellan** is a feminist ethicist, author, psychotherapist and committed activist of long standing. She is Adjunct Associate Professor in the Department of Social Work and Community Welfare and the Centre for Women's Studies at James Cook University, Townsville, and the author of *Overcoming Anxiety* (1991), *Beyond Psychoppression* (1995), *Help! I'm Living with a (Man) Boy* (1999, 2006) and *Unspeakable: A feminist ethic of speech* (2010).

Hiroshi Nakasatomi is a co-founding member of the Anti-Pornography and Prostitution Research Group. He is an Associate Professor of Law at Fukushima University in Japan where he teaches constitutional law, law and gender and peace studies. He has published *Pornography and Sex Violence: In Search of New Approaches to Legal Regulation* (Akashi Shoten, 2007) and co-authored *Evidences: Sex Violence and Harms of Pornography Today* (ShakaifukushiKyougikai, 2010).

Natalie Nenadic is an Assistant Professor of Philosophy at the University of Kentucky, USA. She teaches in the history of philosophy (especially Arendt, Heidegger, and Hegel), ethics, social and political philosophy, and philosophy of law, especially international justice. She has lectured widely on these topics in North America, Europe, and Australasia. With Asja Armanda, she initiated the *Kadic v Karadzic* case in New York against the head of the Bosnian Serbs which pioneered the claim for sexual atrocities as acts of genocide under international law.

Dr **Caroline Norma** is a Lecturer in the School of Global Studies, Social Science, and Planning at RMIT University, and a member of the Coalition Against Trafficking in Women Australia (CATWA).

Dr **Helen Pringle** is in the Faculty of Arts and Social Sciences at the University of New South Wales. Her research has been widely recognised by awards from Princeton University, the Fulbright Foundation, the Australian Federation of University Women, and the Universities of Adelaide, Wollongong and NSW. Her main fields of expertise are human rights, ethics in public life, and political theory.

Diane L. Rosenfeld is a Lecturer on Law at Harvard Law School in Cambridge where she teaches courses on Title IX; Gender Violence, Law and Social Justice; and Theories of Sexual Coercion. She holds a J.D. from University of Wisconsin-Madison, and an LL.M. from Harvard Law School. Diane Rosenfeld served as the Senior Counsel to the Violence Against Women Office at the U.S. Department of Justice before teaching at Harvard.

Diana E.H. Russell, Professor Emerita of Sociology at Mills College, is the author/co-author, editor/co-editor of 17 books, 3 of which are on pornography: *Making Violence Sexy: Feminist Views on Pornography* (1993), *Against Pornography: The Evidence of Harm* (1994), and *Dangerous Relationships: Pornography, Misogyny, and Rape* (1998). Dr Russell has also engaged in numerous actions against pornography since 1976 when she helped found the San Francisco-based organization, Women Against Violence in Pornography & Media (WAVPM).

Dr **Robi Sonderegger** is an internationally renowned clinical psychologist and expert consultant in trauma associated with sexual exploitation, human trafficking, war and natural disaster (with tens of thousands of refugees having graduated from his programs). He is also the Chief Executive of Family Challenge Australia, a nationally registered mental health charity that provides specialist psychology services in Australia and throughout the world.

Stella grew up in rural Victoria before living for some time in America. She worked in offices and restaurants while studying naturopathy before becoming a stripper. After exiting the sex industry she completed a Bachelor of Arts at Melbourne University. She now lives with her partner of 10 years and their 3 daughters in the country. She hopes that by sharing her experience as a stripper, the unglamorous truth of the damage it does to women's lives may be better understood.

Dr **Chyng Sun** is a Clinical Associate Professor of Media Studies at McGhee Division at School of Continuing and Professional Studies at New York University. In addition to various academic research on pornography, she is also the director for the documentary film *The Price of Pleasure: Pornography, Sexuality, and Relationships* (2008), <http://www.thepriceofpleasure.com>.

Melinda Tankard Reist is a writer, speaker, blogger, media commentator and activist against violence against women, objectification of women and sexualisation of girls. Melinda is author/editor of 4 books including *Defiant Birth: Women Who Resist Medical Eugenics* (Spinifex Press, 2006) and *Getting Real: Challenging the Sexualisation of Girls* (Spinifex Press, 2009). Melinda's opinion pieces appear frequently in Australian media and she is a regular on morning television and current affairs programs. She is a co-founder of Collective Shout: for a world free of sexploitation. Melinda is named in the *Who's Who of Australian Women* and the *World Who's Who of Women*. Her Website is <melindatankardreist.com>.

Professor **S. Caroline Taylor** is Foundation Chair in Social Justice at Edith Cowan University, Australia. She is Founder and Chair of Children of Phoenix Inc., a charity that assists survivors of childhood abuse to rebuild their lives through education and mentoring. Dr Taylor is an academic, researcher, social commentator, advocate and provides specialist evidence in child abuse cases, and passionately supports the rights of children to live free from all forms of violence, discrimination and disadvantage.

Linda Thompson is from Northern Ireland where she was involved with youth work, community work and sexual health education, working with young people as peer educators on the HYPE project before moving into HIV and sexual health promotion in Scotland. She is currently the Development Officer with the Women's Support Project and raises awareness of issues around commercial sexual exploitation as a form of violence against women. She is kept busy with a tornado of a toddler and, in her limited free time, volunteers with women's and mother's groups and is a breast-feeding advocate.

Dr **Meagan Tyler** is a Lecturer in the School of Social Sciences and Psychology at Victoria University, Melbourne. She is a member of the Coalition Against Trafficking in Women Australia (CATWA) and the Porn Cultures and Policy Network (PCPN). Her research has been published in *Women's Studies International Forum* and *Women and Therapy*. Her book, *Prostitution in Every Home? The pornographic and sexological construction of women's sexuality in the West*, is forthcoming with Cambridge Scholars Press.

Anna van Heeswijk has a First Class Honours Degree in International Relations and a Masters in Human Rights. Prior to working with OBJECT, Anna campaigned for Disability Rights and Young People's Rights. As well as her feminist activism, she also leads Peer counselling workshops on overcoming the effects of racism, sexism, homophobia, classism and ageism on our lives.

Index

capitalism and 31–2, 107–8
connections with Big Pharma 86–101
exploitative nature of 107–17, 160–5
film investigation of 171–7
ideology of 29–31
in India 239–46
in South Africa 223–9
Internet globalisation of 160–5
links to strip clubs and prostitution
136–42
mass market power of 14–15
pay scales in 153, 176
profits made by xiv, 11, 86, 112
pornsex
campaign against 88
drugs promoted to enhance 86–8
manipulation of women's bodies for
88–90
medical hazards of 90–2
post-feminism, pornification of 118–21
post-traumatic stress disorder, prostitution
and 82, 154, 276
power relations *see also* gender roles
gay male pornography and 54–61
in pornography 254
reinforced by sex therapists' advice 78–83
Pringle, Helen x, xii, xxiv, 86, 101, 299
propaganda
pornography as 25–33
pornography denying genocide 233–5
pornography inciting genocide 231–2
power and 26
prostitution
campaigns against exploitation in 274,
277–8
factors compelling women into 151–2
pornography as 150–7
strip clubs as part of 136–42
violence against women in 151
pseudo child pornography xvi, 181
'incest porn' as sub-genre of 196
childification of women in 182–3
Free Speech Coalition and 4
messages conveyed by 6–8
teen porn 4–8
pubic hair removal, pornography and 5–6, 89

'queer', degrading gay men as 55, 56

Queer Studies 115
Quit Porn Manifesto 291–4

racism
college sexual culture and 46
gay male pornography and 56–7
in pornography 31, 243–4
music lyrics and 47
rape *see also* gang rape; intrafamilial rape
anal, of teenage girls 22
as a weapon of war 230–3
college campuses encouraging 41–3
computer games and 167–70
high rate in South Africa 226
in gay male pornography 57–8
pornography as propaganda for 25–33
US data on incidence of 28
RapeLay 167–70
Reclaim the Night 259, 264, 276
regulation of porn industry xxv–xxvi
attempts at xx–xxi
lack of xx–xxi
religious vilification 252
reproporn 92–6
Rosenfeld, Diane L. xxiii, 41, 300
Royalle, Candida 81, 82
Russell, Diana E.H. xxv, 223, 226, 300
Russell's Theory 181–91

sadomasochism
pornography used to encourage 79–80
torture and 115–17
Schafer, Sue 202–3
self-empowerment
bestiality porn presented as xxiii, 67
challenge to pornography as xiv
prostitution presented as 161, 163–4
sex toys as 118, 121
self-esteem
education to improve 50–1
effect of pornography on 1, 254
working in strip clubs and xxiv, 149
self-image, teen photography and 34–5
self-objectification of women 48
sex education
harm of pornography as xvi–xvii, 20, 272
kits influenced by pornography 80–1
sex shops, sexual 'liberation' in 118–21

Other books from Spinifex Press

Not For Sale: Feminists Resisting Prostitution and Pornography
edited by Christine Stark and Rebecca Whisnant

This international anthology brings together research, heartbreaking personal stories from survivors of the sex industry, and theory from over 30 women and men – activists, survivors, academics and journalists. *Not For Sale* is groundbreaking in its breadth, analysis and honesty.

"The range and quality of the articles makes *Not For Sale* a must read for anyone seeking to understand the opposition to prostitution."

– MAURICE HAMINGTON, *NWSA JOURNAL*

ISBN: 9781876756499

Pornland: How Porn Has Hijacked Our Sexuality
by Gail Dines

Pornland takes an unflinching look at pornography and its effect on our lives, showing that today's pornography is strikingly different from yesterday's *Playboy*. As porn culture has become absorbed into pop culture, a new wave of entrepreneurs are creating porn that is ever more hardcore, violent, sexist, and racist.

"We're now so pornography-saturated that our capacity for sexual delight is being brutalized. Gail Dines brilliantly exposes porn's economics, pervasiveness, and impact with scholarship as impeccable as her tone is reasonable. This book will change your life."

– ROBIN MORGAN, AUTHOR AND ACTIVIST

ISBN: 9781876756871

The Idea of Prostitution
by Sheila Jeffreys

Sheila Jeffreys explodes the distinction between 'forced' and 'free' prostitution, and documents the expanding international traffic in women. She examines the claims of the prostitutes' rights movement and the sex industry, while supporting prostituted women.

"*The Idea of Prostitution* is controversial, yet compelling. It is for me one of a few seminal works that are truly radical and have left an indelible imprint on my thinking. The book questions liberal notions about what it means to be a woman in today's society in which certain practices are still tolerated or have been normalised."

— STIEVE DELANCE, *CHIAROSCURO*

ISBN: 9781876756673

Anticlimax: A Feminist Perspective on the Sexual Revolution
by Sheila Jeffreys

The sexual revolution of the 1960s and 1970s is remembered as a time of great freedom for women. Was the sexual revolution liberation for women or just another insidious form of oppression? Sheila Jeffreys argues that the increasing eroticisation of power differences within heterosexual, lesbian and gay communities was not liberatory. Her alternative vision of sexual relations based on equality is a major statement in the debates over sex and violence that remain relevant in discussions over SlutWalk, sexualisation of girls and the pervasiveness of porn culture.

"A rigorous, savvy contemporary intellectual history ... Read this book."

— ANDREA DWORKIN

ISBN: 9781742198071

Getting Real: Challenging the Sexualisation of Girls
edited by Melinda Tankard Reist

From advertising and merchandising to Bratz and Voodoo Dolls to the Henson affair, *Getting Real* puts the spotlight on the sexualisation and objectification of girls and women in the media, popular culture and society.

"*Getting Real* is powerful, disturbing, confronting. If we don't challenge what we're beginning to accept as the social norm, the risk to our girls will only continue to grow."

— MELINA MARCHETTA, AUTHOR OF *LOOKING FOR ALIBRANDI*

ISBN: 9781876756758

Making Sex Work: A Failed Experiment with Legalised Prostitution
by Mary Lucille Sullivan

Making Sex Work is a compelling read. This book gives an insight into the sex industry, and into a society where women and children have become just another consumer item. If you've ever thought of prostitution as simply a choice some women make, read this book and then ask yourself: Could you do this job? How would you feel if your friend, sister, or daughter chose this career?

"... the evidence is compelling ... prostitution is male sex right in action, and this is where we need to start."

— GRAZYNA ZAJDOW, *ARENA MAGAZINE*

ISBN: 9781876756604

Unmaking War, Remaking Men: How Empathy Can Reshape Our Politics, Our Soldiers and Ourselves
by Kathleen Barry

In *Unmaking War, Remaking Men*, Kathleen Barry explores soldiers' experiences through a politics of empathy. By revealing how men's lives are made expendable for combat, she shows how military training drives them to kill without thinking and without remorse, only to suffer both trauma and loss of their own souls. With the politics of empathy, she sheds new light on the experiences of those who are invaded and occupied and shows how resistance rises among them.

"Kathleen Barry shows in her book how empathy threatens those who promote the militarization of masculinity while simultaneously providing an antidote. She has done deep thinking – thinking that all of us will be made smarter by!"

— CYNTHIA ENLOE, *GLOBALIZATION AND MILITARISM*

ISBN: 9781876756864

Radically Speaking: Feminism Reclaimed
edited by Diane Bell and Renate Klein

They are subversive, reflective, funny, polemical, political, moving, analytical, critical, international, visionary, radical. Seventy writers from every continent discuss their ideas and practice of contemporary feminism.

"*Radically Speaking: Feminism Reclaimed* is the book we've all been waiting for. It is an incredibly powerful collection of articles by radical feminists about radical feminism."

— *WOMEN'S STUDIES INTERNATIONAL FORUM*

ISBN: 9781875559381

Wild Politics: Feminism, Globalisation and Bio/diversity
by Susan Hawthorne

Susan Hawthorne challenges the universal endorsement of global western culture with her concept of biodiversity, arguing that biodiversity is a useful metaphor for understanding social, political, and economic relations in the globalised world of the 21st century.

"One of the many gifts of Susan Hawthorne's *Wild Politics* is the unrelenting analysis and illustration of ways neo-colonialism is promoted under the banner of Western liberalism and economic globalization ... Her goal is to decolonize the Western imagination ... *Wild Politics* is fabulous, and Susan Hawthorne has done us all a tremendous service."

— SARAH LUCIA HOAGLAND, *WOMEN'S REVIEW OF BOOKS*

ISBN: 9781876756246

Unspeakable: A Feminist Ethic of Speech
by Betty McLellan

This is a book about speech and the silencing of speech; about who gets to speak and who does not; about who is listened to and who is ignored. *Unspeakable* focuses on how women are silenced in every nation on earth: through violence, subordination and exclusion.

"Be assured that Betty McLellan has not been silenced ... Recasting debates old and new through the lens of ethics, she marches straight into many a dreary and painful corner, illuminating in the process a true arc of women speaking out against subordination ... Treasure this undying, undaunted voice."

— CATHARINE A. MACKINNON, ELIZABETH A. LONG PROFESSOR OF LAW
AT THE UNIVERSITY OF MICHIGAN LAW SCHOOL

ISBN: 9781742194929

*If you would like to know more about Spinifex Press,
write for a free catalogue or visit our Website.*

SPINIFEX PRESS
PO Box 212 North Melbourne
Victoria 3051 Australia
www.spinifexpress.com.au